STORM CENTER

FIFTH EDITION

Other Books by David M. O'Brien

STORM CENTER

The Supreme Court in American Politics

FIFTH EDITION

DAVID M. O'BRIEN

UNIVERSITY OF VIRGINIA

W • W • Norton & Company

New York • London

Copyright © 2000, 1996, 1993, 1990, 1986 by David M. O'Brien
Printed in the United States of America
Library of Congress Cataloging-in-Publication Data
O'Brien, David M.
Storm center : the Supreme Court in American politics / David M.
O'Brien.—5th ed.
p.   cm.
Includes bibliographical references and index.
ISBN 0-393-97492-8 (pbk.)
1. United States. Supreme Court.   2. Political questions and
judicial power—United States.   3. Judicial process—United States.
I. Title.
KF8742.O27   1999
347.73'26—dc21   99-26041
W. W. Norton & Company, Inc.,
500 Fifth Avenue, New York, N.Y. 10110
www.wwnorton.com
W. W. Norton & Company Ltd.,
10 Coptic Street, London WC1A 1PU
1 2 3 4 5 6 7 8 9 0

For Benjamin, Sara, and Talia

Contents

Illustrations

Tables, Charts, and Graphs

Preface

THE Supreme Court, Justice Oliver Wendell Holmes observed, is a "storm centre" of political controversy. The Court stands as a temple of law—an arbitrator of political disputes, an authoritative organ of law, and an expression of the American ideal of "a government of laws, not of men." But it remains a fundamentally political institution. Behind the marble facade, the justices compete for influence; the Court itself is locked in a larger struggle for power in society. This book is about the political struggles among the justices and between the Court and rival political forces in the country.

Within a week of the publication of the first edition of this book Chief Justice Warren E. Burger resigned, and less than a year later Justice Lewis F. Powell stepped down. With the elevation of William H. Rehnquist from associate to chief justice and the addition of Justices Antonin Scalia and Anthony Kennedy, the Supreme Court changed complexion. The second edition dealt with the changes in the life of the Court that occurred during the first few years of Rehnquist's chief justiceship and due to the addition of President Reagan's last two appointees. Shortly after that edition appeared the Court's leading liberal and one of its most influential members, Justice William J. Brennan, Jr., retired in June 1991. One year later on the last day of the Court's term, his ideological ally, Justice Thurgood Marshall, announced that he would step down. Their replacement on the bench by Justices David H. Souter and Clarence Thomas reinforced the conservative shift in direction of the "Rehnquist Court." The third edition took account of how those further changes affected life within the marble temple and the Rehnquist Court's new uses of judicial power. And the fourth edition took into account President Clinton's two appointees to the high bench, as well as incorporated new material made available in the papers of Justices Thurgood Marshall and Lewis F. Powell, Jr., along with those of President Richard M. Nixon.

This fifth, thoroughly updated, edition incorporates additional materials from the papers of Justices Marshall and Powell as well as interviews and correspondence with a number of the justices. There is also much new research on how changes in the Court's composition affect its internal operations, deference to past rulings, and the doctrine of *stare decisis*, for example, along with the direction of judicial policy-making and constitutional politics. Discussions of the Court's growing docket and the justices' workload, conferences, oral argument sessions, agenda setting, and decision-making processes, as well as opinion-writing practices have thus been thoroughly updated. In addition, readers will find expanded treatments of the Court's relation to public opinion, critical elections, and partisan realignments, along with more emphasis on the politics of judicial policy-making and the institutional constraints and restraints on achieving implementation and compliance with its rulings.

The underlying themes and arguments appearing in the first edition, however, remain. As a political institution, the Court wields an antidemocratic power and is rarely held directly accountable for its decisions. Presidents invariably try to pack the Court and, as Chapter Two shows, thereby influence public policy beyond their limited time in the Oval Office. Through their appointments, especially when filling a crucial seat or a number of vacancies in short order, Presidents may indeed leave their mark on the Court's policy-making. On the bench, however, justices are sovereign and may disappoint their presidential benefactors, as well as find it difficult to refrain from off-the-bench activities. Instead of leaving the world of politics behind, the justices form a small political elite that may wield potentially enormous power.

Life in the marble temple constrains judicial behavior and the politics of making law. In historical perspective, Chapter Three examines the institutional dynamics of the Court and the changing working relations among the justices, and argues that the Court has become increasingly bureaucratic in response to growing caseloads. In addition, unlike any other federal court, the Supreme Court now has virtually complete discretion over its selection of cases and sets its own agenda for policy-making. The justices' control over deciding what to decide and the processes by which they select cases are examined in Chapter Four. In explaining how justices decide cases and the process of opinion writing, Chapter Five shows why there is now less collective deliberation than there used to be and how the Court has come to function more like a legislative body. Critics of unpopular rulings have often castigated the Court for being a "super legislature." I aim to show that the Court has instead come to *function* more like a legislative body because it not only possesses the power to manage its docket but to set its substantive policy-making agenda. The justices now place less of a premium on collegial deliberations leading to institutional decisions and delegate more responsibilities to larger staffs within the Court.

Although the Court has come to function like a roving commission monitoring the governmental process, its rulings are not self-executing. The Court depends on other political institutions and on public opinion to carry out its decisions. But those forces may also curb the Court. The limitations of Supreme Court policy-making are considered in the final chapter, but the basic conclusion may be stated at the outset: the Court by itself holds less power to change the country than either liberals or conservatives often claim. Major confrontations in constitutional politics, like those over school desegregation, school prayer, and abortion, are determined as much by what is possible in a system of free government and in a pluralistic society as by what the Court says. The Court's policy-making, as with its rulings on abortion and school desegregation, also evolves with changes in its composition and in the country. In sum, the Court's influence on American life rests on a paradox. Its political power is at once antidemocratic and countermajoritarian. Yet that power, which flows from giving meaning to the Constitution, truly rests, in Chief Justice Edward White's words, "solely upon the approval of a free people."

Acknowledgments

IN RESEARCHING and writing the first edition of this book, I incurred a large number of debts. It is fair to say that I might never have embarked on the project had it not been for Chief Justice Warren Burger and his assistant, Mark Cannon. The opportunities they afforded me as a judicial fellow, and then as a research associate, in the Office of the Administrative Assistant to the Chief Justice were invaluable. Both later took an interest in the book and generously spent time talking with me and clarifying various matters. Although they may not agree with all my views, I remain grateful for the insights and kindness they gave me.

The experience at the Court provided a perspective, but only began my inquiry. The inquiry led to an examination of the private papers of fifty-eight justices (over half of all the justices who ever sat on the high bench), as well as the papers of seven Presidents. While most of the collections are open to the public, access to some requires special permission. For their permission to use certain collections, I am grateful to Justice William J. Brennan, Jr., Paul Freund, Eugene Gressman, William E. Jackson, Mrs. Carolyn Agger Fortas, Mrs. Hugo Black, Hugo Black, Jr., and Justice Lewis F. Powell, Jr.

Assistance at various libraries was crucial to the study. David Wigdor and his splendid staff in the Manuscripts Division of the Library of Congress were always helpful. Paul Freund, Erika Chadbourn, and Judith Mellins made my stays at the Harvard Law School Library fruitful. Others who deserve mention for their attention and assistance are Bill Cooper of the University of Kentucky Library; Nancy Bressler and Jean Holiday of the Seeley G. Mudd Manuscripts Library at Princeton University; Patricia Bodak Stark of the Yale University Library; Dale Mayer of the Herbert Hoover Presidential Library; Carole Knobil of Special Collections at the University of Texas School of Law Library; Cynthia Fox of the National Archives and Records Service; Marjorie Barritt of the Bentley Historical Library at the University of Michigan; Michael Kohl of Special Collections at Clemson University; Karen Rohrer at the Dwight D. Eisenhower Library; Nancy Smith of the Lyndon Baines Johnson Library; Charles Warren Ohrvall of the Harry S. Truman Library; Dallas R. Lindgren of the Minnesota Historical Society; Gail Galloway and Diane Williams of the Curator's Office of the Supreme Court of the United States; and David Pride of the Supreme Court Historical Society. No less helpful were the staffs of the Manuscripts Division of Alderman Library at the University of Virginia; the John Marshall Papers Project at the College of William and Mary; the John Fitzgerald Kennedy Library; the Gerald R. Ford Library; the Hoover Institution on War, Revolution, and Peace; the Franklin D. Roosevelt Library; the Columbia Oral History Project and the Rare Books and Manuscripts Division in Butler Library at Columbia University; and the library of the Cardozo School of Law at Yeshiva University.

The justices' papers did not end my inquiry, but instead raised further questions. Interviews and discussions of my tentative conclusions saved me from some (though possibly not all) errors of judgment. For their time and insights, I am indebted to Chief Justices Warren Burger and William H. Rehnquist and

Justices William J. Brennan, Jr., Sandra Day O'Connor, Lewis F. Powell, Jr., Potter Stewart, and John Paul Stevens. I am also grateful to Mark Cannon, William T. Gossett, Jr., Fred Graham, Sidney Fine, Paul Freund, Alpheus T. Mason, Walter Murphy, and Benno Schmidt. Justices Harry Blackmun, Thurgood Marshall, and Byron White graciously corresponded with me about the book.

Without the support of a number of individuals and organizations, the research could not have been undertaken. Two grants from the American Philosophical Society got the project under way. The Gerald R. Ford Foundation, the Hoover Presidential Library Association, the Lyndon Baines Johnson Foundation, and the Harry S. Truman Institute made possible the examination of presidential papers. The National Endowment for the Humanities provided a small travel grant. Marshall Robinson and Peter de Janosi of the Russell Sage Foundation, patient supporters of my projects, provided opportunities that contributed to this work. At the University of Virginia, Kenneth Thompson and the Committee on Summer Research Grants, and Dean Merrill Peterson and the Virginia Research Policy Council, provided additional support at crucial times. Henry J. Abraham, Gordon E. Baker, Alpheus T. Mason, Jack Peltason, Philip Phibbs, and C. Herman Pritchett wrote the necessary letters of recommendation. Bunny Stinnett and Kathy Fast faithfully typed the original manuscript.

The book benefited from the comments of John Schmidhauser and Martin Shapiro. There are not words to repay my teacher C. Herman Pritchett for reading two drafts and (as always) offering encouragement. I am no less indebted to my colleague Henry J. Abraham for reading drafts of chapters and supporting me in ways that only he knows.

The second, third, and fourth editions incurred even more debt. I am especially grateful to Erwin N. Griswold for sharing his intimate knowledge of the Court. Steve York, producer of the PBS special "This Honorable Court," was also particularly kind in sharing portions of interviews with members of the Rehnquist Court that, alas, failed to make the final cut for the film but that were immensely helpful in updating this book. Justices William J. Brennan, Arthur Goldberg, Lewis F. Powell, and John Paul Stevens provided me with additional insights. I also benefited when incorporating new material on the battle over Judge Robert H. Bork's nomination from discussions with members of a Twentieth Century Fund Task Force on Judicial Selection, for which I served as rapporteur. Walter Berns, Lloyd N. Cutler, Philip Kurland, Jack W. Peltason, and Michael M. Uhlmann were very helpful, even when we disagreed. Others deserving special acknowledgment include Toni House, the Court's public information officer, and Tony Mauro, Ronald Collins, A. E. Dick Howard, Saul Brenner, William Coleman, Philip Cooper, Louis Fisher, Paul Freund, Herbert Kaufman, Milton Handler, Chief Judge Howard T. Markey, and E. Barrett Prettyman. Christopher Banks, Stephen Bragaw, and Steve Brown, three of my much valued students and research assistants, cheerfully lent their labor on different editions.

This fifth edition incurs still more debt. I am grateful for the favorable reception earlier editions received and for the suggestions and support of colleagues and students. Along with many of those listed above who remain helpful, I remain indebted to the staff of the Manuscripts Room of the Library of Congress for assisting me in working through Justice Thurgood Marshall's papers for this and the fourth edition, as they have for almost two decades on my trips to conduct research in the collections of many other justices. Justice Lewis F. Powell, Jr., also kindly granted permission to consult his papers, for which I am grateful to him and to John Jacobs, the archivist at the Washington and Lee Law School. The staff of the National Archives at College Park, Maryland, were no less helpful in assisting with the Nixon Presidential Materials. In addition, in preparing this edition, I especially benefited from an interview with Chief Justice William H. Rehnquist and from the willingness of Justices Harry

Blackmun, John Paul Stevens, David Souter, Ruth Bader Ginsburg, and Antonin Scalia to meet with me or to correspond about particular matters. William K. Suter, the Clerk of the Court; Dale Bosley, the Marshal; Frank D. Wagner, the Reporter of Decision; Shelley L. Dowling, Librarian of the Court; Mary Ann Willis, Counsel of the Legal Office; the late Toni House, who for sixteen years served as the Court's Public Information Officer; and James Duff, who served as the Administrative Assistant to the Chief Justice, kindly read and commented on portions of the last edition. Their comments helped update and improve this fifth edition, for which I am especially grateful. At Norton, Donald Fusting, Hilary Hinzmann, and Amanda Adams were immensely helpful on the first edition, and Don was a faithful editor on the second and third editions. Steve Dunn served as the editor of the fourth edition, and it was a pleasure to work with Sarah Caldwell on this fifth edition.

Claudine, my wife, continues to make life a joy. With the addition of our daughter, Sara, the second edition was affectionately dedicated to her and her big brother, Benjamin. The fourth edition was rededicated to them as well as to our further addition and their little sister, Talia. This fifth edition is affectionately rededicated to our children.

January 1999   D. M. O.
Charlottesville, Virginia

ONE

A Struggle for Power

O N A HOT NIGHT in August 1969, Norma McCorvey, a twenty-one-year-old carnival worker nicknamed Pixie, was returning to her motel on a side road outside Augusta, Georgia. On her way back to her room, she was gang-raped by three men and a woman. The carnival and Pixie moved on to Texas. There, several weeks later, Pixie found herself pregnant. A high school dropout, who was divorced and had a five-year-old daughter and little money, Norma McCorvey unsuccessfully sought an abortion. Texas, like most other states at the time, prohibited abortions unless necessary to save a woman's life. "No legitimate doctor in Texas would touch me," she remembers. "I found one doctor who offered to abort me for $500. Only he didn't have a license, and I was scared to turn my body over to him. So there I was—pregnant, unmarried, unemployed, alone and stuck."[1]

That was how McCorvey originally told her story of desperation, yet it was only partially true. She was poor and pregnant, but not raped. Nearly twenty years later McCorvey revealed making up the story about being raped, after a doctor told her she could not get an abortion in Texas. "That was a lie—I said it because I was desperate and wanted an abortion very, very bad and thought that would help the situation. It didn't."[2] McCorvey completed her pregnancy and gave up the child she bore for adoption. A Dallas lawyer, Henry McCloskey, Jr., found someone to adopt the baby she never saw. He also introduced her to two recent graduates of the University of Texas Law School, Sarah Weddington and Linda Coffee. The three women decided to challenge the constitutionality of the Texas law forbidding all abortions not necessary "for the purpose of saving the life of the mother." They aimed to establish a woman's constitutional right "to control of her own body" and became part of a larger historical movement and political struggle.

What began as one woman's story of personal struggle unfolded into a saga of political controversy. "Pixie" became "Jane Roe" in a test case against Henry Wade, the district attorney, criminal division, for Dallas County, Texas. Her case led to the Supreme Court's landmark ruling in *Roe v. Wade* (1973). In recognizing a woman's "fundamental right" to control her own body, the Court raised abortion to the national political agenda and, once again, became a storm center of political controversy. Over a quarter of a century later the country remains sharply divided over the issue of abortion. In that time, though, much had changed. The Court's composition altered dramatically and in turn *Roe*'s original mandate failed to stand the test of time, as the Rehnquist Court returned more authority to states and localities to regulate and limit the availability of abortions. Further, Norma McCorvey renounced *Roe* and the abortion-rights movement.[3]

In both the tortuous way the justices reached their decision in *Roe* and in the ensuing controversy, the Court's rulings—from *Roe* and *Webster v. Reproductive Health Services* (1989) to *Planned Parenthood of Southeastern Pennsylvania v. Casey* (1992)—illustrate the political struggles that occur within the Court and over its role in American politics, along with the possibilities and limitations of judicial policy-making. This issue and these cases illustrate how we will examine the Court and the issues before it throughout the book.

Abortion, the Court, and American Politics

Little public attention was paid on May 4, 1971, when *Roe v. Wade* appeared on the Court's order list. It was one of only 163 from more than 4,500 cases on the docket granted oral argument and to be heard the next term. The *New York Times* simply reported that the Court "agreed to consider if state anti-abortion laws violate the constitutional rights of pregnant women by denying their right to decide whether or not to have children." In the end the Court's decision would affect the laws in virtually every state. At the time, though, there was no way of predicting whether or how the Court would decide the issue.

Just one month earlier, in *United States v. Vuitch* (1971), a bare majority had upheld the District of Columbia's statute prohibiting abortions unless "necessary for the preservation of the mother's life or health." By upholding the statute, the Court increased the availability of abortions in Washington, but it did not address the question of whether women have a constitutional right to obtain abortions. Chief Justice Warren Burger and Justices John Harlan, Byron White, and Harry Blackmun joined Hugo Black's opinion for the Court. Black ruled that the law was not unconstitutionally vague in allowing abortions for "health" reasons. The most liberal member of the Court, William Douglas, dissented. He thought the law was "void for vagueness" since it was uncertain whether psychological considerations— such as anxiety and the stigma of having an unwanted or illegitimate child—counted as health factors entitling women to have abortions. The District of Columbia statute, however, unlike the Texas law adopted in 1854, was one of the most liberal in the country at the time, since it allowed abortions not only to save the woman's life but also to maintain her physical and psychological well-being.

The movement to liberalize abortion laws had grown throughout the turbulent 1960s with the "sexual revolution" and demands for women's rights. Yet the legal reforms pushed by women's pro-choice advocates were in some respects little more than a return to the legal status of abortions a century earlier. Until the mid-nineteenth century, most states permitted abortions, except after quickening—the first movement of the fetus—and then an abortion was usually considered only a minor offense. After the Civil War, anti-abortionists persuaded states to toughen their laws. Every state, except Kentucky, had made abortion a felony by 1910. The over-whelming majority of the states permitted abortions only to save a woman's life. But by the late 1960s, fourteen states had liberalized laws to permit abortions when the woman's health was in danger, when there was a likelihood of fetal abnormality, and when the woman had been a victim of rape or incest. Four states—Alaska, Hawaii, New York, and Washington—had gone so far as to repeal all criminal penalties for abortions performed in early pregnancy.

By the time oral arguments were heard in 1971, Black and Harlan had retired. Black had been a leading liberal and Harlan one of the most conservative members within the Court. But neither looked kindly on claims to a constitutional right to an abortion. At the conference discussion of *Vuitch,* Black would not go along "with a woman's claim of [a] constitutional right to use her body as she pleases." Burger shared that view. He rejected any "argument that [a] woman has [an] absolute right to decide what happens to her own body."[4] Without Black and Harlan, the Court was diminished. President Richard Nixon's last two nominations, Lewis Powell, Jr., and William Rehnquist, had not yet been confirmed by the Senate.

On December 13, 1971, Chief Justice Burger opened the Court's oral argument session with the simple announcement "We will hear arguments in No. 18, *Roe* against *Wade.*" Sarah

Weddington was remarkably calm in her first appearance before the high bench. She made no mention of McCorvey's story about being raped. (Nor did Weddington mention the fact that as a twenty-two-year-old daughter of a Texas Methodist minister in the late 1960s she had to cross the border in order to obtain an abortion in Mexico. Although no one knew about her experience, it weighed in her mind when arguing the case before the Court.) Instead, Weddington began by reviewing the lower court's holding that the Texas abortion law violated a woman's right to continue or terminate a pregnancy. But Burger interrupted to ask whether the issues had already been decided by the ruling in *Vuitch v. United States.* Weddington explained that *Vuitch* upheld a law that permitted abortions when necessary to the health or the life of a woman. The Texas law was more restrictive; it allowed abortions only when necessary to save the life of the woman. Doctors were not free to consider the effects of pregnancy on the woman's mental or physical health. *Vuitch* was not considered binding in Texas, and doctors were being prosecuted for performing abortions other than those necessary to save the woman's life. Women who sought to terminate unwanted pregnancies had to go to New York, the District of Columbia, or some other state with liberal abortion laws. Women like Jane Roe, who were poor and for whom abortions were not necessary to save their lives, had no real choice. They faced either unwanted childbirths or medically unsafe self-abortions that could result in their deaths. The irony of the law, moreover, was that women who performed self-abortions were guilty of no crime. The Texas law authorized the prosecution only of doctors who performed abortions, not of the women who sought or performed their own abortions. The victims of the law were women and, Weddington pointed out, "[i]t's so often the poor and disadvantaged in Texas who are not able to escape the effect of the law."

"It's an old joke, but when a man argues against two beautiful ladies like this, they are going to have the last word." There was no laughter in the courtroom, however, at that opening remark by Jay Floyd, the assistant attorney general of Texas, who was before the Court to defend the abortion law. His southern accent and manner embellished the position he was trying to defend. This controversy is not one for the courts, he argued, and arguments about freedom of choice are misleading. Floyd pressed the point:

There are situations in which, of course as the Court knows, no remedy is provided. Now I think she makes her choice prior to the time she becomes pregnant. That is the time of the choice. It's like, more or less, the first three or four years of our life we don't remember anything. But, once a child is born, a woman no longer has a choice, and I think pregnancy then terminates that choice. That's when.

After Weddington's presentation of the realities of abortion in Texas, the argument sounded surreal, strangely out of date and out of place. One of the justices impatiently shot back, "Maybe she makes her choice when she decides to live in Texas." Laughter almost drowned out Floyd's feeble reply: "There is no restriction on moving."

"What is Texas' interest? What is Texas' interest in the statute?" demanded Justice Thurgood Marshall. The state has "recognized the humanness of the embryo, or the fetus," Floyd explained, and has "a compelling interest because of the protection of fetal life." Yet, interjected Justice Potter Stewart, "Texas does not attempt to punish a woman who herself performs an abortion on herself." Floyd replied, "That is correct," and continued:

And the matter has been brought to my attention: Why not punish for murder, since you are destroying what you—or what has been said to be a human being? I don't know, except that I will say this. As medical science progresses, maybe the law will progress along with it. Maybe at one time it could be possible, I suppose, statutes could be passed. Whether or not that would be constitutional or not, I don't know.

But, Stewart countered, "we're dealing with the statute as it is. There's no state, is there, that equates abortion with murder?

Or is there?" There was none, Floyd admitted and then hastened to emphasize that, though courts had not recognized the unborn as having legal rights, states have a legitimate interest in protecting the unborn. As to a woman's choice on abortion, Floyd reiterated, "[W]e feel that this choice is left up to the woman prior to the time she becomes pregnant. This is the time of choice."[5]

When *Roe* was discussed in the justices' private conference, Burger noted that the case had not been very well argued. He also thought because the case presented such a "sensitive issue," it should be set for reargument so that Powell and Rehnquist could participate and a full Court reach a decision. As chief justice, he led the discussion, observing that the Texas law was "certainly arcane," though not unconstitutional. He was inclined to the view that the law should fall for vagueness. Senior Associate Justice William Douglas spoke next. He disagreed and had no doubt that the statute was unconstitutional. For Douglas, the Texas law not only was vague but also impinged on a woman's right of privacy. William Brennan and Stewart agreed, as later did Marshall. White came out on the other side. He could not go along with the argument that women have a constitutional right of privacy, giving them a choice on abortion. A right of privacy is not specifically mentioned in the Constitution. And White did not find persuasive arguments that a right of privacy is one of the unenumerated rights retained by the people under the Ninth Amendment and protected by the Fourteenth Amendment's provision that no state may deprive any person of life, liberty, or property without due process of law. Harry Blackmun, then the newest member of the Court, spoke last: "Don't think there's an absolute right to do what you will with [your] body." But this statute was poorly drawn, Blackmun observed. It's too restrictive—it "doesn't go as far as it should and impinges too far on [Roe's] Ninth Amendment rights."[6] Blackmun appeared in the middle, but inclined toward the position of Douglas, Brennan, Stewart, and Marshall.

After conference the chief justice, if he is in the majority, by tradition assigns a justice to write the opinion justifying the Court's decision. On the abortion cases, Burger appeared to be in the minority, but he nonetheless gave the assignment to Blackmun. When Douglas complained, Burger responded that the issues were so complex and the conference discussion so diverse "that there were, literally, not enough columns to mark up an accurate reflection of the voting" in his docket book. He "therefore marked down no vote and said this was a case that would have to stand or fall on the writing, when it was done."[7]

Assigned to write the Court's opinion in late December 1971, Blackmun did not circulate a first draft until May 18, 1972. The draft immediately troubled Douglas and Brennan. Though striking down the abortion law, Blackmun's opinion did so on Burger's view that the law was vague rather than on the majority's view that it violated a woman's constitutional right of privacy. Douglas and Brennan wanted to know why the opinion failed to address the core issue, "which would make reaching the vagueness issue unnecessary." Blackmun claimed that he was "flexible as to results." He was simply trying his "best to arrive at something which would command a court." With "hope, perhaps forlorn, that we might have a unanimous Court," he explained, "I took the vagueness route."[8]

A "freshman" in his second year on the Court and assigned to write a very difficult opinion, Blackmun found himself in the middle of the cross pressures of a growing dispute. Blackmun was psychologically and intellectually torn. On the one hand, Burger had been his longtime friend and had recommended his appointment to the Court; on the other, Blackmun was attracted to Douglas's position on a woman's right of privacy. He began thinking that it might be better to have the case reargued the next term, as Burger and White had suggested. "Although it would prove costly to [him] personally, in the light of energy and hours expended," Blackmun concluded, he would move for reargument. He explained that "on an issue so sensitive and so emotional as this one, the country deserves the conclusion of a

nine-man, not a seven-man court, whatever the ultimate decision may be."[9]

Douglas was taken aback by the prospect of Nixon's last two
appointees participating; the final decision might go the other
way. If Blackmun withdrew his motion for reargument, it would
fail. But if he didn't, there would be trouble. The vote would be
four to three against reargument, and that could lead to a heated
confrontation. Douglas appealed to Blackmun not to vote for
reargument. Instead of complaining about the initial draft opinion, Douglas commended Blackmun by letter for his "yeoman
service" in a difficult area and emphasized that he had "a firm 5
and the firm 5 will be behind you" on the opinion. Brennan
followed with a similar note.[10]

By tradition, only those justices participating in a case may
vote on its reargument, but then came a memorandum from
Lewis Powell. He noted that during the first months when decisions were made on rearguments he had taken "the position
then, as did Bill Rehnquist, that the other seven Justices were
better qualified to make those decisions." However, Powell further explained, "The present question arises in a different context. I have been on the Court for more than half a term. It may
be that I now have a duty to participate in this decision." He
and Rehnquist would vote for a rehearing.[11] That made a majority of five for carrying *Roe* over to the next term.

Douglas was shocked and threatened: "If the vote of the
Conference is to reargue, then I will file a statement telling what
is happening to us and the tragedy it entails."[12] That would only
have intensified tensions. Douglas was finally persuaded not to
publicize his outrage and instead simply to note that he dissented from the Court's order for reargument. Blackmun also
decided to spend the summer further researching the complex
issues in this increasingly vexing case.

On October 11, 1972, the Court heard rearguments. For a
second time, Weddington stood before the high bench to ask
that it rule that women have a right to choose to continue or

terminate a pregnancy. Since *Vuitch,* she pointed out, more than sixteen hundred Texas women had gone to New York City for abortions, and there were "many other women going to other parts of the country." But Weddington's arguments were repeatedly interrupted by questions from the bench about the rights of the unborn. Justice White put it bluntly: "[W]ould you lose your case if the fetus was a person?" That would require a balancing of interests, Weddington replied, but that was not at issue here, since it had not been asserted that a fetus has any constitutional rights. The issue was simply a conflict between the constitutional rights of women and the statutory interests of the state. The state would have to establish that the fetus is a "person" under the Fourteenth Amendment or some other part of the Constitution, before it would have a compelling interest in prohibiting abortions and require the Court to strike a balance with women's constitutional rights.

"That's what's involved in this case? Weighing one life against another?" White again asked toward the end of Weddington's oral argument time. No, she insisted in her concluding exchange with the justices:

STEWART: Well, if—if it were established that an unborn fetus is a person, with the protection of the Fourteenth Amendment, you would have almost an impossible case here, would you not?

WEDDINGTON: I would have a very difficult case.

STEWART: I'm sure you would. So, if you had the same kind of thing, you'd have to say that this would be the equivalent—after the child was born, if the mother thought it bothered her health any having the child around, she could have it killed. Isn't that correct?

WEDDINGTON: That's correct. That—

BURGER: Could Texas constitutionally, in your view, declare that—by statute, that the fetus is a person, for all constitutional purposes, after the third month of gestation?

WEDDINGTON: I do not believe that the State legislature can determine the meaning of the Federal Constitution. It is up to this Court to make that determination.

Chief Justice Burger then called Robert C. Flowers, who had replaced Floyd and as assistant attorney general represented Texas before the Court. From the outset, Flowers faced a steady barrage of questions about whether a fetus is a "person" under the Constitution. He was driven to concede that no case had recognized the fetus as a "person" and that the Fourteenth Amendment extends protection only to those born or naturalized in the United States. At the prodding of White, he was forced to agree that the case would be lost if the fetus is not recognized as a "person." Yet Flowers continued to insist that the unborn are entitled to constitutional protection. In response to questions from Justices Marshall and Rehnquist, however, he could not supply any medical evidence that a fetus is a "person" at the time of conception. Finally, Flowers confessed that he knew of no way "that any court or any legislature or any doctor anywhere can say that here is the dividing line. Here is not a life; and here is a life, after conception."

Whether a fetus is a "person," Flowers argued, is an issue that should be left to the state legislatures. But that argument underscored the Court's dilemma and aroused Stewart:

Well, if you're right that an unborn fetus is a person, then you can't leave it to the legislature to play fast and loose dealing with that person. In other words, if you're correct, in your basic submission that an unborn fetus is a person, then abortion laws such as that which New York has are grossly unconstitutional, isn't it?

Liberal abortion laws, Flowers urged, allow "the killing of people." But put this way, the matter could not be left to the states, for it ran against the logic of constitutional law to say that a fetus is a "person" in one state but not in another. It is the Court's responsibility to interpret the Constitution. If the Court struck down the Texas law, it would invite attacks by those who believe that the fetus is a "person" entitled to constitutional protection. But even though there may be good, moral arguments for recognizing the personhood of an unborn, there was no constitu-

tional basis for ruling that way. Neither the text nor the history
of the drafting of the Constitution and the Fourteenth Amendment revealed that the unborn are "persons" with constitutionally protected rights. Scientific evidence was not helpful, and the
reform of abortion laws in almost half of the states supported
the conclusion that the unborn were not generally considered
legal persons. If Texas's century-old law were upheld on the
ground that the unborn are "persons" under the Constitution,
then the Court would be making law that ran counter to the text
and history of the Constitution as well as legal and social trends,
and would thus force it to strike down all of the recently enacted
state laws permitting abortions.

Weddington had a few minutes to give a final rebuttal, but
most of her time was consumed by questions from Burger, who
returned to whether *Vuitch* had not already settled the issues
here. Again, she reiterated, the issue of a woman's right to
decide whether to terminate an unwanted pregnancy had not
been decided in *Vuitch,* and that issue had divided the lower
federal courts; nine decisions had favored women in upholding
the constitutionality of liberal abortion laws, and five had not.
The issue was one that the Court could not avoid or leave to
the lower courts or state legislatures. The issue was basically
one of human dignity versus political geography, that of a
woman's struggle for power and for the right to have some
control over her own life on such a fundamental matter versus
allowing each of the fifty states to determine the extent of
women's freedom. "We are not here to advocate abortion,"
Weddington concluded.

We do not ask this Court to rule that abortion is good, or desirable in
any particular situation. We are here to advocate that the decision as
to whether or not a particular woman will continue to carry or will
terminate a pregnancy is a decision that should be made by that individual; that, in fact, she has a constitutional right to make that decision
for herself; and that the State has shown no interest in interfering with
that decision.

The *Roe* v. *Wade* Decision and Its Aftermath

About a month after the Court heard rearguments, Blackmun had finished a new draft of his opinion for *Roe.* "It has been an interesting assignment," he observed when circulating the draft that eventually became the Court's final opinion. The opinion struck down the abortion law, but now along the lines originally advanced by Douglas and Brennan at conference. The opinion announced that the constitutional right of privacy is "broad enough to encompass a woman's decision whether or not to terminate her pregnancy." During the rest of November and most of December, Blackmun continued to rework portions of the opinion in light of other justices' comments. On December 21, he sent around his final draft. Douglas, Brennan, Marshall, and Stewart immediately agreed to join. Soon after the Christmas holidays, Powell also signed on, commending Blackmun for his "exceptional scholarship."[13] By mid-January, Burger had also agreed, though he would add a short concurring opinion, saying that he did not support "abortion on demand." Rehnquist and White were the only dissenters.

States could no longer categorically proscribe abortions or make them unnecessarily difficult to obtain. The promotion of maternal care and the preservation of the life of a fetus were not sufficiently "compelling state interests" to justify restrictive abortion laws. During roughly the first trimester (three months) of a pregnancy, the decision on abortion is that of a woman and her doctor. During the second, the Court ruled, states may regulate abortions, but only in ways reasonably related to its interest in safeguarding the health of women. In the third trimester, states' interests in preserving the life of the unborn become compelling, and they may limit, even ban, abortions, except when necessary to save a woman's life.

At conference, Blackmun had warned that the opinion "will probably result in the Court's being severely criticized." He therefore took special care in preparing the statement announcing the decision that he would read from the bench on January 23, 1973, and even had copies made available for reporters in the hope that they would not go "all the way off the deep end."[14]

But immediate press coverage was muted. President Lyndon Johnson died the day the ruling came down, and so the announcement of the landmark decision shared the headlines in the *New York Times, Los Angeles Times, Chicago Tribune,* and other major newspapers.

Initial reactions to the decision were intense and mixed. The president of the Planned Parenthood Federation of America, Dr. Alan Guttmacher, hailed the ruling as "a wise and courageous stroke for the right of privacy, and for the protection of a woman's physical and emotional health." Others, especially Catholics, took quite a different view. The justices "have made themselves a 'super legislature,' " New York's Terence Cardinal Cooke charged. "Whatever their legal rationale, seven men have made a tragic utilitarian judgment regarding who shall live and who shall die."[15] "Apparently the Court was trying to straddle the fence and give something to everybody," concluded Philadelphia's John Cardinal Krol after reading the opinion: "abortion on demand before three months for those who want that, somewhat more restrictive abortion regulations after three months for those who want that."[16]

Underlying these reactions was the irony of the Court's ruling liberally even though it was packed with "strict constructionists." The final ruling was handed down by a Court that President Nixon had tried to remold in his own image. As a presidential candidate in 1968 Nixon had attacked the "liberal jurisprudence" of the Warren Court (1953–1969) for being unfaithful to the text of the Constitution. Nixon's four appointees—Warren Burger, Harry Blackmun, Lewis Powell, and William Rehnquist—were all selected for their conservative strict constructionist judicial philosophy. Strict constructionists hold that constitutional interpretation should be confined to a literal reading of the Constitution informed by an understanding of its historical context. Yet only Rehnquist and Kennedy appointee White dissented from the Court's ruling that women have a constitutional right to have abortions.

Even those who favored the ruling sharply criticized *Roe* for resting on a constitutional right of privacy. Scholars attacked the legal analysis and reliance on scientific and medical evidence in the opinion.[17] The Court had created the right of privacy out of whole constitutional cloth, when striking down laws limiting the availability of contraceptives in *Griswold v. Connecticut* (1965). In *Griswold*, Douglas held that a constitutional right of privacy may be found in the "penumbras," "emanations," or "shadows" of various guarantees of the Bill of Rights. A right of associational privacy may be found in the penumbra of the First Amendment. The Third Amendment's prohibition against the quartering of soldiers "in any house" without the consent of the owner, Douglas claimed, is another facet of constitutionally protected privacy. The Fourth Amendment explicitly guarantees the right "of the people to be secure in their persons, houses, papers, and effects, against unreasonable searches and seizures." The Fifth Amendment's safeguard against self-incrimination also "enables the citizen to create a zone of privacy." Finally, Douglas noted, the Ninth Amendment provides that "[t]he enumeration in the Constitution, of certain rights, shall not be construed to deny or disparage others retained by the people." Douglas's penumbra theory of a right of privacy was, perhaps, too imaginative to persuade many court watchers. And *Roe* went even further. A woman's interests in abortion appeared to have little to do with those privacy interests identified in *Griswold* with various guarantees of the Bill of Rights. Rather than privacy per se, abortion basically involves a woman's liberty under the Constitution.[18]

Other court watchers critical of *Roe* took their cue from Rehnquist's dissenting opinion. They attacked the Court for becoming a "super legislature" in determining when a state's interests are compelling enough to override a woman's interests in obtaining an abortion. In overturning most abortion laws, the

Court held that states' interests become compelling only at the point of "viability"—the point at which the fetus is "potentially able to live outside the mother's womb, albeit with artificial aid." For states' rights advocates like Rehnquist, the Court impermissibly imposed its own view on state legislatures.

For still others, the Court committed a more fundamental sin: it had written the rights of the unborn out of the Constitution. "In my opinion," Utah's Republican Senator Orrin Hatch proclaimed, "this is clearly the *Dred Scott* issue of this century."[19] In *Dred Scott v. Sandford* (1857) the Court held that under the Constitution blacks were not "persons" entitled to its protection. Chief Justice Roger Taney also held that Congress had unconstitutionally enacted the Missouri Compromise, prohibiting slavery in the Louisiana Territory, except in Missouri. The Court thereby exacerbated tensions between the North and the South and hastened the movement toward the Civil War. In *Roe,* the Court did not resolve the question of when life begins, but held that the unborn do not enjoy protection under the Fourteenth Amendment's guarantee that no state may "deprive any person of life, liberty, or property, without due process of law." The Constitution does not define "person," and, the Court reasoned, the use of the word in the text of the Constitution, as well as the rather permissive abortion practices in the early nineteenth century, indicates that "the word 'person,' as used in the Fourteenth Amendment, does not include the unborn."

While *Roe* sparked political conflict among special-interest groups over abortion policy, the general public remained ambivalent. Rather consistently since 1973, public opinion polls show that over 80 percent approves of abortions if the woman's health is endangered, if a pregnancy is due to rape or incest, and if there is a likelihood of fetal abnormality. A *New York Times/ CBS News* poll found that 49 percent of the country supports continued legalized abortion, whereas 39 percent wants some restrictions, and only 9 percent favors a total ban. But the poll also showed that public opinion splits sharply depending on the reasons for obtaining abortions. When a woman's health is endangered, 87 percent of the public is supportive of abortion, but only 43 percent favors abortions for women who are poor and claim they cannot afford more children; support for abortion drops further (to 26 percent) for women seeking to terminate pregnancies because they interfere with their work or education.[20]

Opponents of *Roe* organized to elect representatives to enact new laws and to pass constitutional amendments, as well as to bring litigation aimed at overturning the decision. But some also took to the streets and turned to civil disobedience and violence. According to the National Abortion Federation, between 1977 and 1987 bombs destroyed thirty-two abortion clinics, thirty-eight others were victimized by arson, and more than six hundred were picketed by demonstrators. In the 1990s, several doctors who perform abortions were murdered or wounded.

Like most Supreme Court policy-making, *Roe* left numerous questions unanswered and afforded ample opportunities for thwarting compliance with its mandate. The Burger Court basically stood its ground, striking down most state and local attempts to limit the impact of *Roe*.[21] However, the Court upheld a city's policy of refusing nontherapeutic abortions in public hospitals and state restrictions on the funding of nontherapeutic abortions.[22] And as the Court's composition changed, pressure mounted with speculation that *Roe* would be further restricted, if not expressly overruled.

Opposition came not only from the states but also from Congress and the President. Constitutional amendments were introduced in Congress to limit or overturn the ruling. Some proposed "right to life" amendments would return to the pre-*Roe* practice of allowing the states to regulate abortion freely. Others, introduced by Senators Hatch and Jesse Helms, would amend the Constitution to recognize the unborn as "persons" with protected rights. Still other bills aimed to limit the federal judiciary's jurisdiction over abortion.[23]

Congress failed to pass a constitutional amendment over-turning *Roe* but succeeded in limiting the reach of the Court's ruling in a number of ways. In the decade following *Roe,* Congress enacted some thirty laws restricting the availability of abortions. Among these statutes, Congress barred the use of funds for programs in which abortion is included as a method of family planning; barred government officials from ordering recipients of federal funds to perform abortions; barred lawyers working in federally funded legal aid programs from giving assistance to those seeking "nontherapeutic" abortions; provided that employers are not required to pay health insurance benefits for abortions except to save a woman's life; prohibited the use of federal employee health benefits to pay for abortions except when a woman's life is imperiled; prohibited the use of foreign aid funds for abortions; and prohibited federal prisons from paying for pregnant inmates' abortions.[24]

The Court responded to Congress's message when hearing challenges to some of its legislation. In *Harris v. McRae* (1980), the justices divided five to four when upholding the so-called Hyde Amendment (named after its sponsor, Republican Representative Henry Hyde of Illinois), which forbids federal funding of nontherapeutic abortions under the Medicaid program. Again, voting five to four in *Bowen v. Kendrick* (1988), the Court upheld the Adolescent Family Life Act, prohibiting federal funding of organizations involved with abortions, while allowing the funding of religious groups advocating self-discipline as a form of birth control.

Throughout the 1980s and into the 1990s the Court's ruling on abortion was an issue in presidential politics as well. In the 1980s and 1990s the Republican platforms, endorsed by Presidents Ronald Reagan and George Bush, supported a constitutional amendment "to restore protection of the right to life for unborn children." It was during Reagan's era that forces opposed to *Roe* gathered momentum and received legitimacy from the President. Although Reagan repeatedly called on Congress "to restore legal protections for the unborn, whether by statute or constitutional amendment," his administration never really pushed for congressional adoption of its stand on abortion. Instead, the strategy of the Reagan administration was to appoint to the federal bench only those opposed to abortion, initiate litigation that might undercut and ultimately lead to overturning *Roe,* and limit access to abortion providers through regulatory reforms.

The Court became ever more a symbol and instrument of political power during the Reagan-Bush era. It was subject to increasing pressure-group activity and litigation geared to reconsidering, if not reversing, *Roe,* as well as efforts to pack it with those opposed to abortion. But even after the retirements of Douglas and Stewart—and the appointments of John Paul Stevens in 1975 and Sandra Day O'Connor in 1981—the Court continued to reaffirm its basic ruling in *Roe.* In *City of Akron v. Akron Center for Reproductive Health* (1983), for example, the Court struck down several restrictions imposed on women seeking abortions, including requirements that they sign "informed consent" forms and wait at least twenty-four hours afterward before having an abortion, along with requiring doctors to perform abortions after the first trimester in a hospital and dispose of fetal remains "in a humane and sanitary way."

Three years later, 1986, the Reagan administration renewed its attack on *Roe.* This time Reagan's second solicitor general, Harvard Law School Professor Charles Fried, dared do what his predecessor had refused: he questioned the Court's wisdom and argued that *Roe* be overturned. In support of Pennsylvania's Governor Richard Thornburgh's appeal of a circuit court ruling, striking down a state law limiting the availability of abortions, Fried filed an extraordinary *amicus curiae* ("friend of the court") brief. He boldly proclaimed that "the textual, doctrinal and historical basis for *Roe v.Wade* is so far flawed and . . . a source of such instability in the law that this Court should reconsider that decision and on reconsideration abandon it."

The Court remained in no mood to reconsider *Roe* and again rebuffed the Reagan administration when handing down *Thornburgh v. American College of Obstetricians* (1986). A majority of the Court, moreover, appeared impatient with the administration's persistence in trying to undo *Roe*. When announcing the decision from the bench, Blackmun exclaimed, "We reaffirm *once again* the general principles of *Roe*." However, Chief Justice Burger broke with *Roe*'s supporters in *Thornburgh,* joining Justices O'Connor, Rehnquist, and White in dissent, and indicated that *Roe* should be "reexamined."

The five-to-four split in *Thornburgh* further escalated speculation about how another Reagan appointee might affect the Court and *Roe*. As the Court's composition changed, support for *Roe* among the justices appeared to decline. Within a week of the ruling on *Thornburgh,* Chief Justice Burger announced that he would step down from the Court. Reagan immediately responded by shrewdly elevating Rehnquist, one of *Roe*'s sharpest critics, to the chief justiceship and naming Antonin Scalia to his seat on the bench.

As an institution the Court does not usually shift course without major changes in its composition. While Justice Powell remained on the Court, he appeared to hold the pivotal vote for upholding *Roe*. The announcement of his retirement in June 1987 and Reagan's nomination of Judge Robert H. Bork— another of *Roe*'s sharpest critics—then set off a political fire storm. Following the mobilization of special-interest groups and weeks of deliberation (discussed in the next chapter), Bork's nomination went down by the widest Senate rejection (fifty-eight to forty-two) of any Supreme Court nominee. Reagan's second nominee, Judge Douglas Ginsburg, was forced to withdraw from consideration, once conservative Republican senators turned against him after revelations about his personal life. Reagan's third nominee, conservative Judge Anthony Kennedy, won easy Senate confirmation.

In the final days of the Reagan administration the Court

seemed poised to reconsider, and possibly to overturn, *Roe*. During the summer of 1988 Assistant Attorney General William Bradford Reynolds and others in Reagan's Department of Justice talked Missouri's attorney general, William Webster, into seizing an opportunity afforded by appealing another appellate court's invalidation of that state's restrictions on abortions.

At issue in *Webster v. Reproductive Health Services* was the constitutionality of four provisions of the 1986 Missouri law: (1) decreeing that life begins at conception and that "unborn children have protectable interest in life, health, and well being"; (2) requiring physicians, prior to performing an abortion on a woman believed to be twenty or more weeks pregnant, to test the fetus's "gestational age, weight, and lung maturity"; (3) prohibiting public employees and facilities from being used to perform abortions not necessary to save a woman's life; and (4) making it unlawful to use public funds, employees, and facilities for the purpose of "encouraging or counseling" a woman to have an abortion except when her life is in danger.

Webster's strategy was to defend Missouri's law as "nothing more than regulat[ing] abortions within the parameters allowed by *Roe v. Wade*." But he was persuaded to repeat word for word in his brief filed before the Court the language Fried used in his *Thornburgh* brief demanding *Roe*'s reversal. *Webster v. Reproductive Health Services* thus became the Reagan administration's parting shot at *Roe* and the Court.

The Court stood even larger as the forum of politics and constitutional principle in the struggle over abortion by the end of the Reagan era. Pressure-group activities surrounding the Court intensified with speculation about how Reagan's justices would line up in *Webster*. The activities of pro-life groups had already become symbolized with an annual "March for Life," attracting greater followings each year in picketing the Court on the anniversary of *Roe*. Unlike legislators, such pressure-group activities rarely touch the justices. But the marches and letter-writing campaigns reflected how the politics of the abortion controversy had been transformed in the years after *Roe*. The groups on both sides of the controversy were greater in number, better organized, and more attuned to the politically strategic uses of litigation. The politics of interest-group litigation are registered in the record number of *amicus* briefs filed in *Webster*. (*Amicus* briefs were originally intended to bring arguments and data not in the main briefs before the Court but became vehicles of advocacy for those seeking to influence the Court directly.) Together, seventy-eight *amicus* briefs were filed, representing a broad range of interests, thousands of individuals, more than four hundred organizations, and various coalitions forged over conflicting interpretations of law, history, science, and medicine.

More than two months passed after hearing oral arguments before the Court announced its decision in *Webster* on the last day of the Court's term. Chief Justice Rehnquist read aloud portions of his opinion upholding Missouri's regulations and reluctantly declining to jettison *Roe*. The justices were bitterly divided. Only Kennedy and White joined Rehnquist's opinion, and O'Connor and Scalia concurred in separate opinions. Visibly distressed, Blackmun, the author of *Roe*, also took the unusual step of reading from the bench his dissenting opinion, which Brennan and Marshall joined. Stevens also read from his separate opinion.

Justice O'Connor had come to hold the balance on the Court and cast the crucial vote. Agreeing with Rehnquist that *Roe*'s trimester approach is "problematic," she was nevertheless unwilling in *Webster* to return to the pre-*Roe* days, when there were no constitutional restraints on states banning abortion. O'Connor reiterated her view that states were free to regulate abortion so long as they do not "unduly burden the right to seek an abortion." Refusing to clarify her position further, she noted simply, "There will be time enough to re-examine *Roe*. And to do so carefully."

Scalia was infuriated by O'Connor's refusal to take a stand on *Roe*. That, lamented Scalia, meant "we can now look forward to at least another term with carts full of mail from the public and streets full of demonstrations." Impatient with the majority's failure expressly to overturn *Roe* and with O'Connor's resisting what he deemed the inevitable outcome, Scalia predicted years of litigation during which, as he put it, "the mansion of constitutionalized abortion law, constructed overnight in *Roe v. Wade*, must be disassembled doorjamb by doorjamb, and never entirely brought down, no matter how wrong it may be."

Rehnquist's plurality opinion thus appeared part of a holding pattern, a pause in the continuing dialogue between the Court and the country, geared toward inviting restrictive abortion laws, bringing litigation, and giving the majority ample opportunities to curtail sharply, if not reverse outright, *Roe*. Rehnquist claimed to "leave [*Roe*] undisturbed" but noted that "[t]o the extent indicated in our opinion, we would modify and narrow *Roe*." His opinion substituted the much more lenient "rational basis" test for *Roe*'s "strict scrutiny" test for reviewing whether abortion restrictions permissibly advance "the State's interest in protecting potential human life." Besides that suggested transformation in the Court's standard of review, Rehnquist included plenty of other language in his opinion to undermine *Roe* and signal the Court's changing course.

THE REHNQUIST COURT AND THE CONTINUING CONTROVERSY OVER ABORTION

Although not expressly overruling *Roe*, the Rehnquist Court shifted course in *Webster*, ensuring a renewed and intensified battle in the states. Both sides of the controversy immediately turned state legislatures into battlegrounds and anticipated bitter fights throughout the 1990s. Some states, like Pennsylvania, quickly passed tougher regulations but stopped short of prohibiting abortions. Louisiana, Utah, and the Territory of Guam, however, enacted laws making abortion a crime with a view to forcing the Court's hand and possibly achieving *Roe*'s reversal.

By the time the first of several challenges to states' post-

Webster abortion laws reached the Court, support for *Roe*'s original mandate had further ebbed on the high bench. The last two staunchly liberal justices, William J. Brennan, Jr., and Thurgood Marshall, had retired and were succeeded by President George Bush's appointees, Justices David H. Souter and Clarence Thomas. Of the seven-member majority in *Roe* only Justice Blackmun remained on the bench. For once both sides in the abortion controversy agreed on something—hat when reviewing the challenge to Pennsylvania's 1989 amendments to its abortion law the Court should make a final decision on *Roe* in *Planned Parenthood of Southeastern Pennsylvania v. Casey,* instead of awaiting another case.

Despite its radically altered composition, when granting *Casey*, the Rehnquist Court appeared in no mood to further fuel the abortion controversy prior to the 1992 presidential election. Notably, the Court did not ask the parties to address the question of whether *Roe* should be reconsidered, as it had done in *Webster*. At issue in *Casey* were provisions in Pennsylvania state law that (1) require doctors to inform women about fetal development, provide a list of medical providers offering "alternatives to abortion," and obtain a woman's "informed consent" before performing an abortion; (2) mandate a twenty-four-hour waiting period after a woman had given her consent before she may obtain an abortion; (3) require minors to obtain the informed consent of at least one parent, or a judge; and (4) require married women to notify their husbands, except when he cannot be located, when the father is not the husband, when a pregnancy is due to "spousal sexual assault" that has been reported to the police, or when a woman "has reason to believe" that notifying her husband might result in "bodily injury." The Court of Appeals for the Third Circuit upheld all of the regulations with the exception of that for husband notification, which it deemed to impose an undue burden on women.

Almost four months after hearing oral arguments, on June 29, 1992, the Court announced its decision in *Planned Parenthood of Southeastern Pennsylvania v. Casey*. The Court's sur-

prising decision was handed down in an unusual joint opinion
written by Justices O'Connor, Kennedy, and Souter, who each
read portions of their opinion for the Court from the bench.
Casey had fragmented the justices four ways, but a bare majority
firmly drew a line in reaffirming *Roe*'s "central holding" and
against state laws that "unduly burden" access to or ban abortions early in a woman's pregnancy. Four justices Chief Justice
Rehnquist and Justices Scalia, Thomas, and White voted to
uphold all of Pennsylvania's restrictions and to overrule *Roe*. By
contrast, Justice Blackmun voted to strike down all of the restrictions, while Justice Stevens voted to uphold the state's informed
consent and reporting requirements but to overturn its provisions for abortion counseling, a twenty-four-hour waiting period,
and spousal notification. The balance on the Court was held by
the plurality: Justices O'Connor, Kennedy, and Souter upheld
all of Pennsylvania's restrictions except for its requirement of
spousal notification and reporting. Besides the plurality's joint
opinion, the Chief Justice and Justices Blackmun, Stevens, and
Scalia filed separate opinions, in part concurring and dissenting,
that totaled 184 pages.

On the first page of their sixty-page opinion, Justices
O'Connor, Kennedy, and Souter observed:

It must be stated at the outset and with clarity that *Roe*'s essential
holding, the holding we reaffirm, has three parts. First is a recognition
of the right of the woman to choose to have an abortion before viability
and to obtain it without undue interference from the State. Before
viability, the State's interests are not strong enough to support a prohibition of abortion or the imposition of a substantial obstacle to the
woman's effective right to elect the procedure. Second is a confirmation of the State's power to restrict abortions after fetal viability, if the
law contains exceptions for pregnancies which endanger a woman's life
or health. And third is the principle that the State has legitimate interests from the outset of the pregnancy in protecting the health of the
woman and the life of the fetus that may become a child.

But the plurality proceeded to reject or significantly redefine
much of what *Roe* stood for. In rejecting *Roe*'s trimester analysis

for balancing the interests of women and the states in protecting the unborn, the plurality also overturned portions of earlier rulings in *Akron v. Akron Center for Reproductive Health, Inc.* (1983) and *Thornburgh v. American College of Obstetricians & Gynecologists* (1986), where, in the latter case, a bare majority had invalidated similar Pennsylvania restrictions to those that the Court now found acceptable. Even more significantly, the plurality (and an overwhelming majority of the justices) no longer recognized *Roe* as guaranteeing women a "fundamental right." Instead, the plurality redefined the "central principle" of *Roe* as guaranteeing a woman a liberty interest under the Fourteenth Amendment "to choose to terminate or continue her pregnancy before viability." And in replacing *Roe*'s analysis with an "undue burden" analysis of women's substantive liberty interests, the plurality drew a line on overly restrictive regulations at the point of viability.

The balance on the Court had clearly shifted to allowing states to impose more conditions and restrictions on the availability of abortions. But the balance had not shifted far enough for Chief Justice Rehnquist and Justices Scalia, Thomas, and White, who attacked the plurality's "undue burden" test as "standardless." They also ridiculed the plurality's invention of a novel theory of *stare decisis*—that is, when the Court should defer to precedents. Indeed, the heart of the plurality's opinion was a sixteen-page section, written by Justice Souter, that defended upholding *Roe* on the grounds that the Court's institutional integrity would otherwise suffer. If the Court overruled *Roe*, he reasoned, it would be perceived as both bowing to political pressure and undercutting its legitimacy for those who believed in and relied on *Roe*. But, the chief justice countered, on the one hand, that the plurality's theory of *stare decisis* appeared incoherent and disingenuous in discarding crucial parts of *Roe* while reaffirming its "central holding." "*Roe* continues to exist," added Rehnquist, "but only in the way a storefront on a western movie set exists: a mere facade to give the illusion of reality." The chief justice in turn criticized the plurality's reasoning for adhering to *stare decisis* because if the Court overturned *Roe* it would be widely perceived as "surrendering to political pressure." But, "there are two sides to every controversy," Rehnquist reminded all, when charging the plurality with giving in to the pressures of those who marched and demonstrated in support of *Roe*.

Casey, in other words, divided the justices not only over *Roe* but over the Court's role and place in American politics. Justices O'Connor, Kennedy, and Souter feared that the Court's legitimacy and institutional integrity would suffer if *Roe* were overturned outright and the Court thereby perceived as just a "naked-power organ"—a political institution whose decisions simply turn on personnel changes in its composition, rather than rest on "principled justifications" that appear essential to the Court's standing as a "temple of law." Chief Justice Rehnquist and three others, however, maintained that neither the Court's legitimacy nor *stare decisis* were served by adhering to a ruling they deemed wrongly and improperly decided in the first place. *Casey* thus confronted the justices with the brute fact that the Court is a political institution whose legitimacy is nonetheless perceived, within the marble temple and the country, to depend largely on the symbolism and reality of judicial independence, impersonal decision making, and "the rule of law." And facing that political reality the justices split not only on *Roe* but on how to preserve the Court's institutional symbolism and myths. "Make no mistake," as Justice Blackmun put it in his opinion, "the joint opinion of Justices O'Connor, Kennedy, and Scalia is an act of personal courage and constitutional principle." The plurality's opinion in *Casey* signaled that a bare majority of the Court would not go along with upholding unduly restrictive regulations, such as spousal notification provisions or bans on abortions performed prior to viability. *Casey* thus represented the kind of political compromise within the Court that was destined to please neither side of the struggle over abortion nor resolve

Proponents on both sides of the abortion issue demonstrate outside the Supreme Court Building. (*Jose R. Lopez/NYT Pictures*)

the continuing controversy. Battles were certain to continue in state legislatures, Congress, and the courts. The Court had struck a new balance and that would not change until the composition of the bench further changed. President Bill Clinton's two appointees, Justices Ruth Bader Ginsburg and Stephen Breyer, reinforced the strength of the centrists on the Court in favor of upholding *Roe.*

No Longer "the Least Dangerous" Branch

Like other rulings on major issues of public policy, *Roe* invited criticism that the Court is no longer, in Alexander Hamilton's words, "the least dangerous" branch. Rather, critics charge, the Court has become a "super legislature." But the Court's responsibility has always been to interpret the Constitution. Political conflicts are raised to the level of constitutional intelligibility. And with its rulings, the Court engages the country in a dialogue over the meaning of the Constitution.

The role and power of the Court have changed with American politics. The Court first struck down an act of Congress in *Marbury v. Madison* (1803), when Chief Justice John Marshall interpreted the Judiciary Act of 1789 to have impermissibly expanded the Court's original jurisdiction under Article III of the Constitution. The Marshall Court also overturned a number of state laws and thereby legitimated the power of the national government and its own power of judicial review. But the Court did not challenge Congress again until the Taney Court's decision in *Dred Scott v. Sandford* in 1857.

Since the late nineteenth century, the Court has assumed a major role in monitoring the governmental process. The Court regularly overturns acts of Congress, of the states, and even of local and municipal governments. The table on page thirty illustrates the trend toward more judicial activism, or willingness to overturn decisions of other political institutions.[25] *Roe v. Wade* dramatically illustrates this trend, because it placed the Court at the center of a great national controversy. But it was by no means an isolated case.

The Court, regardless of its composition, has increasingly

DECISIONS OF THE SUPREME COURT OVERRULED AND
ACTS OF CONGRESS HELD UNCONSTITUTIONAL, 1789–1998;
AND STATE LAWS AND MUNICIPAL ORDINANCES
OVERTURNED, 1789–1998°

Year	Supreme Court Decisions Overruled	Acts of Congress Overturned	State Laws Overturned	Ordinances Overturned
1789–1800, Pre-Marshall				
1801–1835, Marshall Court	3	1	18	
1836–1864, Taney Court	4	1	21	
1865–1873, Chase Court	4	10	33	
1874–1888, Waite Court	13	9	7	
1889–1910, Fuller Court	4	14	73	15
1910–1921, White Court	5	12	107	18
1921–1930, Taft Court	6	12	131	12
1930–1940, Hughes Court	21	14	78	5
1941–1946, Stone Court	15	2	25	7
1947–1952, Vinson Court	13	1	38	7
1953–1969, Warren Court	45	25	150	16
1969–1986, Burger Court	52	34	192	15
1986– , Rehnquist Court	30	17	71	16

°Note that in *Immigration and Naturalization Service v. Chadha* (1983), the Burger Cour struck down a provision for a "one-house" legislative veto in the Immigration and Naturalizatio Act but effectively declared all one- and two-house legislative vetoes unconstitutional. Whil 212 statutes containing provisions for legislative vetoes were implicated by the Court's decision *Chadha* is here counted as a single declaration of the unconstitutionality of congressional leg islation. Note also that the Court's ruling in *Texas v. Johnson* (1989), striking down a Texa law making it a crime to desecrate the American flag, invalidated laws in forty-eight states an a federal statute. It is counted here, however, only once. The data here include the Court 1997–1998 term.

asserted its power. The ideologically conservative Burger and Rehnquist Courts, for example, have been as activist as the liberal Warren Court. Their differences lie in the directions in which they have pushed constitutional law and politics. The Court is a human institution, and as its composition and the country change so does constitutional politics. The reasons why this is so are the subject of this book. The controversial appointment of justices and their struggles for influence, the more bureaucratic structure of the Court, and the political controversies sparked by important cases like *Roe, Webster,* and *Casey* highlight the difficult and vexing role played by the Supreme Court in American political life.

TWO

The Cult of the Robe

THERE is no reason in the world why a President should not 'pack' the Court"—"appoint people to the Court who are sympathetic to his political and philosophical principles."[1] So Justice William Rehnquist answered Democratic charges that President Ronald Reagan could change the direction of Supreme Court policy-making. Because justices serve for life, they furnish a President with historic opportunities to influence the direction of national policy well beyond his own term.

The myth occasionally circulates that appointments should be made strictly on merit. Attorney General Ramsey Clark, for instance, confided to President Lyndon Johnson, "I think a most significant contribution to American government would be the non-political appointment of judges."[2] Yet Johnson's appointments of Abe Fortas and Thurgood Marshall were political, as those of all other Presidents have been.

Once on the bench, justices often forget their political history and complain that Presidents don't know enough about the Court to make intelligent appointments. Justice Felix Frankfurter, for one, felt that President John Kennedy and his attorney general, Robert Kennedy, chose inferior judges. "What does

Bobby understand about the Supreme Court? He understands about as much about it as you understand about the undiscovered 76th star in the galaxy. . . . He said Arthur Goldberg was a scholarly lawyer. I wonder where he got that notion from."[3] What perturbed Frankfurter was that the Kennedy administration did "not adequately appreciate the Supreme Court's role in the country's life and the functions that are entrusted to the Supreme Court and the qualities both intellectual and moral that are necessary to the discharge of its functions." Distinguished individuals were accordingly passed over, in Frankfurter's opinion, in favor of such "wholly inexperienced men as Goldberg and White, without familiarity with the jurisdiction or the jurisprudence of the Court either as practitioners or scholars or judges."[4]

Judges and scholars perpetuate the myth of merit. The reality, however, is that every appointment is political. Merit competes with other political considerations, like personal and ideological compatibility, with the forces of support or opposition in Congress and the White House, and with demands for representative appointments on the bases of geography, religion, race, gender, and ethnicity.

The Myth of Merit

The Supreme Court is not a meritocracy. This is so for essentially two reasons: the difficulties of defining merit and the politics of judicial selection.

Any definition of "judicial merit" is artificial. Henry Abraham, a leading scholar on the appointment of justices, proposes the following six criteria of judicial merit: demonstrated judicial temperament; professional expertise and competence; absolute personal and professional integrity; an able, agile, lucid mind; appropriate professional educational background or training; and the ability to communicate clearly, both orally and in writing.[5] Yet justices themselves have difficulty defining such qualities as "judicial temperament." Judicial merit is perhaps reducible only to the standard of "obscenity" offered by Justice Potter Stewart: "I know it when I see it."[6]

A disproportionate number of justices are appointed from prominent positions in the lower federal and state courts, the legal profession, and the executive branch. The prior positions of the 108 justices who have served on the Court are as follows:[7]

Federal bench	27
Private legal practice	25
Executive branch	21
State bench	21
U.S. Senate	6
State governorship	3
House of Representatives	2
Law school professorship	2
Miscellaneous	1

But legal education and previous judicial experience have not been necessary for appointment to or achievement on the bench. In the first seventy-five years of the nineteenth century, law schools as we know them did not exist, and up until World War I the majority of the legal profession learned law through apprenticeship. Not until 1957, when Justice Charles Whittaker replaced Justice Stanley Reed, did all sitting members of the Court hold law degrees. Lack of prior judicial experience has not been a barrier either. No fewer than 84 of the 108 justices who sat in the Court had less than ten years of previous federal or state court experience. Judicial inexperience does not result in failure on the bench. Six chief justices had no prior experience—John Marshall, Roger Taney, Salmon Chase, Morrison Waite, Melville Fuller, and Earl Warren—as well as some outstanding associate justices, including Joseph Story, Louis Brandeis, Harlan Stone, Charles Evans Hughes, Felix Frankfurter, and Robert Jackson.

Judicial selection, as Justice Stone put it, is like a "lottery" from a pool of more or less qualified individuals. One of Stone's close friends, the Harvard law professor and political scientist Thomas Reed Powell, was even more blunt: "[T]he selection of Supreme Court Justices is pretty much a matter of chance."[8] Political associations and personal friendships often determine the fate of candidates for the Court. Powell saw this illustrated in the fact that:

[President] Taft met [his appointee Mahlon] Pitney at a dinner given to advance Swayze's prospects and preferred him to Swayze; . . . that [Justice Joseph] McKenna was a personal associate of [President William] McKinley; that [Justice William] Day also was and that his appointment by [President Theodore] Roosevelt was a legacy from McKinley; that [Justice Pierce] Butler was known to Taft in the Canadian Railways Valuation work and was a Catholic who could be substituted for Manton without having to turn down a Catholic; . . . that [Justice Stone] had been in college with [President Calvin] Coolidge; that [Justice] Brandeis had a closer relation with [President Woodrow] Wilson than with members of the Boston Bar, etc.[9]

"Luck," along with ability, agrees Justice Ruth Bader Ginsburg, "has a lot to do with who will get [appointed]."[10]

Meritorious individuals are thus passed over. No appointment has been more widely acclaimed as meritorious than that of Benjamin Cardozo, yet it was primarily due to political expediency. Frankfurter, for one, proclaimed, "The appointment of Cardozo is the noble fruit of a large-minded statesmanship on the President's part."[11] When telling President Herbert Hoover of the large number of letters he received hailing the appointment, Harlan Stone noted, "The interesting thing about Judge Cardozo's appointment is that, although there is nothing political in it, it will prove, I believe, to be of immense political advantage to the President. No appointment he has made has been better received."[12]

A leading liberal and chief judge on the New York Court of Appeals, Cardozo was indubitably distinguished. But he had been passed over several times before the Republican President

Hoover nominated him in 1932. He had been mentioned for the seat vacated by William Day in 1922. Leaders of the New York Bar continued to push him for positions filled by Presidents Warren Harding and Calvin Coolidge.[13] Cardozo was first considered by Hoover when Edward Sanford died in 1930. The President wanted to appoint someone from the West, since there was no representation of that region on the Court at the time. However, Hoover's adviser George Wickersham failed to find anyone from that region who merited serious consideration. Wickersham proposed naming Attorney General William Mitchell, the Pennsylvania attorney Owen Roberts, or the prominent attorney and unsuccessful 1924 presidential candidate John W. Davis. Hoover's close friend Justice Stone sent his list of candidates. At the top was Cardozo; at the bottom was the conservative North Carolina circuit court of appeals judge John J. Parker.[14] The President went down the list, eliminating potential nominees on the basis of their geographical location and political leanings, and finally settled on Judge Parker.[15]

Hoover's nomination was immediately attacked by the American Federation of Labor and other labor organizations, because one of Parker's decisions was interpreted as anti-union. The National Association for the Advancement of Colored People (NAACP) also lobbied against his confirmation, because it thought he was an enemy of black voting rights. After a six-week battle, the Senate for the first time in the twentieth century rejected a nomination to the Court, by the narrow margin of forty-one to thirty-nine. The respected Republican attorney Owen Roberts was subsequently nominated and confirmed. Hoover was badly embarrassed by the defeat of Parker. When the opportunity arose to make his next and last appointment, in 1932, he nominated Cardozo, for his reputation was unimpeachable, his nomination politically opportune, and his confirmation certain.

Politics conspired to assure Cardozo's appointment, just as it may defeat meritorious candidates. White House politics

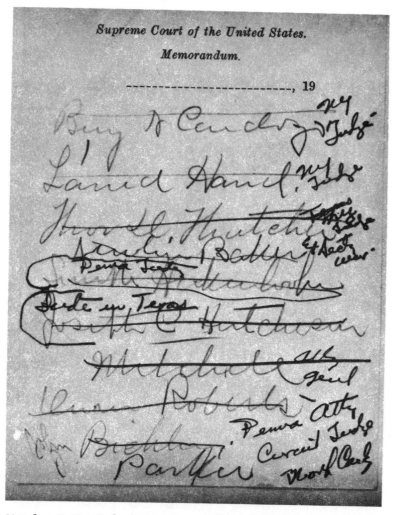

Note from Justice Harlan Stone, recommending individuals for appointment to the Supreme Court in 1930, with President Herbert Hoover's notes. (*Herbert Hoover Presidential Library*)

defeated the selection of Paul Freund, though he unquestion-
ably deserved a seat on the bench. Politics in the Senate
defeated Parker, yet he served with distinction for another
twenty-eight years on the court of appeals and was again considered for an appointment during the Roosevelt and Truman
administrations.[16] The Senate tends to vote for nominees who
are well qualified and ideologically compatible with their constituents.[17] However, senators may turn against nominees who
are viewed as too ideologically extreme. The Senate's rejection
of a nominee may also be affected by whether the President's
party is a minority in the Senate and by whether the nomination
occurs late in a President's term, especially if the occupant of
the Oval Office is a lame-duck President. In addition, the White
House's management or mismanagement of the nominee during
the confirmation process may contribute to success or failure in
the Senate.[18] In any event, the ultimate verdict on candidates
for the Court turns less on merit than on political visibility, support, and circumstance.

Process of Appointment

The appointment of justices is guided by the Constitution
and the competitive politics of the nomination and confirmation
process. Article II, Section 2, of the Constitution stipulates that
the President "shall nominate, and by and with the Advice and
Consent of the Senate, shall appoint" members of the federal
judiciary.* The Senate's power to reject nominees is the crucial

---

*In contrast with the system of appointing federal judges, the methods of
selecting state court judges are rather complex. They vary from state to state
and among different courts within particular states. The methods of selection
include popular—partisan and nonpartisan—election; appointment by governors or legislatures; and some combination of both methods, or so-called merit
system. In the merit system, a nonpartisan commission provides lists of nominees from which the governors legislature makes appointments; then, after
one year of service, the judges have names placed on a ballot and voters decide
whether they should be retained.[19]

obstacle that a President must overcome. Twenty-eight nominees to the Court have fallen prey to partisan politics, either because of the nominee's political views or because the Senate wanted to deny lame-duck Presidents appointments to the high court. Thanks to the tradition of "senatorial courtesy," which began in the 1840s, the Senate may also refuse to confirm an individual opposed by the senators of the President's party and the nominee's home state. Only two nominees—George Williams in 1873 and G. Harrold Carswell in 1970—suffered defeat because of mediocre judicial records and lack of professional qualifications.

The influence of the Senate has declined in the selection of Supreme Court justices but not in that of lower federal court judges. Presidents in fact trade lower-court judgeships for legislation and good relations.[20] Federal judgeships are opportunities for the Senate, no less than for the President, to influence national policy and confer political patronage. The tradition of senatorial courtesy guarantees patronage. During President Jimmy Carter's administration, "merit" commissions were created in an effort to minimize the influence of the Senate over lower-court judgeships. But the commissions did not work well and were abandoned when Reagan took office. Some senators simply refused to give up control over their patronage appointments.

The appointment process has become essentially a bargaining process in which the influence of the Senate is greater in regard to lower-court judgeships and that of the President is greater in regard to the Supreme Court. At the level of federal district courts, in Attorney General Kennedy's words, "Basically, it's senatorial appointment with the advice and consent of the President."[21] Presidents retain greater discretion at the level of circuit courts of appeals, whose jurisdiction spans several states. They may play senators off against each other by claiming the need for representation of different political parties, geographical regions, religions, races, and the like within a circuit. "In the case of the Supreme Court Justices," Hoover's attorney general, William Mitchell, observed, "with the whole country to choose from, the Senators from one state or another are in no position, even if they were so inclined, to attempt a controlling influence. Such an appointment is not a local matter, and the entire nation has an equal interest and responsibility."[22] But the Senate as a whole still has the power to influence the selection of, and even to defeat, a President's nominee.

Most Presidents delegate responsibility to their attorneys general and close advisers for selecting candidates and getting them through the Senate. The assistant attorney general in charge of the Office of Legal Policy usually begins by compiling a list of candidates from recommendations by White House staff, members of Congress, governors, state and local bar associations, and individuals wanting to be considered or suggesting others. A committee of the President's top advisers narrows the number per position down to two or three, on the basis of a political evaluation and (until the Reagan administration) informal approval by the American Bar Association (ABA). An exhaustive FBI investigation is then initiated and a formal evaluation by the ABA requested. Once these reports are reviewed, a recommendation is sent to the President. If he approves, it is formally submitted to the Senate. The Senate Judiciary Committee sends a "blue slip" to the senators of the same state as the nominee for their approval. If there is no objection, a confirmation hearing—typically lasting only a few minutes—is held before a subcommittee of the Judiciary Committee, which finally moves confirmation by the full Senate.

Presidents are now less involved in the process of appointing justices. Their greater reliance on staff has brought the possibility of more infighting at the White House. Appointments have become less a personal presidential decision than a hard choice from among candidates promoted by various vested-interests groups. The appointment of John Paul Stevens in 1975 illustrates the diverse pressures within the contemporary presidency.

SUPREME COURT NOMINATIONS REJECTED, POSTPONED,
OR WITHDRAWN BECAUSE OF SENATE OPPOSITION

Nominee	Year Nominated	Nominated By	Actions[1]
William Paterson[2]	1793	Washington	Withdrawn (for technical reasons)
John Rutledge[3]	1795	Washington	Rejected
Alexander Wolcott	1811	Madison	Rejected
John J. Crittenden	1828	J. Q. Adams	Postponed, 1829
Roger B. Taney[4]	1835	Jackson	Postponed
John C. Spencer	1844	Tyler	Rejected
Reuben H. Walworth	1844	Tyler	Withdrawn
Edward King	1844	Tyler	Postponed
Edward King[5]	1844	Tyler	Withdrawn, 1845
John M. Read	1845	Tyler	No action
George W. Woodward	1845	Polk	Rejected, 1846
Edward A. Bradford	1852	Fillmore	No action
George E. Badger	1853	Fillmore	Postponed
William C. Micou	1853	Fillmore	No action
Jeremiah S. Black	1861	Buchanan	Rejected
Henry Stanbery	1866	Johnson	No action
Ebenezer R. Hoar	1869	Grant	Rejected, 1870
George H. Williams[3]	1873	Grant	Withdrawn, 1874
Caleb Cushing[3]	1874	Grant	Withdrawn
Stanley Matthews[2]	1881	Hayes	No action
William B. Hornblower	1893	Cleveland	Rejected, 1894
Wheeler H. Peckham	1894	Cleveland	Rejected
John J. Parker	1930	Hoover	Rejected
Abe Fortas[6]	1968	Johnson	Withdrawn
Homer Thornberry	1968	Johnson	No action
Clement F. Haynsworth, Jr.	1969	Nixon	Rejected
G. Harrold Carswell	1970	Nixon	Rejected
Robert H. Bork	1987	Reagan	Rejected
Douglas H. Ginsburg	1987	Reagan	Withdrawn

[1] A year is given if different from the year of nomination.
[2] Reappointed and confirmed.
[3] Nominated for chief justice.
[4] Taney was reappointed and confirmed as chief justice.
[5] Second appointment.
[6] Associate justice nominated for chief justice.

James H. Wilson, Jr. *most brilliant + Harvard grad.*
Atlanta, Georgia *test lawyer*
Born 1920

Harvard, ▓▓▓▓▓▓▓▓▓▓▓▓▓▓

2 - Vincent Lee McKusick, Born 1921, Maine   *no Mormon problem*
                                                      confirmation fight
X Dallin Oaks, B. 1932, President of Brigham Young

Philip Areeda, b. 1930

4 Robert Bork, b. 1927

Philip Kurland, b. 1921 (Illinois)

Bennett Boskey, b. 1916 (Washington, D.C.)

Antonin Scalia, 1936

7 — Robert P. Griffin

8 - Charles E. Wiggins

9 - Judge J. Clifford Wallace, Ninth Circuit, 46 (Cal.) *second category*

5 - Judge Alfred T. Goodwin, Ninth Circuit, 52 (Oregon)

X Judge Paul Roney, Fifth Circuit, 53 (Fla)

(12,8)—Judge Philip Tone, 7th Circuit, 52 (Ill.) ✓

6 — Judge William Webster, Eighth Circuit, 51 (Mo.)

3 - Judge Arlin M. Adams, Third Circuit, 54 (Pa.) ✓

1 - Judge John Paul Stevens, 7th Circuit, 55 (Illinois) ✓

(456) —Judge Malcolm R. Wilkey, D.C. Circuit, 56 (Texas)

(4,5,6) - Judge Clarke ✓ ( )

(7,8,9) - Judge Kennedy

(7,8,9) - Carla Hills

President Gerald Ford's list of potential nominees for the Supreme Court in 1975, prepared by his attorney general, on which Ford rank ordered and penciled in other possible candidates, before nominating John Paul Stevens. (*Gerald Ford Presidential Library*)

In an irony of history, the opportunity to fill the seat of the outspoken liberal Justice Douglas fell to the Republican President Ford. As a congressman, Ford had sought to impeach Douglas in 1970. Yet Ford had no electoral mandate. He had been appointed Vice President by President Nixon and had moved into the Oval Office when Nixon resigned rather than face impeachment in 1974. With his own possible election and place in history in mind, Ford faced the forces of competing interests within the White House and the watchful eye of liberal senators. There was considerable pressure on him to appoint the first woman to the Court. Conservatives in the administration, like Ford's presidential adviser and head of the American Enterprise Institute William Baroody, however, urged the nomination of the Yale law professor and AEI associate Robert Bork. Bork, later appointed by Reagan to the Court of Appeals for the District of Columbia Circuit, served as Nixon's solicitor general and acting attorney general during the Watergate episode. "He is young and is a strict Constructionist and," wrote Arizona's Senator Barry Goldwater, "would give continuity to the kind of Court that you want for at least twenty-five years." But for precisely those reasons, the nomination of such a conservative associated with the disgraced Nixon administration would have been extremely controversial. It might have been defeated by Democrats in the Senate and hurt Ford's bid for the 1976 election. As a moderate Republican, Ford leaned toward the advice of Attorney General Edward Levi, who was on leave from the University of Chicago School of Law and who promoted the elevation of John Stevens, a Nixon appointee to the federal court of appeals in Chicago. Ford made a pragmatic, rather than ideologically controversial, nomination based on Stevens's professional qualifications.[23]

The nomination and confirmation process thus involves numerous political compromises and much "horse-trading." The role of the ABA in that process deserves special attention. Its evaluations certify the legal qualification of nominees and thus become political bargaining chips. The ABA's Standing Committee on Federal Judiciary began screening prospective candidates for the Court with the nomination of William Brennan in 1956, rating them as "qualified" or "unqualified." This system continued until the appointment of Harry Blackmun in 1970.

Criticism of the Senate's rejection of Nixon's nomination of Clement Haynsworth and G. Harrold Carswell—whom the committee had ranked as "highly qualified" and "qualified," respectively—led to a change in the ABA system of rating. Nominees for the Court were then rated "highly qualified," "not opposed," or "not qualified." But after a controversy over the ABA's rating of Reagan's unsuccessful nominee, Judge Bork, in 1989 the ABA again changed its system of rating Supreme Court nominees to "well qualified," "qualified," and "not qualified." (Nominees for lower courts are also now rated "well qualified," "qualified," or "not qualified.")[24] After Blackmun's appointment, Nixon's Attorney General John Mitchell refused to submit any further candidates to the ABA committee, because of an unfavorable news story about possible nominees for the seats of retiring Justices John Harlan and Hugo Black. The ABA committee nonetheless conducted its own investigation of Nixon's last two appointments to the Court: it unanimously endorsed Lewis F. Powell, a former ABA president, as "one of the country's best lawyers available," and it gave William Rehnquist, a Nixon administration assistant attorney general, nine votes for a "highly qualified" ranking and three "not opposed" votes for his appointment. With Ford's nomination of Stevens in 1975, the ABA reestablished its formal role in the confirmation process.

The prestige of the ABA serves to legitimize the qualifications of nominees, but does not alter the basic politics of appointments. A former member of the ABA committee, Leon Jaworski, points out that the ABA typically functions as a "buffer" between the White House and the Senate. Senators may be told, "Well, the American Bar Association has turned [your candidate] down, who can we agree on now?"[25] The ABA committee is not above politics, either in rating nominees or in being lobbied by senators, White House officials, and justices.

Political Trade-offs

Packing the Court has come to mean not merely filling the bench with political associates and ideological kin, but accommodating the demands for other kinds of symbolic political representation. Some people maintain that merit rather than political favoritism should govern appointments, and others, like Justice Stone, lament that "the view has come to prevail that in addition to political considerations, considerations of race, religion and sectional interests should influence the appointment."[26] In fact, it is neither merit nor representative factors like geography, religion, race, and gender that proves controlling; instead, it is the competing political considerations in presidential attempts to pack the Court.

IDEOLOGICAL COMPATIBILITY AND GEOGRAPHY

President George Washington initiated the practice of appointing only ideological kin to the Court. When Thomas Jefferson won the election in 1800, President John Adams wanted to ensure the preservation of Federalist philosophy in the national government and appointed his secretary of state, John Marshall, as chief justice. It fell to Andrew Jackson in 1835 to appoint Marshall's successor, and he immediately turned to his longtime supporter and secretary of the treasury, Roger B. Taney. President Abraham Lincoln, in turn, appointed his secretary of the treasury, Salmon Chase, to fill Taney's seat in 1864.

The swing of presidential elections invariably controls judicial appointments. Presidents make little effort to balance the Court by crossing party lines. The party affiliations of those who have served on the Court largely reflect those of their presidential benefactors: thirteen Federalists, one Whig, eight Democratic-Republicans, forty-two Republicans, and forty-four Democrats.

Only two Democratic presidents crossed party lines to fill a vacancy on the Court. Harlan Stone, a Republican, had been elevated to the post of chief justice by Franklin D. Roosevelt in 1941. FDR then filled eight seats with Democrats before he died in the spring of 1945. Harry Truman faced considerable pressure to name a Republican to the seat of retiring Justice Owen Roberts. Although the selection of Harold Burton, a Republican senator, was inspired by political pressure, Truman was perfectly comfortable with his appointment, because they had been close friends for over a decade.[27]

Republican Presidents have more frequently named Democrats, but only when it was politically expedient or as a reward for personal and ideological compatibility. The first crossover appointment was made by President John Tyler, a nominal Whig. After several rejections of earlier nominees, he named the Democrat Samuel Nelson in 1845, just before the Democratic President James Polk took office. Elected by a minority of the popular vote, President Lincoln appointed California's Stephen Field as a gesture to northern and western Democrats in an effort to broaden political support. Benjamin Harrison was defeated for reelection in 1892, and he named Howell Jackson within days of the inauguration of the Democratic President Grover Cleveland. President William Taft elevated Justice Edward White to the post of chief justice and appointed his friend and ideological kin Horace Lurton. His other Democratic appointee, Joseph Lamar, was the only pure crossover to achieve political balance within the Court. Presidents Warren Harding and Dwight D. Eisenhower appointed Pierce Butler and William Brennan because of their Catholic affiliation and reportedly conservative views. Nixon named Lewis Powell, a Democratic-Republican from Virginia, for his conservative and "strict constructionist" views.

Geography used to figure prominently in appointments. During the founding period, geographical representation was considered crucial to establishing the legitimacy of the Court and the national government. Congress encouraged geographical diversity by requiring the justices to ride circuit. From the appointment of John Rutledge from South Carolina in 1789 until the retirement of Hugo Black in 1971, with the exception of the Reconstruction decade of 1866–1876, there was always a southerner on the bench. Until 1867, the sixth seat was reserved as the "southern seat." Until Cardozo's appointment in 1932, the third seat was reserved for New Englanders.

As the country expanded westward, Presidents were inclined to give representation to new states and regions. After the Civil War, the influx of immigrants and the gradual nationalization of the country diminished the importance of geographical regions. Congress's elimination of circuit riding in 1891 reinforced the declining influence of geography. A few appointments in this century turned on geography, but they were exceptional. President Taft selected Willis Van Devanter from Wyoming in 1910 because he was determined to have a westerner on the Court. After he became chief justice, Taft continued to lobby Presidents Harding and Coolidge on the need for geographical balance on the Court.[28]

The appointment of Wiley Rutledge in 1943 illustrates how little geography influences appointments to the modern Court. From FDR's first appointment in 1937, Rutledge, dean of Iowa's law school, was mentioned as a possible nominee because he was a westerner. In 1936, before his own appointment to the high bench, Senator Hugo Black recommended him "as possible material for the Supreme Court." But in 1939 even Black supported the President's decision to pass over Rutledge: "[M]any circumstances," he wrote, "combine to make Felix Frankfurter the only possible nominee at this time, and the balancing of the Court geographically ought to be held back till the next vacancy occurs."[29] Rutledge and geography were repeatedly pushed aside until FDR's last appointment to the Court.[30] Even then, FDR had other reasons for the appointment. Frankfurter made a pest of himself by lobbying for the appointment of Judge Learned Hand, and Roosevelt set his mind against him. During a dinner conversation, Justice William Douglas recalled, FDR said, "Well, this time your Brother Frankfurter has overplayed his hand." He then asked, "Well, in what respect?" The President responded, "Nineteen people have seen me or called me saying that I must appoint Learned Hand. By God, I am not going to do it." Later that evening, Irving Brant, a St. Louis newspaper editor and friend of the President, came by to urge Rutledge's nomination, as he had done many times before. This time FDR agreed: "That's my man."[31]

Rutledge's appointment shows that geography is not insurmountable. And geographical considerations have had even less influence on subsequent appointments to the Court. When the justice from the deep south, Hugo Black, was still on the bench, Clement Haynsworth of South Carolina and G. Harrold Carswell of Florida were nominated. Nixon claimed that southerners "deserve representation on the Court."[32] But after the Senate refused to confirm either, Nixon named Harry Blackmun from Minnesota even though his earlier appointee, Warren Burger, was from that same state. Blackmun was a conservative Republican and best man at Burger's wedding. Burger had recommended his appointment, and in their first years on the Court together the two were known as "the Minnesota Twins." Geography also did not dissuade Reagan from appointing Rehnquist's former Stanford law school classmate Sandra Day O'Connor, though both were from Arizona. Geographical diversity remains important in the selection of lower federal appellate court judges; balance is sought on the basis of population, caseload, and the number of judges from different states in a circuit.[33] But geographical representation on the Court is less compelling: only thirty-one states have been represented by the 108 members of the Court. Over half came from seven states—thirteen from New York; ten from Ohio; nine from Massachusetts; eight from Virginia; six each from Pennsylvania and Tennessee; and five from Kentucky.

RELIGION, RACE, GENDER, AND BEYOND

Religion, race, and gender have historically been barriers to rather than bases for appointments to the Court. The overwhelming majority (93) of the 108 justices have come from established Protestant religions: 55 from old-line faiths—Episcopalian, Unitarian, Congregationalist, and Quaker—and 37 from others, such as Baptist, Methodist, Lutheran, and Disciples of Christ. Of the remaining sixteen, nine were Catholics and seven were Jews.*

Religion has political symbolism, but it played little role in judicial selection until the twentieth century. The "Catholic seat" and the "Jewish seat" were created accidentally, rather than by presidential efforts to give the Court religious balance. Representation, of course, is purely symbolic. Catholics and Jews do not have well-defined positions, for example, on statutory interpretation. Nor does the appointment of a Catholic or a Jew guarantee that the views of each faith will be reflected in the voting of representative justices. Brennan, a Catholic, did not heed Church teachings when voting in *Roe v. Wade* to uphold a woman's right to obtain an abortion. Religious and racial considerations, moreover, appear "highly indefensible and dangerous" to the extent that more qualified individuals are passed over. Frankfurter contended that such considerations are "not only irrelevant for appointments to the bench, but mischievously irrelevant—that to appoint men on the score of race and religion [is] playing with fire."[34]

The first Catholic, Chief Justice Taney, was appointed in 1835, but religion had little to do with Jackson's selection of his friend and adviser. Thirty years after Taney's death, the next

---

*Justice Clarence Thomas is counted here as a Catholic, even though at the time of his appointment in 1991, he belonged to a charismatic Episcopal Church. Thomas was raised a Catholic, went to parochial schools, and later briefly attended a seminary. Moreover, following his appointment to the Court, in 1996 he again began attending a Catholic Church.

Catholic was named. Edward White was appointed in 1894, but again religion played a minor role, though in 1910 President Taft was urged to promote him to the post of chief justice because he was "a democrat, a Catholic, and from the South."[35] From White's appointment until 1949, the Court always included one, and usually two, Catholics: Joseph McKenna served from 1898 to 1925; Pierce Butler from 1923 to 1939; and Frank Murphy from 1940 to 1949. For almost thirty years (from 1898 to 1925), there were two Catholics on the Court, even though Catholics lacked the political influence they later acquired in the New Deal coalition. Roosevelt rewarded Catholic supporters with an unprecedented number of lower federal court judgeships, but he did not do the same with his appointments to the Court.[36] When Murphy died in 1949, Truman did not feel compelled to appoint another Catholic. None sat on the high bench until Eisenhower's appointment of Brennan in 1956. Devoted to bipartisanship, Eisenhower wanted "a very good Catholic, even a conservative Democrat," in order to "show that we mean our declaration that the Court should be nonpartisan."[37] By contrast, Reagan appointed two Catholics, Antonin Scalia and Anthony Kennedy, even though he paid no attention to his nominees' religious affiliations in his quest to infuse a sharply conservative judicial philosophy into the Court.

In 1853, President Millard Fillmore offered a position to Judah Benjamin, but Benjamin wanted to stay in the Senate. Not until President Woodrow Wilson's appointment of Brandeis in 1916 did the Court acquire its first Jewish justice. Opposition was not necessarily anti-Semitic, but based largely on antagonism toward Brandeis's progressive legal views and reform politics. Seven prior ABA presidents, including William Howard Taft, proclaimed that Brandeis was "not a fit person to be a member of the Supreme Court of the United States."[38] After Brandeis's appointment, there developed an expectation of a "Jewish seat." With the confirmation of Cardozo in 1932 and his subsequent replacement by Frankfurter, two Jewish justices sat on the Court until Brandeis retired in 1939. When Frankfurter stepped down in 1962, the Jewish factor mattered, and Kennedy named Arthur Goldberg, his secretary of labor.[39] Three years later, Johnson persuaded Goldberg to become ambassador to the United Nations, and his vacancy was filled by the President's friend Abe Fortas. After Fortas's resignation in 1969, no other Jew sat on the high court until 1993, when it was joined by Justice Ruth Bader Ginsburg. Less than a year later, President Clinton named a second Jewish justice, Stephen Breyer. As a result of Reagan's, Bush's, and Clinton's appointments, in the 1990s the Court had three Catholic and two Jewish justices, more non-Protestants than at any other time in the Court's history.

Although politically symbolic, religious representation on the Court never amounted to a quota system. Catholics and Jews were more often selected because of personal and ideological compatibility with the President. "There is no such thing as a Jewish seat," Goldberg observed, though his religion was a factor that Johnson considered when coaxing him to leave the Court. Johnson was intent on appointing Fortas, regardless of his religion. The two had known each other since the New Deal, and in 1964 LBJ had unsuccessfully urged Fortas to become attorney general. Fortas also initially declined appointment to the Court because he wanted "a few more years of activity."[40] Johnson persisted, and in the end Fortas reluctantly agreed to enter the marble temple.

In 1967, Johnson's advisers told him the time had come for the appointment of a black to the Court.[41] The symbolism of appointing an African American was never lost on the President, nor had LBJ's commitment to naming Thurgood Marshall ever waned. As director of the NAACP Counsel of Legal Defense and Education Fund, Marshall gained national recognition while arguing the landmark school desegregation case, *Brown v. Board of Education* (1954). In 1961, Kennedy named him to the U.S. Court of Appeals for the Second Circuit. Subsequently,

Johnson persuaded him to give up the judgeship and become his solicitor general. LBJ wanted "that image, number one," of having a black solicitor general, Marshall has recalled. The President told him at the time, "You know this has nothing to do with any Supreme Court appointment. I want that distinctly understood. There's no quid pro here at all. You do your job. If you don't do it, you go out. If you do it, you stay here. And that's all there is to it."[42] That, of course, was not all there was to it. The solicitor generalship offers experience in representing the government before the Court and a strategic basis for elevation to the high bench.

When Justice Marshall announced his retirement at the end of the term in 1991, he claimed that poor health at age eighty-two forced him to step down. But his disappointment with the Court's turning 180 degrees also contributed. He was a kind of larger-than-life metaphor for the civil rights movement and an era in American politics. Marshall had joined the Court at the height of its forging a liberal-egalitarian revolution in constitutional law: between 1961 and 1969, over 76 percent of the Warren Court's rulings each term went in the direction of protecting individuals and minorities against the government. But, that did not last long. During the Burger Court years the percentage dropped to below 50 percent, with the exception of one term.[43] Even more disturbing was the Rehnquist Court's threat to reverse many liberal rulings handed down by the Warren and Burger Courts. In his last opinion delivered from the bench, dissenting in *Payne v. Tennessee* (1991), Justice Marshall lamented that the Rehnquist Court was sending "a clear signal that essentially all decisions implementing the personal liberties protected by the Bill of Rights and the Fourteenth Amendment are open to reconsideration."

Four days after Justice Marshall's announcement, President Bush nominated his successor, Judge Clarence Thomas. Despite the president's disclaiming that his nominee was "a quota" and defending him as "the best man for the job on the merits," Thomas's appointment was politically symbolic and his qualifications were immediately called into question. At age forty-three he was one of the youngest ever to join the Court. Thomas also had little prior judicial experience. Just fifteen months earlier Bush had named him to fill Judge Bork's seat on the Court of Appeals for the District of Columbia Circuit. Prior to that Thomas spent eight years as head of the Equal Employment Opportunities Commission (EEOC). Still, he had a law degree from Yale Law School and had pulled himself up from an impoverished childhood in Pin Point, Georgia, where he was raised by his grandparents and attended a Catholic school. More than his qualifications sparked controversy, however. During the 1980s he had established a reputation as a rising black conservative within the Republican party. He had attacked affirmative action, the welfare state, and the judiciary's efforts to integrate public schools. Indeed, Thomas had even questioned the wisdom of *Brown v. Board of Education.* His nomination was thus not unexpected yet bound to invite controversy: Marshall and Thomas, the first two African Americans to sit on the Court, stood for and symbolized very different legal policies and eras in American politics.

Political pressure for the appointment of a woman had been building for decades and intensified in the 1970s with the battle over the adoption of the Equal Rights Amendment to the Constitution. During the Truman administration, the respected federal court of appeals judge Florence Allen was mentioned for an appointment.[44] Later Johnson was urged to consider Barbara Jordan or Sarah Hughes, among other women.[45] Nixon also considered nominating a woman. But he claimed "that in general the women judges and lawyers qualified to be nominated for the Supreme Court were too liberal to meet the strict constructionist criterion" he had set for his appointees.[46] In fact, Nixon submitted the name of Judge Mildred Lillie to the ABA judiciary committee in 1971, but she was unanimously ranked "not qualified." Ford's advisers compiled a list of over twenty women attorneys and judges, including Sandra Day O'Connor, for possible nomination to the vacancy created by the retirement of Douglas.[47]

In 1980, Reagan made a campaign promise to appoint a woman. Less than a year later, he fulfilled that pledge by naming Sandra Day O'Connor. In May 1981, Justice Potter Stewart had privately told the President that he would retire at the end of the term. A two-month search concluded with a woman who shared Reagan's view that "the role of the courts is to interpret the law, not to enact new law by judicial fiat." O'Connor had risen through the ranks of Republican politics, from assistant state attorney general to a seat in the Arizona state senate, where she was a majority leader, and to a state appellate court judgeship. Her nomination was supported by both senators from Arizona and Chief Justice Burger and Justice Rehnquist. The Democratic representative Morris Udall endorsed her nomination with the comment that she was "about as moderate a Republican as you'll ever find being appointed by Reagan." And the president of the National Organization for Women, Eleanor Smeal, claimed "a major victory for women's rights."

Religion, race, and gender are politically symbolic and largely reflect changes in the electorate. In the future, such considerations are likely to compete with expectations for more ethnic representation on the Court—for the appointment of a Hispanic or an Asian. Still, as Justice Ruth Bader Ginsburg put it after becoming the Court's second female, "I don't think we should ever have anything like proportional representation, so that there will be this seat or that for a particular constituency. But, of course, diversity is important."[48] Indeed, "representative appointments" are certain to remain less important than personal and ideological compatibility in presidential attempts to pack the Court.

Justices Ruth Bader Ginsburg (left) and Sandra Day O'Connor, the Court's first two female members. (*Photo by Ken Heinen, Collection of the Supreme Court of the United States*)

Packing the Court

The presidential impulse to pack the Court with politically compatible justices is irresistible. The "tendency to choose a known, rather than an unknown, evil," as Stone put it, "can never be eliminated from the practical administration of government."[49] Yet Court packing depends on the politics of the possible—on presidential prestige and political expediency. The politics of packing the Court is well illustrated by the appointments of Roosevelt, Truman, Eisenhower, Nixon, Reagan, Bush, and Clinton.

With the exception of George Washington, no President has had more opportunities to pack the Court than Franklin Roosevelt. He made eight appointments and elevated Justice Stone to the chief justiceship. Although Nixon and Reagan later achieved remarkable success in remolding the Court in their images, Roosevelt succeeded more than any other President in packing the Court. Moreover, perhaps no other President before Nixon and Reagan had as great a contempt for the Court. Nixon vehemently opposed the "liberal jurisprudence" of the Warren Court, and Reagan attacked many of the social-policy rulings of the more conservative Burger Court, specifically its decisions permitting abortion, allowing affirmative action, and upholding the Fourth Amendment's exclusionary rule. Nixon and Reagan named only those who they believed shared their "strict constructionist" judicial philosophies and agreed with their conservative social-policy positions. By contrast, Roosevelt attacked the conservative economic politics of the Court in the 1930s for thwarting the country's recovery from the Great Depression.

During FDR's first term, the Court invalidated most of the early New Deal program. Yet the President had no opportunity to fill a seat on the bench. After his landslide reelection in 1936, Roosevelt proposed judicial reforms allowing him to expand the size of the Court to fifteen by appointing a new member for every justice over seventy years of age. In the spring of 1937, when the Senate Judiciary Committee was debating his "Court-packing plan," the Court abruptly upheld major pieces of New Deal legislation. The Court had been badly divided five to four in striking down progressive New Deal legislation. George Sutherland, James McReynolds, Pierce Butler, and Willis Van

Nine or Fifteen? The Nation's Eyes Turn to the Supreme Court

The Hughes Court, Supreme Court Building, and Court Room. Clockwise from upper left (*photos credit the* New York Times *except as noted*): **Harlan Fiske Stone, James C. McReynolds, Charles Evans Hughes** (*Harris & Ewing*); **Owen Roberts** (*F. Bachrach*); **Louis Brandeis** (*Harris & Ewing*); **Willis Van Devanter** (*Underwood & Underwood*); **Benjamin Cardozo; George Sutherland;** and **Pierce Butler** (*Harris & Ewing*).

Devanter—the "Four Horsemen"—voted together against economic legislation, while Stone and Cardozo followed Brandeis in supporting progressive economic legislation. Hughes and Roberts were the "swing votes," the latter, more conservative justice casting the crucial fifth vote to strike down FDR's programs. Roberts then changed his mind. In March he abandoned the Four Horsemen in *West Coast Hotel Co. v. Parrish* (1937) to uphold Washington State's minimum-wage law. Two weeks later, in *National Labor Relations Board v. Jones & Laughlin Steel Corporation* (1937), he again switched sides to affirm a major piece of New Deal legislation, the National Labor Relations Act. The Court's "switch in time that saved nine" was widely speculated to have been due to FDR's Court-packing plan. But even though the rulings did not come down until the spring, Roberts had switched his vote at conference in December 1936, two months before FDR announced his plan. The reversal of the Court's position nonetheless contributed to the Senate Judiciary Committee's rejection of FDR's proposal in May. Then Van Devanter—one of the President's staunchest opponents—told the President that he would resign at the end of the term. FDR had the first of eight appointments in the next six years to infuse his own political philosophy into the Court. Although his plan to enlarge the size of the Court failed, FDR eventually succeeded in packing the Court.

When FDR made his first appointment, he was angry at the Senate for defeating his plan to enlarge the Court and angry at the Court for destroying his program for recovery. For the appointment, FDR chose Senator Hugo Black, who had led the unsuccessful fight for the Court-packing plan. Roosevelt, recalled Robert Jackson, wanted to "humiliate [the Senate and the Court] at a single stroke by naming Black." Only in extraordinary circumstances would the Senate refuse to confirm one of its own. "The Senate would have to swallow hard and approve," Jackson observed. "The Court would be humiliated by having to accept one of its most bitter and unfair critics and one completely alien to the judicial tradition."[50]

At Black's confirmation hearings, rumors circulated that he had been a member of the Ku Klux Klan in the mid-1920s, when the Klan membership reached its peak of over four million and virtually assured the election of Democrats in the Deep South. When evidence of Black's prior Klan membership materialized after his confirmation, the revelation confirmed for many that the appointment had been an act of revenge. Roosevelt claimed "that he had not known of any Klan link when he appointed Black to the Court." Black went on national radio to explain briefly, though not to apologize for, his membership in the Klan from 1922 to 1925. Although he denied having any knowledge of the KKK association, Roosevelt must have known. Black, moreover, left a note in his private papers to "correct for posterity any idea about Pres. Roosevelt's having been fooled about my membership in the Klan." He recollected:

President Roosevelt, when I went up to lunch with him, told me that there was no reason for my worrying about having been a member of the Ku Klux Klan. He said that some of the best friends and supporters he had in the State of Georgia were strong members of the organization. He never in any way, by word or attitude, indicated any doubt about my having been in the Klan nor did he indicate any criticism of me for having been a member of that organization. The rumors and statements to the contrary are wrong.[51]

Roosevelt's subsequent appointments all turned on support for the New Deal. When the conservative westerner George Sutherland retired in 1938, the President momentarily considered nominating another senator—either South Carolina's James Byrnes, later appointed in 1941, or Indiana's Sherman Minton, who was forced to await Truman's selection in 1949. But he worried about taking too many supporters from the Senate. Attorney General Homer Cummings urged the elevation of Solicitor General Stanley Reed. Reed was from Kentucky, and the President initially remarked, "Well, McReynolds is from Kentucky, and Stanley will have to wait until McReynolds is no longer with us." Cummings countered that McReynolds was

Justice Hugo Black in his chambers. Black was President Roosevelt's first appointee to the Court and a leader of liberals on the Court. (*Collection of the Supreme Court of the United States*)

"closely identified with New York City" because of his earlier law practice and that Reed's record justified his nomination. Roosevelt agreed: "Tell Stanley to make himself so disagreeable to McReynolds that the latter will retire right away."[52]

Reed joined the Court in 1938, but McReynolds did not retire until 1941, and the pressure for an appointee from the West steadily grew. In 1938 Cardozo died. The vacancy would be hard to fill, for "Cardozo was not only a great Justice, but a great character, a great person and a great soul . . . held in reverence by multitudes of people and," Cummings observed, "whoever followed him, no matter how good a man he might be would suffer by comparison."[53] Roosevelt had long contemplated appointing Frankfurter to Brandeis's seat. Anticipating "a terrible time getting Frankfurter confirmed," he had earlier unsuccessfully urged Frankfurter to become solicitor general. "I want you on the Supreme Court, Felix," Roosevelt told him, "but I can't appoint you out of the Harvard Law School. What will people say? 'He's a Red. He's a professor. He's had no judicial experience.' But I could appoint you to the Court from the Solicitor General's office."[54] When Cardozo died, Roosevelt at first told Frankfurter, "I've got to appoint a fellow west of the Mississippi—I promised the party leaders he'd be a Westerner the next time."[55] A number of westerners were considered, but FDR found lesser-known candidates unacceptable. Frankfurter was appointed, despite criticism that it would put two Jews and an excessive number of justices from the Atlantic seaboard on the Court.

Geography did not dissuade Roosevelt from then filling Brandeis's seat in 1939 with his Securities and Exchange Commission chairman, William O. Douglas. At first, Senator Lewis Schwellenbach was considered, but opposition emerged from the other senator from the state of Washington. Frank Murphy had replaced Cummings as attorney general and urged the President to disregard pressure for the selection of a westerner. "Members of the Supreme Court are not called upon nor expected to represent any single interest or group, area or class of persons," Murphy insisted. "They speak for the country as a whole. Considerations of residential area or class, interest, creed or racial extraction, ought therefore be subordinate if not entirely disregarded."[56] Brandeis had recommended Douglas. Born in Minnesota and raised in Yakima, Washington, Douglas claimed Connecticut as his legal residence because he had taught at Yale Law School before joining the SEC. There was accordingly opposition to naming another nonwesterner, but powerful Senate leaders like Idaho's William Borah endorsed the nomination. Douglas later recalled, "When Roosevelt named me he didn't name me from the State of Washington, but he stuck to the record, and named me from Connecticut."[57]

When the midwesterner Pierce Butler died in 1939, there was even greater pressure on Roosevelt to appoint a westerner and a Catholic. Butler was a Catholic, and Catholics were a crucial part of the New Deal coalition. Roosevelt settled on Attorney General Murphy—a Catholic, an affable "Irish mystic," and a former governor of Michigan. Murphy's midwestern Catholic background, however, was only a politically useful rationalization. No less important, morale within the Department of Justice was abysmally low. Murphy was not intellectually equipped to handle the position of attorney general. His appointment was another example of the President's lack of concern for the Court.[58] Roosevelt was not unaware of Murphy's faults. Assistant Attorney General Robert Jackson told him, "Mr. President, I don't think that Mr. Murphy's temperament is that of a judge." His elevation to the Court was nevertheless politically opportune. The President explained to Jackson, "It's the only way I can appoint you Attorney General."[59]

Roosevelt promised later to make Jackson chief justice if he accepted the attorney generalship. Jackson reluctantly agreed. In 1941, McReynolds retired and Chief Justice Hughes informed the President that he would step down at the end of the term. FDR had the opportunity to fill two more seats and to appoint Jackson. Hughes suggested that the chief justiceship go to Stone. He had long aspired to the position and been disappointed because his friend President Hoover passed him over when appointing Hughes.[60] Frankfurter preferred Jackson but agreed that Stone was "senior and qualified professionally to be C.J." He also told FDR that the elevation of Stone, a Republican, would inspire confidence in him "as a national and not a partisan President."[61] In July, Senator Byrnes was named to McReynolds's seat, Stone elevated to the post of chief justice, and Jackson nominated associate justice. When trying to mollify Jackson, the President noted that Stone was within a couple of years of retirement and explained, "I will have another chance at appointment of a Chief Justice, at which time you'd already be over there [in the Court] and would be familiar with the job." At the moment, the arrangement appeared politically advantageous: "one Republican for Chief Justice and two Democrats will not be too partisan."[62] Roosevelt, however, made his last appointment little over a year later. Byrnes was persuaded to leave the Court to become director of the Office of Economic Stabilization, and Rutledge got his seat on the Court.

Roosevelt's appointments illustrate the importance of presidential prestige. FDR was able to overcome pressures imposed on Presidents for political, geographic, and religious representation on the Court. He turned a conservative Court into a liberal one and changed the direction of the Court's policy-making. As a legacy of FDR's liberalism, Black and Douglas remained on the Court until the 1970s and helped forge the Warren Court's decisions on school desegregation, reapportionment, and criminal procedure.

Chief Justice Stone's death in 1946 presented a ready-made controversy over a successor, but President Truman found a politically expedient solution. The Roosevelt Court had become badly divided. Black led the liberals—Reed, Douglas, Murphy, Rutledge, and Burton—against Jackson and Frankfurter, who tended to advance the basic conservatism of Roberts and Stone.

The Black-Jackson disputes were deep-seated, ideological, and personal. When Stone died, senior Associate Justice Black temporarily assumed the responsibilities of chief justice. Having long labored under Roosevelt's promise to make him chief justice, Jackson immediately became vindictive, convincing himself that his rival would be named chief justice. Unpersuaded by the President's assurances that he had not talked with Black about the position, Jackson made public a telegram sent to the chairman of the House and Senate Judiciary Committees attacking Black and airing the animosities within the Court.[63]

Outraged by the Black-Jackson controversy, Truman lamented, "The Supreme Court has really made a mess of itself."[64] He decided to appoint his friend Fred Vinson. Roosevelt had appointed Vinson to the Court of Appeals for the District of Columbia Circuit in 1938 and director of the Office of Economic Stabilization during World War II. In 1945, Truman successively made him federal loan administrator, director of the Office of War Mobilization and Reconversion, and, finally, secretary of the treasury. Vinson was a loyal friend and an experienced politician with "an uncanny knack of placating opposing minds."[65] That was precisely what Truman thought the Court needed: an outsider and proven negotiator, rather than an insider and legal scholar. What the Court required was someone to keep the justices in line. As William Rogers, Eisenhower's deputy attorney general, later observed, "Fred Vinson would not have been on the Court but for the fact that he was a successful politician."[66]

The appointments of Chief Justices Earl Warren in 1953 and Warren Burger in 1969 both sprang from the 1952 Republican Convention. Why did Eisenhower appoint Warren? Douglas, among others, insisted that Vice President Nixon and Senator William Knowland of California viewed Warren—an extremely popular governor with bipartisan support in California—as "an unorthodox, off-beat kind of Republican." They "went to Eisenhower when Vinson died, and urged that Eisenhower name

Warren as Chief Justice because Nixon and Knowland wanted to get Warren out of the State of California so that they could take over the Republican machine."[67] But the story is too simple to be true.[68] Shortly after the election in November 1952, Eisenhower indicated to Warren that he could have the "first vacancy" on the Court. Later, in the summer of 1953, he persuaded Warren to leave the governorship and become solicitor general so as to gain experience arguing cases before the Court. When Vinson died that summer, his job was immediately offered to Warren.[69]

Eisenhower was committed to appointing Warren because he "was firmly convinced the prestige of the Supreme Court had suffered severely in prior years, and that the only way it could be restored was by the appointment to it of men of nationwide reputation, of integrity, competence in the law, and in statesmanship." He also refused to appoint anyone over sixty-four years of age, and that barred several prominent jurists. As California's favorite-son candidate for the presidency in 1952, Warren had "national stature" and, in Eisenhower's opinion, "unimpeachable integrity," "middle-of-the-road views," and "a splendid record during his years of active law work" as state attorney general. "If the Republicans as a body should try to repudiate" his appointment, the President vowed, "I shall leave the Republican Party and try to organize an intelligent group of independents, no matter how small."[70]

Warren's popularity and role in the 1952 Republican Convention impressed Eisenhower. But what happened at that convention also set the political stage for the eventual appointment of Warren Burger as chief justice. General Eisenhower and Senator Robert Taft (the son of Chief Justice William Taft) were leading contenders, though it remained uncertain right up to the convention who would win the nomination. Herbert Brownell, Eisenhower's campaign manager, was convinced that his candidate could not win without the support of the favorite-son candidates Earl Warren of California and Harold Stassen of

President Dwight D. Eisenhower and Chief Justice Earl Warren with Vice President Richard Nixon, who later appointed Warren Burger chief justice. (*Dwight D. Eisenhower Presidential Library*)

Minnesota. Just before the convention opened, a dispute arose over whether contested delegates could vote on their seating at the convention. If they were allowed to vote, Brownell believed, Taft would have the nomination. If they were not, no candidate could expect a majority on the first ballot, but Eisenhower's chances of getting the nomination would be better. Brownell proposed and secured a "fair play" amendment to the rules of the convention; it forbade any contested delegate from voting, with the result that the Taft candidacy began to disintegrate before the convention opened. During negotiations over the "fair play" amendment, Brownell and Stassen's campaign manager, Warren Burger, came to know and admire each other. Burger worked to get the Minnesota delegation to agree on the amendment. No less helpful was the freshman senator Richard Nixon, who made a moral appeal to the California delegation to vote for the "fair play" amendment. Although pledged as a delegate to support Warren, Nixon was committed to seeing that Eisenhower got the nomination. Warren reluctantly agreed to the amendment, even though it hurt his chances of winning the nomination if there were a deadlock at the convention. When it then looked as though Eisenhower could win the nomination on the first ballot if either the California or Minnesota delegation swung over to him, Burger and others pressed Stassen to turn his delegates over to Eisenhower. Stassen "objected strenuously to it," and his adviser Bernard Shanley later recalled telling him "it was going to happen whether he liked it or not."[71] Toward the end of the first roll-call vote, Stassen released the Minnesota delegation to Eisenhower, giving him a first-ballot nomination, while members of the California delegation continued to support Warren.

Warren's "statesmanship" at the convention impressed Eisenhower. Warren had not opposed the "fair play" amendment, as he might have done. Since he had not turned over any of his delegates on the floor of the convention, Eisenhower felt "there was no possibility of charging that his appointment was made as payment for a political debt."[72] Stassen and his advisers went into the Eisenhower-Nixon administration: Stassen as head of foreign aid, Shanley as special counsel to the President, and Burger as assistant attorney general under Attorney General Brownell. Burger further developed his friendship with Brownell and in 1956 was appointed to the prestigious Court of Appeals for the District of Columbia Circuit.

In 1969, President Nixon's first choice to fill the seat of retiring Chief Justice Warren was Brownell. However, since Brownell "had been Eisenhower's Attorney General in 1957 at the time of the Little Rock school crisis," he concluded that confirmation would be difficult, for "many Southerners were still deeply embittered by his role in the use of federal troops to enforce integration." Nixon's attorney general, Mitchell, told Brownell that "confirmation would be messy," and the latter withdrew from consideration.[73] Nixon could not nominate Mitchell, since that would open him to the charge of "cronyism"—a charge that Republicans had just used to defeat Johnson's effort to promote Fortas to the chief justiceship. The battle over Fortas hurt the morale of the Court. Justice Potter Stewart, another Eisenhower appointee, told the President that under the circumstances it would be unwise for him to be elevated to the position. Nixon also thought about appointing the former New York governor Thomas E. Dewey, but he was too old. The President wanted someone who had judicial experience but was young enough to serve at least ten years. Most important, he wanted someone who shared his own "strict constructionist" philosophy of constitutional interpretation. Nixon's advisors, including Patrick J. Buchanan and Tom Charles Huston, urged him to remold the Court in his more conservative image.[74] The President knew Warren Burger from the days of the Eisenhower administration and had read his speeches on law and order, which Burger had sent him. But Nixon was not close personally to Burger, and so his nomination would not raise charges of cronyism that had dogged LBJ's ill-fated elevation of Justice Fortas to the chief justiceship. Just two weeks before receiving the presidential nod in May 1969, Burger lobbied for the nomination in a letter to Nixon, advising him how to deal with the Court and the controversy over Fortas's extra-judicial activities, as well as lamenting that his first nominee would probably become the media's "whipping boy."[75]

Warren's Court revolutionized constitutional law and American society: with the unanimous 1954 school desegregation ruling, *Brown v. Board of Education;* with the 1962 ruling in *Baker v. Carr* that announced the "reapportionment revolution" guaranteeing equal voting rights; and with a series of rulings on criminal procedure that extended the rights of the accused. Eisenhower later called his appointment of Warren "the biggest damn-fooled mistake" he had ever made. Nixon sought to rectify the mistake. Burger came to the Court with the agenda of reversing the "liberal jurisprudence" of the Warren Court and restoring "law and order."

Nixon's appointments of Burger, Blackmun, Powell, and Rehnquist, however, failed to turn the Court around and to forge a "constitutional counter-revolution." This was because the Burger Court was increasingly fragmented and polarized, dividing six to three or five to four, and pulled in different directions by either its most liberal or most conservative members. There were only modest "adjustments," as Burger put it when announcing his retirement, in the jurisprudential house built by the Warren Court. But the Burger Court also made a few new additions. It upheld abortion, affirmative action, and busing and gave greater scope to the Fourteenth Amendment's equal protection clause. Those rulings, even more than the Warren Court, embittered New Right "movement conservatives" in the 1970s and 1980s. They set the stage for the Reagan era and his attempt to pack the Court anew.

Reagan campaigned in 1980 and 1984 on a promise to appoint only those opposed to abortion and the "judicial activism" of the Warren and Burger Courts. No other President has had as great an impact on the federal judiciary since Roosevelt. Before leaving the Oval Office, Reagan appointed almost half of all lower-court judges (372 out of 736) and elevated Rehnquist to chief justice, as well as appointed three other justices to the Court.[76] Numbers are only part of the story. Reagan put into place the most rigorous process for judicial selection ever. Judges were viewed as symbols and instruments of presidential power and a way to ensure Reagan's legacy. Through judicial appointments, as Attorney General Edwin Meese III claimed, the administration aimed "to institutionalize the Reagan revolution so it can't be set aside no matter what happens in future presidential elections."[77]

While hugely successful in appointing lower-court judges, Reagan failed to win a majority of the Court over to his positions on abortion, affirmative action, and other hotly contested issues until Justice Powell stepped down on June 28, 1987. This was so in spite of his putting Sandra Day O'Connor on the Court in 1981, elevating Rehnquist to the chief justiceship, and appointing Antonin Scalia to Rehnquist's seat as an associate justice in 1986. The balance on the Court did not shift until Powell left because he held a pivotal vote; in his last two terms the justices split five to four in eighty-one cases, with Powell having the deciding vote more than 75 percent of the time. He cast the crucial fifth vote in cases rejecting the Reagan administration's positions on abortion, affirmative action, and some other social-policy issues.

Reagan's first opportunity to name a justice to the Court came with the appointment of Sandra Day O'Connor. Unlike Reagan's other appointees, O'Connor was chosen more for symbolic than for ideological reasons: Reagan had promised to name the first woman to the Court. Her confirmation hearings (the first ever to be televised) generated little controversy.

Reagan's next opportunity to pack the Court came in June 1986, when Burger stepped down to head full time the Commission on the Bicentennial of the Constitution. The decision to elevate Rehnquist from associate to chief justice and appoint Scalia to his seat was politically symbolic and strategic. Both could claim to be intellectual architects of Reagan's legal-policy agenda. Through their writings and judicial opinions, they had largely defined the administration's positions on abortion, affirmative action, federalism, and the role of the courts in American society. Their law clerks regularly came from or went to top positions within Reagan's Justice Department and presidency.

Reagan's White House advisers knew Rehnquist would prove controversial because of his long-standing, often extremely conservative views. But naming him chief justice symbolized Reagan's judicial legacy, and Rehnquist's elevation as a sitting justice made it virtually impossible for the Senate to deny confirmation. Rehnquist had gone to the Court in 1971 from Nixon's Department of Justice, where he had served as an assistant attorney general. His conservative credentials were established years earlier, initially as a law clerk for Justice Robert Jackson (1952–1953) and later as an Arizona attorney and supporter of Arizona Senator Barry Goldwater's presidential candidacy. On the Burger Court, Rehnquist staked out a conservative philosophy. Less willing than others to compromise, he appeared extreme, earning him the nickname Lone Ranger for writing more solo dissents (fifty-four) than any of his colleagues in his fifteen years as an associate justice (although liberal Justice William O. Douglas [1939–1975] holds the record [208] for solo dissents).[78]

The attack on Rehnquist's nomination was spearheaded by Massachusetts's Democratic Senator Edward M. Kennedy, who had also challenged him when he was first named to the Court. Kennedy called Rehnquist "too extreme on race, too extreme on women's rights, too extreme on freedom of speech, too extreme on separation of church and state, too extreme to be Chief Justice." Utah's Republican Senator Orrin Hatch countered that the confirmation hearings threatened to become a "Rehnquisition."

But the Senate Judiciary Committee's televised hearings were less enlightening than an occasion for speeches by supporters and attackers. Rehnquist was repeatedly asked about his judicial opinions, despite his refusal to discuss them. Nor would he answer questions about how he might handle major issues in the future, saying that impinged on judicial independence. He also confronted charges, aimed at tarnishing his integrity and veracity, that as a law clerk in 1953 he had supported segregated schools and in the 1960s had harassed minority voters at polling places.

About all that the committee accomplished was a reassertion of its power to consider the judicial philosophy of nominees, no less than the President does when picking them. Rehnquist was approved by the committee, with five Democrats voting against him and two joining Republicans in a thirteen-to-five vote. Subsequently, the Senate confirmed him by a vote of sixty-five to thirty-three, based on southern Democrats voting with Republicans and two Republicans siding with thirty-one Democrats in opposition.

In contrast with the scrutiny of Rehnquist, the Senate Judiciary Committee spent little time on Scalia; his confirmation hearings were quick and amicable. The differences are reflected in the committee's final reports: Rehnquist's runs 114 pages; Scalia's, only 76 words. On the committee's unanimous recommendation, after barely five minutes of debate, the Senate voted (ninety-eight to zero) for confirmation.

Next to Rehnquist and Bork, no other jurist was closer to the inner circle of Reagan's Justice Department. In the 1970s Scalia made connections with many who were to assume positions of power in Reagan's presidency. After graduating from Harvard Law School, he practiced law for six years before joining the University of Virginia Law School. Then, in 1971–1972, he took a one-year leave to work as general counsel in the Nixon administration. Two years later he was tapped by Ford's attorney general, Edward H. Levi, to head the Office of Legal Counsel in the Justice Department. When Ford left office, Levi returned to the University of Chicago Law School and persuaded Scalia to come along.

Over the years Scalia developed a trenchant judicial philosophy based on a deep antagonism toward affirmative action, abortion, and the "liberal jurisprudence" of the Warren and Burger Courts. In 1982 Reagan placed Scalia on the appellate bench in Washington. There Scalia continued to make his mark as a prolific writer: almost two dozen articles and more than eighty majority opinions and dozens of concurring and dissenting opinions. On the Rehnquist Court, Scalia aligned himself with Rehnquist and later Clarence Thomas. However, he pays less deference than they do to states' rights, and he disappointed some conservatives by adhering to precedents in the area of criminal justice.[79] He also adheres to extreme positions on broad presidential power and takes a rigid view of separation of powers—positions that were advanced by the Reagan administration but that found little support, other than from Scalia, within the Rehnquist Court.[80]

Less than a year after Scalia's confirmation, Justice Powell announced that he would resign. The respected "Virginia gentleman" explained privately to his colleagues that his decision was "motivated by (i) the imminence of my 80th birthday, (ii) by having served 15½ years when I contemplated no more than ten years of service, and (iii) by concern—based on past experience [with three major operations for cancer]—that I could handicap the Court in the event of reoccurrences of serious health problems."[81] Powell's resignation, however, gave way to an extraordinary battle over Reagan's naming Judges Bork and Ginsburg to fill his seat. Instead of becoming the 104th justice, they became the 28th and 29th nominees to be rejected or forced to withdraw. Bork was opposed by the widest margin ever (fifty-eight to forty-two). Allegations that Ginsburg had smoked marijuana as a Harvard Law School professor forced him to withdraw after New Right senators turned against him.

The controversy over Bork underscores the Reagan administration's effort to make the Court a symbol and instrument of his presidency, as well as the power of the Senate to defeat a nominee.[82] Reagan chose, over more moderate Republicans and conservative jurists, one of the most outspoken critics of the Warren and Burger Courts. He did so despite the Democrats' regaining control of the Senate after the 1986 elections, which meant a fight over any nominee closely aligned with New Right Republicans. Reagan also underestimated the extent of the opposition. Yet Powell's seat was considered pivotal since he had often cast the crucial fifth vote in cases upholding abortion and affirmative-action programs and on other divisive issues. In addition, Bork had been passed over three times before, by Ford in 1975 and by Reagan in 1981 (the result of a promise to appoint a woman) and in 1986 (because Reagan's advisers rated Scalia higher than Bork, owing to his industriousness and reputation for being a "team player"). Shortly after Scalia's appointment the White House leaked a rumor that the next vacancy would go to Bork. Liberal interest groups thus studied his record and were prepared to fight his confirmation.

Bork was immediately denounced by Senator Kennedy and by the chairman of the Judiciary Committee, Delaware's Democratic Senator Joseph Biden. More than eighty-three organizations followed. Calling him "unfit" to serve on the high bench, the American Civil Liberties Union (ACLU) abandoned its practice of not opposing nominees. The ACLU had only once before taken such a position; it opposed Rehnquist's nomination in 1971 but took no position on his elevation to chief justice. Promising a "no-holds-barred battle," the AFL-CIO also came out in opposition, something it had not done since joining the coalitions that defeated Nixon's nominations of Judges Haynsworth and Carswell.

New Right organizations were no less active in defending Bork, though they were initially discouraged by White House Chief of Staff Howard Baker from strident support. Over the objections of Meese and others in the Justice Department, the White House advanced the strategy of recasting Bork's conservative record in order to make opponents appear shrill and partisan.

The publicity was extraordinary. What had far greater impact, however, was Bork's own role in the preconfirmation fray and in the confirmation proceedings. Even before the hearings began, Bork took the unusual step of granting an unrivaled number of newspaper interviews. Like Brandeis in 1916, Bork faced charges of being a "radical." Unlike Brandeis and all prior nominees who let their records speak for themselves, Bork sought to explain, clarify, and amend his twenty-five-year record as a Yale Law School law professor, solicitor general, and judge. That broke with tradition and gave the appearance of a public relations campaign.

During his five days of nationally televised testimony before the Judiciary Committee, Bork gave the appearance of refashioning himself into a moderate, "centrist" jurist. A key consideration became, in Senator Patrick Leahy's words, one of "confirmation conversion"—whether Bork was "born again." Besides deserting much of his past record, Bork's lengthy explanations were unprecedented in other ways. Since 1925, when Harlan F. Stone first appeared as a witness during his confirmation hearings, down to Reagan's previous appointees, all nominees had refused to talk about their views on specific cases, let alone discuss how they might vote on issues likely to come before the Court. But Bork gave unusual assurances on how he might vote, if confirmed. Pennsylvania's Republican Senator Arlen Specter and Arizona's Democratic Senator Dennis DeConcini extracted promises (or concessions) on the First Amendment, the Fourteenth Amendment, the commerce clause, and issues like abortion and gender-based discrimination. As much as anything else, Bork strove to assure all that he had "no ideological agenda" and had "great respect for precedent." That proved difficult because of his history of assailing so many watershed rulings and his repeated declarations that "in the field of constitutional law, precedent is not all that important."

By the time Bork finished thirty hours of testifying, he had contradicted much of what he had stood for and for which he had been nominated. Noting the "considerable difference between what Judge Bork has written and what he has testified he will do if confirmed," Specter observed: "I think that what many of us are looking for is some assurance of where you are."

Bork's testimony weighed far more than that of the 110 witnesses assembled for and against him in the following two weeks.

In spite of the publicity and pressure-group activities, the hearings were also remarkably illuminating. They focused on the nature of the Constitution. Is it "the founders' constitution," as identified with Meese's call for "a jurisprudence of original intention" and defended by Bork? Or is the Constitution a "living document," one that amendments and the Court's rulings have made more democratic and protective of civil rights?[83] Put this way, the hearings came close to a national debate, in Biden's words, to "a referendum on the past progress of the Supreme Court and a referendum on the future." The fundamental issue, after all, was the constitutional views shared by Bork and the Reagan administration. That is what had sown divisions with the legal establishment and had broken open with the confirmation battle. It was reflected in the ABA rating Bork "well qualified," but with a third of its committee opposed to his nomination, and in the broad opposition of the legal profession: as many as 1,925 law professors (40 percent of the academic legal profession) signed letters opposing Bork, more than six times the number (300) opposing Carswell.

What captured attention at the end of three weeks of hearings were public opinion polls. A *Washington Post/ABC News* poll found that 52 percent of the public opposed confirmation. But Bork's defeat was not due to public opinion polls. Most senators and their staffs spent an entire summer examining his record; the committee's hearings were more exhaustive than any before. Admittedly, the publicity and pressure-group activities figured in the outcome. Within a couple of days of the Judiciary Committee's vote, seven conservative southern Democrats, led by Louisiana's Senator J. Bennett Johnston, announced their opposition. This, along with similar announcements by Senators Specter and DeConcini, prodded the two remaining Democrats on the committee, Senators Robert C. Byrd and Howell Heflin, to abandon their view that the committee ought not make any recommendation to the full Senate. As a result, the vote of the committee went nine to five against Bork. Ultimately Bork was defeated because of his controversial views and association with the legal-policy goals of the New Right. Other conservative southern Democrats and six moderate Republicans came out against him in the final fifty-eight-to-forty-two vote on the Senate floor.

Bork's defeat was a major setback for Reagan's Justice Department. Meese and others in the department in bitterness blamed White House staff for not pushing hard enough. They vindictively persuaded Reagan to nominate Judge Ginsburg, rather than Ninth Circuit Court of Appeals Judge Anthony M. Kennedy, a less controversial conservative.

Why Ginsburg? Because he was Bork's protégé, sharing more than a nomination and a seat on the same appellate court. Twenty years younger, Ginsburg tracked Bork's path back to law school days at the University of Chicago. After graduating, he followed Bork into the field of antitrust law and an academic career. In 1983 Ginsburg joined the Justice Department as an assistant attorney general in the antitrust division. There he quickly moved it in the direction long advocated by Bork. The Justice Department also expected Ginsburg not to provoke the kind of scrutiny that dogged Bork, since he had written virtually nothing outside of a few articles on antitrust.

In its haste to find a suitable successor to Bork, the Justice Department failed to investigate Ginsburg's background fully. Within ten days of his nomination, Ginsburg was forced to withdraw, amid disclosures about his personal life and growing concerns about his lack of judicial experience. A few days later Reagan nominated Anthony Kennedy.

Kennedy's nomination met with immediate and generally bipartisan praise. He invited little opposition (except from the National Organization for Women) because he was a seasoned jurist who came about as close to Powell as could be expected. After graduating from Harvard Law School, he had practiced law for more than a decade before Ford appointed him to the Ninth Circuit in 1975. Kennedy's reputation was that of a low-profile and nonconfrontational conservative jurist. His record was solidly conservative, but more that of a legal technician than of an outspoken legal philosopher, like Bork.

Kennedy's confirmation hearings were reminiscent of most in the past. Few reporters showed up; none of the commercial television networks broadcast them (as they had Bork's). His testimony was subdued; his answers were reserved, straightforward, and descriptive discourses on developing constitutional law. When pressed on issues such as abortion, he claimed "no fixed view." Kennedy also distanced himself from some of the Reagan administration's and Bork's controversial positions. He expressly rejected, for instance, that "a jurisprudence of original intention" provides a sure guide for constitutional interpretation. The latter, in Kennedy's words, is a "necessary starting point," rather than a "methodology," and "doesn't tell us how to decide a case." Although such responses troubled some New Right conservatives, the Judiciary Committee unanimously approved him, and he was confirmed in 1988.

The conservatism of the Reagan/Rehnquist Court was further reinforced by President George Bush's appointments. In Reagan's shadow, Bush picked his nominees from a list of potential candidates originally compiled during his predecessor's administration. Three days after Justice William Brennan, one of the most liberal and influential justices in the twentieth century, retired in July 1990, Bush nominated Judge David Hackett Souter. Just over a year earlier the fifty-year-old soft-spoken bachelor had been appointed by Bush to the Court of Appeals for the First Circuit. Prior to that, he had served as New Hampshire's attorney general before being elevated to that state's supreme court by then-governor (and later Bush's White House chief of staff) John Sununu. Like Justice Kennedy during his confirmation hearings, Souter endeavored to reassure senators that he had no agenda or rigid jurisprudence. By a vote of thirteen to one (with only Senator Kennedy dissenting), the Senate Judiciary Committee recommended confirmation. Souter was then confirmed by a vote of ninety to nine (with only liberal Democratic senators voting against him).

Major controversy erupted over Bush's second appointee to fill the seat of the first black and last liberal justice when Justice Thurgood Marshall announced his retirement on the last day of the Court's term in June 1991. Women's groups, including NOW and the National Abortion Rights Action League (NARAL), immediately opposed Bush's nomination of Clarence Thomas, a well-known black conservative judge whom the president had named a year earlier to the Court of Appeals for the District of Columbia Circuit, in anticipation of Marshall's eventual retirement. The civil rights community was split on whether and how hard to fight his confirmation. After reviewing his limited judicial record, the ABA Standing Committee on the Federal Judiciary rated Thomas "qualified," though two members of the committee dissented and one abstained; the lowest rating of a nominee for the high court since the ABA began reviewing nominees in 1956.

During his testimony before the Senate Judiciary Committee, Thomas sought to deflect criticism by repeatedly emphasizing his "up-by-the-boot-straps" philosophy and personal struggle in overcoming the poverty of his youth. When asked about his prior writings, however, he followed the practice of Kennedy and Souter in giving only closely guarded answers. Thomas distanced himself from previous statements advocating a "natural law" approach to constitutional interpretation, claiming that he now "did not see a role for the application of natural rights to constitutional adjudication. And in response to more than seventy questions about the constitutionality of *Roe v. Wade*, Thomas steadfastly, though surprisingly, maintained he had never seriously thought about the legitimacy of that controversial ruling on a woman's right to choose an abortion.

After almost two weeks of hearings, the judicial committee was deadlocked. Split seven to seven on whether to recommend him, it finally voted thirteen to one to send Thomas's nomination

Clarence Thomas responding to charges that he had sexually harassed Anita Hill. (*AP/Wide World Photos, Inc.*)

to the full Senate without a recommendation. Several new allegations then surfaced, including one that Thomas had sexually harassed a female assistant a decade earlier when he chaired the EEOC. It was also revealed that the committee's chairman, Delaware's Democratic Senator Joseph Biden, had known of the charges and, though telling several Democratic senators about them, had failed to conduct a full investigation. An FBI report on the allegations was subsequently leaked to the press, and law school professor Anita F. Hill, who had been Thomas's assistant at the EEOC, was forced to come forth at a press conference to explain her charges.

Amid rising public anger over the accusations and counter-charges that Hill was part of a conspiracy to defame Thomas and derail his confirmation, the all white male judiciary committee rushed to hold hearings that pitted Hill against Thomas on nationwide television. Hill cooly and confidently charged that in the early 1980s Thomas had sexually harassed her, repeatedly

Law school professor Anita Hill testifying before the Senate Judiciary Committee. (*AP/Wide World Photos, Inc.*)

asked for dates, frequently talked about pornographic movies, and created a hostile work environment. Thomas in turn categorically denied the accusations and angrily protested that the confirmation process had become "a circus" and "a high-tech lynching for uppity blacks." "The Supreme Court is not worth it," he said. "No job is worth it." Thomas's supporters attacked Hill's motives and Senator Specter went so far as to, misleadingly, charge her with "flat-out perjury." The nasty drama of "she said, he said" raised larger issues of racism and sexism, but failed to resolve the immediate questions about the veracity of either Hill or Thomas. At the end of another week of bitter fighting, the Senate voted fifty-two to forty-eight to confirm Thomas as the 106th justice to serve on the Court.

Finally, after almost a quarter of a century in which Republican Presidents made ten consecutive appointments to the Court, Democratic President Bill Clinton named Justice Ruth Bader Ginsburg in 1993. Clinton wanted a nominee with keen political skills and the know-how to forge coalitions and shape opinions. But, he also did not want to court controversy, both because his first two nominees for attorney general were forced to withdraw and because many within the Washington community thought that the bruising confirmation battles over Bork and Thomas had denigrated the Court.

From an initial list of fifty possible candidates, including New York's Governor Mario Cuomo and Interior Secretary Bruce Babbitt, Clinton's choice came down to two sitting appellate court judges, Stephen Breyer and Ginsburg. Both had the support of the ranking Republican on the Senate Judiciary Committee, Orrin Hatch (R.-Utah). Both won seats on the federal bench as last-minute appointees of Jimmy Carter in 1980. Breyer had been serving as chief counsel to the Senate Judiciary Committee and had the support of both Republicans and Democrats on the committee. Hatch was also instrumental in pushing Ginsburg's appointment through in 1980, when Republicans threatened to block all further nominees of Carter. Hatch agreed to meet her at the request of H. Ross Perot, who was asked to arrange the meeting by his Washington tax attorney and Ginsburg's husband, Martin. Ginsburg had impressed Hatch then, and later with thirteen years of service on the Court of Appeals for the District of Columbia Circuit, during which time she served with future justices Scalia and Thomas, as well as Judge Bork. In 1993, though, Ginsburg's husband, New York Senator Daniel Patrick Moynihan and leaders of prominent women's groups were her strongest supporters.

After meeting Judge Breyer for a widely publicized luncheon amid speculation that he would get the nod, Clinton met with Ginsburg the next day and was touched by the charm and strength of the sixty-year-old Jewish grandmother, jurist, and leader of the women's movement in law in the 1970s. When subsequently announcing his selection, Clinton praised Ginsburg's "pragmatism" and called her the Thurgood Marshall of the women's movement, a comparison drawn earlier by former

Solicitor General Erwin Griswold in 1985, when he observed that "in modern times two appellate advocates altered the nation's course . . . Thurgood Marshall and Ruth Ginsburg."

Born in Brooklyn, Ginsburg went as an undergraduate to Cornell University, where she also met her future husband. Both went on to Harvard Law School, but following her husband's graduation and acceptance of a position in a New York law firm, Ginsburg finished her third year at Columbia Law School, where she tied for first in the class. Following graduation, for two years Ginsburg worked as a law clerk for a federal judge, but then could not find a New York law firm that would hire her. After two more years working as a research assistant, Ginsburg was hired by Rutgers University School of Law, where she taught until 1972, before becoming the first woman law professor at Columbia. While teaching, Ginsburg served as the director of the ACLU's Women's Rights Project and argued six (and won five) important gender-based discrimination cases before the Supreme Court. With little opposition from Republicans and guarded responses during her confirmation hearings, Ginsburg's nomination as the 107th justice sailed through the Senate with a final vote of ninety-six to three.

Less than a year later, in April 1994, Justice Blackmun announced that he would retire at the end of the term and Clinton had his second opportunity to fill a vacancy on the bench. Clinton once again agonized and vacillated in making his decision. He finally settled on the noncontroversial federal judge, Stephen Breyer, whom he had passed over a year earlier. Clinton picked Breyer because his other top two candidates, Bruce Babbitt and Richard Arnold, would have proven more controversial and might have set off a confirmation fight in the Senate.

As expected, Breyer won easy confirmation in the Senate by a vote of eighty-seven to nine. Breyer trained as an undergraduate at Stanford and Oxford universities and later received his law degree from Harvard Law School. He subsequently taught administrative law at Harvard for over a decade. Notably, after graduating from law school, he also served as a law clerk to Justice Arthur Goldberg. During that year the justice handed down his controversial and visionary opinion on the Ninth Amendment in *Griswold v. Connecticut* (1965). Unlike that former very liberal justice, however, Justice Breyer is a centrist and much more of a legal technician. And for that reason the President's advisers correctly anticipated relatively low key confirmation hearings for his second nominee and the 108th member of the Court.

Betrayed by Justice

"Whenever you put a man on the Supreme Court he ceases to be your friend. I'm sure of that." Lamenting that "packing the Supreme Court simply can't be done," Truman confessed, "I've tried and it won't work."[84] Like other disappointed Presidents, Truman felt he had misjudged his appointee. "Tom Clark was my biggest mistake. No question about it." With characteristic bluntness, he expressed his disillusionment:

> That damn fool from Texas that I first made Attorney General and then put on the Supreme Court. I don't know what got into me. He was no damn good as Attorney General, and on the Supreme Court . . . it doesn't seem possible, but he's been even worse. He hasn't made one right decision that I can think of. . . . It's just that he's such a dumb son of a bitch.[85]

In a letter to Douglas, Truman further explained that he could not "see how a Court made up of so-called 'Liberals' could do what that Court did to" him in *Youngstown Sheet & Tube Co. v. Sawyer* (1952).[86] Six members—including two of his appointees, Tom Clark and Harold Burton—held that he had exceeded his power by seizing steel mills in order to avert a nationwide strike that, he claimed, threatened the country's war effort in Korea. Vinson and Minton, his other two appointees, dissented along with Reed. The ruling was Truman's "*Dred Scott* decision." He felt that it "seriously hamstrung" the modern presidency.[87]

Clark's desertion was especially troubling since, earlier as attorney general, Clark had advised Truman that he had the power to deal with such emergencies. That was not the first time, however, that an appointee changed his mind on an important constitutional question after coming to the Court. Lincoln's secretary of the treasury, Salmon Chase, wrote the Legal Tender Acts, allowing the use of paper money to repay the Union's debts incurred in the Civil War. But after his confirmation as chief justice, he struck them down in *Hepburn v. Griswold* (1870) and then dissented when a new majority overturned that decision a year later in the *Legal Tender* cases (1871). Justice Robert Jackson likewise reversed himself on a position he had taken as attorney general, explaining simply, "The matter does not appear to me now as it appears to have appeared to me then."[88]

Like most Presidents, Truman expected loyalty. Yet, justices frequently disappoint their presidential benefactors. Two years after joining the Court, Oliver Wendell Holmes disappointed President Theodore Roosevelt by voting against his administration's antitrust policies. The President was prompted to observe that he "could carve out of a banana a Judge with more backbone than that!"[89] Franklin Roosevelt "thought that Judge Frankfurter was going to be a flaming liberal, but he turned out in many areas to be a rank conservative." Clark also recalled how Eisenhower was "very much disturbed over Chief Justice Warren and Justice Brennan."[90] Byron White disappointed the Kennedys.[91] Nixon was surprised when Burger voted in *United States v. Nixon* (1974) to deny his claim of executive privilege as a shield against having to turn over the "Watergate tapes." Blackmun undoubtedly also proved a disappointment because of his authorship of the ruling on abortion in *Roe v. Wade*. Likewise,

Justices Kennedy, O'Connor, and Souter disappointed supporters of Presidents Reagan and Bush when voting to uphold *Roe*
in *Planned Parenthood of Southeastern Pennsylvania v. Casey*
(1992).

Presidential efforts to pack the Court are only partially successful, for a number of reasons. "Neither the President nor his
appointee can foresee what issues will come before the Court
during the tenure of the appointees," Chief Justice Rehnquist
has pointed out. "Even though they agree as to the proper resolution of [past or] current cases, they may well disagree as to
future cases involving other questions when, as judges, they
study briefs and hear arguments. Longevity of the appointees,
or untimely deaths such as those of Justice [Frank] Murphy and
Justice [Wiley] Rutledge, may also frustrate a President's expectations; so also may the personal antagonism developed between
strong-willed appointees of the same President." Fundamentally, Presidents are disappointed because they fail to understand "that the Supreme Court is an institution far more
dominated by centrifugal forces, pushing towards individuality
and independence, than it is by centripetal forces pulling for
hierarchical ordering and institutional unity."[92]

There is no denying that Presidents influence Supreme
Court decision making through their appointments. One or two
appointments can make a crucial difference in the direction of
Supreme Court policy-making.[93] But life in the marble temple
also frustrates presidential attempts to influence that direction.
"The Court functions in a way," Justice Robert Jackson concluded, "that is pleasing to an individualist." Each justice gets to
the Court "under his own steam" and, Justice William Douglas
observed, becomes "a sovereign in his own right."[94] Unlike the
presidency, the Court does not have a "mission." Phrases like
"the Court as an institution" and "the Court as a team," Frankfurter concluded, amount to question-begging clichés.[95] Each
member serves justice in his or her own way. Justices change
and react differently to life in the marble temple.

Off-the-Bench Activities

The myth of the cult of the robe—that justices are "legal monks" removed from political life—has been perpetuated by justices like Frankfurter who hypocritically proclaim, "When a priest enters a monastery, he must leave—or ought to leave—all sorts of worldly desires behind him. And this Court has no excuse for being unless it's a monastery."[96]

The reality is that justices are political actors and find it more or less hard to refrain from outside political activities. Off-the-bench activities are the norm. More than seventy of those who have sat on the Court have advised Presidents and congressmen about matters of domestic and foreign policy, patronage appointments, judgeships, and legislation affecting the judiciary.[97] Even more justices have made their views on public policy known through speeches and publications.[98] The ethics code of the United States Judicial Conference forbids judges from being "a speaker or the guest of honor at an organization's fund-raising events," and from making partisan endorsements. But, the code does not apply to members of the Supreme Court and occasionally justices invite criticism for not appearing to abide by the code. In 1989, for instance, Justice O'Connor was sharply criticized for sending to a Republican political action committee a letter that cited (incorrectly) cases proclaiming that the United States is a "Christian nation"; she later apologized. And in 1993, Justice Thomas was accused of running afoul of the code for appearing as a guest of honor at a fund-raising dinner for the Georgia Public Policy Foundation, a conservative organization opposed to government regulation. When Thomas was further criticized for his public appearances before other conservative groups, he decided not to attend the national convention of the conservative Concerned Women for America and cut back on his off-the-bench activities.

POLITICAL CAMPAIGNING AND CONSULTING

For much of the Court's early history, justices used their positions for political advantage. Chief Justice John Marshall served for brief periods as secretary of state, and Oliver Ellsworth accepted the post of minister to France. Several other justices campaigned for friends seeking governorships and the presidency. Chief Justice Salmon Chase sought the presidency in 1868, and throughout the rest of the century numerous justices worked actively for presidential candidates. With the growing institutional prestige and responsibilities of the Court in this century, fewer justices sought greener political pastures. Hughes resigned as associate justice after he was nominated Republican presidential candidate in 1916, whereas Douglas, Vinson, and Warren declined opportunities to run as national political candidates.

A far more prevalent activity has been consulting on public policy. Justices on the pre-Marshall Court frequently offered advice. Yet, when President Washington formally requested the Court's views on a treaty in 1793, it responded that there were "considerations which afford strong arguments against the propriety of our extra-judicially deciding such questions."[99] The letter of 1793 remains a precedent for the Court's not rendering advisory opinions. But justices have not felt precluded from giving their individual views on issues of public policy.

In this century, all chief justices served as presidential consultants. Taft pursued the broadest range of activities. He helped shape the 1924 Republican Party platform and regularly advised Presidents Harding and Coolidge on everything from patronage appointments and judicial reform to military expenditures and legislation.[100] Stone was an intimate adviser of Hoover, joining his "Medicine Ball Cabinet," at which policy questions as well as an exercise ball were thrown around. When Roosevelt came into office, Stone thought that his advisory role would end, but he cultivated a relationship with FDR and continued to offer advice on problems with the Court and even on the Department of Justice's strategies and conduct of criminal prosecutions.[101]

Vinson was an intimate adviser of Truman, frequently conferring with him by telephone in the evenings or on fishing trips to Key West.[102] Eisenhower met with Warren and asked his attorney general to seek the chief justice's advice on pending cases before the Court.[103] Both the Kennedy and the Johnson administrations went to Warren for advice on judicial appointments and other matters. According to Nixon's White House aide John Ehrlichman, Burger "sent a steady stream of notes and letters to Nixon" in his campaign to reform judicial administration. Ehrlichman also claimed, though both Nixon and Burger denied, that the President and Attorney General Mitchell sought to keep "in touch with Burger" and "openly discussed with the Chief Justice the pros and cons of issues before the Court."[104] However, Nixon's presidential papers contain numerous letters from Burger, including some advice and historical support for Nixon's claims to White House confidentiality, on which the Court would eventually rule and reject in *United States v. Nixon.*[105]

Just as justices seek to influence Presidents, the latter may try to influence the former. Warren recalled two such instances. The first occurred at the White House when *Brown v. Board of Education* was being considered. At a dinner, the newly appointed chief justice sat next to President Eisenhower and within speaking range of John W. Davis, who was representing the segregation states before the Court in *Brown.* During dinner conversation, the President stressed "what a great man Mr. Davis was." Afterward he took Warren by the arm, and as they walked to another room, and spoke of the southern states in the segregation cases, he observed, "These are not bad people. All they are concerned about is that their sweet little girls are not required to sit in school along side some big overgrown Negroes." The second incident occurred in the first months of the Nixon administration, shortly after the Court ruled against

the government in some wiretapping cases. Attorney General
Mitchell worried that other pending cases might be overturned.
He sent the Department of Justice's public information officer,
Jack C. Landau, to talk with Brennan and Warren. If the Court
disapproved of the government's wiretapping practices, Landau
told them, the electronic surveillance of over forty-eight foreign
embassies might be jeopardized. Warren was appalled at "this
surreptitious attempt to influence the Court."[106]

Isn't it wrong for justices and Presidents to consult with each
other? The traditional view was well expressed by Senator Sam
Ervin, during the confirmation hearing on the nomination of
Fortas as chief justice in 1968:

> I just think it is the height of impropriety for a Supreme Court
> justice, no matter how close he may have been to the President, to
> advise him or consult with him on matters, public matters, that prop-
> erly belong within the realm of the executive branch of Government,
> and which may wind up in the form of litigation before the Court.[107]

History, however, is replete with justices advising Presidents,
and standards of judicial propriety evolve. Ultimately, the crucial
point is whether off-the-bench activities bring the Court into a
political controversy. Abe Fortas's relationship with Lyndon
Johnson and the battle over his confirmation as chief justice
illustrate the politics of off-the-bench activities.

Fortas's relationship with LBJ was by no means unprecedented. FDR in his first term had relied on advice from Brandeis, who had been an adviser to President Wilson. "I need
Brandeis everywhere," Wilson observed, "but I must leave him
somewhere."[108] A respected "prophet of reform," Brandeis stood
as a "judicial idol" for New Deal lawyers. During the early years
of the New Deal, Brandeis used Frankfurter, who was then a
professor at Harvard Law School, as his "scribe," his intermediary for promoting his ideas in the Roosevelt administration.[109]
But the "Brandeis/Frankfurter connection" was neither secret
nor deemed newsworthy or improper in Washington political
circles.[110]

Justice Abe Fortas, with National Security Adviser Clark Clifford, advising President Lyndon Johnson in the Oval Office of the White House. (*Lyndon B. Johnson Presidential Library*)

When Roosevelt filled vacancies on the Court, he continued to feel free to turn to his appointees for advice. Shortly after leaving the post of solicitor general, Reed sent a note requesting a meeting with the President and revealed the attitude of the Roosevelt Court toward its President. "If it is not too much of an intrusion," he wrote, "[our meeting] will help me to maintain, in some degree, my understanding of your objectives."[111] After Frankfurter joined the Court, he continued his advisory relationship, though his constant meddling sometimes backfired. Frankfurter also competed for influence with others on the Court. Stone, Black, and Douglas also advised the President on judicial appointments and other matters of public policy. Murphy frequently met with FDR to discuss the war in the Pacific; and Byrnes, during his brief stay on the bench, continued to offer advice on the constitutionality of legislation.[112] Unlike Frankfurter, Douglas continued, after FDR's death, to offer advice to Truman, Kennedy, and Johnson on concerns ranging from saving the redwoods in the West and protecting the environment to increased Soviet influence in the Middle East and the wisdom of a diplomatic recognition of China.[113] When a President like FDR and justices find commonality of purpose and personal and ideological compatibility, consultations are inevitable and questions of propriety are overlooked.

Johnson's relationship with Fortas was more intimate and extensive than that of FDR with his Court, however. It stemmed from the days of the New Deal and was shaped by the experience of those associated with the inner circle of Democratic politics dating back to the Roosevelt administration. After graduating from and teaching for a year at Yale Law School, Fortas went to Washington in 1934 as an assistant in the Securities and Exchange Commission. The commitment and interaction among New Deal lawyers left an indelible imprint on Fortas, no less than on Johnson, who saw himself as FDR's protégé.

Johnson considered Fortas to be in his elite group of foreign policy advisers. Regularly joining White House meetings on the Vietnam War, Fortas attended more cabinet meetings than the man he replaced on the bench, UN Ambassador Arthur Goldberg, who was one of the few "doves" in the administration.[114] "Should we get out of Vietnam?" was the central question at the November 2, 1967, meeting of the foreign policy advisers (and a question continually debated throughout LBJ's term). "The public would be outraged if we got out," Fortas observed. "What about our course in North Vietnam?" The President asked, "Should we continue as is; go further, moderate it; eliminate the bombing?" Both "hawks" on the war, "Fortas and Clark Clifford recommended continued bombing as we are doing." Less than a year later, in the spring of 1968, the North Vietnamese successfully penetrated South Vietnam in the so-called Tet offensive. General William Westmoreland demanded more troops. Goldberg pressed for a bombing halt and a more vigorous initiative to bring about peace negotiations. Protest against the

Vietnam War was steadily mounting. LBJ was at the crossroads of a major decision affecting the war and his presidency. At a March meeting, Goldberg pushed for direct talks with Hanoi and for a "cessation of the bombing" of North Vietnam. Fortas opposed a pause in the bombing. He urged the President to explain in a speech to the American people the need for troop reinforcement and for American "strength and resoluteness" in the war. Less than ten days later, Johnson announced the most critical decision of his presidency. Bombing would continue, but only in the area south of Hanoi, where the North Vietnamese had a large military force and from where they launched invasions of South Vietnam. He thus opened the possibility for negotiations with the Hanoi government. But he also announced his decision not to seek reelection.[115]

Fortas was no less active in the formulation of domestic policy. He attended meetings on fiscal policy, labor legislation, election reform, and campaign financing, often offering his views on matters that would eventually come before the courts.[116] Senator Thruston Morton remembered making a telephone call to learn LBJ's position on pending legislation and being told, "Well, the President is away, but Mr. Justice Fortas is here and he's managing the bill for the White House."[117] Fortas also helped write LBJ's speeches and messages to Congress on civil rights and criminal justice reform, and he recommended individuals for appointments as attorney general and to federal judgeships.[118]

Fortas's nomination for the post of chief justice was defeated, but not primarily because of his advising LBJ. Even after it was revealed that he had accepted $15,000 for teaching a seminar entitled "Law and the Social Environment" at American University, the public supported confirmation by a two-to-one margin.[119] Several factors contributed to his defeat. Johnson overestimated his influence after announcing that he would not seek reelection. Anticipating Nixon's victory in the 1968 election, Republican senators wanted to deny LBJ any appointments to the Court. White House advisers also told LBJ that it was a mistake to name another close personal friend, Homer Thornberry, to fill the vacancy that would be created by Fortas's promotion.[120]

Senate opposition focused on Fortas's judicial record and his support of the Warren Court's "liberal jurisprudence." Virginia's Senator Harry F. Byrd contended, "[T]he Warren Court has usurped authority to which it is not entitled and is not serving the best interests of our nation. Mr. Fortas appears to have embraced the Warren philosophy, which philosophy I strongly oppose."[121] Senator Eastland asserted, "[T]he main thrust of Justice Fortas' philosophy as expressed in his opinions is to tear down those ideas, ideals, and institutions that have made this country great. . . . "[122]

Defeat, Fortas told Warren, ultimately came from the "bitter, corrosive opposition to all that has been happening in the Court and the country: the racial progress, and the insistence upon increased regard for human rights and dignity in the field of criminal law. Other elements," he added, "contribute to the mix, but it's my guess that they are minor."[123] Shortly before he asked LBJ to withdraw his nomination, Fortas explained to Harlan that he had "not been a governmental 'busybody' " and that he "never 'volunteered' suggestions or participation in the affairs of State. On the other hand," he went on, "I felt that I had no alternative to complying with the President's request for participation in the matters where he sought my help—or more precisely, sought the comfort of hearing my summation before his decision—That's about what it amounted to in the case of President Johnson–Justice Fortas." He had no regrets about his off-the-bench activities and could not believe that he "injured the Court as an institution."[124]

Less than a year later, Fortas resigned from the Court. He did so because of further publicity that he had accepted $20,000 in 1965 as an adviser to the Wolfson Family Foundation, which was devoted to community relations and racial and religious cooperation. Fortas had terminated his relationship with the foundation during his first year on the Court and had returned the $20,000. He conceded "no wrong doing." But, Fortas told Warren, "the public controversy relating to my association with the foundation is likely to continue and adversely affect the work and position of the Court." The Court's prestige, he concluded, "prompts my resignation which, I hope, by terminating the public controversy, will permit the Court to proceed with its work without harassment of debate concerning one of its members."[125]

Off-the-bench consultations and honoraria for justices' lectures and teaching of seminars remain matters of some controversy. Justices often recuse themselves from participating in cases, but they generally do not explain why they are doing so. There are no fixed rules for their recusal, nor do the Judicial Conference's 1990 guidelines on honoraria for lower federal court judges apply to members of the Court. Some of the justices also disagree with and do not feel personally bound by the Court's rulings on when lower federal court judges should recuse themselves. In *Liljeberg v. Health Services Acquisition Corporation* (1988), for instance, Justice Stevens held that judges should recuse themselves when "a reasonable person" knowing the relevant facts would expect them to know of a conflict requiring their disqualification. Yet, Chief Justice Rehnquist and Justices Scalia and White dissented. Moreover, that same term Justice Scalia participated in a legal ethics case, brought by an attorney against the Kentucky Bar Association, despite his having received $2500 earlier that year for a speech given to the Kentucky Bar Association.[126]

SPECIAL ASSIGNMENTS

Justices have either volunteered or given in to presidential pressure to assume the duties of quasi-diplomats, arbitrators of foreign and domestic controversies, and heads of commissions. The practice began when Jay and Ellsworth served as special envoys to Great Britain and France. During the Civil War era,

Samuel Nelson was an intermediary for peace proposals to southern states. In 1876, however, a controversy over off-the-bench public service seriously threatened the Court's prestige. Congress had established a commission to resolve the disputed presidential election of 1876 between the Republican Rutherford Hayes and the Democrat Samuel Tilden. The commission included three Republican and two Democratic senators, two Republican and three Democratic representatives, and five justices—two from each party and the fifth, the Republican Joseph Bradley, designated by the Court. When Bradley cast the deciding vote giving the election to Hayes, attacks on the partisanship of the Court were inexorable.

Justices were more reluctant to assume special assignments after the controversy over the Hayes-Tilden commission. A number still served on nonpartisan commissions and investigatory bodies. But the potential for controversy and the burden of work at the Court in this century persuaded many to resist pressures for taking on additional duties. Harlan Stone was prevailed on by his brethren not to accept Hoover's offer of chairmanship of the Law Enforcement Commission. He declined FDR's plan to make him "rubber czar" during World War II, when rubber products were in short supply and needed for the military; and he turned down Truman's proposal that he head the National Traffic Safety Commission.[127] The patriotic spirit sparked by World War II nonetheless led several justices to accept off-the-bench assignments. Owen Roberts chaired the Commission to Investigate the Pearl Harbor Disaster. Frank Murphy was especially persistent in his endeavor to be helpful. When he was denied a military commission because of his age, he joined the army reserves. He went to boot camp during summer recess, begged FDR for special military assignments, and, much to the ire of Chief Justice Stone, drew a salary both as a justice and as a commissioned army officer.[128]

Robert Jackson's absence from the bench while serving as chief prosecutor at the Nuremberg trials of Nazi war crimes created serious problems and taught a lesson about the dangers of off-the-bench activities. Within the Court, his acceptance of the post was opposed, his absence was resented, and his failure to vote on cases where the others divided four to four was extremely aggravating. Antagonism toward Jackson ran deep and made it manifest to the brethren that, in Harold Burton's words, "the failure of any member to bear his full share of the work immediately results in increasing the burdens of the other members of the Court."[129]

Justices have since been exceedingly reluctant to assume additional time-consuming duties. Warren was hard pressed and finally gave in to LBJ's request that he head the commission to investigate the assassination of President Kennedy. Burger, however, took great pleasure in his responsibilities as chancellor of the Smithsonian Institution, for instance, and traveled to China and the Soviet Union on cultural exchanges as titular head of the federal judiciary. In contrast with Burger, Chief Justice Rehnquist has spent much less time on matters of judicial administration and has less interest in the kinds of extrajudicial activities that preoccupied his predecessor.

The Constitution, however, also assigns chief justices the special role of presiding over Senate trials of presidents who have been impeached by the House of Representatives. In 1868, Chief Justice Salmon Chase presided over the trial of Democratic President Andrew Johnson for firing his Secretary of War in violation of the Tenure in Office Act of 1867. That law was passed over his veto, because he deemed it an unconstitutional limitation on his powers and prohibited the president from removing any official appointed by him without the consent of the Senate. Actually, the Republican-controlled Congress was in a bitter political struggle with Johnson, who had succeeded President Abraham Lincoln after his assassination, over its Reconstruction policies. The Senate failed to muster the two-thirds vote needed for conviction, and Johnson was acquitted by just one vote. In 1999, Chief Justice Rehnquist presided over the trial of President Clinton, the only elected president to be impeached and tried, for allegedly committing perjury before a grand jury and obstructing justice in covering up evidence pertaining to his alleged "sexual" relationship with White House intern, Monica Lewinsky.

Congressional Lobbying

Judicial lobbying for legislation has a long history. On legislation affecting the administration of justice in particular, Chief Justice Burger insisted, "the separation of powers concept was never remotely intended to preclude cooperation, coordination, communication and joint efforts."[130]

Virtually all major legislation affecting the Court's jurisdiction was drafted by justices and was the result of their lobbying. John Jay, James Iredell, and Thomas Johnson lobbied for modifications in the Judiciary Act of 1789 and for the elimination of circuit riding. Joseph Story advised his friend in the House of Representatives, Daniel Webster, on judicial reform and drafted legislation on criminal punishment, bankruptcy, and the jurisdiction of federal courts. In the 1840s, John Catron actively lobbied for judicial improvements.[131] Chief Justice Samuel Chase and Justice Samuel Miller later pushed bills that would give the Court relief from its growing caseload. The latter wrote in 1872, "I have prepared and carried through the House a bill curtailing our jurisdiction and facilitating its exercise. I can do no more, and shall leave the responsibility where it belongs."[132] Miller's proposals achieved some success in 1875 and 1879, but Chief Justices Morrison Waite and Melville Fuller and others continued to press for the elimination of circuit-riding duties and for the expansion of the Court's discretionary power to decide which cases should be granted review. Their lobbying finally succeeded in 1891, when Congress passed the Circuit Court of Appeals Act, which eliminated circuit riding and created courts of appeals.

Chief Justice William Taft championed major reforms in

judicial administration. "If you go pussyfooting," the former President and unblushing judicial lobbyist observed, "my experience convinces me that you will fail."[133] Relying on Willis Van Devanter, William Day, and James McReynolds to draft proposed legislation, Taft successfully lobbied Congress to enact the Judges' Bill, or Judiciary Act of 1925, which established the basic jurisdiction of the modern Supreme Court.[134] Charles Evans Hughes was more reserved but no less shrewd. When Roosevelt sent his Court-packing plan to Congress, Hughes responded with a letter to the Senate Judiciary Committee implying that all the justices opposed the plan. As he hoped, Senator Burton Wheeler proclaimed that the justices were "unanimous with reference to the letter of the Chief Justice." The letter was skillfully written to give that impression, but Hughes had in fact talked only with Van Devanter and Louis Brandeis. Benjamin Cardozo and Harlan Stone strongly disapproved of Hughes's action and would have refused to sign the letter.[135]

Since Taft, chief justices have used a number of organizations in lobbying Congress. The Judicial Conference, established in 1922 and chaired by the chief justice, is the principal policy-making body of the federal judiciary. The conference meets twice a year and brings together senior chief judges from each appellate court and (since 1957) one district court judge from each circuit. It develops rules of procedure for federal courts and recommends or responds to proposed legislation affecting the courts.[136] In 1990, for instance, the Judicial Conference passed a resolution asking Congress to reconsider legislation requiring mandatory minimum sentences for certain federal crimes, in order to reduce the workloads of federal courts and prison overcrowding. The Administrative Office of the United States Courts, created in 1939, studies federal caseloads and helps implement recommendations of the chief justice and the Judicial Conference. Within the Administrative Office, the office of legislative affairs assists in drafting legislation and lobbying the House and Senate Judiciary Committees. The Federal Judicial Center, established in 1969, undertakes research projects aimed at improving the administration of justice and also assists the chief justice and the Judicial Conference.

Chief justices have a number of other ways of coopting congressmen and mobilizing support. After Taft, Burger was the most active in lobbying Congress and getting the assistance of the ABA in promoting his proposals. Although Rehnquist does not share his predecessor's preoccupation with judicial administration, as head of the federal judiciary he has publicly called on Congress not to expand federal courts' jurisdiction "into areas of the law that have traditionally been reserved to state courts," thereby eroding federalism and increasing the caseload of the federal judiciary.

Independence and Accountability

Justices enjoy a remarkable degree of independence. Article III of the Constitution prohibits Congress from diminishing their salary and provides for lifetime tenure, subject to "good behavior." Article II contains the threat of removal by impeachment in the House of Representatives and a trial and conviction by the Senate for "high crimes and misdemeanors."

Salaries have historically ranged somewhat below that of leading members of the legal profession, and so service may involve some financial sacrifice. In 1991, a long-awaited salary increase and cost-of-living adjustment raised the salaries of associate justices to $153,000 and the chief justice's to $160,000. Subsequent cost-of-living adjustments raised associates' salaries to $167,900 and the chief justice's to $175,400 in 1998. While their salaries thus rose, justices and other federal judges may no longer receive additional compensation for off-the-bench speeches or publications, as a result of the Ethics Reform Act of 1989 and rulings of the Judicial Conference of the United States. With the addition of Clinton's appointees, Justices Ginsburg and Breyer, and Justices O'Connor, Souter, Scalia, and Stevens, there are now six independent millionaires on the Court.

Removal from office has never been a serious threat. Impeachment is a "mere scarecrow," concluded Thomas Jefferson, after the unsuccessful 1805 effort to convict Samuel Chase for expounding Federalist philosophy while riding circuit. Forty-seven federal judges have been subject to impeachment proceedings, but only fourteen faced trials and only seven were convicted. Chase and William Douglas were the only two Supreme Court justices to confront the possibility of impeachment. Chase was acquitted. Two impeachment resolutions against Douglas failed to pass the House. Douglas was attacked in 1953 for his temporary stay of the executions of the convicted spies Julius and Ethel Rosenberg, and then again in 1970.

The drive to remove Douglas in 1970 illustrates the political difficulties of impeachment. After Fortas resigned in 1969 and Nixon's first two nominees to fill his seat were defeated, House Republicans sought to impeach Douglas in retaliation. A 1966 *Los Angeles Times* story had disclosed that Douglas was receiving $12,000 a year as a consultant to the Parvin Foundation, which funded seminars on Latin America and on combating the forces of international communism. In light of Fortas's resignation and his association with the Wolfson Foundation, Douglas's activity became newsworthy again. A week after Fortas resigned from the Court, Douglas resigned from the Parvin Foundation.

To the House Republican leader, Gerald Ford, the activities of Fortas and Douglas stretched the ABA's canon of judicial ethics that a "judge's official conduct should be free from impropriety and *the appearance of impropriety.*" Although Douglas's relationship with the Parvin Foundation had been known, the allegation of impropriety was politically opportune for Republicans.

What really disturbed Ford and others was Douglas's lifestyle and judicial philosophy. Ford, as his legislative assistant

Robert Hartmann recalled, "disapproved of Douglas the way a Grand Rapids housewife would deplore the behavior of certain movie stars. The old man [Douglas] took too many wives and he seemed to encourage any new fad in youthful rebellion."[137] He joined the Court's rulings extending First Amendment protection to ostensibly obscene materials. And his publishing agent permitted Ralph Ginsberg, convicted for publishing obscene and libelous magazines, to print an excerpt from one of Douglas's books in *Avant Garde*. Ford alleged a conflict of interest when Douglas participated in the Court's decision denying review of Ginsberg's conviction. Antagonism grew, and House Republicans pressed Ford to do something when an excerpt of Douglas's book *Points of Rebellion* appeared in *Evergreen*, a magazine identified with left-wing radicals.

When Ford finally went to the floor of the House to call for a special committee to investigate Douglas, Representative Andrew Jacobs, a Democrat, beat him to the punch by introducing a resolution for impeachment. Under the rules of the House, the matter immediately went to the Judiciary Committee, which at the time was controlled by Democrats. After the committee found no grounds for impeachment, Ford called it a "travesty." He continued to maintain that "over the past decade Justice Douglas' extensive extra-judicial earnings and activities have impaired his usefulness and clouded his contribution to the United States Supreme Court."[138] Yet the momentum for impeachment had declined by the time of the committee's report. The Senate had confirmed Harry Blackmun, Nixon's third nominee for Fortas's seat. Douglas's association with the Parvin Foundation no longer appeared extraordinary in view of the revelation during Blackmun's confirmation hearing that, as a federal appellate court judge, he was associated with the Mayo Clinic and the Kahler Corporation Foundation, among others, and was a trustee of (Chief Justice Burger's alma mater) the William Mitchell College of Law.

The drive to remove Douglas was also made difficult by disagreement on the standard for removing justices. A number of congressmen contend that judges may be removed for failure to maintain "good behavior" or for "willful misconduct in office, willful and persistent failure to perform duties in the office, habitual intemperance, or other conduct prejudicial to the administration of justice that brings the judicial office into disrepute." By contrast, impeachment requires conviction for an indictable criminal offense. During his attempt to remove Douglas, Ford claimed that the two standards are essentially the same and depend on "historical context and political climate." A justice may be removed, Ford contended, for "whatever a majority of the House of Representatives [decides] at a given moment in history."[139] That position would severely limit judicial independence and make members of the Court sensitive to political opposition in Congress. But the Founding Fathers sought to ensure judicial independence by making removal possible only by impeachment, and no federal judge has ever been impeached except for a criminal offense.

Although impeachment is rare, neither the Court nor the justices are totally unaccountable. The Court is institutionally accountable for its policy-making (as will be discussed further in Chapter Six). Other political institutions and public opinion may thwart and openly defy particular rulings. Justices are subject to the norms of life in the marble temple. A kind of internal institutional accountability is imposed by the processes of decision making and by the competition for influence among the justices. Lower-court judges and leading members of the legal profession impose an additional measure of professional accountability through personal communications and legal publications. Justices also look to their place in history: how their judicial record compares with that of others who sat and will sit on the high bench. Like all political actors, they desire, in the words of Adam Smith, "not only to be loved, but to be lovely."

THREE

Life in the Marble Temple

T HE 'VILLANEOUS' sea-sickness which generally afflicts me in a Stage [coach] has yielded, in some degree, to my suffering from the extreme cold," Justice Levi Woodbury wrote his wife in the 1840s. "I think I never again, at this season of the year, will attempt this mode of journeying. Besides the evils before mentioned I have been elbowed by old women—jammed by young ones—suffocated by cigar smoke—sickened by the vapours of bitters and w[h]iskey—my head knocked through the carriage top by careless drivers and my toes trodden to a jelly by unheeding passengers." In the early nineteenth century, a Supreme Court justice earned much of his pay on rough roads. Justices had to ride circuit and twice a year travel to Washington for the Court's sessions. Travel on horseback or by carriage was a hardship, "amid clouds of dust and torrents of rain," and involved long stays in taverns away from family and friends. Woodbury's wife constantly complained about his long absences, and once on his return he found that his wife had gone on vacation without him. "Why do you talk of regret at my necessary absence on the Circuit to support my family and object to my going to Washington," the devoted justice pleaded, "and are still so unwilling to stay with me when at home?"[1]

The Supreme Court is a human institution that has adapted to changing conditions. "The great tides and currents which engulf the rest of men," Justice Benjamin Cardozo noted, "do not turn aside in their course, and pass judges by."[2] Justices no longer ride circuit, and the caseload now keeps them in Washington for much of the year. These changes have been shaped by American society and politics. But they have also been shaped, in very basic ways, by the institutionalization of the Supreme Court.

Institutionalization is a process by which the Court establishes and maintains its internal procedures and norms and defines and differentiates its role from that of other political branches. Institutionalization reflects justices' interactions, vested interests, and responses to the Court's distinctive history and changing political environment. It remains a central force, conditioning judicial behavior. Whereas the early Court struggled to create procedural norms and an institutional identity, the structure and processes of the contemporary Court have become more bureaucratic. In the past three decades, the number of support and professional staff grew, and the division of labor and responsibility within the Court increased.

Before the Marble Temple

In its first decade (1790–1800), the Court had little business, frequent turnovers in personnel, no chambers or staff of its own, no fixed customs, and no clear institutional identity. It indeed appeared, in Alexander Hamilton's words, to be "the least dangerous" branch. When the Court initially convened, on February 1, 1790, only Chief Justice John Jay and two other justices arrived at the Exchange Building in New York City, where they were to meet. It adjourned until the following day, when Justice

John Blair and Attorney General Edmund Randolph arrived from Virginia. The other two appointed justices of the first Court never arrived: Robert Harrison resigned before the next session, and John Rutledge, though he sat on the circuit court for one year, resigned when appointed chief justice of his state, South Carolina. Its business largely limited to the admission of attorneys who would practice before its bar, the Court concluded its first session in ten days and its second, held in August, in two. Later that year, the capital of the United States moved from New York City to Philadelphia. Thereafter the Court met in Independence Hall, known as The State House, and in Old City Hall, where it shared the courtroom of the Mayor's Court until the capital again moved, to Washington, D.C., in 1800.

In these first years, the justices wore English wigs and colored robes. The wigs soon became controversial and were abandoned; Thomas Jefferson pleaded, "For Heaven's sake, discard the monstrous wig which makes the English Judges look like rats peeping through bunches of oakum!"[3] The justices also adopted, but gradually abandoned, the English practice of rendering *seriatim* opinions, whereby every justice would give his own opinion on each case. Chief Justice Jay initially wore a red robe and the associate justices wore black robes. But since the chief justiceship of John Marshall, all members of the Court have dressed in black robes. However, in January 1995, Chief Justice Rehnquist broke with that long-standing tradition by wearing a black robe with four golden stripes on each sleeve. Rehnquist, a fan of Gilbert and Sullivan and who once appeared in a production of "Trial by Jury," modeled the robe after one worn by the English Lord Chancellor in a production of Gilbert and Sullivan's "Iolanthe."

With few cases, the Court held two sessions a year, one in February and one in August, neither lasting more than two or three weeks. As the workload increased, sessions became somewhat longer, and an annual session, or term, as it is called, was established. By 1840 the Court was convening in January and sitting until March. Yet sessions remained rather short and by the end of the 1860s lasted only about seventeen weeks a year.[4] Because of an increasing workload throughout the late nineteenth century, Congress moved the beginning of each term back in stages to (finally in 1917) its present opening day on the first Monday in October. The term now runs through to the following June or July, depending on when the Court concludes its business.

The problems presented by frequent changes in personnel, few customs, and short sessions were exacerbated by the requirement, under the Judiciary Act of 1789, that the justices ride circuit. Twice a year each justice would hold court, in the company of district judges, in his circuit of the country in order to hear appeals from the trial courts. Circuit riding was the principal means by which the people of the new country became acquainted with the Court, but the justices had to travel long distances on horseback. Justice James Iredell's southern circuit not only carried him through North and South Carolina and Georgia but twice a year also took him back north to attend the Court's sessions. He likened himself to a "travelling postboy." In 1792, the justices urgently requested the President and Congress to find an alternative to circuit riding, insisting that it was "too burdensome" and unfair for them "to pass the greater part of their days on the road, and at inns, and at a distance from their families."[5] Chief Justice Jay complained that serving on the Court "was in a degree intolerable and therefore almost any other office of a suitable rank and emolument was preferable." Rather than ride circuit, Justice Thomas Johnson resigned.

Circuit riding was not merely burdensome; it also diminished the Court's prestige, for a decision by a justice on circuit could afterward be reversed by the whole Court. As Jay observed, "The natural tendency of such fluctuations is obvious; nor can they otherwise be avoided than by confining the Judges to their proper place, *viz.* the Supreme Court."[6] Jay subsequently resigned to become envoy to England and later declined reap-

pointment as chief justice because he "was not perfectly convinced that under a system so defective [the Court] would obtain
the energy, weight and dignity which were essential to its afford-
ing due support for the National Government, nor acquire the
public confidence and respect which, as the last resort of justice
of the nation, it should possess."[7]

The development of the Court's institutional identity was
necessarily difficult because the justices resided primarily in
their circuits rather than in Washington and often felt a greater
allegiance to their circuits than to the Court.[8] Justices not only
faced the problem of divided loyalties but also had opportunities
for teaching, practicing law, and consulting in their circuits,
thereby supplementing (if not surpassing) their judicial salaries.[9]
Accordingly, the important distinction between official status
and personal interests was far from clearly drawn, and, perhaps
inevitably, some justices felt little or no institutional allegiance.
Though Congress periodically altered circuit-riding duties, the
responsibilities and burdens continued to plague the justices
throughout the nineteenth century; they even grew for those
who had to travel west of the Mississippi.[10]

When the capital moved to Washington, D.C., in 1800, no
building or courtroom was specifically provided for the Court.
Between 1801 and 1809, the justices convened in various rooms
in the basement of the Capitol until remodeling took place, and
the Court met for a year in Long's Tavern. In 1810, the justices
returned to the Capitol but now met in a room designed for
their use. At the time, the room was also shared by the circuit
court and the Orphan's Court of the District of Columbia. The
courtroom, however, was rendered unusable in the War of 1812
when the British burned the Capitol on August 24, 1814. For
two years, the Court met in a rented house, the Bell Tavern. In
1817, the Court moved back into the Capitol, where it held its
sessions in a small room, "little better than a dunjeon," until its
courtroom was restored in 1819. A newspaper reporter in 1824
described the courtroom as being

not in a style which comports with the dignity of [the Court], or which bears a comparison with the other Halls of the Capitol. In the first place, it is like going down a cellar to reach it. The room is on the basement story in an obscure part of the north wing. In arriving at it, you pass a labyrinth, and almost need the clue of Ariadne to guide you to the sanctuary of the blind goddess. A stranger might traverse the dark avenues of the Capitol for a week, without finding the remote corner in which Justice is administered to the American Republic.[11]

In this room the Court nevertheless met until 1860, when it moved upstairs to the room previously occupied by the Senate. In the old Senate Chamber, preserved on the ground floor of the Capitol today, the Court met for three-quarters of a century, until the completion of its own building in 1935.

Coincident with the move into the Capitol, John Marshall assumed the position of chief justice, presiding over the Court for the next thirty-four years, until 1835. The Court's internal norms were as uncertain as its institutional identity, but Marshall managed to establish regularized procedures and enhance the Court's prestige. In contrast to the first decade, the entire first half of the nineteenth century saw a remarkable degree of continuity in the Court: seventeen of the twenty-two justices who served were on the bench for fifteen years or more. During this period, with decisions like *Marbury v. Madison*, the Court established, more or less delineated, and maintained its own institutional boundaries, thereby differentiating its role from that of other political institutions. To be sure, the public had little interest in the judicial process, other than attending an occasional session of the Court. Still, after 1811 *Niles' Register* and a few other Washington, New York, and Philadelphia newspapers began covering the Court's decisions. No less important, after 1821 the Court for the first time provided for the filing of written briefs by attorneys, though until 1833 it did not require the printing of records. Briefs and records were rarely preserved until after 1854. Only after 1870 do the yearly sets in the Supreme Court Library become complete.[12]

For most of the nineteenth century, life remained transitory in the Court, as in the Washington community; in the early part of the century, Washington was the capital of the country in search of a city. The justices continued to reside in their districts and to stay in boardinghouses while attending sessions of the Court. Chief Justice Taney (1836–1864) was the first to reside permanently in the city, and as late as the 1880s most justices did not bring their families or maintain homes there. The justices had no offices and shared the law library of Congress in the Capitol. They relied on a single Clerk of the Court to answer correspondence, manage the docket, collect fees, and locate boarding rooms for them on their annual visits. The Marshal of the Court also worked for other courts in the District of Columbia. On days when the Court heard oral arguments, which ran from eleven in the morning to three or four in the afternoon and often carried over for several days, the Marshal would announce the sitting of the justices with the now traditional introduction:

Oyez! Oyez! Oyez! All persons having business before the Honorable, the Supreme Court of the United States, are admonished to draw near and give their attention, for the Court is now sitting. God save the United States, and this Honorable Court.

From across the hall, where they had put on their robes in the presence of spectators, the justices would proceed into the courtroom, following the chief justice in order of their seniority. There they would sit at a long straight bench, the chief justice in the center and the others on both sides in alternating order of their seniority. The Reporter of Decisions recorded arguments and compiled and published the final decisions at his own expense and for his own profit. The Court had no other employees or assistants until the 1860s, when each justice acquired a messenger or servant. Not before the 1880s did the justices gain a secretary or law clerk.[13]

The development of the Court's institutional identity, regularized procedures, and norms of decision making flowed

The Supreme Court in session in the old Senate Chamber of the United States Capitol, where the Court held its sessions from 1860 until 1935, when it moved into the building that now houses the Court. (*Engraving by Carl Becker for* Harper's Weekly, *Collection of the Supreme Court of the United States*)

largely from the creative skills of "the Great Chief Justice," John Marshall. Few fixed customs bound Marshall, and his associates shared his Federalist philosophy. Being chief justice gave him special prerogatives: presiding at public sessions, leading discussion and directing the order of business in private conferences, either writing or assigning to another the Court's opinion, and serving as the executive officer of the Court and the titular head of the federal judiciary. But although the office of chief justice entitled Marshall to lead, his personality—inventive, shrewd, exacting yet amiable and unassuming—enabled him to mass the Court. For other justices, it was "both easy and agreeable to follow his lead" as well as "both hard and unpleasant to differ with him."[14]

One of John Marshall's great legacies has been the Court's

ongoing collegiality. Although he once thought that the Court
had "external & political enemies enough to preserve internal
peace," Marshall sought to maintain "harmony of the bench" by
ensuring that all justices roomed in the same boardinghouse.[15]
He thus turned the disadvantage of transiency into strategic
opportunity. After a day of hearing oral arguments, the justices
would dine together and around seven o'clock begin discussing
cases. Marshall used the talks to achieve his overriding institutional goal—unanimity. He perceived that unanimous decisions
would build the Court's prestige. He discouraged dissenting
opinions, sought to accommodate opposing views, and wrote the
overwhelming number of the Court's opinions, even when he
disagreed with a ruling.[16] Defending his practice, Marshall
observed:

> The course of every tribunal must necessarily be, that the opinion
> which is to be delivered as the opinion of the court, is previously sub-
> mitted to the consideration of all the judges; and, if any part of the
> reasoning be disapproved, it must be so modified as to receive the
> approbation of all, before it can be delivered as the opinion of all.[17]

Justice William Johnson of South Carolina, one of President
Jefferson's appointees, took a different view. When Jefferson
urged him to press for a return to the practice of individual
opinions, Johnson's lengthy reply explained how difficult Marshall made it to disagree:

> While I was on our State-bench I was accustomed to delivering
> *seriatim* Opinions in our Appellate Court, and was not a little surprised
> to find our Chief Justice in the Supreme Court delivering all the opin-
> ions in Cases in which he sat, even in some Instances when contrary
> to his own Judgement and Vote. But I remonstrated in vain; the
> Answer was he is willing to take the trouble and it is a Mark of Respect
> to him. I soon however found out the real Cause. Cushing was incom-
> petent. Chase could not be got to think or write—Paterson was a slow
> man and willingly declined the Trouble, and the other two [Chief Jus-
> tice Marshall and Justice Bushrod Washington] are commonly esti-

mated as one Judge. Some Case soon occurred in which I differed from my Brethren, and I felt it a thing of Course to deliver my Opinion. But, during the rest of the Session I heard nothing but Lectures on the Indecency of Judges cutting at each other, and the Loss of Reputation which the Virginia Appellate Court has sustained by pursuing such a Course. At length I found that I must either submit to Circumstances or become such a Cypher in our Consultations as to effect no good at all. I therefore bent to the Current, and persevered until I got them to adopt the Course they now pursue, which is to appoint someone to deliver the Opinion of the Majority, but to leave it to the rest of the Judges to record their Opinions or not ad Libitum.[18]

The Taney Court emulated the Marshall Court's collegial decision-making practices. Justice John McLean provided the following view of the Court's conferences in that period:

Before any opinion is formed by the Court, the case after being argued at the Bar is thoroughly discussed in consultation. Night after night, this is done, in a case of difficulty, until the mind of every judge is satisfied, and then each judge gives his views of the whole case, embracing every point of it. In this way the opinion of the judges is expressed, and then the Chief Justice requests a particular judge to write, not his opinion, but the opinion of the Court. And after the opinion is read, it is read to all of the judges, and if it does not embrace the views of the judges, it is modified and corrected.[19]

The justice assigned to write the Court's opinion would read his draft at conference but not circulate a printed version. Thus, the justices would typically agree only on the main points of the decision and not on the precise wording of the Court's opinion. The decision would be announced and the opinion read the next day. This practice discouraged dissenting and concurring opinions alike. Occasionally, other justices complained, most notoriously about Taney's opinion in *Dred Scott,* that the opinion read from the bench and the final printed version differed from that agreed to in conference.[20] In the latter part of the nineteenth century, this complaint helped lead to the practice of circulating draft opinions for comments and changes before a

final vote and announcement. Thus, not until the chief justiceship of Melville Fuller (1888–1910) were draft opinions circulated among the justices prior to their delivery,[21] a practice, as
we shall see, that is now central to the Court's decision-making
process.

Chief Justice Charles Evans Hughes once characterized
Dred Scott as one of the Court's "self-inflicted wounds." That
decision and the Civil War changed the Court as well as the
country. During Reconstruction, the capital became a city, the
Court's workload steadily increased, and terms lengthened.
The justices deserted boardinghouses for fashionable hotels
along Pennsylvania Avenue. Instead of dining together and discussing cases after dinner, they held conferences on Saturdays
and announced decisions on Mondays. (The Warren Court
started delivering opinions on any day of open session, and the
Burger Court moved conferences back to Fridays.) Justices still
dined in company, but more frequently they were joined by
members of the Court's bar, with whom they frequently discussed pending cases.[22]

After 1860, the Court met upstairs in the old Senate Chamber in the Capitol between the new chambers of the Senate and
those of the House of Representatives. The justices still had no
offices of their own. In the 1920s, Justices George Sutherland
and Edward Sanford and a few others managed to secure small
rooms on the gallery floor of the Capitol. During the chief justiceships of Salmon Chase (1864–1873) and Morrison Waite
(1874–1888), conferences were held downstairs in a "consultation" room which also served as a library. Chief Justice Melville
Fuller proudly held conferences at his home. The red-brick
house had earlier boarded the Marshall Court in 1831 and
1833.[23] Fuller also inaugurated the customary handshake among
the justices before they ascend the bench or begin conference
deliberations. These marks of conviviality aside, however, Fuller
was unlike his predecessor Waite in spurning Washington social
life. His successor, Chief Justice Edward White (1910–1921),
was similarly austere.

The Supreme Court in 1893. Seated, left to right, front row: Justices Horace Gray and Stephen Field, Chief Justice Melville Fuller, and Justices John M. Harlan and Samuel Blatchford. In the second row: Justices Henry Brown, Lucius Lamar, David Brewer, and George Shiras, Jr. (*Photograph by C. M. Bell, Collection of David M. O'Brien*)

By the turn of the century the justices resided in the capital and for the most part worked at home. Congress provided funds for each justice to maintain a working library and employ a messenger and a secretary or law clerk. In his library, for instance, Oliver Wendell Holmes illegibly wrote his opinions with a sputtering ink pen at a "stand-up" desk inherited from his grandfather. "There is nothing so conclusive to brevity," he often remarked, "as a feeling of weakness in the knees."[24] He had no typewriter. "How I loathe conveniences," Holmes cherished saying.[25] Former Secretary of State Dean Acheson, who clerked for Justice Louis Brandeis, recalled, "Poindexter, the messenger, and I constituted the whole office staff; and Poindexter, half the household staff as well."[26] Law clerks worked in a variety of capacities, from assisting in legal work to serving cocktails at weekly social gatherings. Relations among the justices varied widely, for each worked principally alone at home. Brandeis and Holmes had a warm, lifelong friendship. James McReynolds, a bachelor, was abrasive and worked poorly with others; he even had trouble keeping law clerks.[27]

Since the early part of this century, the Court's collegial procedures have depended less on sociability than on institutional norms and majority rule. The court now functions on the basis of a shared or pooled interdependence. The chief justice has a special role in maintaining certain rules and routines, in scheduling and coordinating conferences, and in assigning and announcing opinions. But the deliberative process—the conference discussions, the voting, and the circulation of draft opinions—entails a mutual adjustment among equals. The Court, Frankfurter once noted, "is an institution in which every man is his own sovereign."[28] The justices' independence, as well as the need for mutual adjustment, was reinforced by the fact that each justice now resided in Washington and worked primarily and independently at home, with little or no assistance. The justices had come to function like "nine little law firms," as Justice Robert Jackson later observed. This was a matter of great pride for justices like Brandeis, who said, "The reason the public thinks so much of the Justices of the Supreme Court is that they are almost the only people in Washington who do their own work."[29]

When William Howard Taft became chief justice in 1921, he set out to construct the Court's own building. His associates balked.[30] In 1896, the justices had unanimously rejected a congressional proposal to move them from the Capitol to the more spacious Congressional Library Building across the street.[31] On Taft's Court, Brandeis thought that there was a more than symbolic importance to the Court's sitting at the center of the Capitol, midway between House and Senate. And he abhorred the opulence of Taft's design. By contrast, Taft envisioned a building that would symbolize the Court's prestige and independence.

Taft tirelessly lobbied Congress and in 1925 persuaded the

Justices Oliver Wendell Holmes (left) and Louis D. Brandeis, two of the Court's "great dissenters." (*Corbis/Bettmann*)

Senate to fund his marble temple. He died before the completion of the building in 1935. Built in the Greek Corinthian style, at a cost of slightly less than $10 million, the four stories above the ground featured Vermont marble outside and Alabama mar-

Members of the Taft Court in 1929 examining a model of the building that now houses the Supreme Court. From left to right: Justices Brandeis and Van Devanter, Chief Justice Taft, and Justices Holmes, Butler, Sanford, and Stone. (*Corbis/Bettmann*)

ble in the interior corridors and in the Great Hall at the entrance; Georgian marble was used for four inner courtyards surrounding the main-floor courtroom, constructed of marble from Italy, Spain, and Africa. Handcrafted American white oak was used throughout the building, with particularly impressive carvings on the arches and ceiling of the library.

The main floor holds two large conference rooms, offices for the marshal and the solicitor general of the United States, and a lawyers' lounge. Circling the four courtyards and the courtroom at the center are the justices' chambers—each a suite of three to four rooms—with the chambers of the chief justice, the justices' robing room, and a private conference room directly behind the courtroom. One floor up are the Office of the Reporter of Decisions, the Legal Office, and the justices' dining room, with smaller private dining rooms on each side. The remaining rooms on the floor house law clerks and records. On the third floor is the library. Half a floor above the library, there is now a basketball court, commonly referred to as the "highest court in the land," where law clerks play basketball and work out on exercise equipment, and where Justice Sandra O'Connor and employees hold an exercise class. On the ground floor, opened to the public by Chief Justice Warren Burger, the curator displays historical exhibits, and the Supreme Court Historical Society has a kiosk. The offices of the Clerk, the Public Information Officer, the Director of Personnel and Organizational Development, the Administrative Assistant to the Chief Justice, and the Curator; the police; and a barbershop, seamstress, nurse, and public cafeteria are also on the ground floor. Below, there are a parking garage for the justices and the Court's printing shop, carpentry shop, and laundry.

Though Chief Justice Taft managed to persuade four other justices—a bare majority—to support his lobbying for the building,[32] he would have found it difficult to get them to move into the marble temple. Chief Justice Hughes himself later referred to the building as simply "a place to hang my hat," and Harlan Stone reportedly commented snidely that the justices would look like nine black beetles in the temple of Karnak. When a guest at one of the Brandeis Sunday teas remarked that Stone was complaining about the building and about the acoustics and lighting in the courtroom, Brandeis, recalled his law clerk Paul Freund, replied hotly, "Well, he voted for it!" Although the Hughes Court (1930–1941) held its sessions and conferences there, Brandeis and the others stayed in their home offices. In 1937, Hugo Black became the first to move in, leading the way for President Roosevelt's seven other appointees. Still, even when Harlan Fiske Stone was elevated from associate to chief justice, he continued to work primarily at home (1941–1946).[33]

The Vinson Court (1946–1953) first saw all nine justices regularly working in the building.

In the Marble Temple

Completion of the marble temple preceded by two years FDR's attack on the Court as a "super legislature" for its invalidation of early New Deal legislation. The building, as Taft envisioned, indeed symbolized the Court's changed role in American politics—its move from being "the least dangerous" to being a coequal branch of government. "The function of the Supreme Court," Taft and later chief justices affirmed, had become "not the remedy of a particular litigant's wrong, but the consideration of cases whose decision involves principles, the application of which are of wide public or governmental interest, and which should be authoritatively declared by the final court."[34] The modern Supreme Court is not, as it once was, a tribunal for the resolution of private disputes; instead, it is an institution devoted to public policy-making through constitutional and statutory interpretation.

The marble temple, however, is more than a symbol of the modern Court. Once again the institutional life of the Court changed. The building further removed and insulated the justices from the political life in the Capitol. The building nonetheless reinforces basic institutional norms—in particular, along with the justices' psychological interdependence and independence from outside political accountability, the norms of secrecy, tradition, and collegiality.

Isolation from the Capitol and the close proximity of the justices' chambers within the Court promote secrecy, to a degree that is remarkable, considering the rather frequent disclosures in the nineteenth century by justices to Presidents, congressmen, and attorneys. The decision in *Dred Scott*, for instance, was leaked well before its announcement from the bench; and

Chief Justice Chase later informed the secretary of the treasury "about two weeks in advance of the delivery of the opinions" in the *Legal Tender* cases.[35] Once justices spent most of their time in the same building, they became more careful about their revelations and certainly more conscious of the consequences of rumors that they had revealed votes or the outcome of cases.[36] The norm of secrecy conditions the employment of the justices' staff and has become more important as the number of employees increases. Messengers were excluded from the justices' conferences because of a leak about the *Carbonic Gas* case (1909), and in 1919 Justice Joseph McKenna's clerk was indicted for disclosing the vote in a pending case to speculators on the New York Stock Exchange.[37]

A current problem, some justices feel, has been that law clerks have discussed cases with reporters and scholars, thus breaking with the Court's tradition of secrecy. As a result, beginning in the 1987 term law clerks were given a thirty-page memorandum, "The Code of Conduct for Supreme Court Law Clerks," instructing them not to discuss the work of the Court with anyone other than the justices or their fellow clerks, even after their clerkship year has ended! When the code of conduct was revised in 1989, law clerks were also admonished that "discussions with law clerks from other chambers should be circumspect" and to "avoid any hint about the Justice's likely action in a pending case." Those injunctions, however, as one of Justice Marshall's clerks observed, do "not match the way clerks work," "may impede discussions among clerks," and unnecessarily interfere with their First Amendment rights.[38] Indeed, the unreliability of the clerks' "code of silence" was underscored in 1998 when Edward Lazarus published *Closed Chambers: The First Eyewitness Account of the Epic Struggles Inside the Supreme Court.*[39] Having clerked during the 1988 term, shortly after the battle over Judge Robert Bork's ill-fated nomination, and drawing on clerks' e-mail messages and private conversations, Lazarus portrayed the justices as "clerk driven" and the clerks as embattled. Although capitalizing on some tantalizing glimpses of behind-the-scenes backbiting, there remained little new in the book apart from tales of clerks' infighting. Within the Court Lazarus's book was dismissed, while reviewers criticized his factual errors and often-exaggerated claims.[40]

Another controversy over the Court's secrecy occurred in 1993, when Justice Marshall's working papers, including memos and draft opinions, became available to the public. A majority of the Rehnquist Court created a minor controversy over what it deemed a breach of confidentiality and pushed to curtail access to the papers. Following his retirement in 1991, Marshall donated his papers to the Library of Congress with the stipulations that the collection, upon his death, be opened to "researchers or scholars engaged in serious research." Less than two years later, he died and the Library made his papers available. Subsequently *The Washington Post* ran a series of articles, based on his papers, that portrayed the conservative shift on the Court and described how close it came to overruling *Roe v. Wade* in *Webster v. Reproductive Health Services* (1989). Chief Justice Rehnquist promptly sent the Library a letter, claiming to "speak for a majority of the active Justices," protesting the "release [of] Justice Marshall's papers dealing with deliberations which occurred as recently as two terms ago," and asking that the papers be closed. The Library, nonetheless, refused to yield.

The release of Justice Marshall's papers, however, was unique only in providing access to the justices' deliberations in cases decided just two years earlier. Even more unprecedented was Justice Brennan making some of his papers available while still sitting on the bench. In the 1980s Brennan made his papers available for his initial years on the Warren Court (1956–1969) and later on the basis of installments that covered cases decided five years earlier. That enabled scholars to write about the workings of the contemporary Court, but angered some of the sitting justices. In 1990, Brennan partially bowed to pressure and changed his policy to allowing only "selective access" for limited periods of time to his papers. But, when doing so he also justified his practice, explaining to the other justices that, "Works published by scholars who have used my papers among other collections have been uniformly substantive and, on the whole, worthwhile."[41]

Justices, of course, differ on whether, when, and to whom their papers should be made available. Indeed, when Rehnquist pressed to end the public's access to Marshall's papers, Justice White sent the Library of Congress a letter disagreeing with the chief justice's view and retired Justice Blackmun donated his papers to the Library of Congress, whereas Chief Justice Burger gave his to the College of William & Mary with severe restrictions on access. No rules govern, nor has there been a common practice with respect to what justices do with their papers. Approximately 40 percent of those who served on the Court destroyed their papers. That is what most of the justices did in the nineteenth century. In the twentieth century, justices have tended to give their papers to the Library of Congress or to a law school. Still, they have usually done so on the condition that they not become available until after their death or until all of the justices with whom they served have left the bench. In addition, Justice Hugo Black burned his docket books and conference notes before turning over case files and correspondence to the Library of Congress. Black and some other justices, however, also inserted personal notes for "posterity." Justice Powell, for instance, inserted notes explaining his decision process and the process of drafting opinions in some important and controversial cases.

The controversies over these disclosures reveal that the Court guards its secrecy carefully. Similar controversies have arisen over access to the Court's deliberations by journalists, scholars, and visitors. For instance, the Court began having oral arguments recorded in 1955. Recordings were made available from the National Archives three years after the date of oral argument and solely for educational purposes. In 1977, a CBS news story aired on television portions of the oral arguments in *New York Times Co. v. United States* (1971)—in which a bitterly divided Court ruled that the government's injunction against the publication of the *Pentagon Papers* (a top-secret history of America's involvement in the Vietnam War) was a prior restraint on freedom of speech in violation of the First Amendment. Subsequently, Burger no longer permitted the recordings to be transferred to the National Archives. But when several of the justices learned about Burger's actions in 1986, they agreed that the recordings would once again be sent to the National Archives.

Since William Rehnquist became chief justice, the Court has become somewhat more open and accessible. The justices have discussed whether television might be introduced into the courtroom. A few justices have favored television coverage of oral arguments. In *Chandler v. Florida* (1981) the Court held that state courts may allow television coverage of their proceedings. And in 1991 two federal appellate courts and six district courts began a three-year experiment in allowing television coverage of their proceedings. But, in 1994 the experiment was ended, in spite of studies by the Federal Judicial Center showing that the cameras in the courtroom had no significant adverse effects. A number of senior judges favor allowing cameras in federal courts and are pushing for reconsideration of the matter, while news organizations are putting pressure on Congress to pass legislation requiring federal courts to permit cameras in federal courts, as forty-seven states now permit in state courts.

A majority on the Court continues to worry that only segments of oral arguments would be shown on the evening news, and that might denigrate the Court. They are also concerned about their own public exposure and loss of privacy. As a result, majorities of the Rehnquist Court have repeatedly rebuffed requests from radio and television companies to broadcast oral arguments in important cases, such as *Morrison v. Olson* (1988).[42] After a consortium of broadcasters in 1989 demonstrated how cameras might be introduced into the Court, Chief Justice Rehnquist again rejected the possibility of television coverage, explaining that, "A majority of the Court remains of the view that we should adhere to our past practice and not allow camera coverage of our proceedings."[43] Only Justices Brennan and Stevens favored permitting television coverage of the Court's proceedings, but they were consistently outvoted when the Court considered requests for not only broadcasting oral arguments, but also the investitures of Justices Kennedy, Souter, Ginsburg, and Breyer. Justices Scalia and Thomas remain the most adamantly opposed to permitting television in the courtroom.[44] In addition, some of the justices' opposition was reinforced by television coverage of Robert Bork's ill-fated Senate confirmation hearings in 1987, and then by the coverage of Clarence Thomas's hearings and Anita Hill's charges that he had sexually harassed her years earlier. Justice Antonin Scalia, for one, has confessed that, "When I first went on the Court, I was in favor of having cameras in the Court. I am less and less so [because] I don't want it to become show biz." Indeed, after his first couple of years on the bench, Scalia even barred C-SPAN from covering his public speeches. On various occasions he offered several explanations for his aversion to television coverage of his off-the-bench speeches: (1) he was "over-exposed" in his first year on the Court, (2) he doesn't want what he says taken out of context, and (3) his legal lectures are "boring" for the public and "comprehensive only to legal experts." "That is why," as he cleverly put it, *"The University of Chicago Law Review* is not sold at 7-Eleven."

In 1993, the Rehnquist Court carried its opposition to broadcasts of oral argument sessions to an angry extreme. Political scientists Peter Irons and Stephanie Guitton produced a collection of six cassettes containing edited recordings of the oral arguments in twenty-three landmark cases, including *Miranda v. Arizona* (1966), *Roe v. Wade* (1973), and *United States v. Nixon* (1973). Like other scholars, Irons had obtained audio copies from the National Archives. But, unlike others, he did not honor his agreement to the Court's conditions for access and use of the tapes. In 1986, when the Burger Court resumed sending the recordings to the archives, it required researchers to sign a form promising to use the tapes "for private, noncommercial purposes only," and "not to give, sell, lend, exchange, or otherwise convey any portion of the audiotape provided under this agreement."[45] Irons defended his broken promise on the ground that the agreement was not valid under the First Amendment. But, a majority of the Rehnquist Court denounced his project, initially threatened legal action, and instructed the Court's marshal not to grant Irons further access to the recordings. The controversy was, perhaps, inevitable and resulting from the Court's unwillingness to come to terms with modern communications technology.[46] Almost two decades earlier, in 1974, the Burger Court had denied permission for the highly respected attorney Jack Greenberg to produce a collection virtually identical to Irons's *May It Please the Court. . . .*[47] In the end, after allowing the controversy to simmer for a few months, the Rehnquist Court instructed the Access to the Motion Picture, Sound, and Video Research Room of the National Archives to make copies of oral arguments on request for $12.75 per one-hour tape. With funding from the National Endowment for the Humanities and the National Science Foundation, political scientist Jerry Goldman started the project "Oyez, Oyez, Oyez," putting oral arguments on to the Internet. Over 300 arguments in leading cases may be heard at ⟨http://oyez.nwu.edu⟩.

One of the major technological changes at the Court aimed at expanding public access, however, has been "Project Hermes"—an experiment inaugurated in 1990 that makes the Court's opinions available immediately after they are announced through a new computer network and various electronic billboards. With a modem and a personal computer, individuals may obtain the opinions on the same day they are handed down through one or more information systems, including Lexis,

The Supreme Court in session, February 8, 1935. This is the only known photograph of the Court in session. (*Photo by Erich Solomon*)

Westlaw, CompuServe, as well as on Internet sites such as FindLaw ⟨http://www.findlaw.com/casecode/supreme.html⟩.

As the controversy over televised hearings demonstrated, the Court has a profound sense of history and tradition. Brass spittoons still flank chairs on the bench, and goose-quill pens and pewter inkwells grace the tables for participating counsel. There have, of course, been changes in the justices' chambers and in other aspects and practices of the Court. From 1790 to 1972, the justices sat in a straight line. Burger modified the straight bench to a half-hexagonal shape, so that the justices seated on the two wings could better hear and see both attorneys and one another. Previously, the Warren Court had amplifying equipment installed because of poor acoustics in the courtroom. Pages abandoned knickers for gray trousers and dark blue blazers in 1963. The tailcoat required of attorneys was abandoned around the turn of the century, though the solicitor general and his staff continue to wear tailcoats when appearing before the Court. In 1981, shortly before Justice O'Connor's appointment, the practice of addressing a member of the Court as "Mr. Justice" was dropped; with the exception of the chief justice, each member of the Court is now referred to as "Justice." In 1982, after a complaint, the Court started using the term "Esquire" when addressing female and male attorneys. Down through Chief Justice Warren's time, almost all of the justices' messengers were black—virtually the only black employees in the Court until the first black page was appointed in 1954.[48] The first black law clerk, William Coleman, was chosen by Felix Frankfurter in 1948. The first woman was picked by William Douglas in 1944, but no others were until Black selected the daughter of his New Deal friend and Washington lawyer-lobbyist Thomas ("Tommy the Cork") Corcoran in 1966. Under Chief Justice Burger, the racial, ethnic, and religious character of Court employees became more diverse, and employment became more professional with the posting of job openings, the establishment of pay scales and time sheets for Court personnel, and the creation of an officer of personnel and organizational development.[49]

While altering working relations among the justices, the building to some extent also reinforces collegiality. Justices collectively decide (usually by majority vote) not only cases but also changes in procedures and other organizational matters. In Chief Justice Waite's time, for instance, the justices agreed (over two dissents) that the Reporter of Decisions should live in Washington during the term and not participate in pending cases while the Court is in session.[50]

Most matters come to a vote: the printing of Court opinions within the building, the transcribing of oral arguments, the posting in the robing room of opinions to be announced, and the setting of salaries for the Court's officers.[51] Typically, a committee of three justices studies proposed changes affecting life in the marble temple, and then makes a recommendation on which the justices vote at conference. In recent years, the Court adopted regulations and policies on such matters as smoking in the building, the number of group photographs that the justices will sign each year, guidelines for tours of the Court, and a code of conduct for law clerks.[52] If a majority fails to agree on proposed changes, then past practice prevails. Chief Justice Burger, for instance, unsuccessfully proposed to save the Court's time by ending the tradition of formally admitting attorneys to the Supreme Court's bar,[53] and Justice Blackmun failed to persuade the others to abandon the custom of forbidding the public from taking notes or writing during oral argument sessions.[54]

Majority rule on organizational matters occasionally proves unsatisfactory, for as Frankfurter observed:

Of course votes—a majority vote—must decide judicial business, and such votes must be acted upon. But very different considerations apply to the family life of the Court—the way it should carry on in its corporate life, its relations to the other branches of Government, to the Bar, and the public. In such matters, the controlling considerations are those that relate to the best way of assuring inner harmony, whatever intellectual differences there may be. And that means not votes but accommodation—the give-and-take of comradeship, accommodation to the purpose and not mere counting of heads.[55]

After his retirement, Chief Justice Warren recollected, "When you are going to serve on a court of that kind for the rest of your productive days, you accustom yourself to the institution like you do to the institution of marriage, and you realize that you can't be in a brawl every day and still get any satisfaction out of life."[56] But the Court under Chief Justice Burger became much less collegial, and the justices socialized less with each other. There was a time when, on the days that oral arguments were heard, the justices would have lunch together. But that almost never happened during the Burger Court years. Under Chief Justice Rehnquist, though, the tradition of justices lunching together has been revived.

Even though the Court depends on accommodation and compromise, it is also, in Justice Lewis Powell's words, "one of the last citadels of jealousy preserved individualism."[57] Some justices have no friends on the bench. McReynolds refused to sign letters of tribute from the Court to Justices Brandeis, Cardozo, and John Clarke on their retirement. Black refused to sign any joint letter of tribute from the justices to Owen Roberts that expressed regret "that our association within the daily work of the Court must come to an end."[58]

The internal dynamics and institutional life of the Court reflect the norms, vested interests, and interplay of personalities among the justices and their staffs. The modern Court still functions more or less like nine little law firms, but life in the marble temple has also become more bureaucratic. As caseloads have increased dramatically over the last thirty years, the number of law clerks has more than tripled and the number of other employees increased by more than 65 percent.[59] Most of the justices' chambers have grown in proportion.

Justice and Company — Nine Little Law Firms

When Potter Stewart joined the Court in 1958, he expected to find "one law firm with nine partners, if you will, the law clerks being the associates." But Justice Harlan told him, "No, you will find here it is like nine firms, sometimes practicing law against one another."[60] Each justice and his staff work in rather secluded chambers with virtually none of the direct daily interaction that occurs in lower federal appellate courts. No one today follows Frankfurter's practice of sending clerks—"Felix's happy hot-dogs"—scurrying around the building. "As much as 90 percent of our total time," Powell underscored, "we function as nine small, independent law firms."

I emphasize the words *small* and *independent*. There is the equivalent of one partner in each chamber, three or four law clerks [seven of the justices each use four clerks, while Chief Justice Rehnquist and Justice John Paul Stevens rely on three], two secretaries, and a messenger. The informal interchange between chambers is minimal, with most exchanges of views being by correspondence or memoranda. Indeed, a justice may go through an entire term without being once in the chambers of all of the other eight members of the Court.[61]

A number of factors isolate the justices. The Court's members decide together, but each justice deliberates alone. Their interaction and decision making depend on how each and all of the nine justices view their roles and common institutional goals. According to John Harlan, "decisions of the Court are not the product of an institutional approach, as with a professional deci-sion of a law firm or policy determination of a business enter-prise. They are the result merely of a tally of individual votes cast after the illuminating influences of collective debate."[62] Intellectual and personal compatibility and leadership may determine whether justices embrace an institutional, consensual approach to their work or stress their own policy objectives. Chief Justice Rehnquist has said, "When one puts on the robe, one enters a world . . . which sets great store by individual per-formance, and much less store upon the virtue of being a 'team player.' " At worst, as Harry Blackmun observed, the justices are "all primadonnas."[63]

The growing caseload has affected the contemporary Court

in several ways. By Chief Justice Stone's time, it was well established for each justice to have one law clerk and for the chief justice to have one additional clerk. During Fred Vinson's chief justiceship, the number increased to two and more or less remained the same through the years of the Warren Court. Beginning in 1970, the number gradually grew to three and to four, with Burger having a fifth senior clerk. (Rehnquist, even after his elevation to chief justice, however, relies on only three clerks.) The number of secretaries likewise increased, at first in place of additional clerks and later to help the growing number of clerks.[64] The Legal Office was created in 1975 to assist the justices; subsequently, the staff of research librarians was increased and the secretarial pool was enlarged.

Computer technology also affects the operation of the chambers. In the late 1970s, each chamber acquired a photocopying machine and five or more terminals for word processing and computerized legal research in the library. Justices once circulated eight carbon copies—called flimsies—of their draft opinions for comments and return by other justices. But they now send and receive, in duplicate, drafts and other justices' comments; typically, justices respond with a one-page, one-line reply such as "Please join me" or "I am still with you."[65] In 1990, each chamber also acquired a fax machine for sending and receiving documents in capital cases.[66]

The justices' chambers tend to resemble, in Chief Justice Rehnquist's words, "opinion writing bureaus."[67] Each chamber now averages about seven people: the justice, three to four law clerks, two secretaries, and a messenger. The managing of chambers and supervising of paperwork consume more time than in the past and keep the justices apart. They talk less to each other and read and write more memoranda and opinions.

Law Clerks in the Chambers

Law clerks have been in the Court just over a century. As the Court's caseload increased, the justices acquired more clerks and delegated more of their work. But in addition to relieving some of the justices' workload pressures, clerks bring fresh perspectives to the Court. For young lawyers one or two years out of law school, the opportunity of clerking is invaluable for their later careers. After their year at the Court, clerks have gone on to teach at leading law schools or to work for prestigious law firms.

On his appointment in 1882, Horace Gray initiated (at first at his own expense) the practice of hiring each year a graduate of Harvard Law School as "secretary" or law clerk. When Oliver Wendell Holmes succeeded Gray, he continued the practice, and other justices gradually followed him. Most justices have had clerks serve for only one year. There are some notable exceptions: one clerk for Pierce Butler served sixteen years; McKenna's first clerk worked for twelve; Frank Murphy kept Eugene Gressman for six; and Owen Roberts had a husband-and-wife team as his permanent clerk and secretary. Chief Justices Stone and Vinson had overlapping terms for one of their two clerks each year; and Burger had his special legal assistant sign on for three to four years.

The selection of clerks is entirely a personal matter and may be one of the most important decisions that a justice makes in any given year.[68] The selection process varies with each justice. But four considerations appear to enter into everyone's selection process: the justice's preference for (1) certain law schools, (2) special geographic regions, (3) prior clerking experience on certain courts or with particular judges, and (4) personal compatibility.

Following Gray and Holmes, Brandeis, Frankfurter, and Brennan chose graduates of Harvard Law School. Some other justices also tended to choose graduates of their alma maters, while several others tended to favor particular geographical regions when selecting clerks. Most of the justices now rely on former clerks to screen candidates, though Justice O'Connor wades through the some 500 applications that annually arrive in her chambers.

As the Court's caseload and the number of law clerks grew,

the justices started drawing clerks from lower federal or state courts. Consequently, clerking for a respected judge or on a leading lower court in the country is now just as important as attending a top law school. As indicated below, the typical clerk is twenty-five years old, white, male, and a year out of Harvard or Yale law school. Of the 394 clerks who served justices sitting on the Rehnquist Court, nearly forty percent attended Harvard or Yale. More than two-thirds of them (285) were graduates of six law schools: Harvard (92), Yale (64), Chicago (47), Stanford (35), Columbia (26), and Virginia (21). Among the lower federal court "feeder" judges whose clerks tend to go on to the Court are Fourth Circuit Court of Appeals Judge Michael Luttig and Ninth Circuit Judge Alex Kozinski (both former clerks to Chief Justice Burger), and District of Columbia Circuit Judge Laurence Silberman.[69]

The position and duties of clerks naturally vary with the justice and with the historical development of the institution. Oliver Wendell Holmes initially had little casual contact with his clerks, but when his eyesight began to fade in his later years, they served as companions and often read aloud to him. According to Walter Gellhorn, Stone "made one feel a co-worker—a very junior and subordinate co-worker, to be sure, but nevertheless one whose opinions counted and whose assistance was valued."[70] Likewise, Harold Burton told his law clerks that he wanted each "to feel a keen personal interest in our joint product," and he encouraged "the most complete possible exchange of views and the utmost freedom of expression of opinion on all matters to the end that the best possible product may result."[71] Earl Warren's law clerks communicated with him almost always by memorandum.[72] By contrast, Rehnquist, Scalia, Souter, and Stevens set up rather warm working relationships with their clerks.

The level of work and responsibility depends on the capabilities and the number of the clerks and varies from justice to justice and over the course of the clerkship year. At one extreme, perhaps, is Dean Acheson, who said of his working with Brandeis

A PORTRAIT OF THE LAW CLERKS TO JUSTICES (1971–1998)

Justice	Number Of Clerks	Male	Female	White	Black	Hispanic	Asian
Rehnquist (1972–1998)	79	68	11	78		1	
Stevens (1975–1998)	58	42	16	50	3		5
O'Connor (1981–1998)	68	39	29	62	1	1	4
Scalia (1986–1998)	48	41	7	48			
Kennedy (1988–1998)	45	38	7	41		1	3
Souter (1990–1998)	31	26	5	29		1	1
Thomas (1991–1998)	29	24	5	25	1		3
Ginsburg (1993–1998)	20	12	8	18	1		1
Breyer (1994–1998)	16	8	8	14	1		1

in the 1930s, "He wrote the opinion; I wrote the footnotes."[73] At the other are clerks like Butler's, Byrnes's, and Murphy's, who in the 1940s and 1950s drafted almost all of a justice's written work. Indeed, within the Court, Murphy's law clerks were snidely referred to as "Mr. Justice Huddleson" and "Mr. Justice Gressman."[74] In one instance, Wiley Rutledge wrote to the chief justice, "After discussion with Justices Black and Douglas and Justice Murphy's clerk, Mr. Gressman, it has been agreed that I should inform you that the four of us" agree that the petition should be granted review and that "the case should be set for argument forthwith." On another occasion, Gressman wrote Rutledge, "I have tried in vain to reach Justice Murphy. But I know that he would want to join Black's statement if he files it. It certainly expresses his sentiments. I feel it perfectly O.K. to put his name on it—he would want it that way, especially since you are putting your name on it."[75]

In historical perspective, most clerks' roles typically fall somewhere between these two extremes. Stone let his clerks craft footnotes that often announced novel principles of law.[76] Stone's technique, in the view of his clerk Herbert Wechsler, was like that of "a squirrel storing nuts to be pulled out at some later time."[77] Frankfurter had his clerks prepare lengthy memoranda, such as the ninety-one-page examination of segregation prepared by Alexander Bickel in 1954, as well as some of his better-known opinions, such as his dissent in the landmark reapportionment case, *Baker v. Carr* (1962).[78]

From the perspective of other justices, Frankfurter "used his law clerks as flying squadrons against the law clerks of other Justices and even against the Justices themselves. Frankfurter, a proselytizer, never missed a chance to line up a vote."[79] Similarly, "F. F.'s" former student at Harvard Law School Justice William Brennan used the informal communications network among the law clerks to find out other justices' views. Unlike Frankfurter, however, Brennan rarely tried to directly lobby his colleagues. Instead, as one of his law clerks recalled, Brennan used his clerks "to talk to other clerks and find out what their Justices [were] thinking." Brennan then would pitch his points at conference or in draft opinions at particular justices in order to mass and hold onto a majority.

A justice's background, facility in writing, dedication, and age affect his style of work and his reliance on law clerks. Few are academic lawyers like Stone, "a New England wood carver" devoted to craftsmanship. Most come from an administrative-political background, where they learned law in government law offices and were accustomed to the assistance of large staffs. As two of his former clerks observed, "The fact that [Chief Justice Vinson] wasn't going to sit down with a blank yellow pad and start from scratch was characteristic of an administrator." Moreover, unlike Frankfurter, he "was not a legal scholar who took great delight in the intellectual approach to the law for its own sake."[80] Exceptional are justices who have the ability of a William

Douglas or a Robert Jackson to write quickly and with flair. Stanley Reed, for one, struggled to write what he wanted to say. "Wouldn't it be nice if we could write the way we think," he once lamented.[81] Like many of his successors, Reed for the most part relied on his clerks for first drafts—"the clerk had the first word and he had the last word."[82]

By all accounts, most justices now delegate the preliminary writing of opinions to their clerks. Chief Justice Rehnquist, for instance, usually has one of his clerks do a first draft, without bothering about style, and gives him about ten days to prepare it. Before having a clerk begin work on an opinion, Rehnquist goes over the conference discussion with the clerk and explains how he thinks "an opinion can be written supporting the result reached by the majority." It is not "a very sweeping original type of assignment," he emphasizes. "It is not telling the clerk just figure out how you'd like to decide this case and write something about. It's not that at all." Once the clerk has finished a preliminary draft, Rehnquist reworks the opinion—using some, none, or all of the draft—to get his own style down. The draft opinion then typically circulates three or four times among the clerks in his chambers, before Rehnquist sends it to the other justices for their comments. As a result, Chief Justice Rehnquist concedes that his "original contributions to [some opinions] are definitely a minor part of them; other opinions, my original contributions are a major part of them."[83]

Even though they delegate the preliminary opinion writing, justices differ in their approach when revising first drafts. If a clerk's draft is "in the ball park," they often edit rather than rewrite. But some, like Burton, virtually rewrite their clerks' drafts, while others, like Reed, tend to insert paragraphs in the draft opinions prepared by their clerks. As one former clerk recalled, Reed simply "didn't like to start from the beginning and go to the ending." Consequently, his opinions tend to read like a dialogue with "a change of voice from paragraph to paragraph."[84] Reed's patchwork opinions did not stem from excessive delegation of responsibility or lack of dedication. At least in his early years on the Court, he took opinion writing seriously but found that words did not flow easily for him. "The problem with Stanley," Frankfurter once said, "is that he doesn't let his law clerks do enough of the work. The trouble with Murphy is that he lets them do too much of the work."[85] In time, as Reed grew older and the pressures of the caseload increased, he, like others on the Court, found it necessary to delegate more and more opinion writing to law clerks.

Though there are differences in the duties and manner in which clerks function, certain responsibilities are now commonly assigned in all chambers. Clerks play an indispensable role in the justices' deciding what to decide. As the number of filings each year rose, justices delegated the responsibility of initially reading all filings: appeals, which required mandatory review, and petitions for *certiorari*—"pets for *cert*.," as Justice Holmes referred to them—which seek review but may be denied or granted at the Court's own discretion. Clerks then write a one- to two-page summary of the facts, the questions presented, and the recommended course of action—that is, whether the case should be denied, dismissed, or granted full briefing and plenary consideration.

This practice originated with the handling of indigents' petitions—*in forma pauperis* petitions, or "Ifps"—by Chief Justice Hughes and his clerks. Unlike paid petitions and appeals, which are filed in multiple copies, petitions of indigents are typically filed without the assistance of an attorney in a single, handwritten copy. From the time of Hughes through that of Warren, these petitions were solely the responsibility of the chief justice and his law clerks (and this also explains why the chief justice had one more law clerk than the other justices). Except when an Ifp raised important legal issues or involved a capital case, Chief Justice Hughes as a matter of course neither circulated the petition to the other justices nor placed it on the conference list for discussion. Stone, Vinson, and Warren had their law clerks' *certiorari* memos routinely circulated to the other chambers. Chief justices, of course, differ in how carefully they study Ifps. Hughes and Warren were especially conscientious and scrupulous about Ifps; the latter told his clerks, "[I]t is necessary for you to be their counsel, in a sense."[86] As the number of Ifps and other filings grew, they became too much for the chief's chambers to handle alone. They were thus distributed along with other paid petitions and jurisdictional statements to all chambers for each justice's consideration. Accordingly, almost all filings, with the exception of those handled by the Legal Office, are now circulated to the chambers, where clerks draft short memos on most.

With the mounting workload in the 1970s and 1980s, the role of law clerks in the screening process changed again. In 1972, at the suggestion of Lewis Powell, a majority of the Court's members began to pool their clerks, dividing up all filings and having a single clerk's *certiorari* memo then circulate to all those participating in the *"cert.* pool." Eight justices—Rehnquist, O'Connor, Scalia, Kennedy, Souter, Thomas, Ginsburg, and Breyer—now share the memos prepared by their pool of clerks. Former law clerks have estimated that the preparation of a *cert.* memo may take anywhere from 15 minutes to, in a rare case, a full day.[87] When the memos from the *cert.* pool are circulated, each justice typically has one of his or her clerks go over each memo and make a recommendation on whether the case should be granted or denied.

Those justices who objected to the establishment of the *cert.* pool and who refuse to join nevertheless find it necessary to have their clerks prepare memos on the most important of those one hundred or more filings that come in each week. Brennan described his use of clerks this way: Although "I try not to delegate any of the screening function to my law clerks and to do the complete task myself," he reported,

I make exceptions during the summer recess when their initial screening of petitions is invaluable training for next Term's new law clerks. And I also must make some few exceptions during the Term on occasions when opinion work must take precedence. When law clerks do screening, they prepare a memorandum of not more than a page or two in each case, noting whether the case is properly before the Court, what federal issues are presented, how they were decided by the courts below, and summarizing the positions of the parties pro and con the grant of the case.[88]

Stevens, who alone does not participate in the *cert.* pool, has a somewhat different practice. "I have found it necessary to delegate a great deal of responsibility in the review of certiorari petitions to my clerks," Stevens has said. "They examine them all and select a small minority that they believe I should read myself. As a result, I do not even look at the papers in over 80 percent of the cases that are filed."[89] Stevens's three clerks write memos on only those petitions they deem important. He reviews those and reads the lower-court opinions on all cases to be discussed at conference. For Stevens, the preliminary screening of cases consumes about a day and a half per week. Newly appointed justices may also find it impossible to read all of the *certiorari* petitions that accumulate over the summer and to stay abreast of the Court's workload. Justice Scalia, for instance, at the beginning of his service in 1986 found it necessary to limit himself to reading only those memos in cases on which three justices had voted to grant *certiorari* and to set over for discussion at another conference.[90]

After the justices vote in conference to hear a case, each usually assigns that case to a clerk. The clerk then researches the background and prepares a "bench memo." Bench memos outline pertinent facts and issues, propose possible questions to be put to participating attorneys during oral arguments, and address the merits of the cases.[91] The clerk stays with the case as long as the justice does, helping with research and draft opinions. The nature of the work at this stage varies with the justice and the case, but it includes research, a hand in drafting the opinion and in commenting on other justices' responses to it, and the subsequent checking of citations and proofreading of the final version. Justices may also tell their clerks to draft concurring or dissenting opinions, while they themselves concentrate on the opinions they are assigned to write for the Court. As each term draws to a close and the justices feel the pressure of completing their opinions by the end of June or the first week of July, clerks perhaps inevitably assume an even greater role in the opinion-writing process.[92]

Has too much responsibility been delegated to law clerks? Do they substantively influence the justices' voting and the final disposition of cases? After thirty-six years on the bench, Douglas claimed that circumstances were such that "many law clerks did much of the work of the justices."[93] Rehnquist has provided one perspective on the function of law clerks: "I don't think people are shocked any longer to learn that an appellate judge receives a draft of a proposed opinion from a law clerk." He added, however:

I think they would be shocked, and properly shocked, to learn that an appellate judge simply "signed off" on such a draft without fully understanding its import and in all probability making some changes in it. The line between having law clerks help one with one's work, and supervising subordinates in the performance of *their* work, may be a hazy one, but it is at the heart . . . [of] the fundamental concept of "judging."[94]

Almost fifty years ago, Rehnquist, who clerked for one-and-a-half years with Robert Jackson, had charged that law clerks—who he also claimed tended to be more "liberal" than the justices for whom they worked—had a substantive influence on the justices when preparing both *certiorari* memos and first drafts of opinions.[95] The degree to which law clerks substantively influence justices' voting and opinion writing is difficult to gauge, and it certainly varies from justice to justice. With the increasing caseload, justices have perhaps inevitably come to rely more heavily on their law clerks' recommendations when voting in conference. Yet even when Rehnquist served as a clerk and the caseload was less than a third of its present size, justices no doubt voted overwhelmingly along the lines recommended by their law clerks. Vinson, for one, tallied the number of times he differed with his clerks. There were differences in less than 5 percent of the cases.[96]

Clerks would look very powerful indeed if they were not transients in the Court. Clerks, as Alexander Bickel once noted, "are in no respect any kind of a powerful kitchen cabinet."[97] As a clerk, Rehnquist, for instance, was unable to dissuade Justice Jackson from eventually going along with the decision in the landmark school desegregation ruling in *Brown v. Board of Education* (1954). In a memorandum entitled "A Random Thought on the Segregation Cases," Rehnquist charged that if the Court struck down segregated schools, it would do so by reading "its own sociological views into the Constitution," just as a majority of the Court had read its own economic philosophy into the Constitution when it struck down most of the early New Deal legislation. Later, at his confirmation hearing in 1971, Rehnquist claimed that the memo was written at Jackson's request and reflected the justice's views rather than his own. And he maintained that position during his 1986 confirmation hearings on being elevated to chief justice. But the content and the style of the memo (as well as the fact that there are several other similar memos written by Rehnquist in Justice Jackson's private papers) indicate that it was Rehnquist's own handiwork. Rehnquist wrote in the conclusion of the memo, "I realize that it is an unpopular and unhumanitarian position, but I think *Plessy v. Ferguson* [1896] was right and should be reaffirmed. If the Fourteenth Amendment did not enact Spencer's *Social Statics*, it just as surely did not enact Myrdal's *American Dilemma*."*[98]

---

*Social Statics (1866), by the English philosopher Herbert Spencer, profoundly influenced late-nineteenth-century American legal, political, and economic thought by popularizing Charles Darwin's evolutionary theory of the "survival of the fittest" and by inspiring the movement of Social Dawinism. The Court was not immune from the intellectual currents of its time. A majority legitimated lassiez-faire capitalism by striking down economic regulation

CASE SELECTION: CHIEF JUSTICE VINSON AND HIS
CLERKS' RECOMMENDATIONS

Term	Number of Cases Disposed	Number of Times Chief Justice Vinson's Vote Diverged from Law Clerks' Recommendation
1947	1,331	38 (2.8%)
1948	1,434	53 (3.6%)
1949	1,308	52 (3.9%)
1950	1,216	51 (4.1%)
1952	1,286	46 (3.5%)

As part of the institutionalization of the Court, law clerks have assumed a greater role in conducting the business of the Court, particularly in the last quarter of a century. Their role in the justices' screening process is now considerably greater than it was in the past. At the stage of opinion writing, the substantive influence of law clerks varies from justice to justice, and from

---

under the guise of a "liberty of contract," which it invented and inserted into the Fourteenth Amendment's prohibition against any state depriving a person of "life, liberty, or property, without due process of law." When *Lochner v. New York* (1905) overturned a New York statute regulating the number of hours that bakers could work, the dissenting Justice Holmes charged that the Court had become a "super legislature" by impermissibly reading into the Constitution a "liberty of contract" in order to enforce its own conservative social-economic theory. As Holmes put it, "The Fourteenth Amendment does not enact Mr. Herbert Spencer's *Social Statics*." Later, when enforcing the Fourteenth Amendment in the landmark school segregation ruling in *Brown v. Board of Education* (1954), the Warren Court cited seven social science studies in support of overturning the racial doctrine of "separate but equal facilities." Among those studies showing the adverse social and psychological effects of racial segregation was the Swedish economist and sociologist Gunnar Myrdal's book *An American Dilemma* (1944), the premier work on race relations in America. The Court's mention of *An American Dilemma* intensified the antagonism of powerful southerners, such as the South Carolina governor and former Supreme Court justice James F. Byrnes and the Mississippi senator James O. Eastland. They and others attacked the Court for citing the work of "foreign sociologists," for bad social science research, and, most of all, for drawing on social science in the first place, rather than simply sticking to the text and historical context of the Constitution.

time to time in each chamber, as well as from case to case. No less important, the greater numbers of law clerks and of delegated responsibilities have contributed to an increase in the volume of concurring and dissenting opinions and to the production of longer and more heavily footnoted opinions.

THE LEGAL OFFICE—A TENTH LITTLE LAW FIRM

Louis Brandeis, who spoke proudly of the justices' doing their own work, would have abhorred the Legal Office. In the 1970s, the Court hired two legal officers, or staff counsel—a legal assistant and a legal intern. A growing caseload was only one reason for creating this tenth little law firm. Several of the justices also thought they needed more permanent and specialized help because law clerks are transients.

Staff counsel serve two to three years. They advise the justices and other Court officers on procedure and jurisdiction. They recommend action on special motions and applications, such as requests for expedited proceedings. For example, in *United States v. Nixon* (1974), in the heat of the Watergate crisis, the Legal Office advised the Court to expedite the case, ordering the President to turn over secret White House tapes before the court of appeals had ruled on his claim of executive privilege. At the time, Congress had not finished investigating the Watergate break-in and the possibility of impeaching the President for conspiracy and obstruction of justice.[99] The Legal Office also handles cases that come on original jurisdiction under Article III of the Constitution. Those cases tend to carry over from one year to the next and involve, for example, complex land and water disputes. In addition, they may advise the justices on personal legal matters. And they serve as liaison to the Department of Justice when disgruntled individuals file nuisance suits against individual justices.[100] Finally, the Legal Office prepares memoranda for the chief justice on such matters as proposed changes in the Federal Rules of Evidence and Criminal Procedure, as well as how new legislation may affect the Court and on inquires from Court officers.

LEGAL OFFICE'S WORK ON ITEMS DISCUSSED AT
CONFERENCE, 1985–1990

Term	1989–90	1988–89	1987–88	1986–87	1985–86
Motions memoranda	157	123	133	124	96
Applications	40	35	37	41	30
Petitions for extraordinary relief	84	97	84	77	90
Memoranda on original cases	18	22	20	15	19
Certiorari petitions	3	0	8	9	10
Petitions for rehearing	274	225	199	187	180
Application to the Supreme Court's Bar	42	37	38	41	44
Summaries on miscellaneous motions	172	153	128	163	145
Total number of matters	618	539	519	494	469

As the business of the Court has steadily increased, so has
the work of the Legal Office. The data above on the number
and kinds of memoranda prepared for the justices are indicative
of the Legal Office's work and the increasing role that it plays
in the conduct of the business of the Court.[101] During the 1997
term, the Legal Office reviewed 911 such matters.[102]

Administrative Staff and Political Struggles

The days of unassisted justices are long past. Within the
chambers, the justices and their clerks and secretaries do all
their work. But the court as an institution embraces five officers
outside the chambers: the Clerk, the Reporter of Decisions, the
Marshal, the Librarian, and the Administrative Assistant to the
Chief Justice. After they moved into the marble temple, their
offices gradually became more professional and acquired larger
separate staffs. These developments have tended to further the
bureaucratization of the contemporary Court. More employees
handle the Court's caseload and manage its administration.
There is a greater division of labor and delegation of responsibility within the Court and an increasingly specialized and professional staff.

THE CLERK OF THE COURT

The Office of the Clerk is central to the Court's administration. It has also traditionally served as the primary liaison with attorneys practicing in the Court.

For most of the Court's history, the Clerk earned no salary. Instead, he pocketed filing fees and attorneys' admission fees. Thus, even at the turn of this century, the Clerk's income often exceeded that of the justices. In 1883, the Court cut off the Clerk's access to filing fees at $6,000 a year. The Clerk still took in all admission fees until 1921, when Taft became chief justice. The Clerk died the same year, and with the change in the office, Taft lobbied for legislation that put the office in his hands. The Clerk became a salaried employee, paid out of fees but receiving a salary fixed by the justices.[103]

The Clerks' early financial independence often made them players in the Court's internal politics. From the very first, justices were lobbied by those seeking the position.[104] After their appointment, Clerks often rendered personal favors to the justices. In the last century, for example, they secured lodgings for the justices—occasionally with considerable diplomacy, as when the aging and feeble Justice Robert Grier proposed living in the Capitol itself. At other times, the Clerk became involved in rather bitter conflicts with the justices and other officers. One of the more astonishing incidents arose when the Clerk, at Chief Justice Taney's request, refused to give Justice Benjamin Curtis a copy of the final written opinion in *Dred Scott* so that he could prepare his dissent from the Court's decision. Curtis was furious, but the Clerk and Taney stood firm.[105]

Over the years, the responsibilities and size of the Clerk's office became greater and more crucial to the conducting of the Court's business. The office continues to collect filing and admission fees; to receive and record all motions, petitions, jurisdictional statements, briefs, and other documents; and to circulate those necessary items to each chamber. The Clerk establishes the Court's argument calendar; approximately 100 cases are heard each term at the rate of one hour each, four cases a day, three days a week, for two weeks out of every month, from the first of October through April. In addition to managing the docket and answering correspondence and notifying attorneys of the Court's decisions, the office prepares and maintains the order list of cases granted or denied review and formal judgments, as well as the *Supreme Court Journal* (containing the minutes of its sessions). In the 1990s, due to the rising number of death row inmates and the Court's rulings expediting executions, the number of death penalty appeals and motions for stays of executions increased dramatically. As a result, the clerk's office now employs a so-called "death penalty clerk" to oversee the processing of death penalty cases. In 1996 it also inaugurated an electronic bulletin board giving the public access via a modem to the Court's opinions, the docket, and the oral argument calendar.

In 1975, the Clerk's office acquired a computer system. The system automatically notifies counsel in over 95 percent of all cases of the disposition of their filings; produces conference and order lists; and prints out the majority of simple Court orders and opinions. The Clerk may also conduct case searches and statistical computations with the system. Under the direction of William K. Suter, the nineteenth clerk of the Court, in the 1990s the office became even more automated and electronically efficient. For example, there is an automated phone service that allows the public to call in and, with the press of a few buttons, find out the status of any case; the automated service receives about 2,000 calls a month.

THE REPORTER OF DECISIONS

For the first quarter century of the Court, there was no official Reporter of Decisions, and not until 1835 were the justices' opinions given to the Clerk. In 1816, the Court officially appointed a Reporter, Henry Wheaton, an action that preceded congressional authorization by almost a year. Early Reporters, following the English custom, worked at their own expense and for their own profit and prestige. For most of the nineteenth century, the Reporter could practice law before the Court or serve as a judge in a lower court. In publishing the Court's decisions, the Reporter could advertise his legal services as well. Until the chief justiceship of Taft, the Reporter continued to engage in this semiprivate enterprise and supplemented his salary by negotiating contracts with publishers and by selling to the public the *United States Reports* (containing the final opinions of the Court). In 1922, Congress established the present arrangement: the Reporter's salary is fixed by the justices and paid by the government, and the Government Printing Office oversees the printing and binding, now done by private firms, of the *United States Reports*.[106]

The practices of early Reporters engendered numerous controversies over the reporting of decisions. When Richard Peters succeeded Henry Wheaton in 1827, for instance, he updated and revised the entire series of prior Court decisions, omitting a good deal of Wheaton's headnotes (which summarized the opinions) and other matter that Wheaton had included. Wheaton was furious and sued Peters. The latter countered with the argument, rather novel at the time, that "the opinions of the Court are public property." The Court eventually held in *Wheaton v. Peters* (1834) that its opinions were indeed in the public domain but that Wheaton's notations were private property subject to copyright. Though Peters won, he had other problems. In 1831, he published the decision in *Cherokee Nation*—denying Indians the right to sue under the Court's original jurisdiction—as a separate pamphlet along with, in his words, "Mr. Wirt's great argument in behalf of the Cherokees, which had been taken down by stenographers employed for that purpose."[107] This displeased Jacksonian populists—and Justice Henry Baldwin, in particular. A decade later he had his revenge. In the absence of Justice Joseph Story, a close friend of the

Reporter, the Court voted four to three to fire Peters and hire Benjamin Howard, a Jacksonian.[108] Considering the status of the Reporter in the nineteenth century, it is not surprising that there were other such instances of patronage and ideological divisions within the Court over the selection and tenure of its Reporter.[109]

The responsibilities of writing headnotes or syllabi (or "syllabuses," according to the Reporter of Decisions), making editorial suggestions, and supervising the publication of the Court's opinions invite controversy. Though at the turn of the century Justice Horace Gray wrote headnotes for his opinions, most justices did not bother. Headnotes are now considered the work of the Reporter and not part of the Court's decision.[110] Still, besides being useful for attorneys and the press, headnotes have tangible and symbolic importance.

There is perhaps no better illustration of the consequence of a headnote than in *Santa Clara County v. Southern Pacific Railroad Company* (1886). There, after consulting Chief Justice Waite, the Reporter at his own discretion decided to note in an otherwise uninteresting tax case that the Court considered corporations "legal persons" entitled to protection under the Fourteenth Amendment.[111] Corporations, like individual citizens, could thereafter challenge the constitutionality of congressional and state legislation impinging on their interests. With decisions like this in the late nineteenth and early twentieth centuries, the Court encouraged and protected the interests of business and fortified the basis of American capitalism.

Editing was especially difficult when justices wrote their opinions by hand. When asked to decipher one of his opinions, Justice Stephen Field replied, "How the Hell should I know!"[112] The Court's word-processing system is now integrated with the printing and publishing of decisions, and the Reporter has a staff of ten. Still, editing approximately 225 opinions each term takes time and painstaking care. As each term closes, the work becomes relentless and mistakes happen. In 1983, one opinion referred to a second that had not yet been announced.[113] Following that mistake, in 1984 the Reporter instituted a cite and quote checking service. Without careful attention even to the statement of facts in a case, mistakes may become part of a permanent record and distort the Court's decision.[114] For this reason the final bound volumes of the Court's decisions sometimes include corrections, and, rarely, additions to the opinions initially issued.[115]

Sometimes errors and disagreements are inescapable, even for the Court's Reporter, who considers himself a "double-revolving peripatetic nitpicker." For example, not until 1986 did the Court consistently spell the word "marijuana." According to Henry C. Lind, a former reporter, it had six acceptable spellings and some justices would spell it "marihuana" and others would spell it "marijuana." In one opinion, it was spelled both ways in the same footnote! After a memo was circulated to all the justices, it was finally agreed henceforth to use "marijuana."[116]

The Reporter's editorial changes must be approved by the author of an opinion; significant changes in an opinion for the Court must be approved by a majority of the justices.

THE MARSHAL

For most of the first century, order in the courtroom was preserved by U.S. marshals. At the request of Chief Justice Salmon P. Chase, Congress created the Office of the Marshal of the Supreme Court in 1867. Like other Court employees, the Marshal tended to get his job either through personal friendship with the justices or through previous employment in some other capacity at the Court. The first Marshal, Richard Parsons, was an intimate friend of Chief Justice Chase. Others, like Thomas Waggaman, the Marshal from 1938 to 1952, first came to the Court as a page. More professional criteria have now replaced personal patronage.

The Marshal maintains order in the courtroom and times oral arguments. He is authorized to set regulations, subject to the chief justice's approval, for ensuring the decorum of the courtroom. But there are few fixed standards other than those of tradition. For example, women (but not men) may wear hats in the courtroom, although Orthodox Jewish men may wear yarmulkes; no visitor wearing a swimming suit is allowed to enter.[117] Rarely do incidents occur when the Court is in session. In 1983 Larry Flynt, the owner of *Hustler* magazine, was forcibly removed from the courtroom after making a profane outburst during the oral arguments of *Keeton v. Hustler Magazine, Inc.*[118] In 1989 another incident occurred just before the Court's 1:00 P.M. argument. A woman visitor in the courtroom stood up and shouted, "The Supreme Court has declared war on women, and I'm here to declare war on the Supreme Court." Both Flynt and the woman were promptly arrested and charged with "being disruptive," an offense that carried a thirty-day jail sentence and a $100 fine.

In addition to overseeing building maintenance and security (there are 85 Supreme Court police), the Marshal serves as business and payroll manager. The Office of the Marshal now manages over 350 employees—messengers, carpenters, police, workmen, a nurse, a physiotherapist, a barber, a seamstress, and cafeteria workers.

THE LIBRARIAN

In the Court's early years, the justices relied on their own personal libraries as well as those of friends and in local courthouses. Thirty years after the establishment of the Library of Congress, in 1832 Congress directed the Librarian of Congress to create a separate collection of law books for use by the Court. A decade later, this collection was moved closer to where the Court heard oral arguments, in the old Senate chamber, and became known as the Conference Room collection. In 1887, the Court appointed its first librarian, Henry DeForest Clarke, but it was not until 1948 that the librarian was designated a statutory officer of the Court. By 1901, the Court's collection had grown to 11,000 volumes and provided the foundation for the modern

Court's library, which it acquired with the move into the Supreme Court building in 1935. Located on the third floor, the library is a breathtaking room with hand-carved American white oak walls, medallions, and arches, representing various disciplines of study and learning. It, however, is not open to the public and remains for the exclusive use of the justices, their clerks, members of the Supreme Court bar, and Congress.

The library now has a staff of twenty-five, including twelve professionals who have law and library degrees. It houses half a million volumes in paper, microform, and digital formats. There is access to the Internet; national bibliographic databases; and online resources, such as Lexis, Westlaw, Legislate, Dow-Jones, and library catalogs from around the world. Although in the 1990s the justices and their clerks do most of their work on their own computers in their chambers, and thus few people actually work in the library, the librarians remain busy. The library annually responds to approximately 9,000 questions, circulates an average of 5,000 books, and receives over 3,500 requests a year for use of the bound Records and Briefs of Supreme Court cases.[119]

THE CHIEF JUSTICE, THE ADMINISTRATIVE ASSISTANT, AND THE PUBLIC INFORMATION OFFICER

The chief justice is more than primus inter pares—first among equals—in terms of administrative responsibilities within the Court and for the federal judiciary. Since the chief justice-ship of Taft, the responsibilities and demands for leadership have grown enormously. By statute and custom, the chief justice is the executive officer of the Court. Over eighty statutes confer additional administrative duties, ranging from serving as chairman of the Judicial Conference and of the Board of the Federal Judicial Center to supervising the Administrative Office of the U.S. Courts and serving as chancellor of the Smithsonian Institution.[120]

Unlike Taft and Hughes, Chief Justice Stone felt overwhelmed by the duties. He wrote President Harry Truman just two months before he died:

Few are aware that neither my predecessor, nor I in more than twenty years since I have been a Justice of the Supreme Court, have been able to meet the daily demands upon us without working nights and holidays and Sunday. The administrative duties of the Chief Justice have increased, and many other duties have been imposed on him by acts of Congress which my predecessors were not called on to perform.[121]

Stone had told Truman that the duties of a chief justice, unlike those of executive branch officials, could not be delegated. His successor, Fred Vinson, however, immediately increased the number of his law clerks and appointed an administrative assistant or executive officer to deal with internal administrative matters and to work with the Administrative Office of the U.S. Courts. This prompted a number of the justices to refer to his chamber as "Vinson, Ltd." But Vinson's staff, like that of Earl Warren later, remained rather small, at least by later comparison with Warren Burger's.

Burger's interest in judicial administration and efficiency antedated his appointment. Shortly after he arrived, he pushed for technological and managerial improvements both in the Court and in lower federal courts. In his view, a "sort of overhaul [was] needed up and down the line."[122] He brought photocopying machines and computers to the Court. He also asked Congress to create an Office of Administrative Assistant and to reexamine the Court's jurisdiction.

Burger got his Administrative Assistant in 1972, after Congress created a fifth legal officer of the Court. The duties and qualifications were not legislated, and the Administrative Assistant serves at the pleasure of the chief justice. Burger wanted someone to handle day-to-day administration and act as a liaison with judicial and legal committees, organizations, and interest groups outside the Court. The office received a cool reception from justices who saw it as "empire-building" and from other officers of the Court who felt it diminished their access to the chief. Burger wanted an individual with "high administrative and managerial talents, but also a lawyer of substantial experience or a Judge."[123]

The office grew to include a special assistant or research associate, four secretaries, a judicial fellows program—in which administrators, lawyers, judges, and academics were selected to work for one year at the Court—and an internship program for undergraduates and law students. The Administrative Assistant also gradually became the Court's chief executive officer, along with promoting the chief justice's agenda for judicial reform.[124]

The Office of the Administrative Assistant is but one example of Burger's effort to bring Taft's marble temple into the world of modern technology and managerial practices. Those efforts included new personnel (both more people and a greater diversity of people); new technology; and new, specialized offices (Legal Office, Budget and Personnel Office, Curator's Office, and Data Systems Division), as well as an enlarged secretarial pool and Public Information Office.

Since 1973, the Court has had a full-time Public Information Officer. Prior to that, beginning in 1935 there was a "press clerk," later called "the press officer." The Public Information Office has grown to include a staff of four, plus interns. It is with the press, however, not the public, that the office primarily works. It furnishes reporters with copies of the justices' opinions and speeches, as well as maintains a room, with copies of all the filings before the Court, for the use of the Court's press corps. Unlike other government public relations offices, the Public Information Officer does not explain or comment on the Court's decisions. As the late Toni House, who headed the office from 1982 to 1998, put it: "We do not do spin."[125]

Chief Justice Rehnquist has less interest in judicial administration than Burger had and remains more concerned with the intellectual and adjudicative business of the Court. He, for example, institutionalized the executive committee of the Judicial Conference. He also opened up opportunities for more judges to serve on Judicial Conference committees. The Judicial Conference prepares proposals for changes in the operation of the federal judiciary and responds to those proposed by Congress. However, Rehnquist has continued a number of the programs created by Burger, including the judicial fellows and intern programs. Unlike Burger, though, Rehnquist has appointed his Administrative Assistants to serve for only two-to-three-year terms. And each of Rehnquist's Administrative Assistants have also kept low profiles when working as the chief justice's liaison with other judicial organizations, Congress, and the executive branch. Rehnquist, nonetheless, estimates that he "spends on average 20 to 25 percent of his time on administrative matters."[126]

Managing the Caseload

Throughout the Court's history, justices have complained of "relentless schedules" and "unremitting toil." The caseload has stimulated institutional reform, procedural change, and the evolution of internal norms and practices.

AN INCREASING CASELOAD

The Court's docket has grown phenomenally. The following graph illustrates the increase in filings, in total docket, and in number of cases disposed of each term.[127] Sometimes a ruling of the Court swells the docket. For example, decisions on the constitutional rights of indigents significantly contributed to an increase in filings. But by and large, the docket reflects the course of legislation and broad socioeconomic and political change.

During the first half of the nineteenth century, the caseload grew largely because of population growth, territorial expansion, and the incremental development of federal regulation. The

Civil War and Reconstruction, both great sources of legal conflict, and the late-nineteenth-century business boom dramatically swelled the docket. No less important, Congress greatly expanded the jurisdiction of all federal courts. In particular, federal jurisdiction reached out to include civil rights, *habeas corpus* appeals, questions of federal law decided by state courts, and all suits over $500 arising under the Constitution or federal legislation.[128]

By the 1870s, the Court was confronting a growing backlog of cases. In response, Congress first raised the jurisdictional amount in diversity cases (cases between citizens of different states) to $2,000. In the 1891 Evarts Act, Congress provided immediate (if not long-lasting) relief by creating circuit courts of appeals. These courts were given final jurisdiction over most appeals, with the exception of certain civil cases and cases involving capital or otherwise infamous crimes. The courts of appeals had final say in admiralty and diversity suits, criminal prosecutions, and violations of revenue and patent law. The act preserved access to the Court by providing, instead of mandatory rights of appeal, for petitions for writs of *certiorari,* which the Court could refuse to grant. The act thus for the first time gave the Court the power of discretionary review.

In the early twentieth century, the Court's docket grew again, in part because of further population increases. Economic changes and World War I brought a rash of disputes over war contracts and suits against the government. A large measure of the Court's congested docket was nonetheless due to expanding congressional legislation and regulation. Congress inflated the Court's docket by enlarging the opportunities both for government and for special-interest groups to appeal directly to the Court. Mandatory review was extended, for instance, to government appeals from dismissals of criminal prosecutions. Individuals and businesses challenging administrative decisions under antitrust and interstate commerce laws, the Federal Employer's Liability Act (FELA), and injunctions issued by three-judge courts were also given the right of appeal to the Court.

DOCKET AND FILINGS, 1800–1998

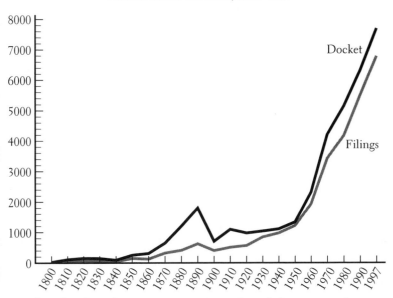

Based on data from the U.S. Supreme Court, through the 1997–1998 term.

The Court once again could not stay abreast of its caseload. Congress initially responded piecemeal. It slightly enlarged the Court's discretionary jurisdiction by eliminating mandatory rights of appeal in narrow, though important, areas, such as under the FELA. Then, as a result of a campaign waged by Chief Justice Taft for further relief for the Court, Congress passed the "Judges' Bill," or the Judiciary Act of February 13, 1925, which basically established the jurisdiction of the modern Court.[129] That act replaced mandatory review of appeals with discretionary review of petitions for writs of *certiorari*. The act enabled the Court largely to set its own agenda and to decide only cases of national importance.[130]

Since World War II, the Court's business has increased yet again. In the 1970s Congress provided incremental relief by eliminating many provisions for mandatory review of appeals,

MAJOR LEGISLATION AFFECTING THE JURISDICTION
AND BUSINESS OF THE SUPREME COURT°

Legislation	Commentary
Judiciary Act of 1789	Provided basic appellate jurisdiction; a 3-tier judiciary system staffed by justices and district court judges; required circuit riding
Acts of 1793, 1801, 1802, and 1803	Provided rotation system for circuit riding, then eliminated the responsibilities, only to have Jeffersonians reinstate circuit-riding duties
Act of 1807	Added 7th circuit and justice
Act of 1837	Divided country into 9 circuits and brought number of justices to 9 (Court's jurisdiction was also expanded to include appeals from new states and territories in 1825, 1828, and 1848)
Acts of 1855 and 1863	California added as 10th circuit, and 10th justice
Acts of 1866, 1867, 1869, and 1871	Expanded federal jurisdiction over civil rights; reorganized country into 9 circuits and reduced number of justices to 7, and later fixed the number at 9; and expanded jurisdiction over habeas corpus and state court decisions
Act of 1875	Greatly expanded jurisdiction over civil disputes, and given review of writs of error, and granted full federal question review from state courts
Act of 1887	Curbed access by raising amount of dispute in diversity cases; and provided writ of error in all capital cases
Circuit Court of Appeals Act of 1891	Established 9 circuit courts, and judgeships; broadened review of criminal cases and provided for limited discretionary review via writs of *certorari*
Act of 1892	Provided for *in forma pauperis* filings
Act of 1893	Created District of Columbia Circuit

Legislation	Commentary
Acts of 1903 and 1907	Provided direct appeal under antitrust and interstate commerce acts; granted government right of direct appeal in dismissals of criminal prosecutions
Acts of 1910, 1911, and 1913	Altered federal injunctive power; established 3-judge courts because of abuses by single judges in enjoining state economic regulation; and later extended the jurisdiction of 3-judge courts and direct appeals to Court
Acts of 1914, 1915, and 1916	Jurisdiction over some state cases made discretionary and eliminated right to review in bankruptcy, trademark, and FELA
Judiciary Act of 1925	Greatly extended the Court's discretionary jurisdiction by replacing mandatory appeals with petitions for *certiorari*
Act of 1928	Appeals became the sole method of mandatory appellate review
Act of 1939	Expanded review of decisions by Court of Claims over both law and fact
Act of 1948	Judicial code revised, codified, and enacted into law
Act of 1950 (Hobbes Act)	Eliminated 3-judge court requirement in certain areas
Voting Rights Act of 1965	Provided direct appeal over decisions of 3-judge courts in area of voting rights
Acts of 1970, 1971, 1974, 1975, and 1976	Reorganized District of Columbia courts; expanded Court's discretionary review; repealed direct government appeals under Act of 1907; eliminated direct appeals in antitrust and ICC cases; further cut back jurisdiction and direct appeals from 3-judge courts, with the exception of areas of voting rights and reapportionment
Federal Courts Improvement Act of 1982	Created Court of Appeals for the Federal Circuit, by joining the Court of Claims with the Court of Customs and Patent Appeals

Legislation	Commentary
1988 Act to Improve the Administration of Justice	Eliminated virtually all of the Court's non-discretionary appellate jurisdiction, except for appeals in reapportionment cases, suits under the Civil Rights and Voting Rights acts, antitrust laws, and the Presidential Election Campaign Fund Act

*Excluded, necessarily, is the vast amount of legislation expanding the administrative state and providing opportunities for challenging law and policy in federal courts.

particularly those from three-judge courts. As a result, the number of mandatory appeals coming to the Court declined from 311 in 1976 to 248 in 1987. Still, the justices unanimously agreed that Congress should eliminate most of the remaining provisions requiring the Court to review cases involving lower federal and state courts' invalidation of federal and state laws, as well as their rulings on certain other statutory matters. In 1988 Congress finally passed and President Reagan signed legislation eliminating virtually all of the Court's nondiscretionary appellate jurisdiction. The only mandatory appeals that the Court must now review are those that involve reapportionment, some antitrust matters, and cases under the Civil Rights and Voting Rights acts and the Presidential Election Campaign Fund Act. The table above summarizes the principal legislation altering the Court's jurisdiction and extending its power of discretionary review, enabling it to gain control over its docket.

ALTERNATIVE INSTITUTIONAL RESPONSES

In historical perspective, the process of institutionalization paralleled the growth of the caseload. There are basically three ways in which the Court has responded to a rising caseload and workload.

First, a *bureaucratic response:* the Court may make managerial and technological changes. In the late nineteenth century, for example, the Court's terms were lengthened, the time allowed for oral arguments was shortened, and the justices gradually acquired staff. In this century and especially during the Burger Court years (1969–1986), the justices hired larger and more professional staffs and bought modern office equipment.

The bureaucratic response, however, may prove counterproductive in a collegial institution like the Court. One problem is that caseload is not equivalent to workload. Filings and cases are not fungible; some take a great deal more time than others. Another problem is that larger staffs and the delegation of work force justices to spend more time supervising their chambers. Consequently, the nature of the justices' workload may change but need not diminish. The justices, moreover, have less opportunity and inclination to talk and try to reach accommodations with each other. The present pattern of formal written communications among the chambers, in turn, encourages even greater reliance on dictaphones, secretaries, law clerks, and staff counsel for the preparation of draft opinions. Justices accordingly spend more time reading and revising and have, as Burger and Rehnquist agree, less "time and freshness of mind for private study and reflection . . . [and] fruitful interchange . . . indispensable to thoughtful, unhurried decision."[131]

In 1991, two justices—O'Connor and Scalia—conceded that adding more law clerks and secretaries would not necessarily help in managing the increasing docket, and might even prove counterproductive. "You reach a point of diminishing returns with law clerks." Justice Scalia told Arkansas's Democratic Senator Dale Bumpers, during a hearing on funding for the federal judiciary. "It's not healthy," he added, "It's not necessarily the case that the more clerks you have, the more cases you can pump out."

A second response to the burgeoning docket has been the introduction of *jurisdictional* changes. Such changes include a further enlarging of the Court's power of discretionary review and the creating of new lower appellate courts so that the justices may decide only those cases of national importance which can adequately be considered in any given term. The Court must decide cases arising under its original jurisdiction, as is specified in Article III of the Constitution. But over 95 percent of all filings now come under appellate jurisdiction, which Congress provides and may change. Since the Judiciary Act of 1925, Congress has incrementally enlarged the Court's discretionary jurisdiction, allowing the justices to deny review to more cases. In Justice White's words, "the power to deny cases helps to keep us current."[132] In 1988, after years of urging by the Court, Congress eliminated remaining provisions for mandatory appellate review.[133] The Court now enjoys virtually complete discretionary jurisdiction, with the exception of those few cases coming under its original jurisdiction. This jurisdictional change, however, did not reduce the Court's caseload; it only affects the justices' workload and the process of deciding what to decide. Still, the 1988 Act to Improve the Administration of Justice has allowed the Court to grant fewer cases review, and thereby ease their opinion-writing pressures.

The contemporary Court's docket is now so large, in the view of Burger and Rehnquist, that they both endorsed the idea of Congress's establishing a national intermediate appellate court, located between the court of appeals and the Supreme Court. Such a national intermediate appellate court would either screen and decide cases or have cases referred to it by the Court.

In 1971, Burger initially appointed a committee, chaired by the Harvard law professor Paul Freund, to study the Court's caseload and to make recommendations for reform. The Freund report proposed the establishment of a national court of appeals. The court would screen all filings, other than those on original jurisdiction, and refer some four hundred each year to the Supreme Court and deny without appeal the rest (in terms of the present docket, around 4,400 cases a year). The Court could then decide which of those cases merit consideration and either deny or remand the remaining cases back to the national court of appeals for decision.[134] The Freund report was widely criticized, most notably by retired Chief Justice Warren and Justices Douglas and Brennan.[135] They argued that whereas the Constitution provides for only "one Supreme Court," the Freund proposal would block many cases, issues, and factual circumstances from ever coming to the attention of the Court. Thus, a national court of appeals would function as the court of last resort in most cases, ostensibly in violation of the Constitution. Douglas and Brennan further contended that they were not overworked but underworked. The latter eventually agreed that the Court had a workload problem, but he still profoundly objected to the creation of a court that would screen cases and diminish the Court's power to set its own agenda. At one time, though, Stevens and Rehnquist also endorsed the idea as a way of reducing both the caseload and the workload of the Court.[136]

An alternative way of addressing the Court's problems was proposed by the Hruska Commission, established by Congress in 1972 as the Commission on Revision of the Federal Court Appellate System, chaired by Senator Roman Hruska. When its final report was released in 1975, the Hruska Commission also recommended a national court of appeals, but, instead of screening cases, one that would hear cases referred to it by the Court or transferred over by courts of appeals.[137] Although this proposal received more support than Freund's did, it too invited criticism. A central concern in regard to the Hruska proposal was that such a court would neither reduce the Supreme Court's caseload (except where cases were transferred by other courts of appeals) nor substantially reduce the Court's workload. Indeed, the Court's workload might actually increase since filings would still have to be screened and the justices would have to decide not merely whether to grant or deny a case but also whether a case merited reference to the national court of appeals for decision.

Shortly before his resignation from the Court, Burger lobbied Congress to establish a temporary five-year experimental intermediate tribunal, staffed by judges drawn from the various courts of appeals. The tribunal would decide cases involving circuit conflicts—that is, cases where two or more courts of appeals have ruled differently on the same issue—and any other cases referred to it by the Court. At the time, O'Connor, White, and Powell endorsed the idea, as did Rehnquist, but the Department of Justice refused to endorse the creation of such a court.[138] Other justices and numerous federal appellate court judges, moreover, opposed and lobbied against the proposal.[139] Stevens wrote Congressman Robert Kastenmeier that there were too few intercircuit conflict cases to merit creation of such a court. He also pointed out that most of these cases were decided by the Court because of the constitutional and statutory issues presented, not because of a conflict among the circuits, and that there were alternative ways of securing national uniformity in the law and judiciary.[140] Stevens further maintained that the Court's workload problems in the 1970s and 1980s arose because the justices lacked self-restraint and simply granted review to too many cases.

A final and third institutional response relates to the Court's internal *procedures and processes:* formal procedural rules and informal processes and practices in the screening and disposing of cases may be modified by the justices. The Court has often changed formal requirements for accepting cases, raised filing fees, and imposed penalties for filing "frivolous" cases, for example. It has also altered internal processes and practices of judicial review. Such changes in procedure and process will be examined in the next chapter, on how the Court decides what to decide.

The kinds of major institutional changes championed by Chief Justice Burger appear unlikely in the near future. That is because, as discussed further in the next chapter, in the 1990s the Rehnquist Court cut back very sharply on the number of cases granted review, thereby undercutting further arguments that the justices have a workload problem that they cannot resolve themselves.

FOUR

Deciding What to Decide

I'LL TAKE my case all the way to the Supreme Court." People say that when they feel they have been treated unjustly and want a fair hearing. But few actually do take their cases all the way to the Court, and even fewer are granted a hearing. Clarence Earl Gideon was one who succeeded in getting his case accepted by the Court. Gideon, a fifty-one-year-old rambler, in and out of jails for most of his life, was convicted of breaking and entering into the Bay Harbor Poolroom in Panama City, Florida. At his trial, he claimed he was too poor to afford an attorney and requested that one be provided. The judge refused, but Gideon persisted. While serving a five-year sentence for petty larceny in the Florida State Prison in 1961, he mailed a petition, printed childishly on lined paper obtained from a prison guard. His petition led to the landmark ruling in *Gideon v. Wainwright* (1963) that indigents have a right to counsel in all felony cases.

Gideon was exceptional, for the overwhelming number of all petitions are denied. Only about one percent of the cases on the Court's docket are granted and decided by written opinion. Out of the over 8,000 cases that now arrive each term, only about

100 get the Court's full attention. Unlike other federal judges, the justices have virtually complete discretion to screen out of the many cases they receive the few they will decide. By deciding what to decide, the Court can stay abreast of its caseload. The cornerstone of the modern Court's operation, as Justice John Harlan remarked, "is the control it possesses over the amount and character of its business."[1]

The power to decide what to decide also enables the Court to set its own agenda. Like other courts, the Court must await issues brought by lawsuits. One hundred and fifty years ago, the court's docket did not include issues of personal privacy raised by the possibility of electronic surveillance and computer data banks, for instance, or controversies over abortion and the "right to die." As technology develops and society changes, courts respond. Law evolves (more or less quickly) in response to social change. Unlike any other court, however, the Supreme Court, as its caseload changed and grew, got the power to pick which issues it would decide. The Court now functions like a roving commission, or legislative body, in responding to social forces.

Gideon's petition provided a vehicle for the Warren Court to change the course of American law. Gideon was wrong in claiming that the Court had said that the poor have a right to a court-appointed attorney. He did not know that he was asking the Court to reverse itself. The Sixth Amendment provides simply that in criminal cases the accused has the right "to have the Assistance of Counsel for his defense." The guarantee applied only in federal, not in state, courts; and it did not require that the government provide attorneys for indigent defendants. The Court had first addressed the issue of a right to counsel in *Powell v. Alabama* (1932). Nine black youths—the Scottsboro boys, as they were called—were convicted of raping a white girl by an all-white jury in a small southern town. Under these circumstances, the Court ruled, without the benefit of counsel "the defendants, young, ignorant, illiterate [and] surrounded by hostile sentiment," were denied a fair hearing. Six years later, in

Johnson v. Zerbst (1938), Hugo Black wrote for a bare majority that the Sixth Amendment requires counsel for indigents in all federal criminal cases. A majority of the Court nonetheless refused to apply that ruling to indigents in state courts. In *Betts v. Brady* (1942), the Court held that only in "special circumstances," like those in the Scottsboro case, was counsel required. Black, along with William Douglas and Frank Murphy, dissented. Anticipating his eventual opinion for the Court in *Gideon* that overturned *Betts,* Black insisted that no one should be "deprived of counsel merely because of his poverty." He added, "Any other practice seems to me to defeat the promise of our democratic society to provide equal justice under the law."

Gideon was not known to the justices, nor was he part of a special-interest group seeking legal reform. Yet he "was part of a current history," as the Pulitzer Prize winner Anthony Lewis observed; "there were working for him forces in law and society larger than he could understand."[2] Constitutional law is a constantly changing dialogue between the Court and the country. *Betts*'s special-circumstances rule stood for two decades, but it was increasingly criticized by Black and others. Only three members of the Court that decided *Betts* remained when Gideon's petition was granted: two of the dissenters, Black and Douglas; and Felix Frankfurter, who was eighty years old, ill, and in his last year on the bench. They had been joined by Tom Clark and Eisenhower's appointees—Earl Warren, John Harlan, William Brennan, Charles Whittaker, and Potter Stewart. By the time *Gideon* was decided, Frankfurter had retired and Whittaker was disabled. They had been replaced by Kennedy's appointees—Arthur Goldberg and Byron White.

Gideon fit the agenda of a majority of the Warren Court. In cases like Gideon's, their "liberal jurisprudence" revolutionized criminal law by extending the guarantees of the Bill of Rights to the poor and others in state as well as in federal courts. By contrast, members of the Burger and Rehnquist Courts selected cases in order to cut back, if not reverse, the direction of Warren

Court policy-making. The Warren Court, in *Douglas v. California* (1963), for example, extended the ruling in *Gideon* to require counsel for indigents appealing their convictions. But in *Ross v. Moffitt* (1974), over the dissents of Douglas, Brennan, and Thurgood Marshall, the Burger Court held that indigents have a right to counsel only on their first appeal to a state supreme court or the U.S. Supreme Court. The Burger Court also cut back on *Gideon* by holding in *Argersinger v. Hamlin* (1972) that counsel is required only when there is a possibility of a defendant's imprisonment and by then holding in *Scott v. Illinois* (1979) that it is required only when a defendant is actually imprisoned for committing a felony.

The Rehnquist Court is much more conservative than either the Warren or Burger Courts and (as discussed further in this chapter) has taken steps to discourage indigents from filing what it considers frivolous appeals. Still, jailhouse lawyers, like Gideon, may on occasion command the Court's attention. Keith J. Hudson, an inmate in the Louisiana State Penitentiary in Angola, was one who persuaded the justices to grant his petition. While serving a twenty-year sentence for armed robbery in 1983, Hudson was beaten repeatedly by prison guards. Early one morning he had been cleaning his clothes in the toilet in his cell, when a guard ordered him to stop flushing the toilet and to go back to sleep. When Hudson continued doing his laundry, the guards handcuffed and shackled him in order to take him to an isolation cell known as the dungeon. On their way, he was beaten and kicked, under the supervision of another guard who warned them, "Not to have too much fun." The encounter left Hudson with a split lip, broken dental plate, and some bruises, but no other "significant harm." Hudson later filed a complaint and eventually won $800 in damages for his "mental and physical anguish." That award, though, was subsequently overturned by the Court of Appeals for the Fifth Circuit. And Hudson appealed to the Supreme Court, arguing that the appellate court had misread the Constitution and that the guards had violated his rights under the Eighth Amendment's prohibition against "cruel and unusual punishment" and the Fourteenth Amendment's due process and equal protection clauses. By a seven-to-two vote, the justices agreed. Writing for the majority in *Hudson v. McMillian* (1992), Justice Sandra Day O'Connor held that the Eighth Amendment forbids the gratuitous use of excessive force in the treatment of prisoners. By contrast, dissenting Justices Clarence Thomas and Antonin Scalia repudiated the idea that the Eighth Amendment even applies to the treatment of prisoners and charged that the majority's ruling was "yet another manifestation of the pervasive view that the Federal Constitution must address all ills in our society."

Each Court, with its unique combination of justices, sets its own agenda. Justices, of course, differ on what cases they think should be decided. "There is an ideological division on the Court," Chief Justice William Rehnquist has admitted, "and each of us has some cases we would like to see granted, and on the contrary some of the other members would not like to see them granted."[3] Justices compete for influence in setting the Court's agenda. That competition flows from the jurisdictional rules and doctrines governing access to the Court's power.

Access to Justice

Jurisdiction is power over access to justice and the exercise of judicial review. The Court's jurisdiction derives from three sources: (1) Article III of the Constitution, which defines the Court's original jurisdiction; (2) congressional legislation, providing appellate jurisdiction; and (3) the Court's own interpretation of one and two together with its own rules for accepting cases.

Article III of the Constitution provides that the judicial power extends to all federal questions—that is, "all Cases, in Law and Equity, arising under this Constitution, the Laws of the United States, and Treaties." The Court also has original jurisdiction over specific kinds of "cases or controversies": those affecting ambassadors, other public ministers, and consuls; disputes to which the United States is a party, between two or more states, between a state and a citizen of another state, and between a state (or its citizens) and foreign countries. The Court today has only a handful of such cases each term coming on original jurisdiction. Most involve states suing each other over land and water rights, and they tend to be rather complex and carried over for several terms before they are finally decided. In 1998, for instance, the Court held in *New Jersey v. New York* that 90 percent of Ellis Island's 27.5 acres, created by landfill long after an 1834 agreement dividing the island, belongs to New Jersey, thereby ending a 164-year dispute between those two states.

Congress establishes (and may change) the appellate jurisdiction of the federal judiciary, including the Supreme Court.[4] Most cases used to come as direct appeals, requiring obligatory review. But as the caseload increased, Congress expanded the Court's discretionary jurisdiction by replacing appeals with petitions for *certiorari*, which the Court may in its discretion grant or deny. Before the Judiciary Act of 1925, which broadened the Court's discretionary jurisdiction, appeals amounted to 80 percent of the docket and petitions for *certiorari* less than 20 percent. Today virtually 99 percent of the docket comes on *certiorari*.

Although most cases now come as *certiorari* petitions, Congress provides that appellate courts may also submit a writ of certification to the Court, requesting the justices to clarify or "make more certain" a point of federal law. The Court receives only a handful of such cases each term. Congress also gave the Court the power to issue certain extraordinary writs, or orders. In a few cases, the Court may issue writs of mandamus and prohibition, ordering lower courts or public officials either to do something or to refrain from some action. In addition, the Court has the power to grant writs of *habeas corpus* ("produce the body"), enabling it to review cases by prisoners who claim that their constitutional rights have been violated and that they are unlawfully imprisoned.

Congress also established the practice of giving poor citizens, like Gideon, the right to file without the payment of fees.[5] When filing an appeal or petition for *certiorari*, indigents may file an affidavit requesting that they be allowed to proceed *in forma pauperis* ("in the manner of a pauper"), without the usual filing fees and forms. Gideon's first petition, for example, was returned because he failed to include a statement that he was an indigent and unable to pay the cost of filing his petition. The Court sets both the rules governing filing fees and the form that appeals, *certiorari* petitions, and other documents must take. Except for indigents, the Court now requires $300 for filing any case and another $100 if a case is granted oral argument, as well as a $200 fee for filing a petition for a rehearing. Indigents are exempt as well from the Court's rule specifying particular colors and lengths of paper for various kinds of filings. All *certiorari* petitions, for instance, must have a white color, whereas opposing briefs are light orange. Any document filed by the federal government has a gray cover. No petition or appeal may exceed forty pages; for those few cases granted oral argument, briefs on the merits of cases are limited to fifty pages. In 1995, the Court also changed its rules to require pauper petitioners to file ten copies, instead of one, of their petitions, unless they are incarcerated and without counsel.

The Constitution and Congress thus stipulate the kinds of cases and controversies the Court may consider. Yet, as Chief Justice Charles Evans Hughes candidly remarked, "We are under the Constitution, but the Constitution is what the judges say it is."[6] The Court has developed its own doctrines for denying review to a large number of cases and for setting its own agenda. These doctrines depend, in one justice's words, upon "our sense of self-restraint."[7]

Jurisdictional Doctrines and Policies
Each "case or controversy" has, Earl Warren observed,

an iceberg quality, containing beneath [the] surface simplicity, submerged complexities which go to the very heart of our constitutional form of government. Embodied in the words "cases" and "controversies" are two complementary but somewhat different limitations. In part those words limit the business of federal courts to questions presented in an adversary context and in a form historically viewed as capable of resolution through the judicial process. And in part those words define the role assigned to the judiciary in a tripartite allocation of power to assure that the federal courts will not intrude into areas committed to the other branches of government. Justiciability is a term of art employed to give expression to this dual limitation placed upon federal courts by the case and controversy doctrine.[8]

In other words, the Court considers first whether it had jurisdiction over a "case or controversy" and then whether that dispute is justiciable, capable of judicial resolution. Justices thus may (or may not) deny a case if it (1) lacks adverseness; (2) is brought by parties who lack "standing to sue"; or poses issues that either (3) are not "ripe" or (4) have become "moot"; or (5) involves a "political question."

Adverseness and Advisory Opinions • The Court generally maintains that litigants must be real and adverse in seeking a decision that will resolve their dispute and not some hypothetical issue. The requirement of real and adverse parties means that the Court will not decide "friendly suits" (in which the parties do not have adverse interests in the outcome of a case). Nor will the Court give "advisory opinions" on issues not raised in an actual lawsuit. The Jay Court denied two requests for advisory opinions: one, in 1790, by Secretary of the Treasury Alexander Hamilton for advice on the national government's power to assume state Revolutionary War debts, and another, in 1793, by

AVENUES OF APPEAL: THE TWO MAIN ROUTES TO THE SUPREME COURT

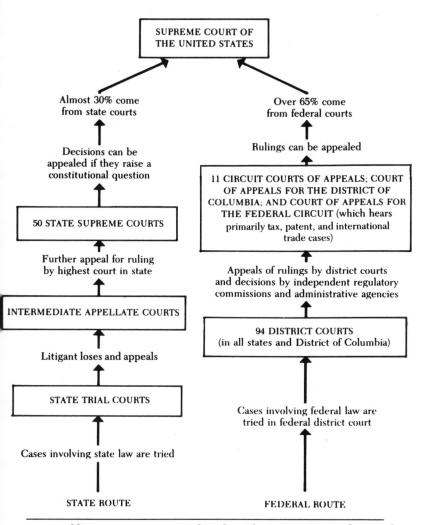

Note: In addition, some cases come directly to the Supreme Court from trial courts when they involve reapportionment or civil rights disputes. Appeals from the Court of Military Appeals also go directly to the Supreme Court. A few cases come on "original jurisdiction" and involve disputes between state governments.

Secretary of State Thomas Jefferson for an interpretation of certain treaties and international law. Chief Justice John Jay held that it would be improper for the Court to judge such matters because the President might call on cabinet heads for advice. In doing so, the Jay Court broke with the English practice of advisory opinions and set a precedent,[9] The Court continues to maintain that it is inappropriate "to give opinions in the nature of advice concerning legislative action, a function never conferred upon it by the Constitution and against the exercise of which this court has steadily set its face from the beginning."[10]

Historically, justices have nevertheless extrajudicially advised attorneys, congressmen, and Presidents. They occasionally even accuse each other of including in opinions *dicta* (statements of personal opinion or philosophy not necessary to the decision handed down)—an inclusion that is tantamount to "giving legal advice."[11] The Court, furthermore, upheld the constitutionality of the Declaratory Judgment Act, authorizing federal courts to declare, or make clear, rights and legal relationships even before a law has taken effect, though only in "cases of actual controversy."[12]

The requirement of adverseness and the prohibition against advisory opinions from time to time admit of exceptions. When both parties in a suit agree on how an issue should be decided but need a judicial ruling, the Court will approve a special counsel or *amicus curiae* ("friend of the court") to argue the other side and assure opposition. This occurred in the 1983 one-house veto case, *Immigration and Naturalization Service v. Chadha.* Jagdish Rai Chadha came to the United States on a nonimmigrant student visa, but remained after it expired. The Immigration and Naturalization Service (INS) moved to deport him, but the attorney general suspended deportation and, as required, reported his decision to Congress. One house of Congress then passed a resolution vetoing the suspension of Chadha's deportation. The INS, the Department of Justice, and Chadha all agreed that that action was unconstitutional. The Court of

Appeals for the Ninth Circuit, which initially heard the case, requested Congress to submit *amicus* briefs arguing the opposite. Ultimately, the Supreme Court held that one-house vetos of executive branch agencies' decisions are unconstitutional.

Standing to Sue • Standing, like adverseness, is a threshold requirement for getting into court. "Generalizations about standing to sue," Douglas discouragingly but candidly put it, "are largely worthless as such."[13] Nonetheless, the basic requirement is that an individual show injury to a legally protected interest or right and demonstrate that other opportunities for defending that claim (before an administrative tribunal or a lower court) have been exhausted. The claim of an injury "must be of a personal and not official nature" and of "some specialized interest of [the individual's] own to vindicate, apart from political concerns which belong to it."[14] The interest must be real as opposed to speculative or hypothetical.

The injuries and legal interests that were claimed traditionally turned on a showing of personal or proprietary damage. Typically, plaintiffs had suffered some "pocketbook" or monetary injury. In the last twenty years, however, individuals have sought standing in order to represent nonmonetary injuries and "the public interest."

The law of standing is a combination of judge-made law and congressional legislation, as interpreted by the Court. The Warren Court era substantially lowered the threshold for standing and permitted more litigation of public policy issues. In *Frothingham v. Mellon* (1923), the Taft Court had denied individual taxpayers standing to challenge the constitutionality of federal legislation. Mrs. Frothingham, a taxpayer, attacked a congressional appropriation to the states for a maternal and infant care program. She claimed that Congress exceeded its power and intruded on "the reserved rights of the states" under the Tenth Amendment. The Taft Court avoided confronting the merits of the claim by denying standing. It did so on the ground that an individual taxpayer's interest in the financing of federal programs is "comparatively minute and indeterminable," when viewed in light of all taxpayers. Frothingham's injury was neither direct nor immediate, and the issue raised was basically "political, not judicial."[15] The government relied on the ruling in *Frothingham* to provide an absolute barrier to subsequent taxpayer suits.

The Warren Court repudiated that view in *Flast v. Cohen* (1968). *Flast* involved a taxpayer's challenge, under the First Amendment establishment clause, of the appropriation of funds for private religious schools in the Elementary and Secondary Education Act of 1965. Here the Warren Court found that Mrs. Florance Flast, unlike Mrs. Frothingham, had standing. The Court ruled that she had a "personal stake in the outcome," which assured concrete adverseness and litigation that would illuminate the constitutional issues presented. In so doing, the Warren Court created standing where there is a logical relationship between a taxpayer's status and the challenged legislative statute as well as a connection between that status and the "precise nature of the constitutional infringement alleged." The Warren Court's two-pronged test invited more taxpayer lawsuits.

The Burger Court tightened the requirements for standing in some cases, but relaxed it in others. In 1972, in two closely divided decisions, the Burger Court denied standing to a group challenging military surveillance of lawful political protests in public places and to the Sierra Club when challenging the construction of a ski resort in Mineral King National Park. In both cases a bare majority found that the groups failed to show a "personal stake in the outcome" of the litigation.[16] The following year, however, the Burger Court granted standing to a group of law students attacking a proposed surcharge on railroad freight. The students contended that the surcharge would discourage the recycling of bottles and cans by making recycling more expensive, and thus contribute to environmental pollution. In *United States v. Students Challenging Regulatory Agency*

Procedures (SCRAP) (1973), the Burger Court granted standing, observing:

Aesthetic and environmental well-being, like economic well-being, are important ingredients of the quality of life in our society, and the fact that particular environmental interests are shared by the many rather than the few does not make them less deserving of legal protection through the judicial process.

Plaintiffs must still claim a personal injury, but they could now act as surrogates for special-interest groups. The personal injuries claimed thus embrace a public injury. Congress at the same time expanded the principle even more by providing that any individual "adversely affected or aggrieved" may challenge administrative decisions. Health, safety, and environmental legislation passed in the 1970s mandated such "citizen suits" and right to judicial review of regulatory action. Even when legislation does not provide for the "citizen suits," individuals may claim personal injuries, or a "private cause of action," to gain access to the courts and to force agency compliance with the law.

The Court has restricted standing requirements in two ways. First, it has refused to recognize new interests and injuries in granting standing. In one 1973 case, an unwed mother sought enforcement of child support under the Texas penal code. The local prosecutor refused to enforce the statute against fathers of illegitimate children. A majority of the Burger Court ruled that she had no recognizable interest or injury, no standing, since she could not prove that payments stopped because the statute was unenforced. White and Douglas, in dissent, argued that unwed mothers and illegitimate children were thus rendered nonpersons: "Texas prosecutes fathers of legitimate children on the complaint of the mother asserting nonsupport and refuses to entertain like complaints from the mother of an illegitimate child. [We] see no basis for saying that the latter mother has no standing to demand that the discrimination be ended, one way or another."[17] In a later ruling in *Paul v. Davis* (1976), a majority of the Burger Court rejected a claim of injury to personal reputation by an individual who objected to the circulation of a flier to local merchants that carried his photograph along with that of other alleged "Active Shoplifters." Rehnquist dismissed the claim out of hand. However, Brennan in dissent responded, "The Court by mere fiat and with no analysis wholly excludes personal interest in reputation from the ambit of 'life, liberty, or property' under the Fifth and Fourteenth Amendments, thus rendering due process concerns *never* applicable to the official stigmatization however arbitrary." Both of these cases illustrate the judicial politics involved in the law of standing, and the importance of legal definitions of interests and injuries.

The second way the Court has tried to dilute *Flast* is to say that standing is not a citizen's right but instead a set of prudential rules. In *Warth v. Seldin* (1975), the majority denied review to a group claiming that zoning laws excluded persons of low income from living in a township outside Rochester, New York. In a dissenting opinion joined by White and Marshall, Brennan charged that the majority had denied standing simply because it unfavorably viewed the merits of the case:

While the Court gives lip service to the principle, often repeated in recent years, that "standing in no way depends on the merits of the plaintiff's contention that particular conduct is illegal," . . . in fact the opinion, which tosses out of court almost every conceivable kind of plaintiff who could be injured by the activity claimed to be unconstitutional can be explained only by an indefensible hostility to the claim on the merits.

In addition, the Court has made it more difficult to bring class action suits and for consumer, environmental, and civil rights organizations to challenge governmental policies. Under Rule 23 of the Federal Rules of Civil Procedure, individuals may bring suits for themselves and all others similarly situated. This enabled individuals to bring suits over environmental damages, defective consumer products, and other matters that affect large numbers of people. But in *Eisen v. Carlisle & Jacquelin* (1974) the Court held that individuals bringing suits under Rule 23 must bear the cost of actually notifying all those potentially in the class action suit, thereby making these suits more expensive, if not prohibitive. Then, in *Valley Forge Christian College v. Americans United for Separation of Church and State* (1982), the Court denied standing to an organization challenging the Department of Health, Education, and Welfare (now the Department of Health and Human Services) for giving a former military hospital to a religious college. Writing for a bare majority, Rehnquist held that standing under *Flast* was limited to challenging congressional actions and did not extend to decisions of administration agencies.

Almost twenty years after the Burger Court liberalized the law of standing in the area of environmental litigation, in *United States v. SCRAP* (1973) and other cases, the Rehnquist Court began tightening those requirements and raising new obstacles for citizens bringing environmental lawsuits. In *Lujan v. Defenders of Wildlife* (1992), for example, the Court denied two environmentalists standing to sue the Department of Interior under the Endangered Species Act (ESA) of 1973 for reinterpreting the ESA to no longer apply to federally funded projects abroad and for failing, as required under the act, to consult with other agencies about a federally funded irrigation project on the Mahaweli River in Sri Lanka, and a redevelopment project on the Nile River in Egypt. In asserting standing, the president of Defenders of Wildlife, Joyce Kelly, and another member, claimed those projects threatened endangered elephants and leopards in Sri Lanka and crocodiles in Egypt. They testified that they were environmentalists who had traveled to each of the sites and would again visit, though they did not specify when. Writing for the majority, Justice Scalia denied standing because of the failure to show "imminent injury." "That the two women 'had visited' the areas of the projects," as Scalia put it, "proves nothing." Dissenting Justices Blackmun and O'Connor, however, charged the majority with "what amounts to a slash-and-burn expedition through the law of environmental standing" and, along with Justice Stevens, would have granted standing, even under the Court's "imminent personal injury" test.

Ripeness and Mootness • With these doctrines the Court wields a double-edged sword. A plaintiff may discover that a case is dismissed because it was brought too early or because the issues are moot and the case was brought too late. A case is usually rejected as not ripe if the injury claimed has not yet occurred or if other avenues of appeal have not yet been exhausted. Alternatively, a case may be dismissed if pertinent facts or law change so that there is no longer real adverseness or an actual case or controversy. The issue becomes moot since "there is no subject matter on which the judgment of the court can operate," and hence a ruling would not prove "conclusive" and final.[18]

In practice, both doctrines bend to the Court's will. The requirement of ripeness, for instance, permits the Court to avoid or delay deciding certain issues. Between 1943 and 1965, the Court refused standing to individuals attacking the constitutionality of a late-nineteenth-century Connecticut statute. The law prohibited virtually all single and married individuals from using contraceptives and physicians from giving advice about their use. In *Tileston v. Ullman* (1943), a doctor sued, charging that the statute prevented him from giving information to patients. But the Court ruled that he had no real interest or personal injury, since he had not been arrested.

Over a decade later, in *Poe v. Ullman* (1961), a doctor and a patient were likewise denied standing on the ground that the law had not been enforced for eighty years, even though the state had begun to close birth control clinics. Finally, after two individuals were found guilty of prescribing contraceptives to a married couple, the Warren Court in *Griswold v. Connecticut*

(1965) struck down what Stewart called Connecticut's "uncommonly silly law." The ruling was limited to the privacy and marital decisions of couples. Consequently, in *Eisenstadt v. Baird* (1972), in order to gain standing to claim that single individuals also have a right to acquire and use contraceptives, a doctor arranged to be arrested after delivering a public lecture on contraceptives and handing out samples to single women in the audience. The Burger Court accepted the case and ruled that single women also have the right to acquire and use contraceptives.

A finding of mootness likewise enables the Court to avoid, if not escape, deciding controversial political issues. *DeFunis v. Odegaard* (1974), for example, involved a white student who was denied admission to the University of Washington Law School. The student claimed that the school's affirmative-action program discriminated against him and allowed the entrance of minorities with lower Law School Admission Test scores. After the trial judge's ruling in his favor, he was admitted into law school, but by the time his case reached the Supreme Court he was completing his final year and assured of graduation. Over four dissenters, the majority held that the case was moot. Yet, as the dissenters predicted, the issue would not go away. Within four years, the Burger Court reconsidered the issue of reverse discrimination in university affirmative-action programs in *Regents of the University of California v. Bakke* (1978). In *Bakke*, Lewis Powell held not only that quota systems for minorities in college admissions are unconstitutional but also that the Constitution is not "color blind" and that affirmative-action programs are permissible in order to achieve a diverse student body in colleges and universities.

The issue of mootness presented no serious problem when the Burger Court tackled abortion in *Roe v. Wade* (1973). Here, we saw, a Texas criminal statute prohibiting abortions, except when necessary to save a mother's life, was attacked as infringing on a woman's right of privacy recognized in *Griswold*. In defending the law, the state attorney general argued that the plaintiff was a single woman whose pregnancy had terminated by the time the case reached the Court and that hence her claim was moot. Harry Blackmun, writing for the Court, rejected that view:

[W]hen, as here, pregnancy is a significant fact in the litigation, the normal 266-day human gestation period is so short that the pregnancy will come to term before the usual appellate process is complete. If that termination makes a case moot, pregnancy litigation seldom will survive much beyond the trial stage, and appellate review will be effectively denied. Our law should not be that rigid. Pregnancy often comes more than once to the same woman, and in the general population, if man is to survive, it will always be with us. Pregnancy provides a classic justification for a conclusion of nonmootness. It truly could be "capable of repetition, yet evading review."

Political Questions • Even when the Court has jurisdiction over a properly framed suit, it may decline to rule because it decides that a case raises a political question that should be resolved by other political branches. Like other jurisdictional doctrines, the political-question doctrine means what the justices say it means.

The doctrine has its origin in the following observation by Chief Justice John Marshall in *Marbury v. Madison* (1803): "The province of the Court, is, solely, to decide on the rights of individuals. . . . Questions in the nature political, or which are, by the constitution and laws, submitted to the executive can never be made in this Court." Yet, as Alexis de Tocqueville noted in the 1830s, "Scarcely any political question arises in the United States that is not resolved, sooner or later, into a judicial question."[19] Litigation that reaches the Court is political, and the justices for political reasons decide what and how to decide cases on their docket.

The Taney Court first developed the doctrine in *Luther v. Borden* (1849). There the Court was called on to decide whether Rhode Island had a "republican form of government," as guaranteed by Article IV of the Constitution. Taney reasoned that Article I gave Congress and not the Court "the right to decide." Subsequent rulings elaborated other reasons for the doctrine besides deference to separation of powers. The Court may lack information and resources needed for a ruling. In some areas, as in foreign policy and international relations, the Court lacks both adequate standards for resolving disputes and the means to enforce its decisions.

For many decades, the Court relied on the doctrine to avoid entering the "political thicket" of state representation and apportionment.[20] Yet blacks and other minorities in urban areas were often denied equal voting rights. The Court finally responded and reversed itself in *Baker v. Carr* (1962). The Court reasserted its power to decide what is and is not a "political question" when it held that disputes over state representation and apportionment are within its jurisdiction and justiciable. The Warren Court thus forced state and local governments to provide equal voting rights and established the principle of "one person, one vote."

The doctrine's logic is circular. "Political questions are matters not soluble by the judicial process; matters not soluble by the judicial process are political questions. As an early dictionary explained," the political scientist John Roche has said, "violins are small cellos, and cellos are large violins."[21] Still, as the Columbia Law professor Louis Henkin has pointed out, even when denying review because of a political question, "the court does not refuse judicial review; it exercises it. It is not dismissing the case or the issue as nonjusticiable; it adjudicates it. It is not refusing to pass on the power of the political branches; it passes upon it, only to affirm that they had the power which had been challenged and that nothing in the Constitution prohibited the particular exercise of it."[22]

Stare Decisis and Other Policies • The justices occasionally also rely on other self-denying policies to avoid reaching issues.

They may, for example, invoke what has been called the doctrine of strict necessity and thereupon formulate and decide only the narrowest possible issue.

The doctrine of *stare decisis* ("let the prior decision stand") is also not a mechanical formula. It is, rather, a judicial policy that promotes "the certainty, uniformity, and stability of the law." Even the conservative Justice George Sutherland recognized that members of the Court "are not infallible, and when convinced that a prior decision was not originally based on, or that conditions have so changed as to render the decision no longer in accordance with, sound reason, [they] should not hesitate to say so."[23]

"*Stare decisis* is usually the wise policy," Louis Brandeis remarked, "because in most matters it is more important that the applicable rule of law be settled than that it be settled right."[24] On constitutional matters, however, Douglas among others emphasized, "*stare decisis*—that is, established law—was really no sure guideline because what did . . . the judges who sat there in 1875 know about, say, electronic surveillance? They didn't know anything about it."[25] At the time of his ill-fated nomination to the Court, Judge Robert Bork agreed and raised serious questions about the value of judicial precedents, though for somewhat different reasons from Douglas. Bork contended that "the real meaning of the Constitution ought to prevail over a prior mistake by the Court" and "the Court ought to be always open to rethink constitutional problems." But he also maintained that "certain precedents [are] so fixed, some issues so settled, that regardless of how you felt about them you shouldn't vote to overrule them." Bork gave as an example nineteenth-century cases dealing with Congress's commerce power, which, however wrongly decided, should be upheld. By contrast, he did "not include *Roe v. Wade* in that category."[26]

The Rehnquist Court's deference to *stare decisis* has been a matter of controversy on and off the bench. The justices have debated the value of adhering to the doctrine of *stare decisis* in several cases, most notably in their 1989 abortion ruling in *Webster v. Reproductive Health Services,* and in a 1991 decision, *Payne v. Tennessee,* which overruled two earlier rulings that had prohibited the use of "victim-impact statements" during the sentencing stage of capital murder trials. Concurring in *Webster,* Scalia lamented the majority's refusal to expressly overturn *Roe* and that "the mansion of constitutionalized abortion-law" would have to "be disassembled door-jamb by door-jamb." Scalia's views drew an unusual response from retired Justice Lewis Powell, who in a speech on *"Stare Decisis* and Judicial Restraint" countered that,

> Those who would eliminate *stare decisis* in constitutional cases argue that the doctrine is simply one of convenience. . . . But elimination of constitutional *stare decisis* would represent explicit endorsement of the idea that the Constitution is nothing more than what five Justices say it is. This would undermine the rule of law . . . .
>
> It is evident that I consider *stare decisis* essential to the rule of law. . . . After two centuries of vast change, the original intent of the Founders is difficult to discern or is irrelevant. Indeed, there may be no evidence of intent. The Framers of the Constitution were wise enough to write broadly, using language that must be construed in light of changing conditions that could not be foreseen. Yet the doctrine of *stare decisis* has remained a constant thread in preserving continuity and stability.[27]

In the first four terms of the Rehnquist Court, however, only eleven prior decisions were overturned. More often the Court appeared content to simply chip away at controversial landmark rulings like *Miranda v. Arizona* (1966), which held that police must inform suspects of their rights to remain silent and to have attorneys present during police questioning. Over the years the Court has allowed so many exceptions that *Miranda* survives only as a hollow symbol of the Warren Court. *Pennsylvania v. Bruder* (1988), for instance, held that police do not have to honor *Miranda* when making routine traffic stops that result in a driver's arrest. Nor do police have to use the exact language of *Miranda* when informing suspects of their rights, the Rehnquist Court held in *Duckworth v. Egan* (1989). The strategy of the Rehnquist Court was initially to reinterpret a precedent in such a way as to reverse it without explicitly saying so. In *Wards Cove Packing Co. v. Atonio* (1989), a major ruling making it more difficult for minorities to prove on-the-job bias, a bare majority held that statistics may no longer be used to prove discrimination and that an earlier ruling, in *Greggs v. Duke Power Company* (1971), "should have been understood to mean" that!

With the appointments of Justices David Souter and Clarence Thomas, the Rehnquist Court appeared to grow more willing to reconsider past rulings. When granting *Payne v. Tennessee,* for example, the Court directed the parties to address the question of whether it should overturn prior decisions barring the use of victim-impact statements, despite the fact that neither party had raised that issue. In 1987 when that issue was initially addressed in *Booth v. Maryland,* Justice Powell had cast the crucial fifth vote for disallowing the use of victim-impact statements. Following his retirement and the arrival of his successor, Justice Anthony Kennedy, the Rehnquist Court reconsidered the issue in *South Carolina v. Gathers* (1989). This time, Justice White switched sides and voted with a bare majority to reaffirm *Booth*. With Justice Brennan's retirement in 1990, the composition of the Rehnquist Court changed again with the arrival of Justice Souter. And by a six-to-three vote (with White again switching his position, without explanation) *Payne v. Tennessee* reversed both *Booth* and *Gathers*.

In handing down *Payne,* Chief Justice Rehnquist observed that "*Stare decisis* is not an inexorable command," and set forth some guidelines for adhering to the doctrine of *stare decisis*. Prior rulings dealing with property and contract rights deserve great respect but, according to Rehnquist, "the opposite is true in cases such as the present one involving procedural and evidentiary rules." Moreover, precedents in areas of civil rights and liberties that commanded the support of a bare majority, or were "decided by the narrowest of margins," Rehnquist deemed especially open to reconsideration. By contrast, dissenting Justice Marshall charged that, "Power, not reason, is the new currency of this Court's decision making," and pointed out that, "Neither the law nor the facts supporting *Booth* and *Gathers* underwent any change in the last four years. Only the personnel of this Court did."

The Court's reversal of prior rulings registers the politics of the changing composition of the bench. In historical perspective, the Court reversed itself on average about once each term between 1791 and 1998. Last century, reversals were more infrequent, if only because there were fewer decisions to overturn. There were just 32 reversals, whereas there have been 215 reversals in this century, and 189 of those since 1937. Notably, when the Court's composition changes dramatically in a short period of time, or a pivotal justice leaves the bench, the Court tends to overturn prior rulings. The Warren Court (1953–1969) was even more activist than the Roosevelt Court in reversing forty-five precedents. The Roosevelt Court, with FDR's eight successive appointees and elevation of Justice Harlan Stone to the chief justiceship, overturned thirty precedents between 1937 and 1946. The Warren Court's record, moreover, reveals how crucial the timing of one or two changes on the bench may prove for the direction of the Court. From its landmark school desegregation ruling in *Brown v. Board of Education* (1954) to the appointment of Justice Stewart in 1959, only six precedents were reversed. With Stewart's arrival, six more were overturned in the next four years. In 1962, then, the composition of the bench changed again with President John F. Kennedy's appointments of Justices White and Goldberg. In the remaining seven years another twenty were reversed, as the Warren Court pushed constitutional law in even more liberal and egalitarian directions. During Chief Justice Burger's tenure (1969–1986), the Court gradually became more conservative, particularly in the area of criminal procedure. And as its composition changed, the Burger

Court also continued reconsidering precedents—though typically liberal ones—reversing a total of fifty-two prior rulings.[28] The Rehnquist Court's initial rush to overrule liberal precedents abated, however, as more moderate centrists came to command a majority and were joined by Clinton's appointees. Whereas in the first four terms of the Rehnquist Court, eleven precedents were abandoned, and twelve more in the next two terms, for a total of twenty-three, by the 1992 term only two more were overturned, none in the 1993 term, only one in each 1994 and 1995 term, two in the 1996 term, and just one in the 1997 term.

In sum, *stare decisis* and the precedential value of the Court's jurisdictional doctrines and policies, as Justice Robert Jackson quipped, "are accepted only at their current valuation and have a mortality rate as high as their authors."[29]

Formal Rules and Practices

Except for government attorneys and members of the practicing bar, few people pay any attention to the technical rules of the Court. Yet the rules are an exercise of political power and determine the nation's access to justice. They govern the admission and activities of attorneys in filing appeals, petitions, and motions and in conducting oral arguments. They stipulate the fees, forms, and length of filings, as well as the size of pages submitted (in 1990 the Court changed its rules to require all documents submitted in typewritten form to be on letter size, instead of legal size paper). Most important, they explain the Court's formal grounds for granting and disposing of cases.

The justices, however, do not explain why they recuse themselves from participating in decisions to grant and decide cases. There are no fixed rules for a justice's recusal, nor do the justices even have to explain to their colleagues why they think they have a potential financial or personal conflict of interest that disqualifies them from voting on a case. Justice O'Connor, for instance, withdrew from consideration of one case because, as she explained to the others, she had "learned that [her] mother's estate, in which I have a remainder interest, includes some AT&T stock." In another case, O'Connor recused herself after finding that her "sister's husband participated as a judge in the lower court."[30] In still another case involving the constitutionality of "single sex clubs," a number of justices persuaded her not to recuse herself because they too belonged to such clubs.[31] Moreover, in some corporate law cases all of the justices would have to disqualify themselves due to their stock holdings, as Justice Blackmun pointed out, because "counsel have put the case together in such a way that it represents almost the entire heavy industrial structure in the United States."[32]

Some Court watchers find this practice of unexplained judicial disqualification disturbing because of the large number of cases in which one or more of the justices recuse themselves. In 1987–1988, for example, as former solicitor general Erwin Griswold pointed out when criticizing the Court, one out of every fifteen cases was decided without a full Court.[33] Griswold's criticisms hit home and launched the justices on a five-year search for a policy on recusals.[34] Among the proposals considered and dismissed was that of asking Congress to enact legislation permitting retired justices to sit on cases in which one or more justices had recused themselves. Although Stevens advocated that policy, he failed to win the other justices over. Finally, in 1993 seven justices—all except Blackmun and Souter—agreed to issue a public statement explaining that they would recuse themselves from cases in which relatives participated as a lawyer or when their or a relative's compensation would be substantially affected by the outcome of a case. However, they also cautioned that, "We think that a relative's partnership in the firm appearing before us, or his or her previous work as a lawyer on a case that later comes before us, does not automatically trigger these provisions."

In order to expedite the process of deciding what to decide, the Court periodically revises its rules. For example, even after the Judiciary Act of 1925 expanded the Court's discretionary jurisdiction, the justices still felt burdened by mandatory appeals. Accordingly, in 1928 the Court required the filing of a jurisdictional statement, explaining the circumstances of an appeal, the questions presented, and the reasons why the Court should grant review. The requirement, as Justice Stone explained, "enabled us to dispose of many questions without bringing counsel to argue them, but it has also helped to enlighten counsel as to the nature of our jurisdiction and the burden which always rests on an appellant to establish jurisdiction."[35] The requirement also allowed the justices to screen appeals just as they screened petitions for *certiorari*. As the Clerk of the Court in 1945 remarked:

> Most attorneys are well aware of the fact that the Court may and does exercise its discretion in passing on applications for *certiorari* but insofar as appeals are concerned they harbor the mistaken impression that review is obligatory and that where they have an appeal "as of right" they are entitled to oral argument on the merits. On the contrary, at least fifty percent of the appeals are dismissed or the judgments affirmed upon consideration of the jurisdictional statements, before records are printed and without oral arguments. Jurisdictional statements and petitions for *certiorari* now stand on practically the same footing.[36]

The vast majority of filings can now be quickly scanned.

One of the reasons for granting *certiorari* that the Court's rules give is that "a federal court of appeals has rendered a decision in conflict with the decision of another federal court of appeals on the same matter." This rule is especially advantageous for the federal government. The Department of Justice has a relitigation policy. If it receives an adverse ruling from a circuit court of appeals, it will relitigate the issue in other circuits in order to obtain favorable decisions and generate a conflict among the circuits, which then may be brought to the Court. One function of the Court, in Chief Justice Vinson's words, has become the resolution of "conflicts of opinion on federal questions that have arisen among lower courts."[37] Yet each term the Court denies review to between fifty and sixty such conflicts.[38]

The rule for granting circuit conflicts, however, does not control mechanically the justices' practice of granting *certiorari*. The Rehnquist Court has been less willing than the Burger Court to grant cases review because they involve alleged conflicts among the circuit courts; a case must typically present a "deep conflict," involving more than two circuit courts, in order for the Court to grant review. In general, the Court will not grant cases review unless there is a genuine conflict on an important issue. The circuit conflict must also be neither too old nor too new, or too narrow, or in need of "percolation" among the circuits, and it must be a conflict that cannot be resolved by Congress or an administrative agency.[39]

Most crucial in granting *certiorari* is simply the majority's agreement on the importance of the issue presented. In 1995, the Court underscored that point when changing Rule 10 to indicate that *cert.* would be granted for only "important" matters or for "compelling reasons." This fact is also underscored by the justices' screening process. The justices rely primarily on law clerks' memos when granting *certiorari*. But these memos only summarize the facts, questions, and arguments presented. On that basis, they recommend whether a case should be granted or denied. Clerks' memos do not fully explore whether an alleged conflict is "real," "tolerable," or "square" and must be decided. The workload usually precludes such an examination until a case has already been granted and set for oral argument.

That the Court's rules for granting or denying cases do not dictate judicial behavior should not be surprising. But we should not conclude that justices do not take the rules seriously. A majority of the Rehnquist Court also has firmly indicated that it will no longer abide "frivolous" petitions filed by indigents. For the first time, in 1989, a bare majority took the extraordinary step of denying an individual the right to ever again file an *in forma pauperis* petition.[40] Subsequently, after denying several other indigents the right to file Ifp petitions, in 1991 the Rehnquist Court amended its rule governing motions to proceed *in forma pauperis* to provide for their denial whenever a majority deemed the petition frivolous or malicious.[41] Rule 39 was amended to provide that, "If satisfied that a petition for a writ of certorari, jurisdictional statement, or petition for an extraordinary writ, as the case may be, is frivolous or malicious, the Court may deny a motion for leave to proceed *in forma pauperis*." Although admitting that "frequent filers" did not consume any of the justices' conference time, Chief Justice Rehnquist and Justice Scalia spearheaded the change in the rules because they "consume the time of law clerks and of the Clerk's office." Dissenting Justices Marshall, Stevens, and Blackmun, however, lamented the political symbolism of the Court's action. In the words of dissenting Justice Marshall, "This Court once had a great tradition [echoed in the oath taken by the justices when sworn into office]: 'All men and women are entitled to their day in Court.' That guarantee has now been conditioned on monetary worth. It now will read: 'All men and women are entitled to their day in Court only if they have the *means* and the *money*.'"

Setting the Agenda

The justices' interpretations of their jurisdiction and rules govern access to the Court. But the justices also need flexible procedures for screening cases and deciding what to decide. The Court is a collegial institution in which all nine justices have an equal vote, and so justices need room for compromise. Attempts at streamlining the process and imposing strict procedures can get in the way of compromise and sharply divide the justices.

Justice Frankfurter's unsuccessful efforts to persuade his brethren to adopt formal rules for conducting their deliberations illustrate the dynamics of the Court. A persistent meddler, Frankfurter circulated a memorandum every year from 1951 until his last term on the bench, in 1961 (often the same each year but with minor editorial changes), proposing formal procedural rules for conducting the Court's deliberative process.[42] Always a hyper-self-conscious law professor, he became increasingly concerned with a fact of life in the Court that Justice Brandeis initially pointed out to him in 1923, while Frankfurter was still a professor at Harvard. "Nothing is decided without consideration," Brandeis had told him, "but hardly anything is decided with adequate consideration. . . . [Y]ou must constantly bear in mind the large part played by personal considerations and inadequacy of consideration."[43] Once on the bench, Frankfurter campaigned for procedures *he* thought would ensure "adequate consideration" of the Court's business. He succeeded only in distancing himself from Chief Justice Warren and the others.[44] In particular, Douglas protested:

If we unanimously adopted rules on such matters we would be plagued by them, bogged down, and interminably delayed. If we were not unanimous, the rules would be ineffective. I, for one, could not agree to give anyone any more control over when I vote than over how I vote.[45]

Likewise, Black opposed the adoption of formal rules. "I am satisfied with our present flexible procedures," he wrote Frankfurter, adding, "The majority, I suppose, could not by mechanical rules bind individual Justices as to the exercise of their discretion."[46]

SCREENING CASES

When any appeal or *certiorari* petition arrives at the Court, it immediately goes to the Clerk's office. There staff determines whether it satisfies requirements regarding form, length, and fees and, if the filing is from an indigent, whether there is an affidavit stating that the petitioner is too poor to pay fees. All unpaid cases are assigned numbers, in the order they arrive, and placed on what is called the Miscellaneous Docket. Paid cases are also assigned numbers but placed on the Appellate Docket. The other party, or respondent, in each case must file a brief in response within thirty days. After receiving briefs from respondents, the Clerk circulates to the justices' chambers a list of cases ready for consideration and a set of briefs for each case.

For much of the Court's history, every justice was responsible for reviewing each case. The justices did not work by panels or delegate responsibility for screening cases to others. That is no longer true. As the size of the Court's docket grew, so did the amount of paperwork and demands on the justices' time in screening cases. In the 1930s Attorney General Homer Cummings observed that the number of filings was so large that every justice in reviewing them would have to read the equivalent of *Gone with the Wind* every day before breakfast. In the last sixty years the number of filings and amount of paperwork have so dramatically increased that the justices have had to delegate much of their responsibility for screening cases to their law clerks. The justices or their clerks must now consider before selecting those few cases granted review over an estimated

    250,000 pages of appeals and petitions for review
     62,500 pages of responses opposing review
     25,000 pages of replies favoring review
     37,500 pages of law clerks' memoranda on the cases

That amounts to more than 375,000 pages of filings that must be reviewed, in addition to the briefs on the merits of the 100 or so cases that are granted review and oral argument each term.[47]

Changes in the screening of cases began because of the increasing number of unpaid petitions (as is indicated in the chart on page 195).[48] In historical perspective, the number of unpaid filings has fluctuated with changes in the Court's direction and in the criminal justice system as well as with socioeconomic forces in the country. Prior to the 1930s, the number of unpaid filings was negligible, less than eighty a year. But as the Court began to review more cases involving civil liberties

PAID AND UNPAID FILINGS, 1935–1998°

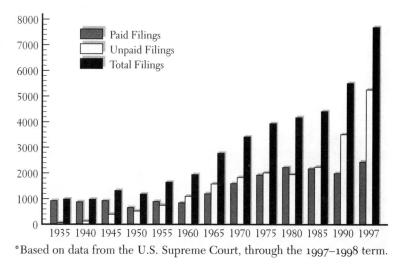

°Based on data from the U.S. Supreme Court, through the 1997–1998 term.

and the rights of the accused, unpaid filings incrementally increased during the 1940s and 1950s. By Chief Justice Warren's first year on the bench (1953) the number of unpaid and paid cases was about the same (618 unpaid and 884 paid cases). When the Warren Court then forged its "revolution in criminal procedure" the number of unpaid cases swelled to 1,947 (while paid cases grew to only 1,324) by 1968. The rising tide of unpaid filings went unabated in the 1970s, but so did that of paid cases. By 1979 paid cases slightly outnumbered unpaid cases and that remained so until the mid-1980s. Since 1985, however, the number of "jailhouse lawyers" and indigents filing petitions has steadily grown, largely due to the dramatic increase in prison populations as a result of tougher sentencing laws and the "war on drugs." Unpaid filings now outnumber paid cases.

Each justice traditionally received copies of the briefs in all paid cases. But beginning with the Taft Court (1921–1930), justices deferred to the chief justice and his law clerks' recommen-

Chief Justice William Rehnquist discussing cases with his law clerks in his chambers. (© *Yoichi Okamoto, Photo Researchers*)

dations on whether unpaid cases should be granted. When the number was still manageable in the 1930s, Chief Justice Hughes examined all unpaid petitions and orally reported his findings at conference. Only exceptional cases were distributed to other justices. Yet, as Frankfurter noted, Hughes's concern for indigents was such that it "made him the leader of the legal aid movement." Stone initially continued the practice, but in conference, rather than briefly stating his views, he read his law clerks' memos on each petition. "After two or three Stone terms a spontaneous feeling developed among [the justices] that instead of having Stone merely read the memorandum, full as it was, by his law clerk, it would be better to have multiple copies made of it for circulation among the brethren prior to conference."[49] During his last two years, Stone had copies of his clerks' memos sent to all the justices. At conference, the justices discussed only those Stone or others placed on a "take-up list," appended to the regular conference list that included appeals and other paid cases. Fred Vinson and Earl Warren continued this practice, except that gradually petitions in death penalty and other extraordinary cases were routinely circulated to all justices and discussed at conference. Only those unpaid cases thought to be important by a chief justice, or by another justice, were discussed at conference. All other unpaid cases were placed on a "Dead List" and formally denied at conference.

When Burger arrived at the Court, in the summer of 1969, the number of unpaid cases constituted almost half of the total docket. He immediately sought congressional approval for nine additional law clerks but succeeded in obtaining only three. These three "general" law clerks, along with one of the chief's, wrote memos on all unpaid cases. Their memos were photocopied (on the Court's newly acquired and, at the time, only copier) and sent around to the other justices. This "inordinate burden" on the chief justice's chambers, however, was not one that Burger was "willing to bear, along with an average of at least 20 hours a week on administrative duties."[50]

During his first term, Burger had the National Archives and Records Service (NARS) study the paperwork involved in processing the caseload and estimate the cost-effectiveness of alternative practices. At conference, Burger proposed three alternatives: a revolving panel of senior judges to act as "Special Masters" who would (1) review all unpaid cases and recommend a few for the justices' consideration; (2) divide all the unpaid cases among the justices, with each examining one-ninth; and (3) copy and circulate all unpaid cases, along with paid cases, to each chamber. There was vehement opposition to the first proposal. The justices refused to give up control over their docket and agenda setting. The second alternative also met opposition, and NARS estimated that it would be the most expensive and would greatly increase the workload of each chamber. The conference settled on the third option, having all unpaid cases circulated to each chamber. The increased workload would be offset by the addition of one law clerk per justice.[51]

Subsequently, in 1972, at the suggestion of Powell, the *"cert.*

pool" was established. Initially, only five justices shared their collective law clerks' memos on all paid and unpaid cases. The four most senior and liberal justices—Justices Douglas, Stewart, Brennan, and Marshall—refused to join. In particular, Douglas staunchly opposed on the grounds that petitions would receive inadequate attention from the justices and that the *cert.* pool amounted to a "Junior Supreme Court," screening cases for the justices.[52] Basically, the *cert.* pool accomplished internally what Paul Freund's Study Group proposed in 1973 as an external solution to the Court's workload problem, namely, the creation of a national appellate court to screen appeals. Freund, who had clerked for Justice Brandeis in the 1930s, took the "moral stance" that a separate appellate court was preferable to having law clerks do the screening, since such a court would be more "professional, visible, and institutionally accountable."[53] Nonetheless, with the exception of Justice Stevens, every justice appointed in the last quarter of a century joined the pool. Stevens remains the only justice to have his clerks screen all cases and write memos on those they deem important enough for him to consider.

The expanded role of law clerks in screening cases is significant and problematic. Although bright, the clerks are much less experienced than the justices. As Harlan noted, "Frequently the question whether a case is 'certworthy' is more a matter of 'feel' than of precisely ascertainable rules."[54] Indeed, the *cert.* pool and the justices' delegation of so much of their work to clerks has come into increasing criticism. Kenneth W. Starr, who clerked for Chief Justice Burger in 1975–1977, for one, urged the Court to "[d]isband the *cert.* pool," because it has come to exert too much influence with the consequence that there is not enough independent review by the justices and important cases are passed over.[55] Even within the Court, some justices have expressed concerns. In 1991, at the time of Justice Thomas's nomination, Justice Kennedy urged the chief justice to encourage the new justice to join the pool but added, "That would mean, though, that only John [Stevens] would be reviewing the petitions without the use of a pool memo." He thus proposed a change in the *cert.* pool; namely, for each case one justice would not receive a pool memo and instead would prepare a separate one, resulting in two memos. "This suggestion would impose a slight additional burden," he conceded, "but the benefit of an alternative form of review within the pool system may justify the extra effort." Blackmun agreed. "So long as there are three or four not in the pool," he explained, "there was a brake against errors that might be committed by pool members." For his part, Rehnquist admitted the "obvious weakness" in the *cert.* pool "as the number of justices who participated in it grows."[56] Yet neither he nor others were moved to change the system. Justice Stevens, though, concedes that law clerks may wield too much influence and prove "risk averse" when recommending whether or not to grant cases. Stevens, who clerked for Justice Rutledge in 1947–1948, also admits that fifty years ago he "had a lot less responsibility than some of the clerks now. They are much more involved in the entire process now."[57]

The problems of relying too much on clerks are apparent at the beginning of each term. The term runs from October to the end of June, but filings come in year-round. Until justices delegated to their clerks the responsibility of screening filings, bags of petitions and appeals were sent out by the Clerk throughout the summer to the justices wherever they were vacationing; this was done when Hughes spent his summers in Jasper Park, Canada, Stone retreated to the Isle au Haute, and Douglas made his annual trek to Goose Prairie, in the Pacific Northwest. The justices now initiate their clerks, who come aboard in July, by having them write memos on the filings that arrive in the summer. The justices review these memos before their conference at the beginning of the term. Yet these memos are written by clerks who have little experience with the Court's rules and norms.[58]

Moreover, law clerks in their initial two or three months at the Court screen about one-fifth of the cases for a term. The number of filings has grown so much that the Court now has a docket of about 2,000 cases before it even starts its term. As the caseload increased, the justices' initial conference grew longer and carried over for several days during the first week of each term.[59] The Burger Court found it necessary to begin meeting the last week of September, prior to its formal opening on the first Monday in October. During this preterm conference the justices dispose of about a thousand cases, discussing fewer than two hundred. In Burger's years as chief justice, the conference usually lasted four or five days. But Rehnquist manages to get the conference to pass on about the same number of cases in half the time, typically in two days. Thus, before the start of its term, the Court has already disposed of approximately one-fifth of its entire docket. Over four-fifths of those cases are screened out by law clerks and are never collectively discussed and considered by the justices.

Conference Discussions

The justices meet alone in conference to decide which cases to accept and to discuss the merits of those few cases on which they hear oral arguments. Throughout the term, during the weeks in which the Court hears oral arguments, it holds conferences on Wednesday afternoons to take up the four cases argued on Monday, and then on Fridays to discuss new filings and the eight cases on which it heard oral argument on Tuesday and Wednesday. In May and June, when the Court does not hear oral arguments, conferences are held on Thursdays, from ten in the morning until the mid-afternoon, with the justices breaking for a forty-five-minute lunch around twelve-thirty. A majority may vote to hold a special session during the summer months, when extraordinarily urgent cases arise—such as President Nixon's claim of "executive privilege" in *United States v. Nixon* (1974) during the Watergate episode.

Summoned by a buzzer five minutes before the hour, the

justices meet in the conference room, located directly behind the courtroom itself and next to the chief justice's chambers. The oak-paneled room is lined with *United States Reports* (containing the Court's decisions). Over the mantel of an exquisite fireplace at one end hangs a portrait of Chief Justice Marshall. Next to the fireplace stands a large rectangular table, where the justices sit. The chief justice sits at the one end and the senior associate justice at the other. Along the right-hand side of the chief justice, next to the fireplace, sit Stevens, O'Connor, and Scalia; on the left-hand side, Kennedy, Souter, Thomas, Ginsburg, and Breyer, the most junior justice.

The seating of the justices has traditionally been on the basis of seniority. But variations occur because of individual justices' preferences. In the late nineteenth century, for instance, Justice Rufus Peckham grew accustomed to the seat at the foot of the table; on Joseph McKenna's appointment, he refused to move one seat up and thus retained the junior justice's place. Sitting closest to the outside double door, the junior justice by tradition receives and sends messages that come and go by way of knocks on the door—a tradition that led Tom Clark to comment wryly, "For five years I was the highest paid doorkeeper in the world."[60]

Two conference lists are circulated to each chamber by noon on the Wednesday before the Friday conference. They structure conference discussion and enable the justices to get through their caseload. On the first list—Special List I, or the Discuss List—are jurisdictional statements, petitions for *certiorari,* and motions that are ready and worth discussing. The Discuss List typically includes between forty and fifty cases for each conference. Attached is a second list—Special List II, or what was called the Dead List—containing those cases considered unworthy of discussion. Any justice may request that a case be put on the Discuss List, and only after the chief's conference secretary has heard from all chambers do the lists become final. In addition, Chief Justice Rehnquist circulates another weekly memorandum with summaries and recommendations for miscellaneous motions that would be discussed at conference, along with another "Dead List" of motions that would simply be approved without discussion.[61] Although some of the justices favored ending the practice of automatically placing all capital cases on the Discuss List, Rehnquist decided against that change, despite the fact that capital cases are not discussed unless one or more justices specifically ask for a conference discussion of the merits of a case.[62]

At least 70 to 80 percent of the cases on the conference lists are automatically denied without discussion, and most of those that do make the Discuss List are denied as well.[63] The conference lists are an important technique for saving time and focusing attention on the few cases deemed worthy of consideration.

Each conference begins with the customary shaking of hands, which reminded Justice James Byrnes of "the usual instruction of the referee in the prize ring, 'Shake hands, go to your corner and come out fighting.' "[64] A typical conference, Rehnquist revealed in an interview, begins with those cases for which opinions have already been written and are ready to be announced the following week and moves to a consideration of motions and finally to those cases on which oral arguments were heard earlier in the week.[65] The chief justice begins discussions, which then pass from one justice to another in order of their seniority. In the absence of the chief justice, the senior associate justice leads the conference.[66]

Chief justices have significant opportunities for structuring and influencing conference discussions. As Rehnquist put it, "what the conference shapes up like is pretty much what the chief justice makes it."[67] Chief justices vary in their skills, style, and ideological orientations. Hughes is widely considered to be the greatest chief justice in this century. "Warren was closer to Hughes than any others." And in Douglas's view, "Burger was close to Vinson. Stone was somewhere in between."[68]

Hughes's photographic memory, authoritative demeanor, and personal charisma made him a respected task and social

The conference room in the Supreme Court. During a break for lunch, the chief justice's secretary arranges docket books and other materials. (*Collection of the Supreme Court of the United States*)

leader. At conference, Hughes strove to limit discussion by giving crisp three-and-a-half-minute summaries of each filing. His "machine gun style" was largely successful. Owen Roberts recalled that "so complete were his summaries that in many cases nothing needed to be added by any of his associates."[69] But Stone, a former Columbia law professor always interested in a searching examination of every issue, took a different view. He found it annoying that Hughes conducted conferences "much like a drill sergeant."[70] When Stone was elevated to the post of chief justice, he encouraged lengthy discussions, at the cost of prolonging conferences and carrying unfinished business over to special conferences later in the week. Personally inclined to debate every point, Stone was not disposed to cut short the debates that erupted from disagreements between Black and Frankfurter or Jackson. As a result, under Stone, Douglas observed, the justices were "almost in a continuous Conference." Vinson was not as intellectually equipped or as interested in the law as Stone. But he was more business-minded, though Douglas claimed that "he would filibuster for hours to have his way on a case."

Earl Warren was more of a politician, a big bear of a man with great personal charm. "We all loved him," Stewart fondly recalled. But when Warren first arrived, he was totally unprepared and unfamiliar with Court ways. Frankfurter immediately tried to bring him under his sphere of influence and to some extent succeeded in the first couple of terms. By the end of the 1956 term, however, Warren had grown wary of Frankfurter, and thereafter the latter became an increasingly overbearing pest. Warren developed a warm working relationship with Brennan. They had a practice of meeting in Brennan's chambers on Thursday afternoons to discuss the cases that would be taken up at the Friday conference. Warren still had some problems stifling Frankfurter, who irritated all by trying to dominate conference discussions. Yet Warren gradually came into his own at conference. Though not a legal scholar, he showed that he was more than a skilled politician and that he had more intellectual ability than many critics gave him credit for. Warren drew on his experiences as a former attorney general and governor of California and grew intellectually with his role as chief justice.

Burger tended to be more like Vinson. Outside of the area of criminal procedure, he did not have a "legal mind" or a "taste for the law." He was more interested (and his great accomplishments lie) in the area of judicial administration. With considerable personal charm and a good sense of humor, but also a temper, Burger did about all he could to promote collegial relations within the Court. But like Vinson, he was basically managerial in his approach, believing that the Court can adequately decide only around one hundred cases each term.

At conference, Burger likewise tended to rely heavily on his clerks' memos when opening conference discussions of cases. He claimed to make a conscious attempt not to mention every point raised in a case, in order to let the others pick up on those points and contribute to the discussion. But Burger's discussion of cases left some of the justices feeling that he was "the least prepared member of the Court." Moreover, retired Justice Powell recalled that under Chief Justice Burger, "the justices at conference [had] a great deal of latitude. You could speak as long as you wanted, and you could interrupt another justice if you wanted to." In contrast, Rehnquist, who was a junior associate justice during the Burger Court years, has said he often felt there was little for him to say by the time it came for him to give his views at conference. That was because Burger allowed more senior justices to interrupt and debate with each other. Since becoming chief justice, Rehnquist has thus discouraged such exchanges at conference in the belief that it is "very important for every one of the members of the Court to speak once on a subject before there is cross questioning . . . or second bites of the apple."[71]

During Burger's years, conference discussions occasionally became heated. Following one such conference, Rehnquist wrote his brethren, "I had a feeling that at the very close of today's Conference we may have fitted Matthew Arnold's closing lines in 'Dover Beach' wherein he refers to those 'Swept with confused alarms of Struggle and flight Where ignorant armies clash by night.' "[72] Confusion occasionally resulted over who voted how and which justices later switched votes.[73] But Burger's lack of precision, contributing to confusion, at conference permitted him to join a perceived majority and later to assign the opinion, thereby allowing him to continue to try to influence the outcome.

With Rehnquist's elevation from associate to chief justice in 1986, conferences greatly improved. Even "liberal" Justices Brennan and Marshall praised Rehnquist as a "splendid" chief justice. This is in part because Burger was not equipped to lead conference discussions of cases. By contrast, Rehnquist has the intellectual and temperamental wherewithal to be a leader, in Marshall's words, "a great chief justice." Rehnquist moves conferences along quickly; as Blackmun observed, "He gets through the agenda in a hurry" and "cuts down [on the] interchange between the justices and always says, well, that can come out in the writing."[74] Unlike his predecessor, Chief Justice Burger, Rehnquist does not allow other justices to interrupt or engage in cross-exchanges until all of the justices have spoken once and voted, in descending order of seniority. As a result, conference deliberations consume much less time and the post-conference opinion-writing and circulation process have become even more pivotal to the Court's decision-making process.

A shrewdly articulate advocate of his own views, Rehnquist has the sense of humor of a practical joker, which also helps during conferences. Besides cutting back on exchanges among the justices, Rehnquist moves conferences along by concisely and firmly discussing cases, as well as by bringing his sense of timing and humor to conference deliberations. When circulating the fourth and substantially revised draft of his opinion for the majority in *Barnes v. Glen Theatre, Inc.* (1991), in which the Court upheld Indiana's ban on "totally nude dancing," Rehnquist wrote his colleagues: "The theme of this fourth draft is a very positive one, and it can be summed up in the following verse from a once popular song."

Accentuate the positive
Eliminate the negative
Latch on to the affirmative
Don't mess with Mr. In Between

By virtually all accounts, Rehnquist's success as chief justice is attributable to his strong "social" and "task" leadership, in addition to his sense of humor and congenial manner. Rehnquist reintroduced an informal "End of Term" dinner for the justices, and more of them gather together for lunch after hearing oral arguments than did during the Burger Court years.[75] Rehnquist also generally succeeded in bringing the Court's annual term to a close by the end of June. He did so by adopting certain opinion-assignment rules and by establishing the norm that "*all* majority opinions are expected to circulate by June 1, and *all* dissents by June 15."[76] As to his opinion assignments, Rehnquist generally sought to "give everyone approximately the same number of assignments of opinions for the Court during any one term," except that after the midterm point he gave more weight to whether a justice (1) already had for a month or more an uncirculated majority opinion, or (2) an uncirculated dissenting opinion, and (3) had not "voted in a case in which both majority and dissenting opinions [had] circulated."[77] Although Rehnquist's strategy for managing the Court's work largely succeeded, it drew some criticism. Justice Stevens complained that "although the prompt completion of a Supreme Court opinion is important, the quality of our work product is even more so. Too much emphasis on speed can have an adverse effect on quality." Moreover, Stevens pointed out that justices usually work on several opinions at once and the chief justice's deadlines could "adversely affect the orderly production of a group of opinions."[78]

There was once a good deal of give-and-take in conference, but that is no longer possible in light of the Court's heavy caseload. There is simply no longer time for each justice to discuss and deliberate over what the others have said and then to vote on each case. Some justices, particularly those newly appointed, find this disturbing and hoped for "more of a roundtable discussion." "In fact," Scalia said, "to call our discussion of a case a conference is really something of a misnomer. It's much more a statement of the views of each of the nine justices."[79] More discussion, however, he admits, would probably not contribute much or lead justices to change their minds when voting on cases. This is because the justices confront similar issues year after year, and as Rehnquist noted, "it would be surprising if [justices] voted differently than they had the previous time."[80]

The justices come to conference prepared to vote and to explain very briefly their position on each case. "By the time that everyone has had his say," Justice White explained, "the vote is usually quite clear; but, if not, it will be formally taken."[81] The justices once voted in ascending order of seniority. Clark, for one, gave the following rationale for this manner of voting: "Ever since Chief Justice Marshall's day the formal vote begins with the junior Justice and moves up through the ranks of seniority, the Chief Justice voting last. Hence the juniors are not influenced by the vote of their elders."[82] A quaint rationale, but the procedure has not been regularly followed since Hughes was chief justice. A number of the justices have said that that procedure broke down during Stone's time as chief justice (1941–1946) because he was unable to control conference discussions of cases, but there is also some evidence that his successor, Chief Justice Vinson (1946–1953), renewed the procedure.[83] In interviews, however, neither Brennan nor Burger could recall when that procedure was last strictly adhered to by the Court. In any event, the caseload is now so heavy that there is no longer time for each justice to discuss and deliberate over what the others have said, and then vote on each case. The justices come prepared to vote when explaining how they view each case. As Black emphasized, it is "a fiction that everybody always waits for the youngest man to express himself, or vote, as they say. Well that's fiction."[84] Likewise, Blackmun affirmed, "we vote by seniority, as you know, despite [the fact] that some texts say we vote by juniority."[85] Moreover, shortly after Rehnquist was elevated to the chief justiceship in 1986, Justice Stevens, when approving certain changes in the docket book, jested that, "Since we now have a Chief Justice who experienced the disadvantage of speaking only after most of his colleagues had already voted," perhaps "he might be sympathetic to considering a return to the Court's old practice of having the discussion of argued cases proceed down the ladder but have the voting then go up the ladder?"[86]

Immediately after conference, the chief justice traditionally had the task of reporting the votes to the Clerk. Burger delegated this task to a junior justice, initially to Rehnquist and then to O'Connor. This was done in part because Burger occasionally made mistakes recording conference votes. All the justices have large docket books in which they may note votes and discussions for their personal records. But the junior justice now tells the Clerk which cases have been granted oral arguments and which have been denied. The Clerk then notifies both sides in a case granted review. The petitioner has forty-five days to file briefs on the merits, and the respondent then has thirty days to file briefs on the merits. Once all briefs (forty copies of each) are submitted, the Clerk schedules the case for oral argument.

Considering the volume of the Court's business and the justices' ideological differences, unanimity in case selection is remarkably high. Unanimity is a rather consistent pattern in case selection, regardless of the Court's composition. During the chief justiceships of Vinson and Warren, the political scientist Marie Provine found, on the basis of a study of Harold Burton's docket books for the period 1947–1957, 82 percent of all cases were unanimously disposed; and of these, 79 percent were denied and 3 percent were granted review.[87] During that period, the Court disposed of approximately fifteen hundred cases each term.

The Court's docket has since more than doubled, but an examination of Brennan's docket book for the 1973 term nevertheless reveals comparable unanimity. Almost 79 percent of all petitions and appeals were initially unanimously disposed. Some 72 percent of the denials of *certiorari* were unanimous. But the number of petitions unanimously granted dropped by half, to less than 2 percent.

Despite the Court's increasing caseload in the 1980s and

1990s, its internal norms for discussing a limited number of cases and granting fewer cases review were only strengthened. During his time on the bench, Justice White periodically had his law clerks keep track of the flow of the Court's business. For the October 1985–1986 term, for instance, he determined that on average only 26 percent of the cases on the Court's conference lists were discussed and just 3 percent of the total cases were granted review.[88] As Justice Brennan's 1973 docket books already revealed, White found that the overwhelming number of cases were simply denied, dismissed for lack of jurisdiction, or "granted, vacated, and remanded." In addition, as the case-load steadily increased and Congress expanded the Court's discretionary jurisdiction by further eliminating mandatory appeals under the 1988 Act to Improve the Administration of Justice, the number of petitions unanimously denied rose to 88 percent in the 1990–1991 term, registering the institutional norm or consensus within the Court that only a limited number of cases may be granted. The extent of greater unanimity in case selection is illustrated on page 211.[89]

What explains the patterns of unanimity in case selection, despite the changing composition of the Court?

Agreement by a majority or more on case selection reflects the interplay of a number of factors. Most important, institutional norms promote a shared conception of the role of the Court as a tribunal for resolving only issues of national importance. With the increasing business of the Court, the justices have come to accept the following view, first expressed by Chief Justice William Taft:

No litigant is entitled to more than two chances, namely, to the original trial and to a review, and the intermediate courts of review are provided for that purpose. When a case goes beyond that, it is not primarily to preserve the rights of the litigants. The Supreme Court's function is for the purpose of expounding and stabilizing principles of law for the benefit of the people of the country, passing upon constitutional questions and other important questions of law for the public benefit.[90]

DISPOSITION IN CASE SELECTION, 1990–1991 TERM

Disposition	Unanimous (%)	Divided (%)	Total Number (%)
Denied petition	3,852 (88.0)	222 (5.0)	4,074 (93.1)
Granted petition	70 (1.6)	97 (2.2)	168 (3.8)
Appeal accepted	3 (0.06)		3 (0.06)
Appeal affirmed	2 (0.04)	2 (0.04)	4 (0.09)
Appeal dismissed	1 (0.02)	1 (0.02)	2 (0.04)
Miscellaneous	117 (2.67)	5 (0.01)	122 (2.78)
Total	4,046 (92.5)	327 (7.47)	4,373

Justices agree that the overwhelming proportion of cases are "frivolous" and that there are a limited number of cases to which they may give full consideration.

These factors tend to overshadow ideological divisions in case selection. Ideological differences appear less pronounced in voting on case selection than in voting on the merits of cases disposed by written opinions. The selection process may appear as "the first battleground on the merits,"[91] but principally for those justices at either end of the Court's ideological spectrum.

THE RULE OF FOUR AND WHAT IT MEANS

When Congress gave the Court discretionary jurisdiction in the Judiciary Act of 1925, by substituting petitions for *certiorari* for mandatory appeals, the justices developed the informal rule of four to decide which petitions they would grant. During conference, at least four justices must agree that a case warrants oral argument and consideration by the full Court.

The rule of four evolved in a flexible, collegial manner. But when urging Congress to pass the Judiciary Act of 1925, Justice Willis Van Devanter contended that the rule of four would ensure that important cases would still be granted and that expanding the Court's discretionary jurisdiction would not impair the administration of justice. "We always grant the petitions when as many as four think that it should be granted and sometimes when as many as three think that way. We proceed upon the theory," he explained, "that, if that number out of the nine are impressed with the thought that the case is one that ought to be heard and decided by us, the petition should be granted."[92]

When the caseload was lighter than it is today, exceptions were often made to the rule of four. Influential justices and persuasive arguments occasionally won cases a hearing on fewer than four votes.[93] Even during the 1930s, under Chief Justice Hughes, the rule was rather liberally applied. As he explained, "*certiorari* is always granted if four justices think it should be, and not infrequently, when 3, or even 2, justices strongly urge the grant."[94] Justice Stanley Reed once pleaded with Hughes:

Won't you consider further the soundness of the suggestions made yesterday in Conference that three votes should be sufficient to bring up Bethlehem [*United States v. Bethlehem Steel Corporation* (1940)]? There is really no absolute rule that four votes are necessary when a full Court sits. Certainly when there are only six justices sitting, it seems that three should be sufficient to justify a hearing on the merits.[95]

To pressure the chief justice further, Reed emphasized the agreement with his view of two others, Frankfurter and Douglas, who often were at odds with each other. On another occasion, when a petition in a capital punishment case was denied, Frankfurter appealed to emotion: "On any view, these petitioners are worthless creatures. But the fact that worthless creatures may invoke the protection of the Constitution is not the least of the glories of our country."[96] Yet another time, Douglas adopted a different tactic. He agreed to supply the necessary fourth vote if the other three justices would limit their grant of a case to one of several issues presented.[97]

After a conference vote denying a case, three justices may still find or persuade another to vote to grant the case at the next conference.[98] A strategy sometimes employed by justices in order to win votes to grant *cert.* is the circulation of dissents from the denial of *certiorari*. Such a tactic may be particularly effective if it is joined by one or more justices. It also became a rather common practice in the 1970s and 1980s, after some justices regularly began to publish their votes to grant and dissents from the denial of *cert.* In the 1940s and 1950s, when Justices Black and Douglas occasionally noted their dissents from denial, they provoked debate within the Court.[99] Justice Frankfurter, for one, complained that such dissents threatened the "integrity of the *certiorari* process."[100] Nevertheless, dissents from denials greatly increased in the 1970s and 1980s, largely due to Justice Douglas's making it a practice to publish every dissent from denial of review. He did so in opposition to the creation of the *cert.* pool in 1972 and some others followed his practice. Notably, as illustrated below, Justice White started publishing his dissents in 1973 and continued doing so throughout his career.[101] He did so largely to flag cases in which he identified a conflict among circuit court rulings that he deemed to demand the Court's resolution. Moreover, as the plenary docket began to shrink, his notations increased significantly.

But, with the retirement of White and others in the late 1980s and early 1990s, the publication of dissents from denial largely fell out of practice; except when justices want to record strong opposition to the denial of *cert.*, such dissents are now rarely published.

The rule of four, to be sure, operates in a fraction of cases because of the increasing caseload. Whereas in 1941 the Court acted on 951 petitions, that number had doubled by 1961; it doubled again, with a total of 4,066 petitions, by 1981, and then rose to 5,191 in 1990–1991.[102] Stevens estimated, on the basis of the docket books of Harold Burton, that during the Vinson Court, in 1946–1947, over 25 percent of the cases granted had the support of no more than four justices. Brennan's docket book for 1973 reveals that 19 percent of the cases accepted for oral argument received less than a majority vote. Of those cases granted, 80 percent were on the basis of a vote of five or more of the justices, and only 27 percent as the result of a bare

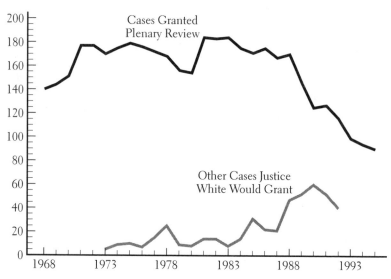

DISSENTS FROM DENIAL: ADDITIONAL CASES JUSTICE WHITE VOTED TO GRANT, 1968–1995

majority. By contrast, in the 1990–1991 term the number of cases granted by less than a majority rose to 22 percent, and 77 percent were granted on the basis of a vote of five or more justices, of which only 19 percent was the result of a bare majority vote.[103]

The small number of petitions granted upon the rule of four raises two important questions about the Court's agenda setting. First, since the rule of four operates in a small number of cases, is it useful any longer? Second, since only about 2 percent of *all* petitions are granted on less than a majority vote, what is the meaning of a denial of *certiorari?*

The caseload and institutional norms push toward a limiting of the operation of the rule of four. But the rule remains useful, particularly if there is a bloc of justices who share the same ideological orientation. For they may work together in picking cases and setting the Court's agenda. The rule of four is also instrumental in establishing a threshold for granting cases and

**NOTATIONS OF VOTES TO GRANT AND
DISSENTS FROM DENIAL OF REVIEW, 1981–1995°**

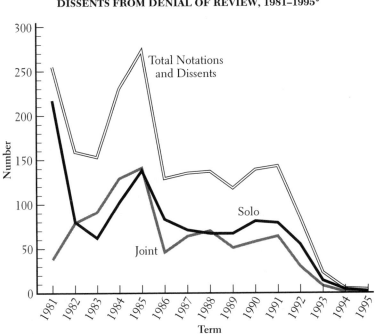

°Total Notations of Votes to Grant and Dissents from the Denial of Review includes the number of individual and joint notations and dissents. Solo notations and dissents include the number of cases in which a single justice noted his or her vote to grant or dissent from denial of review. Joint notations and dissents indicate the number issued by two or more justices together.

thus managing the Court's plenary docket. In the early 1980s, when the Court was granting and deciding over 180 cases a year, Justice Stevens once proposed abandoning the rule of four and instead granting petitions only on a majority vote.[104] He did so as a counter to Burger's 1983 proposal that Congress establish a special tribunal to which one-fourth to one-third of the cases on which the Court now hears oral argument might be referred (and thereby relieve the justices' workload). Stevens estimated that abandoning the rule of four would eliminate as many as one-fourth of the cases granted. In 1973, 19 percent of the cases granted were on the basis of four votes, but Stevens's docket books show that percentage rose from 1979 to 1981 to between 23 and 30 percent of the cases accepted for oral argument.

Justice Stevens's proposal for discarding the rule of four met strong opposition, however. In particular, Justice Marshall contended that the Court could not abandon the rule without consulting Congress, since Van Devanter and others had promised to abide by it when pressing for the enactment of the Judiciary Act of 1925.[105] But, as Stevens noted, "Since [the Judiciary Act of 1925] the Court has made a number of changes—most notably abandoning the practice of discussing every petition at conference and making extensive use of law clerks' memoranda—without worrying about congressional approval, and I see no reason why we could not decide to adopt a Rule of Five if we thought it prudent to do so."[106]

With the diminished plenary docket, Stevens no longer favors abandoning the rule of four.[107] Yet, his proposal remains instructive, for it highlights the importance of the rule of four as a threshold for granting cases and imposing self-discipline in setting the plenary docket. As Stevens repeatedly reminded his colleagues, who complained about the workload in the 1970s and 1980s, "if we simply acted with greater restraint during the case selection process, we might be able to manage the docket effectively under the Rule of Four."

What Stevens did not mention at the time was that other justices were casting so-called "Join-3 votes."[108] A Join-3 vote is a vote to provide a fourth vote if others vote to grant review, but is otherwise considered as voting to deny. The rule of four was firmly in place until the Burger Court years, though neither Chief Justice Rehnquist nor Justices Blackmun and Stevens have recalled "any definitive discussion about the use of the [Join-3] vote."[109] One possible explanation for the practice of casting Join-3 votes in the 1970s and 1980s is that when leading conferences, Burger began voting to join three and others did the same. He may have done so because his discussion of cases was often vague and also because he felt pressures to fill the expanded space on the oral argument calendar once the time allotted each side was reduced from one hour to thirty minutes in 1970, permitting the granting and hearing of more cases. In addition, as earlier noted, in response to the creation of the *cert*. pool in 1972 several justices began threatening and publishing dissents from denial, often joined by one or more other justices. And in anticipation of them, Burger and others may have been inclined to cast Join-3 votes. In any event, it is clear from Justice Marshall's bench memos and docket books that some justices cast a large number of Join-3 votes, whereas others rarely (if ever) did, as indicated on page 218.

Join-3 votes arguably lowered the threshold for granting cases, thereby weakening the self-discipline imposed by the rule of four and contributing to the inflation of the plenary docket in the 1970s and early 1980s, when between 150 and 180 cases were annually decided. The plenary docket in turn, then, may have declined in the late 1980s and 1990s (as illustrated on page 219) in part because of the retirements of those who cast such votes and their replacement on the bench with justices, like Scalia and Thomas, who instead simply vote to grant or deny review.

What remains the significance of this Court's denial of *certiorari?*[110] Denial of *certiorari* purportedly "imparts no expression of opinion upon the merits of the case."[111] The Court, however, is "not quite of one mind on the subject," as Jackson observed. "Some say denial means nothing, others say it means nothing much. Realistically, the first position is untenable and the second is unintelligible."[112]

Justice Frankfurter explained the orthodox view that "a denial no wise implies agreement" on the merits of a case: "It simply means that fewer than four members of the Court deemed it desirable to review a decision of the lower court as a matter of 'sound judicial discretion.' Pertinent considerations of judicial policy here come into play."[113]

JUSTICES CASTING JOIN-3 VOTES, 1979–1990

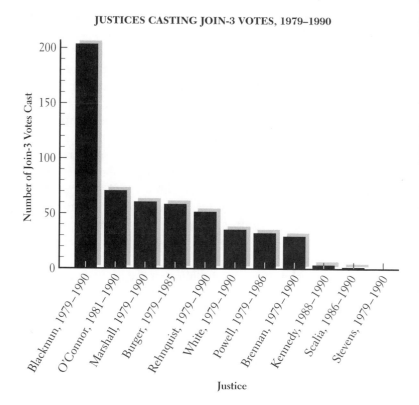

Justices may have any number of reasons for denying *certiorari*. But as Jackson observed, "Because no one knows all that a denial means, does it mean that it means nothing?"[114] A denial cannot mean "nothing much." The Court does not grant *certiorari* to review the facts of cases. Do denials thus convey approval of the lower-court ruling? In *Brown v. Allen* (1953), involving federal courts' jurisdiction over *habeas corpus* appeals from state courts, three justices indicated that when issues are repetitiously raised, denials should be understood as affirming the lower court's ruling. Yet if a grant or a denial is based on the justices' view of the merits of a case, then a paradox results

NUMBER OF CASES GRANTED PLENARY REVIEW, 1968–1998

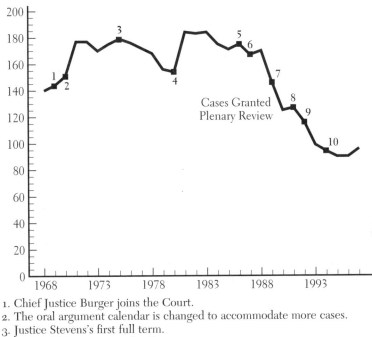

Cases Granted Plenary Review

1. Chief Justice Burger joins the Court.
2. The oral argument calendar is changed to accommodate more cases.
3. Justice Stevens's first full term.
4. Justice O'Connor joins the Court.
5. Rehnquist's first term as chief justice.
6. Justice Powell's last term.
7. Justice Brennan's last term.
8. Justice Marshall's last term.
9. Justice White's last term.
10. Justice Blackmun's last term.

in voting on case selection. Since only four justices may grant a case, a minority binds the majority to deciding the merits of a case that they do not think need to be considered. In all other respects, the Court operates by majority vote. "Even though a minority may bring a case here for oral argument," Frankfurter contended, "that does not mean that the majority has given up its right to vote on the ultimate disposition of the case as conscience dictates."[115] Frankfurter made a practice of refusing to vote on the merits of some cases that he thought the Court had improperly granted.[116] If Frankfurter's practice were widely accepted, the rule of four would be superfluous. As Douglas objected, "If four can grant and the opposing five dismiss, then the four cannot get a decision of the case on the merits. The integrity of the four vote rule would then be impaired."[117]

Because the Court declines to take a case, it does not follow that "[i]t means nothing else."[118] The denial of *certiorari* cannot be considered completely meaningless, for a number of reasons. Brennan's docket books from 1973 show that 98 percent of the cases granted or denied were on the basis of a vote of a majority or more. Stevens's proposal for replacing the rule of four by a majority vote would have simply acknowledged what already basically occurs in practice. Adoption of a rule of five, even more than the present voting pattern, of course, would legitimize the view that denials amount to passing on the merits of cases. Denials inevitably send signals as to which and what kind of cases "do not present questions of sufficient gravity."[119]

Why don't the justices simply explain what they are doing, why they are denying review? They don't, because the power to deny review enables the Court to dispose of its caseload, and to explain each denial would increase the justices' workload. As Justice Stone put it, "to state a reason which would be accurately expressed and would satisfy the members of the Court, would require an amount of time and energy that is simply impossible to give."[120] A denial without explanation also gives the justices greater flexibility in agenda setting. They may let an issue percolate in the lower courts and then take it up in a later case without feeling bound by their earlier denial.[121]

Because denials are usually not explained, there may be no way of knowing how a majority views the merits of particular cases. Liberal members of the Burger and Rehnquist Courts dissented from the denial of a large number of cases dealing with obscenity and capital punishment. And their dissents illustrate the difficulties of determining the meaning of a denial of *certiorari*.

After a bare majority of the Burger Court redefined the standards for obscenity and pornography in *Miller v. California* (1973), Brennan and Marshall dissented from the denial of later similar cases. Stevens, in an unusual concurring opinion to the denial of one such case, explained the futility of granting cases based on the rule of four when a majority of the Court has already expressed its view of the merits:

> For there is no reason to believe that the majority of the Court which decided *Miller v. California* . . . is any less adamant than the minority. Accordingly, regardless of how I might vote on the merits after full argument, it would be pointless to grant *certiorari* in case after case of this character only to have *Miller* reaffirmed time after time . . . . [U]ntil a valid reason for voting to grant one of these petitions is put forward, I shall continue to vote to deny. In the interest of conserving scarce law library space, I shall not repeat this explanation every time I cast such a vote.[122]

Brennan and Marshall also opposed the Court's upholding of the constitutionality of capital punishment, and they had programmed into the Court's computer system an opinion dissenting from denial of review and expressing their position on the death penalty which automatically accompanied every such case denied review. Shortly before announcing that he would retire at the end of the 1994–1995 term, Blackmun also anounced in a dissent from the denial of *certiorari* that he opposed the imposition of capital punishment. And in his remaining time on the bench he followed Brennan's and Marshall's practice of noting his dissent from the Court's denial of each case involving the death penalty.[123]

Denial of *certiorari* is an important technique for managing the Court's caseload. But its meaning in particular cases may be far from clear. The Court has few fixed rules, and even the rule of four is not "an absolutely inflexible rule." In 1980, in two capital punishment cases, *four* justices issued dissenting opinions from the denial of review of both cases. Each justice indicated that, but for one more vote, he would have granted the case, vacated the ruling below, and remanded the case to the lower court.[124]

So too, in 1990 *four* justices dissented from the majority's denial of an application to stay an injunction against protesters claiming that they were denied their First Amendment right of freedom of speech in *Hirsh v. City of Atlanta.* Justice Kennedy, joined by Justices Brennan, Marshall, and Scalia, argued that an application for a stay of the enforcement of a court order should be treated as a petition for *certiorari* and that the case should have been granted review. In another ironic twist of fate, in 1992 four justices voted to grant review of a death sentence imposed on James Edward Smith. But before oral arguments could be heard, Smith was scheduled for execution and a majority of the Rehnquist Court declined to grant a stay of his execution, despite four votes for granting review and hearing oral arguments in the case. Following his execution, the Rehnquist Court simply declared the case moot.

Again, in 1992, four justices dissented from the denial of *certiorari* in *McCleary v. Navarro,* which appealed a decision concerning whether a police officer, who had a warrant but had broken into the wrong house, was entitled to immunity from being sued. The appellate court's ruling came down just a few days after the Court announced in *Hunter v. Bryant* (1991) a new legal standard for determining immunity in such cases. By denying *certiorari* in *McCleary* the majority left the lower court's decision and reliance on a standard rejected in *Hunter* undisturbed. And Chief Justice Rehnquist, along with Justices O'Connor, Thomas, and White, dissented. They would have summarily reversed and remanded the case back for reconsideration in light of *Hunter,* however, rather than grant *certiorari* and allocate scarce oral argument time to the case. In sum, as the rule of four has evolved and the caseload grown it rather strictly applies only to granting petitions plenary consideration. Even if four justices think that an application ought to be treated like a *certiorari* petition, as in *Hirsh,* or a summary judgment entered instead of denying *certiorari*, as in *McCleary,* they may be forced to silently acquiesce in or dissent from the majority's disposition. In addition, the Court's majority may override the rule of four, after a case has been granted and oral arguments heard, with a vote to "DIG," that is, to "dismiss as improvidently granted." Not surprisingly, when that occurs the other four may become outraged and dissent. One such controversy led Justices Brennan and Rehnquist to suggest a procedure for handling "Digs and the Rule of Four." While rejecting the view that "there *should* be an absolute rule against" such dismissing, they agreed that "comity to our colleagues and respect for the Rule of Four should make DIG'ing . . . relatively rare." They therefore proposed that "the five voting to DIG set out their reasons in a published opinion," but also that "our policy on this issue is a matter best left unpublished and should be treated as an internal rule."[125]

Thus, the rule of four has come to operate only with regard to granting cases oral argument; on all other matters the majority's will prevails. Although enabling the Court to manage its business, denials invite confusion and the suspicion, as Justice Jackson once observed, "that this Court no longer respects impersonal rules of law but is guided in these matters by personal impression which from time to time may be shared by a majority of the justices."

DECIDING CASES WITHOUT FULL CONSIDERATION

The distinction between mandatory and discretionary review of appeals and *certiorari* petitions has basically disappeared in the Court's process of deciding what to decide. Before Congress eliminated virtually all of the remaining mandatory appeals in

1988, fewer than 20 percent of all appeals were granted oral argument and full consideration. Instead of giving mandatory appeals the full-dress treatment, however, the Court summarily decided them. In other words, without hearing oral arguments, the Court simply affirmed, vacated, or reversed the lower court ruling, or dismissed the appeal for failing to present a substantial federal question or for want of jurisdiction. As the caseload grew, the number of summary decisions increased as well, until 1988 when Congress replaced most provisions for mandatory appeals with provisions for *certiorari* petitions. The number disposed summarily was very small in the 1940s but in the 1950s and 1960s rose to about fifty, and in the 1970s and 1980s frequently exceeded eighty per term.[126]

A large number of summary dispositions of appeals were unanimous. Like *certiorari* petitions, most appeals were thought to be insubstantial and frivolous. In a 1982 letter to Congressman Robert Kastenmeier urging the elimination of the Court's remaining mandatory appellate jurisdiction (which Congress finally did in 1988), the justices explained:

It is impossible for the Court to give plenary consideration to all the mandatory appeals it receives; to have done so, for example, during the 1980 Term would have required at least 9 additional weeks of oral argument or a seventy-five percent increase in the argument calendar. To handle the volume of appeals presently being received, the Court must dispose of many cases summarily, often without written opinion.[127]

Summarily decided cases enable the Court to cut down on its workload. But they may also engender confusion among the lower courts. Summary decisions take the form of rather cryptic orders or *per curiam* (unsigned) opinions. Like denials of *certiorari* petitions, they invite confusion over how the Court views the merits of a case and the lower-court ruling. The problem is one of the Court's own making. The Court holds that summarily decided cases do not have the same precedential weight as plenary decisions but that they are nonetheless binding on lower courts "until such time as the Court informs [them] that [they] are not."[128]

Another problem is that some cases deserving a full consideration may besummarily decided by the Court. In *Goldwater v. Carter* (1979), for example, the Court issued an order vacating the lower-court decision in a dispute between several congressmen and the President over the termination of a defense treaty with Taiwan. Blackmun and White viewed the decision as "indefensible" in failing to "set the case for oral argument and giv[ing] it the plenary consideration it so obviously deserved."

The justices also occasionally *grant certiorari, vacate* the judgment below, and *remand* the case to the lower court, or, as it is known within the Court, summarily disposing of cases with a "GVR" order. This is done with cases raising an issue that has been decided in another case, and thus they are granted, vacated, and remanded for reconsideration in light of the Court's recent ruling on the issue. The Court has also made it clear that it will issue GVRs when the federal government confesses making an error in the lower court and switches its position on the issues presented.[129]

Agenda for Policy-making — Who Benefits, Who Loses?

The power to decide what to decide entails more than merely selecting a manageable number of cases for oral argument and full consideration. The Court also sets its own substantive agenda for policy-making.

The Court did not always have the power to set its own agenda, nor did its docket include the kinds of major issues of public policy that arrive today. During its first decade, the Court had little important business. Over 40 percent consisted in admiralty and prize cases. About 50 percent raised issues of common law, and the remaining 10 percent dealt with matters

like equity, including one probate case.[130] Not until the chief
justiceship of John Marshall did the Court assert its power of
judicial review. Still, only a tiny fraction of its business raised
important issues of public policy. By the late nineteenth century,
the Court's business had gradually changed in response to developments in American society. The number of admiralty cases,
for instance, had by 1882 dwindled to less than 4 percent of the
total. Almost 40 percent of the decisions handed down still dealt
with either disputes at common law or questions of jurisdiction
and procedure in federal courts. Over 43 percent of the Court's
business, however, involved interpreting congressional statutes.
Less than 4 percent of the cases raised issues of constitutional
law. The decline in admiralty and common law litigation, and
the increase in statutory interpretation, reflected the impact of
the Industrial Revolution and the growing governmental regulation of social and economic relations. In this century, the trend
has continued. Throughout the 1980s and into the 1990s, about
47 percent of the cases decided by opinion involved matters of
constitutional law. Around 38 percent dealt with the interpretation of congressional statutes. The remaining 15 percent
resolved issues of administrative law, taxation, patents, and
claims. The table on page 227 illustrates the changing nature of
the Court's business.[131]

The current Court's power to pick the cases it wants from a
very large docket enables it to assume the role of a super legislature. The overwhelming number of cases on the docket
involve indigents' claims and issues of criminal procedure. Yet,
as is indicated below, few are selected and decided on merits.
Cases raising other issues of constitutional law have a better
chance of being selected; so do cases involving statutory, administrative, and regulatory matters. These are all areas in which the
government has an interest in legitimating its policies. The Court
thus functions like a roving commission, selecting and deciding
only issues of national importance for the governmental process.

The Court directly and indirectly encourages interest groups

The Business of the Supreme Court, October Terms, 1825–1995

Subject of Court Opinions	1825	1875	1925	1930	1935	1945	1955	1965	1975	1985	1995
Admiralty	2	5	8	2	1	3	1	0	0	2	3
Antitrust	0	0	2	5	3	2	2	8	3	4	1
Bankruptcy	0	13	9	1	9	7	1	5	0	1	2
Bill of Rights (civil liberties; except rights of accused)	0	2	3	3	3	9	6	15	8	22	9
Commerce clause											
1. Constitutionality *and* construction of Federal legislation, regulation, and administrative action	0	0	31	17	13	28	28	13	31	36	13
2. Constitutionality of state regulation	0	2	2	4	11	4	1	8	27	2	2
Common law	10	81	11	5	3	3	0	0	0	2	2
Misc. statutory interpretation	4	16	15	14	16	9	16	12	4	1	11
Due process											
1. Economic interests	0	0	20	8	8	3	1	0	0	3	3
2. Procedure of rights of accused contained in Bill of Rights	0	2	3	3	2	5	7	18	34	41	16
Impairment of contract/just compensation	0	1	4	0	6	1	0	1	0	1	1
Native Americans	0	0	7	3	0	2	1	0	4	4	1
International law, war, and peace	2	5	6	0	2	12	3	0	1	2	2
Jurisdiction, procedure, and practice	4	30	29	21	27	27	17	16	4	27	16
Land legislation	0	11	3	0	3	0	0	0	0	1	0
Patents, copyright, and trademarks	1	8	4	12	5	2	1	1	1	0	2
Slaves	3	0	0	0	0	0	0	0	0	0	0
Other suits against the government and officials	0	12	17	1	1	2	0	5	16	8	3
Suits by states	0	0	8	6	5	0	2	5	6	0	4
Taxation (federal and state)	0	5	27	59	40	19	7	5	4	5	1

and the government to litigate issues of public policy. The Court selects and decides "only those cases which present questions whose resolution will have immediate importance far beyond the particular facts and parties involved." Attorneys whose cases are accepted by the Court "are, in a sense, prosecuting or defending class actions"; as Chief Justice Vinson emphasized, "you represent your clients, but [more crucially] tremendously important principles, upon which are based the plans, hopes and aspirations of a great many people throughout the country."[132]

For the poor, minorities, and interest groups, as the Warren Court observed in *NAACP v. Button* (1963), "under the conditions of modern government, litigation may well be the sole practicable avenue open to a minority to petition for redress of grievances."[133] Interest-group litigation, however, is by no means confined to the poor and minorities. Pointing to the successes of the American Civil Liberties Union (ACLU), Lewis Powell, shortly before his appointment to the Court, urged the Chamber of Commerce of the United States to consider that "the judiciary may be the most important instrument for social, economic and political change."[134]

Interest groups from the entire political spectrum look to the Court to decide issues of public policy: from business organizations and corporations in the late nineteenth century to the Jehovah's Witnesses in the 1930s; the ACLU and NAACP in the 1950s and 1960s; "liberal" women's rights groups and consumer and environmental protection groups, such as the National Organization for Women (NOW), Common Cause, "Nader's Raiders," the Sierra Club, the Environmental Defense Fund, and the Natural Resources Defense Council; as well as a growing number of conservative "public-interest" law firms like the Pacific Legal Foundation, the Mountain States Legal Foundation, and the Washington Legal Foundation.[135] "This is government by lawsuit," Justice Jackson declared. "These constitutional lawsuits are the stuff of power politics in America."[136]

Interest-group activities and "public-interest" law firms offer a number of advantages for litigating policy disputes. They command greater financial resources than the average individual. A single suit may settle a large number of claims, and the issues are not as likely to be compromised or settled out of court. Interest-group law firms typically specialize in particular kinds of lawsuits. They are therefore able to litigate more skillfully and over a longer period of time. There are also tactical opportunities. Litigants may be chosen to bring "test cases," and those cases may be coordinated with other litigation and the activities of other organizations.

Interest-group litigation has proceeded and proliferated on the theory that politically disadvantaged groups are more successful in achieving their legal-policy goals through a litigation campaign in the courts, instead of pursuing their causes in legislatures and through the political process. The NAACP Legal Defense Fund's litigation strategy for ending segregated public schools resulted in *Brown v. Board of Education* (1954) and provided a model for planned litigation that other interest groups have followed.[137] However, not all of the litigation engaged in by the NAACP Legal Defense Fund, and most other interest groups, is planned or organized. Much is "responsive and reflexive,"[138] and recent studies suggest that interest-group litigation may not fare any better than individual and nongroup lawsuits.[139] Interest groups may also champion litigation to command media attention and publicity for their causes, to maintain or attract supporters, as well as to give or keep an issue like abortion salient in electoral politics.[140]

In addition, interest groups may enter litigation as third parties by filing *amicus curiae* briefs, which are no longer neutral or friendly, but partisan. In the reverse discrimination case of *Regents of the University of California v. Bakke* (1978), 120 organizations joined 58 *amicus* briefs filed before the Court: 83 for the University of California, 32 for Bakke, and 5 urging the Court not to accept the case. The number of *amicus* briefs filed in *Bakke,* however, was exceeded during the abortion controversy over *Webster v. Reproductive Health Services* (1989), when a record number 78 briefs were filed. When the Court handed down its ruling in *Webster* the justices cited 29 separate *amicus* briefs, several more than once, for a total of 43 citations. Chief Justice Rehnquist and Justice O'Connor each had ten citations to *amici* briefs in their opinions, while dissenting Justices Blackmun and Stevens had seven and sixteen, respectively. Only Justice Scalia's concurring opinion made no reference to the briefs or other sources. In *Webster amici* briefs on both sides clearly helped shape the debate over abortion within the Court.[141] Justices increasingly cite *amici* briefs, though of course they differ in their propensity to do so. From the 1953 to 1991 terms, for example, *amici* briefs were most often cited in the opinions of Justices Brennan (755), White (660), Stevens (607), Blackmun (531), Marshall (509), Powell (458), Rehnquist (453), and Douglas (416). Yet, when *amici* brief citations relative to the total number of opinions are compared, Justices Powell and O'Connor lead as the top citers, followed by Justices Stevens and Marshall, Blackmun, White, Burger, and Brennan.[142]

Do justices select cases because they are brought by particular interest groups? There is no evidence that they do and considerable evidence that they do not. One study has found that *certiorari* petitions are more likely to be granted when they are accompanied by one or more *amicus* briefs urging the Court to grant review.[143] Some political scientists hypothesize that justices select cases on the basis of certain "cues" in the filings.[144] According to "cue theory," justices disproportionately grant cases in which one or more of the following "cues" are present: (1) a civil liberties issue, (2) disagreement in lower courts, and (3) the involvement of the federal government as the petitioner. Studies of Burton's docket books for 1947–1957 and of samples drawn from the petitions granted and denied during 1967–1968 and 1976–1977, however, indicate that the strongest correlation between any of these "cues" and the acceptance of a case is the participation of the federal government. Although justices' attitudes toward upperdogs (the government and corporations) or underdogs (individuals and minorities) may predispose their voting on whether to grant a case,[145] the overwhelming number of filings are unanimously denied. Institutional norms promote a shared conception of the work appropriate for the Court. Besides, the justices tend not to look for "cues" to reduce their workload but simply to rely on their clerks to screen cases.

The government has a distinct advantage in getting cases accepted, but its higher rate of success is not surprising. Since the creation of the office in 1870, the solicitor general of the United States assumed responsibility for representing the federal government. From the Court's perspective, the solicitor general performs an invaluable service. He screens all prospective federal appeals and petitions and decides which should be taken to the Court. Unlike any other petitioner, the solicitor general has the opportunity of selecting from a large number of cases around the country and appealing only those likely to win Court approval. Since he typically argues all government cases before the Court, the solicitor general has intimate knowledge of the justices and has been characterized as the Court's "ninth-and-a-half" member. Given these tactical advantages, the government's applications for review are usually granted. Between 1954 and 1985, some 71 percent of the government's cases were granted each year, whereas less than 6 percent of all others were. The government also participates in about one-half of all cases decided on merits, and between 1953 and 1991, the Court annually decided on average 63 percent of the cases in favor of the government.[146] Because of the position and the high reputation of the attorneys working in the office of the solicitor general, the justices often defer and simply vote to "go with the S.G."[147]

By contrast, indigents are unlikely to have their cases given full consideration. With the increasing number of unpaid cases, the percentage of those granted declined sharply. During the Vinson and Warren Courts, the number dropped from around

9 percent to less than 3 percent and then to about 1 percent during the Burger and Rehnquist Courts. The decline is due to a number of factors. First and foremost is simply the reality that the more filings, the larger the number of those considered "frivolous." "The claims made are often fantastic, surpassing credulity," Douglas observed. Although "98 or 99% of them are frivolous," he added, "[w]e read them all because they produce classic situations like *Gideon* and *Miranda* and so on."[148] Most members of the Court no longer individually consider indigents' petitions. Instead, they rely on their law clerks' *certiorari* memos and recommendations. Moreover, a majority on the Burger and Rehnquist Courts, unlike the Warren Court, are increasingly unsympathetic to claims brought by indigents. And whereas the Warren Court tended to take criminal cases brought by defendants appealing their convictions in order to reverse lower court decisions, the Burger Court tended to select appeals from and decide in favor of the government in criminal procedure cases.[149] Still, 21 percent of the 99 cases granted oral arguments by the Rehnquist Court in its 1993–1994 term were filed by indigents.

The transformation of the Court's agenda registers the interplay between changes in the composition and direction of the Court and the issues brought by litigants and broader socioeconomic forces. On economic issues, for example, changes in the composition of the bench led to eras in which the Court pursued alternatively conservative or liberal policy-making. From 1790 to 1835 the Court staunchly defended property rights. But from the presidency of Andrew Jackson and his appointments of Chief Justice Roger Taney and four other justices, through the Civil War and the Reconstruction—the period of the Industrial Revolution (1836–1890)—the Court generally tolerated governmental regulation of economic interests. That period was in turn followed by a second conservative era (1890–1937) in which the Court defended laissez-faire capitalism against progressive legislation. The Court's "switch in time that saved nine" in 1937 and FDR's subsequent appointments then ushered in a second era of liberal economic judicial philosophy. Fewer economic regulation cases were granted (despite the fact that the number of such cases arriving on the docket did not decline), and those decided upheld, rather than overturned, governmental regulations. With the successive appointments of Republican Presidents Nixon, Ford, Reagan, and Bush, some legal scholars argue that the Court entered a third conservative era that will continue into the next century.[150] Yet during the Burger Court years (1969–1986) a move toward conservatism on economic matters did not take place, as it did with respect to the rights of the accused and criminal justice. Still, that may change as the Rehnquist Court directs more attention to cases involving the rights of property owners and economic regulations.

The Court's agenda generally changes incrementally, though sudden shifts in direction may take place. Over the long haul it also registers policy-making cycles. During such cycles the Court commits itself to a new legal-policy area—such as school desegregation or capital punishment—and opens a window of opportunity for some litigants. For a time (sometimes several decades) the Court continues addressing related "spill-over" issues, challenges to legislation passed in response to its rulings, conflicts generated in the lower courts over applying its holdings to different fact patterns, and fine-tunes its doctrinal policy-making. The Warren Court's watershed rulings advancing a broad principle of equality by giving "strict scrutiny" to racial and other forms of invidious discrimination, for instance, set the stage for women and other non-racial groups to bring Fourteenth Amendment challenges. And the Burger Court in turn confronted whether "strict scrutiny" or some other standard should apply in cases involving non-racial discrimination. In time the Court either comes to regard particular legal policies settled and redirects its attention to other issues or, as its composition changes, reconsiders prior rulings and charts a new course.

In a study of decisions handed down between 1933 and

1988, political scientist Richard L. Pacelle, Jr., further demonstrates how the Court's agenda is transformed through the interaction of the issues brought by litigants and changes in the Court's ideological composition.[151] The economic issues that preoccupied the Court prior to 1937 were gradually eliminated and, after a brief flury of federalism challenges to the expansion of the administrative state after the New Deal, civil rights and civil liberties cases filled the docket and received more attention. Initially, due process claims, followed by substantive rights claims, and later equal protection cases commanded a larger share of the Court's policy-making agenda. The pace of the movement in those directions proceeded slowly yet steadily until a dramatic shift in the 1960s when the Warren Court built an agenda for constitutional revolution and accelerated legal-policy changes. The Burger and Rehnquist Courts then limited or reversed some of those rulings, expanded others, addressed new issues—such as abortion, busing, and affirmative action—and closed windows of opportunity for still other issues, as with claims to homosexual rights. Changes in the composition of the Rehnquist Court may bring a new series of dynamics that again will alter the Court's policy-making agenda, leading to renewed attention to federalism, intergovernmental relations, property rights, and a corresponding decline in the agenda space devoted to claims of new substantive rights and civil liberties.

Review Denied, Justice Denied?

The Court now decides only about one percent of the cases annually arriving on its docket. That is far less than twenty-five years ago, when about three percent of a much smaller docket were granted and decided, leading David J. Garrow to conclude that this change is "one of the most striking developments of the Rehnquist years."[152] A quarter of a century ago the docket was just reaching 5,000 cases and the justices decided between 150 and 180 cases a term. The docket now hovers around 8,000, yet the justices decide less than 100 a year. That is the same number decided by the Court in 1955 when the docket remained under 2,000.

Even some of the justices have been "amazed" by the trend and have speculated on possible explanations. It "just happened," according to Justice Souter, "Nobody set a quota; nobody sits at the conference table and says, 'We've taken too much. We must pull back.' . . . It simply has happened."[153] Even if the Court in the 1990s had continued to grant as many cases as the Burger Court did in the 1970s and 1980s, the percentage granted would have declined, of course, due to the continued growth in the caseload. Still, the diminished plenary docket is striking and probably reflects a combination of factors internal and external to the Court. As discussed earlier in this chapter, these factors undoubtedly contributed to the inflation of the plenary docket during the Burger Court years (1969–1986) and to its contraction thereafter. Early in his chief justiceship, Burger expanded the size of the oral argument calendar in order to accommodate more cases, because of his concern about the Court's declining supervisory capacity. During Burger's tenure, the discipline imposed by the rule of four was also weakened by the emergence of the practice of casting Join-3 votes and the increased circulation of dissents from denial of review. As the Court's composition changed in the late 1980s and 1990s, so did the justices' voting practices when deciding what to decide: both Join-3 votes and dissents from denial became no longer commonplace and justices in the 1990s, unlike White and others on the Burger Court, became more tolerant of intercircuit conflicts. In addition, the Judicial Improvements and Access to Justice Act of 1988 eliminated virtually all remaining non-discretionary appellate jurisdiction, thereby increasing the Court's "managerial capacity" for controlling the plenary docket by denying *cert.* to more cases. Finally, as Justice Stevens underscores, the institutionalization of the *cert.* pool over the last quarter of a century undoubtedly contributed in several ways: more justices now rely, and rely to a greater degree than before, on their law clerks' *cert.* memos; there is, thus, less independent review of petitions by the justices themselves; and, as Stevens emphasizes, the clerks tend to be "risk averse" when recommending that cases be granted.[154]

Even when the Court granted more cases and its docket was smaller, the question often arose: Is this not a matter of review denied, justice denied? Hugo Black once offered a partial response to that question:

I don't think it can fairly be said that we give no consideration to all who apply. I think we do. You can't decide the case, you can't write long opinions, but when we meet, we take up the cases that are on our docket that have been brought up since we adjourned. Frequently I'll mark up at the top [of a petition] "Denied—not of sufficient importance." "No dispute among the circuits," or something else. And I'll go in and vote to deny it. Well, I've considered it to that extent. And every judge does that same thing in [our] conference.[155]

As Black indicated, every case is given some consideration, though now more often by law clerks than by the justices. No case, of course, is entitled to unlimited review. And the justices appear to agree that the Court no longer functions to correct errors in particular cases, but rather to resolve only controversies of nationwide importance. As Chief Justice Rehnquist repeatedly stresses, "no litigant is entitled to more than one review by an appellate court."

No less crucial, the justices generally agree that the vast majority of filings are frivolous. Testifying before Congress in 1937, Chief Justice Hughes observed:

I think that it is safe to say that almost 60 percent of the applications for *certiorari* are wholly without merit and ought never to have been made. There are probably about 20 percent or so in addition which have a fair degree of plausibility, but which fail to survive critical examination. The remainder, falling short, I believe, of 20 percent, show substantial grounds and are granted.[156]

Even prior to the expansion of the Court's discretionary jurisdiction, Justice John Clarke in 1922 was surprised "at the great number of cases finding their way into court which are of entirely negligible importance, whether considered from the point of view of the principles of law or of the property involved in them. That impression has been intensified as time has passed, for their number constantly increases."[157] Justices as ideologically opposed as Douglas and Harlan agreed that more "than nine-tenths of the unpaid petitions [are] so insubstantial that they never should have been filed" and that "more than one-half of all appeals are so untenable that they never should have been filed." In Rehnquist's words, "a lot of the filings are junk."[158]

But what are "frivolous" cases? Clarence Brummett, for one, repeatedly asked the Court to assist him in a war of extermination he vowed to wage against Turkey.[159] Brennan gave further illustrations of the kinds of frivolous cases that arrive at the Court:

Are Negroes in fact Indians and therefore entitled to Indians' exemptions from federal income taxes? Are the federal income tax laws unconstitutional insofar as they do not provide a deduction for depletion of the human body? Is the 16th Amendment unconstitutional as violative of the 14th Amendment? and . . . Does a ban on drivers turning right on a red light constitute an unreasonable burden on interstate commerce?[160]

The largest category of "frivolous" cases comes from "jailhouse lawyers" such as the Reverend Clovis Green, founder of the Church of the New Song and the Human Awareness Universal Life Church, who, from his prison cell, alone filed an estimated seven hundred cases in federal and state courts during the 1970s.[161] In amending its rule for granting *in forma pauperis* petitions in 1991, however, the Rehnquist Court emphasized that it does not look kindly on such petitions and would summarily deny those it deems "frivolous or malicious."

Which cases appear "frivolous" and which merit the Court's attention, of course, depend on the justices. In *Cohen v. California* (1971), for example, the Court overturned as inconsistent with the First Amendment the criminal conviction of a man who wore in a courthouse a jacket bearing the words "Fuck the Draft." The Court established the important First Amendment principle that four-letter words are not obscene per se and may symbolically express political ideas as well. But, in a circulated and unpublished dissent, Burger protested

that this Court's limited resources of time should be devoted to such a case as this. It is a measure of a lack of a sense of priorities . . . . It is nothing short of absurd nonsense that juvenile delinquents and their emotionally unstable outbursts should command the attention of this Court. The appeal should be dismissed for failure to present a substantial federal question.[162]

Whether justice is denied depends on who sits on the Court and the process of deciding what to decide. In Douglas's words, "The electronics industry—resourceful as it is—will never produce a machine to handle these problems. They require at times the economist's understanding, the poet's insight, the executive's experience, the political scientist's understanding, the historian's perspective."[163]

FIVE

Deciding Cases and Writing Opinions

THE COURT grants a full hearing to only around one hundred of the over eight thousand cases on the docket each term. When cases are granted full consideration, attorneys for each side submit briefs "on the merits" setting forth their arguments and how they think the case should be decided. The Clerk of the Court circulates the briefs to each chamber and sets a date for the attorneys to argue their views orally before the justices. After hearing oral arguments, the justices in private conference vote on how to decide the issues presented in a case.

Cases are decided by majority rule on the basis of a tally of the justices' votes. But conference votes by no means end the work or resolve conflicts. Votes are tentative until an opinion announcing the Court's decision is handed down. After conference, a justice assigned to write the Court's opinion must circulate drafts to all the other justices for their comments and then usually revise the opinion before delivering it in open Court. Justices are free to switch their votes and to write separate opinions concurring in or dissenting from the Court's decision. They thus continue after conference to compete for influence on the final decision and opinion.

How tentative votes may sometimes be at conference and how crucial the later opinion-writing process is for the Court's final decisions are exemplified by *Bowers v. Hardwick* (1986). There the justices, five to four, with Justice Lewis Powell casting the controlling vote, upheld Georgia's law making heterosexual and homosexual sodomy a crime. But when the case was initially discussed at conference, Powell had indicated that he would go the other way, and if he had not later changed his mind, the law would have gone down as unconstitutional.

The issue of sodomy and homosexual rights was divisive and one justices preferred to avoid.[1] Just a year before *Hardwick,* in Powell's absence, the justices split four to four in a decision leaving intact a lower-court ruling overturning an Oklahoma law that provided for the dismissal of teachers who advocated homosexual activities.[2] Thus, when the Harvard Law School professor Laurence H. Tribe argued his side of *Hardwick* before the Court, he pitched his arguments for overturning Georgia's law at Powell. Yet Powell continued to think the Court should not have taken "this troublesome case" in the first place. In fact, only Rehnquist and White had voted initially to grant review. But, a week later White circulated a dissent from the proposed denial of *certiorari,* contending that the case should have been granted because of conflicting federal appellate court rulings on the matter.[3] While Powell remained firm, *Bowers v. Hardwick* was relisted for conference discussion. This time there were four votes to grant. The Court's last two liberal justices, Brennan and Marshall, voted with Rehnquist and White to hear the case.

Powell was torn over the case. "In view of my age, general background and convictions as to what is best for society," he explained in a memo to his law clerk, Michael Mosman, "I think a good deal can be said for the validity of statutes that criminalize sodomy. If it becomes sufficiently wide-spread, civilization itself will be severely weakened as the perpetuation of the human race depends on normal sexual relations just as is true in the animal world."[4] Mosman, a Mormon and even more conservative than the justice he served, agreed. Powell's reaction was visceral and he found "repellent" Tribe's references to the "sanctity of the home." He claimed to have never met a homosexual and simply could not understand homosexuality. Another of his clerks tried to explain that for some the pull of homosexual love was just as strong and natural as heterosexual love for others. (This clerk, however, could not come to tell the justice of his own homosexuality.[5]) Powell, though, conceded that "if I were in the state legislature I would vote to decriminalize sodomy. It is widely prevalent in some places (e.g., San Francisco), and is a criminal statute that almost never is enforced. Moreover, police have more important responsibilities than snooping around trying to catch people in the act of sodomy. But the question here," Powell stressed, "is not what a legislator would do." The bottom line, from which Powell did not waiver, was that he did not agree with Hardwick's argument for a "fundamental right" or substantive right of privacy under the due process clause.

At the same time, Powell remained troubled by the facts in the case. Michael Hardwick was arrested in his bedroom after a police officer discovered him in bed with another male. The officer was there to serve an arrest warrant for Hardwick's failure to appear in court on a charge of drinking in public. One of his housemates had answered the door and told the officer that Hardwick was not at home but that he could look in his room. After Hardwick's arrest, the local prosecutor decided not to seek an indictment and dropped the sodomy charge. In the meantime, though, Hardwick had joined forces with the American Civil Liberties Union in challenging the constitutionality of the law. A federal district court dismissed the suit, but the Eleventh Circuit Court of Appeals reversed and held that the right of privacy protects individuals from punishment for their "consensual sexual behavior." That ruling was in turn appealed by Georgia's Attorney General Michael Bowers. Powell agreed that individuals enjoy a right of privacy in their homes, but disagreed that they had a "fundamental right" to sodomy, even there. Always one "to take each case on its own merits," however, Powell remained disturbed by two facts pointing in opposite directions. Punishment for sodomy in Georgia carried twenty years imprisonment, which seemed harsh and unfair. Still, Powell was concerned about overturning the law because Hardwick had not been tried and convicted.

"This case is about the limits of government power," Tribe argued during oral arguments, repeatedly reminding the justices that they had held that individuals have constitutionally protected privacy interests in their homes. But, Tribe's "torrent of words," as Powell characterized them in his notes, left him unpersuaded; he was inclined to go his way but saw no "limiting principle" to Tribe's argument. In this case, unlike most cases by the time of oral argument, Powell remained undecided on how to vote on the merits. Prior to conference, Powell thus discussed the case with Mosman, the clerk assigned to the case, and asked him to prepare a memo outlining possible bases for affirming the lower court. Mosman's memo dissuaded Powell from following up on his suggestion "that the constitution might protect homosexual relationships that resemble marriage— stable, monogamous relationships involving members of the same sex." Instead, if he were to vote to affirm, Mosman recommended two "middle courses," both based on the Eighth Amendment's ban on cruel and unusual punishment. First, drawing on *Robinson v. California* (1962), which invalidated a law making it a crime to be a drug addict, Georgia's sodomy law might be invalidated for stigmatizing homosexuals, "for criminalizing private, consensual sexual conduct between consenting adults, when the conduct does not cause demonstrable physical or psychological injury." Alternatively, Powell might rely on his earlier ruling, in *Solem v. Helm* (1983), to "hold that it is constitutionally disproportionate to sentence someone to 1 year or more in jail merely for a consensual, private sex act." Mosman, though, continued to lobby the justice "to vote to reverse and write separately to introduce the [latter] argument, since it was not presented"[6] in the briefs or oral arguments.

At conference, Chief Justice Burger led off the discussion, observing that "sodomy has been criminalized for centuries" and there is "no fundamental right to engage in sodomy." He expressed concerns as well about extending past rulings on the right of privacy and substantive due process because there was "no limiting principle." What about, he asked, laws against incest, adultery, and prostitution? He voted to reverse. Justice Brennan took the opposite view, "the conduct is intimate and private." "As to a limiting principle," he said, it was simple: "hurt to home and privacy." The states' interests were also assuredly far greater in criminalizing incest, adultery, and the like. Marshall agreed, but White disagreed and would vote to reverse. He also continued to think that Powell had gone "too far" in *Moore v. City of East Cleveland* (1977), when striking down a zoning law limiting rental housing to "single families." In that case a grandmother ran afoul of the law and was ordered to move from her home because she took in her grandson after his mother died. Powell had affirmed her right of privacy in her home, but also never dreamed that would be a basis for limiting the state's power to regulate sodomy, as Tribe had argued. Justice Blackmun, then, voted to affirm and Rehnquist to reverse. Powell in turn said he could not support a ruling on a "fundamental due process right," but would vote to affirm based on his view of the Eighth Amendment. Stevens also voted to affirm and indicated he "might agree" with Powell, while O'Connor went the other way. The "Court has repeated[ly] said [that the] right of privacy is not absolute," and in her view the "constitutional framework does not preclude state laws like this one." The vote, as Powell recorded in his docket book, was four to affirm on privacy grounds, his vote to afffirm on the Eighth Amendment, and four to reverse.[7]

As in *Bakke* (1978), the controversial ruling on affirmative action, and many other cases during the Burger Court years, Powell held the pivotal vote and was lobbied by the others. The day after their conference, Burger sent him a three-page letter attacking his positions on the Eighth Amendment. His arguments were "extremely dangerous because they prove far too much," in the chief's words, they had "no limiting principle" and invited a "slippery slope" of challenges to laws against "incest, exhibition, rape, and drug possession." "Are we to excuse every 'Jack the Ripper'?" asked Burger. He could see no reason for indulging Hardwick's desire "for sexual gratification." Burger ended with, Powell thought, the "incredible statement" that "the case presents for me the most far reaching issue" of his thirty years on the federal bench. Powell noted on the top of the letter that, "There is both sense and non-sense in this letter—mostly the latter."[8] But, the letter did the trick. Unlike in *Bakke* where he stood his ground, Powell switched his vote to reverse, abandoning his view that Georgia's law unconstitutionally stigmatized homosexuals while adhering to his view that the law's punishment was disproportionate to the offense.

Burger promptly assigned the majority's opinion to Justice White and Blackmun undertook to write for the dissenters. Powell, as Mosman had suggested, issued a brief concurrence reflecting his pragmatic "middle of the road" philosophy. He returned to Hardwick's not having been tried and convicted, and explained later that there was "no threat to him and the law was not being enforced, hadn't been enforced since the 1930s."[9] He thought sodomy laws were "moribund" yet wanted to avoid overturning them "in the abstract." For that reason he stressed that penalties for sodomy (such as the twenty-year sentence that Hardwick would face if he were tried and convicted) might violate the Eighth Amendment. However, three years after retiring from the Court, Powell publicly regretted switching positions and confessed that, "I think I probably made a mistake in that one."[10]

"The business of the Court," Potter Stewart said, "is to give

institutional opinions for its decisions."[11] The Court's opinion
serves to communicate an institutional decision. It should also
convey the politically symbolic values of certainty, stability, and
impartiality in the law. In most cases, justices therefore try to
persuade as many others as possible to join an opinion. Sometimes when the justices cannot agree on an opinion for their
decision, or in minor cases, an unsigned (*per curiam*) opinion is
handed down.

In extraordinary cases all the justices may sign an opinion to
emphasize their agreement. This happened in *Cooper v. Aaron*
(1958), when the Warren Court reaffirmed the unanimous ruling in *Brown v. Board of Education* (1954) and refused to permit
delays in school desegregation in Little Rock, Arkansas. Brennan
initially prepared a draft of the opinion, but then all nine justices
gathered around a table and rewrote portions of the opinion.
The justices' collective drafting of *Cooper v. Aaron* was exceptional, though reminiscent of the nineteenth-century opinion-
writing practice. The justices also took the unusual step of noting
in the opinion that three—Brennan, Stewart, and Whittaker—
were not on the Court when the landmark ruling in *Brown* was
handed down but that they would have joined that unanimous
decision if they had been. All nine justices then signed the
Court's opinion in order to emphasize their unanimity and
because Frankfurter insisted on adding a concurring opinion.
This departure from the usual practice of having one justice sign
the opinion was strongly opposed by Douglas. But all agreed to
depart in this way so that Frankfurter's concurring opinion
"would not be accepted as any dilution or interpretation of the
views expressed in the Court's joint opinion."[12]

What is significant about opinions for the Court is that they
are not statements of a particular justice's jurisprudence. Rather,
they are negotiated documents forged from ideological divisions
within the Court. On rare occasions, the justice delivering the
Court's opinion may add his own separate concurring opinion.[13]
But historically, justices have sought compromise, if not pride

of authorship, because the Court's opinion must serve as an institutional justification for a collective decision.

The unanimous ruling in *United States v. Nixon* (1974) provides a good, even if extreme, example of the justices working toward an institutional decision and opinion. The case against President Richard Nixon grew out of the scandal of Watergate that began in the summer of 1972. By the time the case reached the Court, a major constitutional crisis loomed over the country.

The Watergate complex in Washington housed the headquarters of the national Democratic party. On the night of June 17, 1972, five men broke in to plant bugging devices so they could monitor the Democratic party's campaign plans for the fall presidential election. The plumbers, as they were called, were caught by some off-duty policemen. On the next day, it was learned that one of them, E. Howard Hunt, a former agent for the Central Intelligence Agency (CIA), worked for Nixon's reelection committee. Within two weeks Nixon's former attorney general, John Mitchell, resigned as chairman of the Committee for the Re-election of the President.

Nixon and his associates managed to cover up involvement in the break-in and won reelection in November 1972. But reporters and congressional committees continued to search for links between the break-in and the White House. Judge John Sirica presided over the trial of the five burglars and pressed for a full disclosure of White House involvement. These investigations led to further cover-ups.

A year later, the Nixon administration was implicated in the break-in and the cover-up. To give the impression of cleaning house, Nixon dismissed his chief aides, H. R. Haldeman and John Ehrlichman; his counsel, John Dean; and Mitchell's replacement as attorney general, Richard Kleindienst. In the spring of 1973, however, the Senate Select Committee on Presidential Activities of 1972, chaired by North Carolina's Senator Sam Ervin, began its investigations, carried over national television. Nixon's former counsel, John Dean, became the star witness, revealing much of the President's involvement in the cover-up. A surprise witness and former Haldeman deputy, Alexander Butterfield, then disclosed that Nixon had installed listening devices in order to tape conversations in the Oval Office. The possibility of evidence in the tapes showing Nixon's direct involvement in the cover-up deepened the Watergate crisis.

The Senate committee and a special prosecutor, Archibald Cox, appointed to investigate illegal activities of the White House, immediately sought a small number of the tapes. Nixon refused to relinquish them. He claimed an executive privilege to withhold information that might damage national security interests. The President's attorney, Charles Alan Wright of the University of Texas School of Law, denied that Congress or the special prosecutor could force the release of the tapes. Congress, contended Wright, could impeach Nixon but not compel him to produce the tapes. Congress was not yet willing to go that far. Its investigations, however, had already revealed that the Nixon administration had engaged in a wide range of illegal activities. It turned out that Nixon had approved "hush money" for Hunt and had had the CIA pressure the FBI to curtail its investigation of Watergate. The Watergate break-in was part of a larger domestic spying operation. White House plumbers had also broken into the office of Daniel Ellsberg's psychiatrist looking for information with which to discredit Ellsberg. Ellsberg had angered the Nixon administration by giving the *New York Times* a top-secret report, the so-called *Pentagon Papers,* detailing America's involvement in the Vietnam War. Other government officials, senators, newspaper reporters, and antiwar protesters were subject to illegal wiretaps and surveillance by the Nixon administration.

The special prosecutor subpoenaed Nixon's attorneys to hand over the tapes. When Nixon again refused, Sirica ordered the release of the tapes. Nixon would still not comply. Cox appealed to the Court of Appeals for the District of Columbia

Circuit, whose judges urged that some compromise be found. When none could be reached, the court ruled that Nixon had to surrender the tapes.

After the court of appeals ruling, Nixon announced his own compromise. On Friday, October 19, 1973, he offered to provide summaries of relevant conversations. Cox found the deal unacceptable. Nixon then ordered the "Saturday Night Massacre." His chief of staff, Alexander Haig, told Attorney General Elliot Richardson to fire the special prosecutor. Instead, Richardson resigned. So did the deputy attorney general, William Ruckelshaus. Finally, Solicitor General Robert Bork became acting attorney general, and he fired Cox. The Saturday Night Massacre unleashed a wave of public anger. Within four days, Nixon was forced to tell Sirica that nine tapes would be forthcoming.

The public outcry against Nixon would not subside, nor did the release of the nine tapes end the controversy. It was soon discovered that an eighteen-and-a-half-minute segment of the first conversation after the break-in, between Nixon and Haldeman, had been erased. That and other revelations by mid-November 1973 prodded the House of Representatives to establish a committee to investigate the possibility of impeachment. Three months later, in February 1974, the House directed its Judiciary Committee to begin hearings on impeachment.

Nixon continued to refuse to give additional tapes to the Judiciary Committee and Leon Jaworski, who had replaced Cox as special prosecutor. Then, on March 1, 1974, the federal grand jury investigating Watergate indicted top White House aides. The grand jury also secretly named Nixon as an unindicted co-conspirator and asked that the information against him be turned over to the House Judiciary Committee.

The Judiciary Committee subpoenaed the release of all documents and tapes related to Watergate. Nixon remained adamant about his right to decide what to release. Jaworski countered by asking Sirica to enforce the subpoena for sixty-four tapes. When Nixon would not yield, Jaworski appealed to the Court of Appeals for the District of Columbia Circuit and, not waiting for its decision, also filed a petition for *certiorari* in the Supreme Court.

In his petition Jaworski asked that the case be granted and expedited because of the constitutional issues at stake and so that the trial of Mitchell and the other conspirators might proceed. On May 31, 1974, the Court announced it would hear the appeal in *United States v. Nixon*. At conference, Justice Rehnquist, a former assistant attorney general in the Nixon administration, had disqualified himself from participating. He did so not because of the case at hand but because of his "close professional association with three of the named defendants" in the criminal prosecution of Mitchell and the others.[14] Blackmun and White wanted to deny *certiorari* and an expedited hearing, but they were outvoted and later changed their minds.

Before the Court received the briefs on the merits of the case, on June 21, Nixon had surrendered the transcripts—but not the tapes—of some of his conversations. Although incomplete, the transcripts proved damaging to the President. Public opposition steadily mounted. The House Judiciary Committee moved toward recommending the impeachment of Nixon for obstructing justice, misusing government agencies, and defying his constitutional duty "to see that the laws be faithfully executed."

The Court heard oral arguments on July 8, 1974. The fundamental issue, Jaworski argued, was "Who is to be the arbiter of what the Constitution says?" Nixon's claim of executive privilege in withholding the tapes, Jaworski insisted, placed the President above the law. Douglas pointed out that nowhere in the Constitution is the President granted such a privilege. But Burger twice interrupted to point out that courts had recognized a privilege of executives to withhold information in certain circumstances. Jaworski conceded that much. He did not deny that the Constitution might provide "for such a thing as executive privilege." What Jaworski denied was that Nixon, or any President, had the power to claim an absolute, unreviewable privilege. If he had that power, the President, not the Court, would be the supreme interpreter of the Constitution.

After Jaworski argued for an hour, it was time for Nixon's attorney, James St. Clair, to respond. As in his brief, St. Clair asked that the case be dismissed. He argued that there was a "fusion" between the criminal prosecution of Mitchell and the others, on the one hand, and the impeachment proceedings against Nixon, on the other. Information used at the trial of the Watergate conspirators would be turned over to Congress for use against the President. That, he claimed, violated the principle of separation of powers. Moreover, St. Clair pressed Nixon's view that the President should decide as a political matter what should be made available to the House Judiciary Committee. The dispute, he unsuccessfully urged, "is essentially a political dispute. It is a dispute that this Court ought not be drawn into."[15]

When the justices later discussed *Nixon* in conference, all agreed that the Court had jurisdiction, that the case did not raise a "political question," and that the case should be decided as soon as possible.[16] All agreed, furthermore, that Nixon's claim of executive privilege could not withstand scrutiny. They nonetheless differed in their deference to the President. Those differences had to be reconciled during the opinion-writing process.

Given unanimity on the outcome, and the symbolism and tactical advantages of drafting the Court's opinion, Burger took the case for himself. But what followed in the weeks after conference was truly a process of collective deliberation and drafting. It soon became clear that Burger was too deferential to the President, who had appointed him for his strict constructionism and advocacy of judicial self-restraint. An exchange of memoranda suggesting possible treatment of various sections of the opinion circulated from chamber to chamber. "My effort to

accommodate everyone by sending out 'first drafts' is not working out," Burger wrote, and at one point was driven to respond,
"I do not contemplate sending out any more material until it is
ready."[17]

The importance of the case compelled the justices to try to
arrive at an opinion acceptable to all. The case had been heard
at the end of the term, and by then the Court had already
handed down most of its decisions. The justices had more time
to devote to the case than they might otherwise have had. Blackmun worked on the statement of facts. Douglas offered suggestions on issues of standing and jurisdiction. Brennan worked on
issues of justiciability and intrabranch disputes, while White
focused on issues involving the power to subpoena the President. Powell and Stewart tried to sharpen the treatment of the
merits of the claim of executive privilege to establish unequi-
vocally that any such privilege is neither absolute nor unreviewable.

In the evenings and over the weekend, the justices met "in
the interest of a cooperative effort" to find common ground.
"After individually going over the circulation," Stewart
explained, "we collected our joint and several specific suggestions and met with the Chief Justice in order to convey these
suggestions to him."[18] When submitting another revision of a
section to Burger, Powell wrote Brennan, "I have tried to move
fairly close to your original memo on this point, as I understand
it and what you said at conference."[19]

In such circumstances, when there is an implicit agreement
on the importance of achieving a unanimous opinion for the
Court, the spirit of cooperation prevails. At the same time,
threats of a concurring or dissenting opinion carry more weight.
Burger's initial draft appeared not merely deferential but weak
in treating the authority and power of judicial review. According
to Burger, judicial review and executive privilege are on the
same constitutional footing: neither is specifically mentioned in
the Constitution, but both derive legitimacy from the operation

of government. Stewart offered revisions, which White supported in a memo to Burger, stating:

Because I am one of those who thinks [*sic*] that the Constitution on its face provides for judicial review; especially if construed in the light of what those who drafted it said at the time or later. I always wince when it is inferred that the Court created the power or even when it is said that the "power of judicial review [was] first announced in *Marbury v. Madison.*" See page 4 of your draft. But perhaps this is only personal idiosyncrasy.

"Perhaps none of these matters is of earthshaking importance," White continued, "but it is likely that I shall write separately if your draft becomes the opinion of the Court."[20]

What emerged as a unanimous opinion was the result of negotiations and compromises among the justices. In the end, various justices had assumed a major role in drafting different sections of the final opinion. Blackmun's work became incorporated in the statement of facts. The first section, on matters of jurisdiction, reflected Douglas's work. The second, on justiciability, was a compromised version of drafts by Burger and Brennan. The third, dealing with subpoenaing the President, drew on White's early work. Powell, Stewart, and Brennan had a hand in drafting various parts of the final section, on judicial review of claims to executive privilege.

Before the decision was to come down, Brennan suggested that all the justices sign the final opinion, as was done in *Cooper v. Aaron,* because of their cooperative drafting. But Burger insisted on delivering the opinion. The others agreed since he had accommodated their views and since landmark and unanimous rulings have historically been handed down by the chief justice. In addition, some no doubt relished the irony in having forced Burger to accept their revisions and then having Burger deliver the Court's ruling against the President who had appointed him.

On July 24, 1974, just sixteen days after hearing oral arguments, the Court handed down its ruling. In the thirty-one-page opinion delivered by Burger, the Court rejected Nixon's claim of executive privilege as inconsistent with "the fundamental demands of due process of law in the fair administration of justice." The announcement was dramatic and devastating for the President. Later that day, the House Judiciary Committee began televised debates on the exact wording of its articles of impeachment. Two weeks later, on August 8, 1974, Nixon resigned.

The unanimous decision and opinion in *United States v. Nixon* were exceptional. The justices have worked together to reach an institutional decision and opinion in this way, Justice Brennan recalled, only two or three times in the last forty years.[21] The trend is now toward less consensus on the Court's rulings. The justices tend to be increasingly divided over their decisions. Individual opinions have become more highly prized than institutional opinions. The Court now functions more like a legislative body relying simply on a tally of the votes to decide cases than like a collegial body working toward collective decisions and opinions.

The Role of Oral Argument

For those outside the Court, the role of oral argument in deciding cases is vague, if not bewildering. Visitors at the Court must often stand in line for an hour or more before they are seated in the courtroom to hear oral arguments. They are then given only three or four minutes to listen and watch attorneys argue cases, before they are ushered out. That is because the courtroom has only 355 seats for the public, the news media, and members of the Supreme Court's bar. Only by special request, and subject to available seats, may members of the public hear entire arguments in a case. There are reserved seats for the press, so it may hear all oral arguments. And in major cases, reporters may be allocated additional seats from the public section. Approximately 50,000 people annually view oral arguments during the Court's term.

The importance of oral argument, Chief Justice Hughes observed, lies in the fact that often "the impression that a judge has at the close of a full oral argument accords with the conviction which controls his final vote."[22] The justices hold conference and take their initial, usually decisive vote on cases within a day or two after hearing arguments. Oral arguments come at a crucial time. They focus the minds of the justices and present the possibility for fresh perspectives on a case. "Often my idea of how a case shapes up is changed by oral argument," Brennan conceded, adding, "I have had too many occasions when my judgment or a decision has turned on what happened in oral argument."[23]

The role of oral argument was more prominent in the business of the Court in the nineteenth century. Virtually unlimited time for oral argument was once allowed. In the important case of *Gibbons v. Ogden* (1824), the Court heard twenty hours of oral arguments over five days. In *Gibbons,* the Marshall Court held that Congress's power over interstate commerce limits the power of states to regulate commerce and transportation within their borders. By contrast, the Burger Court gave only two hours to *Dames & Moore v. Regan* (1981). Yet *Dames & Moore,* as Rehnquist has pointed out, was "a similarly important commercial case."[24] There the Court upheld President Jimmy Carter's agreement with Iran securing the release of fifty-two American hostages, but also canceling attachments of Iranian assets and transferring the claims of businesses against Iran from courts in the United States to an international tribunal. Those two hours of oral argument in *Dames & Moore* were an exception to the present practice. Cases are now given only one hour, unless time is extended.

The Court began cutting back on time for oral arguments in 1848. The 1848 rule allowed eight hours per case—two hours for two counsel on each side. In 1871, the Court cut the amount of time in half, permitting two hours for each side. Subsequently, in 1911, each side got an hour and a half; in 1925, though, time was limited to one hour per side. Finally, in 1970, Burger persuaded the Court to limit arguments to thirty minutes per side.

The Court's current argument calendar permits the hearing of between 150 and 180 cases each year, even though it now annually takes only about 100. For fourteen weeks each term, from the first Monday in October until the end of April, the Court hears arguments from ten to twelve and from one to three on Monday, Tuesday, and Wednesday about every two weeks. Although the amount of time per case was substantially reduced by the Burger Court, more cases may be heard than thirty years ago. At the turn of the century, the Court heard between 170 and 190 cases. After the Judiciary Act of 1925 enlarged the Court's power to deny cases review, the number of cases accepted for oral argument dropped. During the chief justiceship of Fred Vinson, the Court heard an average of 137 cases each term, and during that of Warren about 138. By cutting back on the time allowed for oral arguments, the Court increased the number of cases it could hear to between 150 and 180 each term. But after a few years the justices then began complaining that they were deciding too many cases. With Rehnquist's tenure as chief justice, the Court has gradually cut back on the number of cases granted oral arguments and spends only about 100 hours each term hearing oral arguments.

Oral argument usually takes place four months after a case has been accepted. The major exception is in cases granted after February. By then the Court's calendar typically has already been filled, so the case may be put over to the beginning of the next term. Occasionally, in very pressing cases, the Court will advance a case for oral argument. It did so in the Little Rock School case, *Cooper v. Aaron* (1958), argued three days after the petition was filed, and in *United States v. Nixon* (1974), heard less than six weeks after being granted. In *New York Times Co. v. United States* (1971), the Nixon administration sought to suppress publication of the *Pentagon Papers,* a history of America's involvement in Vietnam. And the Court moved at a "frenzied" pace to decide the case, over the protests of Burger and others. On the morning of Thursday, June 24, 1971, the Court received the *New York Times*'s petition. That of the government arrived later that day. The following morning Chief Justice Burger called Solicitor General Erwin N. Griswold, who argued the case for the government, and told him that the Court had granted the petition and scheduled oral arguments for 10:00 A.M. the next day, Saturday, June 26. The briefs on the merits of the case arrived just minutes before oral argument took place. Four days later, in a single-paragraph *per curiam* opinion, the Court upheld the First Amendment right to publish without prior restraint. But all nine justices filed separate opinions, six concurring and three dissenting, for a total of ten opinions!

The reduction in the amount of time devoted to oral arguments was only partly due to an increasing caseload. No less important, some justices had grown dissatisfied with the quality of advocacy.

For most of the nineteenth century, a relatively small number of attorneys, like Daniel Webster and William Wirt, argued before the Court and excelled in the art of oratory. The Court's sessions were short, and the difficulties of transportation precluded many attorneys from traveling to Washington to argue their cases. Hence, attorneys hired Washington lawyers and members of the Court's bar to make oral presentations. The Court's bar was small, and there was usually a close friendship between the justices and counsel. Daniel Webster epitomizes the best of nineteenth-century oratory and the mutual respect of the Court and its bar. At issue in one of his early cases, *Dartmouth College v. Woodward* (1819), was whether, without abridging the contract clause of the Constitution, New Hampshire could revise a college charter, granted originally by the crown of England, in order to replace a board of trustees with one more to its liking. With his sonorous and histrionic power Webster concluded his argument in a grand manner:

Sir, you may destroy this little institution. It is weak. It is in your hands! I know it is one of the lesser lights in the literary horizon of the country. You may put it out. But if you do so, you must carry through your work. You must extinguish, one after another, all those great lights of science which, for more than a century, have thrown their radiance over our land.

It is, Sir, as I have said, a small college and yet, there are those who love it . . . .

Sir, I care not how others may feel, but, for myself, when I see my Alma Mater surrounded, like Caesar in the senate-house, by those who are reiterating stab on stab, I would not, for this right hand, have her turn to me, and say *et tu quoque, mi fili!*[25]

Webster's oratory won the day, as it often did. He described his feelings when later arguing *Gibbons v. Ogden* (1824) before Chief Justice Marshall: "I think I never experienced more intellectual pleasure arguing [a] novel question to a great man who appreciates it and takes it in; and he did take it in, as a baby takes in its mother's milk."[26] The Court also appreciated Webster's presence, as is evident from Justice Samuel Miller's praise of a case "argued at much length by Mr. Webster, Mr. Sergeant and Mr. Clayton whose names are a sufficient guarantee that the matter was well considered."[27]

As travel became easier in the late nineteenth century, attorneys journeyed more often to Washington for the publicity of arguing cases before the highest court in the land. But their lack of experience became all too evident. The quality of advocacy declined. Oral presentations seemed to Justice John Clarke to "stretch out as if to the crack of doom."[28] Oliver Wendell Holmes used the time to write letters, confessing, "[W]e don't shut up bores, one has to listen to discourses dragging slowly along after one has seen the point and made up one's mind. That is what is happening now and I take the chance to write as I sit with my brethren. I hope I shall be supposed to be taking notes."[29] Once Felix Frankfurter passed a note to Hugo Black asking, "You are more indulgent of poor advocacy than I am—so please tell me why a lawyer having limited time wastes 10 minutes before he comes to the point 'on which the case turns'?"[30] Indeed, in 1996 Chief Justice Rehnquist lectured the ABA on sloppy, "slipshod," advocacy before the Court and warned lawyers to be prepared for hypotheticals during oral arguments.[31]

Although since World War II the Court has annually admitted over 2,000 attorneys to practice in its bar, most never have any opportunity to argue a case before the justices. Moreover, while the Washington legal community has grown enormously, as political scientist Kevin T. McGuire points out, the increase in interest-group litigation and Washington-branch offices of large corporate law firms has resulted in the reemergence of an elite group of attorneys who specialize in Supreme Court litigation.[32] The contemporary "legal elite" or "repeat players" is composed of former law clerks at the Court, solicitors general, deputy solicitors general, and law professors.

Even before time was limited to thirty minutes per side, a number of justices agreed that the best arguments were those presented in half an hour. In Frankfurter's words, "A number of lawyers think it is a constitutional duty to use an hour when they have got it."[33] Some on the Court continue to complain about the quality of oral argument.

Oral argument remains the only opportunity for attorneys to communicate directly with the justices. Two basic factors appear to control the relative importance of oral argument. As Wiley Rutledge observed, "One is brevity. The other is the preparation with which the judge comes to it."[34]

The justices have enforced their interest in brevity in several ways. Chief Justice Edward Douglass White invented what was called the summary docket: if an appeal could not be dismissed but the Court did not deem a case worth full argument time, each side was allowed thirty minutes. William Taft had a practice of announcing, "The Court does not care to hear the respondent," if the appellate or petitioner failed to sustain his contention in opening argument.[35] A rigorous enforcer of rules governing oral arguments, Charles Evans Hughes reportedly called time on a lawyer in the middle of the word "if." But the Court became somewhat "more liberal," Burger claimed. "We allow a lawyer to finish the sentence that is unfolding when the red light goes on, provided, of course, the sentence is not too long." However, when the Court revised its rules in 1980, the justices underscored their admonishment: *"The Court looks with disfavor on any oral argument that is read from a prepared text."*

Central to preparation and delivery is a bird's-eye view of the case, the issues and facts, and the reasoning behind legal developments. Crisp, concise, and conversational presentations are what the justices want. An attorney must never forget, in Rehnquist's words, that "he is not, after all, presenting his case to some abstract, platonic embodiment of appellate judges as a class, but . . . [to] nine flesh and blood men and women." Oral argument is definitely not a "brief with gestures."[36]

In 1993, the Court's Clerk began sending lawyers a booklet offering advice on preparing and presenting oral arguments. Among the recommendations: *"Never under any circumstance* interrupt a Justice when he or she is addressing you. Give the Justice your attention while being addressed by the Justice! If you are speaking and a Justice interrupts you, you should cease talking immediately and listen." Attorneys are advised to "[m]ake every effort to answer the questions directly. If at all possible, use 'yes' or 'no' and then expand upon your answer." They are also counseled on responding to hypotheticals: "In the past, attorneys have responded, 'But those aren't the facts in this case!' Please be advised that the Justice who poses the hypothetical question is aware that there are different facts in your case, but the Justice wants your answer to the posed hypothetical question." And on making effective arguments, the booklet advises: "If a question seems hostile to you, do not answer with a short and abrupt response. It is far more effective to be polite and accurate. . . . Rebuttal can be very effective. But you can be even more effective if you thoughtfully waive it when your opponent has not been impressive." Finally, the booklet warns that,

"Attempts at humor usually fall flat. The same is true for attempts at familiarity. For example, do not say something like this: 'This is similar to a case argued when I clerked here.' "

Justices differ in their own preparation. Douglas insisted that "oral arguments win or lose a case," but Warren found them "not highly persuasive."[37] By contrast, Holmes rarely found oral arguments influential. If not writing letters, he took catnaps while on the bench. Both Frankfurter and Douglas claimed never to read briefs before oral arguments, but once they were on the bench their styles and strategies varied markedly. Frankfurter consumed large segments of time with questions, exasperating counsel and other justices. Frankfurter once interrupted a lawyer ninety-three times during a 120-minute oral argument.[38]

Most justices now come to hear oral arguments armed with bench memos drafted by their law clerks. Bench memos identify the central facts, issues, and possible questions raised by a case. Because of the workload, Scalia explained, "you have to have done all the work you think is necessary for that case before you hear the argument." He no longer thinks, as he did before his appointment, of oral arguments as "a dog and pony show," and he goes over each case with clerks before hearing oral arguments. "Things," he said, "can be put in perspective during oral argument in a way that they can't in a written brief." Justice Kennedy also emphasizes, "When the people come . . . to see our arguments, they often see a dialogue between the justices asking a question and the attorney answering it. And they think of the argument as a series of these dialogues. It isn't that. As John [Stevens] points out, what is happening is the court is having a conversation with itself through the intermediary of the attorney."[39]

Justices also vary in their style and approach to the questioning of attorneys during oral arguments. And consequently oral arguments have a different flavor depending on the Court's composition; in the 1970s and early 1980s, for instance, very few justices on the Burger Court asked questions from the bench. By contrast, with the exception of Justice Thomas, every justice on the Rehnquist Court tends to ask questions aggressively and to demand precision in language and legal reasoning. In particular, Scalia, like Frankfurter before him, has a reputation for outspokenness, which some justices and attorneys find irritating. "He asks far too many questions," claimed Blackmun, "and he takes over the whole argument of counsel." During one of Scalia's lengthy questionings of an attorney, Rehnquist finally interrupted to tell the attorney, "You have fifteen minutes remaining. I hope when you're given the opportunity to do so, you'll address some of your remarks to the question on which the Court voted to grant *certiorari*." Scalia concedes that he is sometimes overbearing in his questioning but explains, "It is the academic in me. I fight against it. The devil makes me do it."[40] Ginsburg is also an aggressive questioner who at times even interrupts other justices and has prompted O'Connor and Kennedy to respond "excuse me," before continuing their questioning of attorneys.

"Does oral argument make a difference? Of course it makes a difference," according to Justice Kennedy, explaining, "It has to make a difference. That's the passion and the power, and the poetry of the law—that a rhetorical case can make a difference, because abstract principles have to be applied in a real-life situation. And that's what the lawyer is there to remind the Court about."[41]

Conference on Merits

The justices hold a private conference on Wednesday afternoons to discuss the merits of the four cases heard on Monday, and then another on Friday to discuss the eight cases they heard on Tuesday and Wednesday. Conference discussions are secret, except for revelations in justices' opinions, off-the-bench communications, or, when available, private papers. "The integrity of decision making would be impaired seriously if we had to reach our judgments in the atmosphere of an ongoing town meeting," Powell asserted. "There must be candid discussion, a willingness to consider arguments advanced by other Justices, and a continuing examination and reexamination of one's own views."[42]

Since the content of conference discussions is not revealed, their importance apart from the voting on cases is difficult to determine. But the significance of conference discussions has certainly changed with the increasing caseload. "Our tasks involve deliberation, reflection and mediation," Douglas observed in 1961.[43] Those tasks no longer take place at conference; they now revolve around the activities in and among the chambers before and after conference.

Conference discussions do not play the role that they once did. When the docket was smaller, in the nineteenth century, conferences were integral to the justices' collective deliberations. Cases were discussed in detail and differences hammered out. The justices not only decided how to dispose of cases but also reached agreement on an institutional opinion for the Court. As the caseload grew, conferences became largely symbolic of past collective deliberations. They now serve only to discover consensus. There is no longer time for justices to reach agreement and compromise on opinions for the Court.

With the limited time available, Douglas commented, "[c]onference discussion sometimes changes one's view of a case, but usually not."[44] Rehnquist agrees that persuading others to change their positions is "the exception." When examining the Court's workload in the late 1950s, the Harvard Law School professor Henry Hart estimated that the justices heard oral arguments about 140 hours and deliberated in conference about 132 hours each term.[45] The Court's docket included around 2,000 cases, meaning that each case could have been given an average of three to four minutes at conference. A large number, however, were never brought up for discussion. If we assume (on the basis of the discussion of the Court's screening process in Chapter Four) that at least 80 percent of the cases are not discussed, each remaining case could have been given at most eleven minutes. Assuming further (and unrealistically) that the Court devoted entire conferences to only those cases argued and decided on merits (around 125 cases at the time), each case would have received an average of sixty-three minutes or almost seven minutes of conference discussion per justice.

The docket is now four times as large (over 8,000 cases). But the justices spend only slightly more time in conference and have a little less time to discuss each case. The Court hears oral argument on fewer cases (about 100) in less time (about 100 hours) and spends a little more time in conference (at most 150 hours) each term.[46] Yet at least 80 percent of all cases now never make the Discuss List. The placement of more cases on the Dead List leaves each of the remaining cases eligible for six minutes of conference consideration, compared with the eleven minutes thirty years ago. Each justice has less than a minute to discuss each case on the Discuss List. If we assume further (and again unrealistically) that entire conferences were devoted only to the discussion of cases on which the Court heard oral arguments, then each case would receive up to fifty-two minutes, compared with over an hour's time in the 1950s. But the justices now hold short conferences (for about an hour and a half) on Wednesdays during the weeks when they hear oral arguments. At those conferences they vote on the four cases on which they heard arguments on Monday. Each of those cases is given an average of twenty-two minutes of discussion. If we assume that the justices devote about half of their regular Friday conferences to discussing the merits of the cases on which they heard arguments on Tuesday and Wednesday, then each case granted full consideration would receive about twenty-nine minutes of collective deliberation. And justices may express their views on the merits of each case for an average of three minutes. In sum, the

Court's caseload and conference schedule permits an average of six minutes per pending case on the Discuss List and about twenty-nine minutes for each case granted full consideration.

Some cases undoubtedly are discussed at greater length and even at more than one conference. But conference discussions have less significance in the Court's decision making. The cost of the practice of devoting less time to collective deliberation and consensus building is more divided decisions and less agreement on the Court's rulings. Because the justices no longer have the time or inclination to agree on opinions for the Court, they file a greater number of separate opinions. The reality of cases and less collective deliberation discourage the reaching of compromises necessary for institutional opinions. Ideological and personal differences in the Court are reinforced.

STRATEGIES DURING CONFERENCE

Justices vary in the weight they place on conference deliberations. They all come prepared to vote. Some, like Douglas, have little interest in discussions. Others take copious notes. Much depends on a justice's intellectual ability, self-confidence, and style. At conference, some junior justices have been said to experience a so-called freshman effect. That is, since senior justices speak first, newly appointed members may be somewhat circumspect and often have little to say after the others have spoken. Hughes once observed that "it takes three or four years to get the hang of it, and that so extraordinary an intellect as Brandeis said that it took him four or five years to feel that he understood the jurisdictional problems of the Court."[47] Likewise, Justice Blackmun recalled that it took him "five years to become comfortable" at the Court.[48] Justice Thomas agrees that it takes "three to five years to adjust to the work of the Court." Calling his first five years his "rookie year," he added, "In your first five years, you wonder how you got here. After that you wonder how your colleagues got here."[49]

Justice Antonin Scalia recalls his "biggest surprise" on arriving at the Court was "the enormity of the workload. I don't think I worked as hard in my life," he adds, "including first-year law school, as I did my first year on the Court." Yet Scalia did not give any indication of experiencing a freshman effect; far from being circumspect, he quickly staked out his sharply conservative positions.[50] Nor did Justice Anthony Kennedy give any evidence of experiencing a freshman effect during his first few terms on the Court. He quickly aligned himself with other conservatives on the bench and wrote his fair share of opinions, including some important non-unanimous opinions dealing with such vexing issues as mandatory drug testing and racial harassment in the workplace.[51] Likewise, Justices Ginsburg and Breyer gave no indication of experiencing a "freshman effect" in their first terms, but they also each had over a decade of experience on the appellate bench before their elevation to the Court.

The justices' interaction at conference has been analyzed by the political scientist David Danelski in terms of small-group behavior. He specifically examined the role of the chief justice, distinguishing between two kinds of influence—"task" and "social" leadership.[52] Task leadership relates to the managing of the workload, even at the cost of ignoring personal relations among the justices. By contrast, social leadership addresses the interpersonal relations among the justices that are crucial for a collegial body. Danelski found that some chief justices tend to be either more task-or more social leadership–oriented. Few assume both roles, and some fail at both.

Though the chief justice is the titular head of the Court, it by no means follows that he has a monopoly on leadership. Taft was good-humored but, recognizing his own intellectual limitations, relied on Van Devanter for task leadership.[53] Warren, likewise socially oriented, found it useful to consult with Brennan when planning conferences. On the Burger Court, Powell showed considerable task leadership with suggestions for expediting the processing of the Court's caseload.

Any justice may assume task or social leadership. He or she

may also assert a third kind of leadership—policy leadership. Justices demonstrate policy leadership by persuading others to vote in ways (in the short and long run) favorable to their policy goals. Some members of the Court deny the possibility of such influence. "It may well be that, since the days of John Marshall, an individual Justice or Chief Justice cannot 'lead,' " Blackmun suggested. "The Court pretty much goes its own way."[54] But all three kinds of influence—task, social, and policy leadership—are intertwined and present various strategies for justices trying to affect the outcome of the Court's decisions.

On especially controversial cases, one strategy may be simply to confer but not to vote. Forcing a vote may sharply divide the justices and foreclose negotiations. Warren adopted this approach with *Brown v. Board of Education* (1954). When Earl Warren arrived at the Court in 1953, *Brown* had already been on the docket for over a year. Oral arguments were then held in November, but he carried the case over week after week at conference. No vote was taken until the middle of February. Warren's strategy, statement of the moral issue at stake, and persistence made the ruling unanimous. Warren wanted a unanimous ruling because *Brown* would inevitably engender resistance. If *Brown* had been decided when it first arrived, the vote would probably have been six to three or five to four. Fred Vinson was still chief justice then. Robert Jackson's notes of conference discussions indicate that Stanley Reed would "uphold segregation as constitutional," as Vinson would have. Tom Clark and Jackson were also inclined to let segregated schools stand. Yet Warren persuaded all the justices to join the ruling striking down segregation. At the last minute, Warren got Jackson, who was in the hospital recovering from a heart attack, to suppress a concurring opinion he had written. Jackson had a practice of writing separate opinions, with a view to clarifying his thinking and bargaining with the others, and then withholding their publication when the Court's final ruling came along. But, as Harold Burton noted in his diary, Warren did a "magnificent job in getting a unanimous Court (This would have been impossible a year ago—probably 6–3 with the Chief Justice at that time one of the dissenters)."*55

The strategy of postponing a vote is not one open only to the chief justice. Since the chief justiceship of Vinson, the practice has been "to pass any argued case upon the request of any member of the Court."56 Obviously, there are limits to how often this can be done if the Court is to complete its work. Vinson's experience during 1946–1950 indicates that less than 9 percent of the cases were decided "upon votes not cast at the first conference following argument."57

Another strategy may prove more prudent and afford a justice additional opportunities to influence others. "The practice has grown up," according to Burger, "of assigning one Justice to simply prepare a memorandum about the case, and at that time all other Justices are invited if they want to submit a memorandum; and then out of that memorandum usually a consensus is formed and someone is identified who can write an opinion that will command a majority of the Court."58 The practice sharpens the confrontation between opposing policy preferences. This occurred, for instance, with the circulation of rival opinions in the important obscenity case *Miller v. California* (1973). Burger and Brennan directly competed for votes to support their respective draft opinions. In the end, a bare majority accepted Burger's analysis and more restrictive definition of obscenity based on local community standards of what appeals to a prurient interest in sex.59

A justice who decides to draft a memorandum on a case for conference discussion gains time for refining ideas and trying

---

*Although Warren managed to bring the Court's full prestige to the ruling, opposition to *Brown* was nevertheless intense and widespread, as will be further discussed in Chapter Six, and perhaps, as Stevens has said, a nonunanimous decision would have been preferable since southerners might have felt that at least some of the members of the Court understood their traditions and the inexorable problems of ending segregation.

rationally to persuade others. This strategy so appealed to Frank-furter that he often circulated memos on cases pending before conference and urged the others to do the same. The disadvan-tage of such preconference reports is the inevitable increase in the workload. Such a practice, Douglas thought, would also "launch the Court into the law review business, multiplying our volumes, and load them with irrelevances."[60] No member of the Rehnquist Court follows Frankfurter's practice of writing and circulating memos on pending cases, with the exception of Jus-tice Antonin Scalia. A prolific writer, Scalia's memos are known within the Court as "Ninograms."

At conference justices may try to reason with each other, but there is little time for that considering the Court's current workload. Their success depends on how much time they have and on their style as much as on the reasons they offer. Frank-furter was inclined to try to monopolize discussions, occasionally standing up and lecturing. Stewart was prompted to tell him "that he held forth for exactly fifty minutes, the length of a law school class period at Harvard."[61] Once, when Frankfurter refused to answer one of Douglas's questions, the latter pro-tested but added, "We all know what a great burden your long discourses are. So I am not complaining."[62] Frankfurter's ten-dency to try to monopolize conference discussions so irritated Douglas that on occasion, recalled Brennan, Douglas "would rise from his seat, approach the chief justice and say, 'When Felix finishes, Chief, I'll be back,' and leave the conference."[63] In contrast, Frankfurter's ideological ally on the matter of judi-cial self-restraint, John Harlan, never talked at great length. He always focused on the facts he thought controlling, and fre-quently concluded, "Now that we have the whole case before us it is clear this is a 'peewee' but it is here and we should deal with it."[64]

During Justice Thurgood Marshall's time on the bench (1967–1991), he frequently recounted his earlier days as a civil rights attorney encountering racism in the deep South. A great storyteller, Marshall's anecdotal memory and rhetorical gifts embellished his compassionate judicial philosophy. As a result, his influence at conferences was that of a raconteur, who downplayed personal hardships while underscoring for others his unique perspective on criminal justice and racial discrimination. Justice O'Connor recalls being especially moved by his discussion of a case in which an African American defendant challenged his death sentence as racially biased. "That reminds of a story," he interjected. "You know," Marshall said:

> I had an innocent man once. He was accused of raping a white woman. The government told me if he would plead guilty, he'd only get life. I said I couldn't make that decision; I'd have to ask my client. So I told him that if he plead guilty, he wouldn't get the death sentence. He said, "Plead guilty to what?" I said, "Plead guilty to rape." He said, "Raping that woman? You gotta be kidding. I won't do it." That's when I knew I had an innocent man.

"When the judge sent the jurors out," Marshall continued, "he told them that they had three choices: Not guilty, guilty, or guilty with mercy. 'You understand those are the three different possible choices,' he instructed. But after the jury left, the judge told the people in the courtroom that they were not to move before the bailiff took the defendant away. I said, 'What happened to "not guilty?"' The judge looked at me, and said, 'Are you kidding?' Just like that. And he was the 'judge.'" With his characteristic signal of the finale, Marshall concluded: "E-e-e-end of the Story. The guy was found guilty and sentenced to death. But he never raped that woman. Oh well," Marshall could not resist adding, "he was just a Negro." Such stories, according to Justice O'Connor, often had a "profound influence" on the others. "I had no personal sense," she explained, "of being a minority in a society that cared primarily for the majority."[65]

Other justices have used similar tactics, appealing to emotions and egos rather than to reason. Jackson once observed of another that "you just can't disagree with him. You must go to war with him if you disagree."[66] Actual physical aggression, of course, is rare. However, Douglas recalled one time when Chief Justice Vinson became so perturbed that he got up from the conference table and headed around the room, shouting at Frankfurter, "No son-of-a-bitch can ever say that to Fred Vinson."[67] Personal animosities sometimes prevail. The most extreme were those of Justice James McReynolds. He was anti-Semitic, and whenever Brandeis spoke at conference, he would get up from his chair and go out of the conference room. But he would leave the door open a crack and peek in until Brandeis was through, and then he would come back and take his seat. For the most part, justices do not let professional differences become personal. They must disagree without being disagreeable.

When discussions become heated, humor may prove useful. As Rehnquist puts it, the only effective power a chief justice has at conference is that of "making a frown" to cut down on heated debates. There is also the story of Holmes's interrupting one of the senior John Harlan's discourses, violating the unwritten rule against interruptions. "But that just won't wash," he said, outraging Harlan. Thereupon Chief Justice Melville Fuller quickly started a washboard motion with his hands and said, "But I just keep scrubbing away, scrubbing away."[68] During another heated debate at conference, Frankfurter and Chief Justice Harlan Stone squared off. Again, humor helped to relieve the tensions. After Stone made one of his long presentations on a case, Frankfurter snapped, "I suppose you know more than those who drafted the Constitution." To which Stone shot back, "I know some things better than those who drafted the Constitution." "Yes, wine and cheese," Frankfurter quipped, drawing an uproar of laughter from the justices.[69]

At other times, justices may more or less subtly appeal to each other's egos. Personally offended by a remark at a conference, Frank Murphy passed a note to Black stating, "Hugo: I appreciate your sentiments because you are the bravest and keenest man on this Court."[70] By contrast, Sherman Minton thought Black a "Demagogue" after he made "one of his inflammatory outbursts at Conference."[71]

Justice Douglas contended that Frankfurter "was always a divisive influence." In particular, he claimed that Frankfurter abused Murphy for his own purposes. "Frankfurter did more [to] tear down Murphy, to ridicule him, make fun of him," Douglas maintained. "It was very sad and pathetic that he spent hours every week talking to people about Murphy, laughing behind Frank Murphy's back."[72] Frankfurter himself once told Murphy, "You have some false friends—those who flatter you and play on you for your place in history, not in tomorrow's columns, as lasting as yesterday's snow."[73] Murphy was not oblivious to Frankfurter's duplicity. As he once wrote Frankfurter, "My grievance against you grows out of 1st—1. My belief in you—2. My many acts of friendship toward you.—3. That you, too, believed statements, stories . . . brought to you by unworthy characters.—4. That—as I see it—you were ungrateful and chose to undo me . . . [and] 5. That you have espoused legal views that seemed to me not only wrong but contrary to all that your early gospel stood for."[74]

Even ideological foes, like Black and Frankfurter, may nonetheless appeal to, if not retain, each other's self-esteem. Black once wrote to the latter:

More than a quarter of a century's close association between us in the Supreme Court's exacting intellectual activities had enabled both of us, I suspect, to anticipate with reasonable accuracy the basic position both are likely to take on questions that importantly involve the public welfare and tranquility. Our differences, which have been many, have rarely been over the ultimate and desired, but rather have related to the means that were most likely to achieve the end we both envisioned. Our years together, and these differences, have but added to the respect and admiration that I had for *Professor* Frankfurter even before I knew him—his love of country, steadfast devotion to what he believed to be right, and to his wisdom.[75]

TENTATIVE VOTES

Voting presents each justice with opportunities for negotiating on which issues are finally decided and how. "*Votes* count,"
one of Black's colleagues reminded him in a note passed at conference. "I vote to reverse, if there were two more of my mind
there would be a reversal."[76] But the justices' votes are always
tentative until the day the Court hands down its decision and
opinion. Before, during, and after conference, justices may use
their votes in strategic ways to influence the disposition of a case.
"The books on voting are never closed until the decision actually
comes down," Harlan explained. "Until then any member of the
Court is perfectly free to change his vote, and it is not an
unheard of occurrence for a persuasive minority opinion to
eventuate as the prevailing opinion."[77]

At conference, a justice may vote with others if they appear
to constitute a majority, even though he or she disagrees with
their treatment of a case. The justice may then bargain and try
to minimize the damage, from his or her policy perspective, of
the Court's decision. Alternatively, justices may threaten dissenting opinions or try to form a voting bloc, and thereby influence the final decision and written opinion.

The utility of such voting strategies depends on how the
justices line up at conference. They may prove quite useful if
the initial vote is five to four or six to three. But their effective-
ness also depends on institutional norms and practices.

The importance of voting strategies at conference is also conditioned by the complexity of the issues presented and by their
divisiveness. Complex cases may result in confusion at conference. When the Court considered the issue of abortion in *Roe
v. Wade* (1973), for example, Burger claimed that there was too
much confusion at conference about how the justices stood on
the issues. "At the close of discussion of this case there were,
literally, not enough columns to mark up an accurate reflection
of the voting," he explained afterward. Burger "therefore

For my friend and colleagues
William O. Douglas who will always
climb new mountains as long
as they are there
With best wishes,
Warren E. Burger

Chief Justice Warren Burger (right) and Justice William O. Douglas. (*Office of the Curator, Supreme Court of the United States*)

marked down no vote and said this was a case that would have to stand or fall on the writing, when it was done."[78]

In two other controversial cases, involving claims by the press to a First Amendment right of access to visit and interview prisoners, Burger switched his vote after conference. During the conference discussion of *Pell v. Procuiner* (1974) and *Saxbe v.*

Washington Post (1974), the vote went five to four for recognizing that the press has a First Amendment right of access. But Burger later changed his mind and explained that the final outcome of the cases depended on how the opinions were written:

> This difficult case has few very clear cut and fixed positions but my further study over the weekend leads me to see my position as closer for those who would sustain the authority of the corrections administrators than those who would not! I would therefore reverse in 73–754, affirm in 73–918 and reverse in 73–1265.
>
> This is another one of those cases that will depend a good deal on "how it is written." The solution to the problem must be allowed time for experimentation and I fear an "absolute" constitutional holding adverse to administrators will tend to "freeze" progress.[79]

The Court ultimately divided five to four, but held that the press does not have a First Amendment right of access to interview inmates of prisons. Like *Roe,* these examples illustrate how important postconference deliberations and communications among the chambers have become for the Court's decision making.

Opinion-Writing Process

Opinions justify or explain votes at conference. The opinion for the Court is the most important and most difficult to write because it represents a collective judgment. Writing the Court's opinion, as Holmes put it, requires that a "judge can dance the sword dance; that is he can justify an obvious result without stepping on either blade of opposing fallacies."[80] Holmes in his good-natured way often complained about the compromises he had to make when writing an opinion for the Court. "I am sorry that my moderation," he wrote Chief Justice Edward White, "did not soften your inexorable heart—But I stand like St. Sebastian ready for your arrows."[81]

Before he retired from the Court, Justice Blackmun agreed, in a 1993 interview, that opinions must often be revised "because other justices say, if you put in this kind of a paragraph or say this, I'll join your opinion. So you put it in. And many times the final result is a compromise. I think the public doesn't always appreciate this but many times the final result is not what the author would originally have liked to have. But five votes are the answer and that's what the coached judgment is. So you swallow your pride and go along with it if you can."[82]

Since conference votes are tentative, the assignment, drafting, and circulation of opinions are crucial to the Court's rulings. At each stage, justices compete for influence in determining the Court's final decision and opinion.

OPINION ASSIGNMENT

The power of opinion assignment is perhaps a chief justice's "single most influential function" and, as Tom Clark emphasized, an exercise in "judicial-political discretion."[83] By tradition, when the chief justice is in the majority, he assigns the Court's opinion. If the chief justice did not vote with the majority, then the senior associate justice who was in the majority either writes the opinion or assigns it to another.

Chief justices may keep cases for themselves. This is in the tradition of Chief Justice Marshall, but as modified by the workload and other justices' expectations of equitable opinion assignments. In unanimous decisions and landmark cases, the chief justice often self-assigns the Court's opinion. "The great cases are written," Justice John Clarke observed, "as they should be, by the Chief Justice."[84] But chief justices differ. Fuller, even against the advice of other justices, frequently "gave away" important cases;[85] Taft, by contrast, retained 34 percent, Hughes 28 percent, and Stone 11 percent of "the important cases."[86] Various considerations may lie behind a chief justice's self-assignment, such as how much time he has already invested in a case and how he finally decides to vote.

Chief justices approach opinion assignment differently. Hughes tended to write most of the Court's opinions and was "notoriously inclined to keep the 'plums' for himself." Between 1930 and 1938, Hughes wrote an average of twenty-one opinions for the Court, while other justices averaged only sixteen each term. Hughes also made all assignments immediately after conference. Typically, "assignments would arrive at each Justice's home within a half hour or so" of his return from the Court.[87] Since conference tended to drag on under Stone, he was not as prompt in his assignments. Like Hughes, however, Stone tended to take more of the opinions for himself. He averaged about nineteen, whereas other justices each wrote only about fifteen opinions for the Court every term.

The inequities in opinion assignments by Hughes and Stone angered some justices. When Vinson became chief justice, he strove to distribute opinions more equitably. The increase in the business of the Court also led Vinson to safeguard against justices' piling up of too many opinions and forcing the Court to sit for extra weeks while they were completed at the end of the term. On a large chart, he kept track of the opinions assigned, when they were completed, and which remained outstanding.[88] Vinson was remarkably successful in achieving parity in opinion assignments. All justices on the Vinson Court averaged about ten opinions for the Court every term. Warren followed that practice and achieved the same result. Warren "was the Super Chief," in Brennan's view, and "bent over backwards in assigning opinions to assure that each Justice, including himself, wrote approximately the same number of Court opinions and received a fair share of the more desirable opinions."[89] Burger likewise paid attention to equity in opinion writing, but tended to write slightly more opinions for the Court each term than the other justices. During his years as chief justice (1969–1986), Burger averaged 15.3 opinions for the Court each term, whereas the other justices averaged 13.9 opinions.[90] By comparison, Chief Justice Rehnquist strives for more equal distribution of the workload.[91] In a 1989 memorandum Rehnquist said that "the principal rule" he followed in opinion assignments was "to give everyone approximately the same number of assignments of opinions for the Court during any one term." However, this policy did not take into account the difficulty of a case or the work backed up in different chambers, and Rehnquist explained that he therefore would henceforth give additional weight to whether "(1) A chambers has one or more uncirculated majority opinions that were assigned more than four weeks previously; (2) A chambers has one or more uncirculated dissenting opinions in which the majority opinion has circulated more than four weeks previously; and (3) A chambers has not voted in a case in both majority and dissenting opinions have circulated."[92] In these ways, Chief Justice Rehnquist aimed to achieve both equity in and expeditious processing of opinions for the Court.

Parity in opinion assignment now generally prevails. But the practice of immediately assigning opinions after conference, as Hughes did, or within a day or two, as Stone did, was gradually abandoned by the end of Vinson's tenure as chief justice. Following Warren and Burger, Rehnquist assigns opinions after each two-week session of oral arguments and conferences. With more assignments to make at any given time, they thus acquired greater flexibility in distributing the workload. Chief justices also enhanced their own opportunities for influencing the final outcome of cases through their assignment of opinions.

Assignment of opinions is complicated in controversial cases. Occasionally, a justice assigned to write an opinion discovers that it "just won't write," and it must then be reassigned.[93] Chief Justice Taft once assigned himself an opinion but wrote it reversing the vote taken at conference. He explained to his colleagues, "I think we made a mistake in this case and have written the opinion the other way. Hope you will agree."[94]

Sometimes other justices switch votes after an opinion has been assigned, and thus necessitate reassignment. Rather dramatically in the course of writing an opinion for a bare majority

in *Garcia v. San Antonio Metropolitan Transit Authority* (1985),
Justice Blackmun changed his mind and wrote the opinion so as
to reach the opposite result. Instead of extending an earlier controversial five-to-four ruling handed down by Rehnquist in
National League of Cities v. Usery (1976), Blackmun wrote his
Garcia opinion the other way and expressly overturned *Usery*.
Rehnquist's opinion in *Usery* was divisive because the Court had
not limited Congress's power under the commerce clause since
striking down much of the early New Deal legislation, which
precipitated the "constitutional crisis" of 1937. Yet Rehnquist
had managed to persuade Blackmun, along with three others,
to strike down Congress's setting of minimum wage and maxi-
mum hour standards for all state, county, and municipal employees under the Fair Labor Standards Act. He did so on a novel
reading of the Tenth Amendment guarantee that powers not
delegated to the federal government "are reserved to the States"
and by claiming that the Court should defend states' sovereignty
against federal intrusions on their "traditional" and "integral"
state activities. The justices remained sharply divided on Rehnquist's position in *Usery*.[95] Finally, when assigned *Garcia*, Blackmun was to write an opinion striking down the extension of
federal wage and overtime standards to municipal transit workers. But he changed his mind about the wisdom of Rehnquist's
earlier opinion and attempt to draw a line between "traditional"
and "nontraditional" state activities in limiting congressional
power. So he wrote his *Garcia* opinion in line with the views of
the four dissenters in *Usery*, upholding Congress's power and
overturning Rehnquist's earlier ruling.*

---

*Notably, seven years later, after four appointees of Reagan and Bush joined
the Court and only three justices who made up the majority in *Garcia* remained
on the bench, the Court again reconsidered *Usery* and *Garcia*. At issue in *New
York v. United States* (1992) was the constitutionality of Congress's imposing
in 1985 a deadline for each state to provide disposal sites for all low-level
radioactive waste generated within its borders by 1996. New York authorities
contended that Congress had infringed on states' rights under the Tenth

Dramatic instances of vote switching and opinion reassignment, however, are rare. Changes in voting alignments usually only increase the size of the majority.[96] The unpublished opinions of John Harlan during his service on the Court (1955–1971) reveal that of some sixty-one undelivered opinions only nine were abandoned because of a reversal of a majority on the treatment of a case. Typically, Harlan withdrew a draft of a concurrence or a dissent because the author of the Court's opinion accommodated his views. Harlan did so in twelve cases. In thirteen cases, he substantially revised his own initial separate opinion in light of changes made in the opinion for the Court. In four cases, he abandoned an initial concurrence or dissent in favor of joining another. And in about one case each term, Harlan suppressed an opinion because the Court was so divided that the final vote was to issue a brief *per curiam* opinion, affirming the lower-court ruling by an equally divided Court, or to carry the case over for reargument the next term.[97]

Since justices may switch their votes and since opinions for the Court require compromise, chief justices may assign opin-

Amendment, but an appellate court rejected that argument on the basis of the ruling in *Garcia*. On appeal, moreover, the Rehnquist Court declined to reconsider and overrule *Garcia*. While strongly defending federalism in her opinion for the Court, Justice O'Connor tried to set that controversy aside. In a narrowly drawn opinion, O'Connor upheld all of the requirements imposed on the states by Congress except for a provision requiring states that failed to provide for radioactive waste disposal sites by 1996 to take title of and assume all liability for wastes generated and not disposed within their jurisdictions. That requirement intruded on states' sovereignty, O'Connor claimed, though dissenting Justices Blackmun, Stevens, and White sharply disagreed. In another bare majority ruling the Rehnquist Court further limited Congress's power under the Commerce Clause, but again declined to overrule *Garcia*. In *United States v. Lopez* (1995), Chief Justice Rehnquist held that Congress exceeded its power and infringed upon states' power in enacting the Gun-Free School Zones Act of 1990, which made it a federal crime to possess a firearm within 1,000 feet of a school. Justices Breyer, Ginsburg, Souter, and Stevens dissented. Subsequently, in *Printz v. United States* and *Mack v. United States* (1997) the same bare majority struck down the Brady Handgun Violence Prevention Act of 1993, but still declined to reverse *Garcia*.

ions on the basis of a "voting paradox" or, as David Danelski has explained, "assign the case to the justice whose views are closest to the dissenters on the ground that his opinion would take a middle approach upon which both majority and minority could agree."[98]

Some chief justices employ the strategy of assigning opinions to pivotal justices more than others do. Hughes, Vinson, and Warren tended to favor justices likely to hold on to a majority, and perhaps even win over some of the dissenters. Taft and Stone were not so inclined.[99] Assigning opinions to pivotal justices presents a chief justice with additional opportunities for influencing the Court's final ruling. Because votes are always tentative, a chief justice may vote with a majority and assign the case to a marginal justice, but later switch his vote or even write a dissenting opinion.

Chief justices may take other factors into account in assigning opinions. What kind of reaction a case is likely to engender may be important. Hughes apparently took this into account when giving Frankfurter the first flag-salute case, *Minersville School District v. Gobitis* (1940), because he was a Jewish immigrant. There the Court, with only Stone dissenting, denied the Jehovah's Witnesses' claim that requiring schoolchildren to salute the American flag at the start of classes violates the First Amendment. But three years later, in a second case, the Court reversed itself. In *West Virginia Board of Education v. Barnette* (1943), the Court held that the First Amendment guarantee of freedom of religion prohibits states from compelling schoolchildren to recite the pledge of allegiance to the flag.

Hughes was also inclined to give "liberal" opinions to "conservative" justices in order to defuse opposition to rulings striking down early New Deal legislation. Later, when the Court decided the Texas *White Primary* case, *Smith v. Allwright* (1944), ruling that blacks may not be excluded from voting in state primary elections, Stone assigned the Court's opinion to Frankfurter. But Jackson immediately expressed his concerns about the assignment. Frankfurter was a Vienna-born Jew, raised in New England, and a former professor at the elite Harvard Law School. Stone and Frankfurter were persuaded of the wisdom of reassigning the opinion to Reed, a native-born Protestant from Kentucky, long associated with the Democratic party. The justices thought that they might thereby diminish some of the opposition in the South to the ruling.[100]

A number of other cases illustrate that public relations may enter into a chief justice's calculations. The leading civil libertarian on the Court, Hugo Black, wrote the opinion in *Korematsu v. United States* (1944), upholding the constitutionality of the relocation of Japanese Americans during World War II. A former attorney general experienced in law enforcement, Tom Clark, wrote the opinion in the landmark exclusionary rule case, *Mapp v. Ohio* (1961), holding that evidence obtained in violation of the Fourth Amendment's requirements for a reasonable search and seizure may not be used against criminal suspects at trial. And a former counsel for the Mayo Clinic, experienced in the law of medicine, Harry Blackmun, was assigned the abortion case *Roe v. Wade* (1973).

These examples also suggest that chief justices may look for expertise in particular areas of law. Taney gave Peter Daniel a large number of land, title, and equity cases, but few involving constitutional matters.[101] Taft was especially apt to assign opinions on the basis of expertise: John Clarke and Joseph McKenna wrote patent cases; Louis Brandeis, tax and rate opinions; and James McReynolds was "the boss on Admiralty," while Willis Van Devanter and George Sutherland, both from "out West," were given land and Indian disputes.[102] Burger tended to give First Amendment cases to White and Stewart and those involving federalism to Powell or Rehnquist, depending on the size of the conference vote. By contrast, Warren expressly disapproved of specialization. He thought that it both discouraged collective decision making and might make a "specialist" defensive when challenged.[103] Yet Brennan wrote the watershed opinions on the

First Amendment and became a kind of custodian of obscenity cases during the Warren Court.

Some political scientists have argued that in their first couple of years on the bench "freshman" justices are assigned to write fewer opinions for the Court.[104] Junior justices may be given fewer opinions due to the complexities of the cases granted review, the Court's workload, and because they still may not have well-developed ideological positions on the issues coming before the Court. By tradition, new justices are usually given a unanimous decision to write as their first opinion for the Court. And some justices (Frank Murphy, Sandra O'Connor, and David Souter, for instance) did write significantly fewer opinions in their first year on the bench. However, in a major study of opinion assignment ratios (OAR) of senior and junior justices from 1921 to 1991, political scientists Terry Bowen and John Scheb found no confirmation for the theory that junior justices are necessarily less likely to write opinions for the Court or are less likely to be assigned difficult opinions.[105] Moreover, recent appointees with extensive prior experience on the appellate bench, Justices Ginsburg and Breyer, gave no indication of a "freshman effect" in their first years on the Court.[106]

The power of opinion assignment may invite resentment and lobbying by the other members of the Court. Justice Frank Murphy, for instance, was known within the Court to delegate his opinion writing largely to his clerks. Neither Stone nor Vinson had much confidence in his work. Accordingly, he received few opinions in important cases from either chief justice. Murphy once complained to Vinson, when tendering back his "sole assignment to date": "I have done my best to write an opinion acceptable to the majority who voted as I did at the conference. I have failed in this task and a majority has now voted the other way."[107] Only when Murphy's ideological ally, Hugo Black, as the senior associate, assigned opinions did he receive major cases.

"During all the years," Warren claimed, "I never had any of

the Justices urge me to give them opinions to write, nor did I have anyone object to any opinion that I assigned to him or anyone else."[108] Warren's experience was exceptional, but he also often conferred with other justices before making his assignments.[109] Black and Douglas, for instance, urged Warren to assign Brennan the landmark case on reapportionment, *Baker v. Carr* (1962). They did so because Brennan's views were closest to those of Stewart, the crucial fifth vote, and his draft would be most likely to command a majority.[110] Most chief justices find themselves lobbied, to a greater or lesser degree, when they assign opinions.[111]

WRITING AND CIRCULATING OPINIONS

Writing opinions is the justices' most difficult and time-consuming task. As Frankfurter once put it, when appealing to Brennan to suppress a proposed opinion, "psychologically speaking, voting is one thing and expressing views in support of a vote quite another."[112]

Justices differ in their styles and approaches to opinion writing. They now more or less delegate responsibility to their clerks for assistance in the preparation of opinions (as was discussed in Chapter Three). On the Rehnquist Court only Justice Stevens still regularly does the first draft of his opinions; he does them, he says, "for self-discipline." For opinions in cases that they deem important, Justice Scalia and Souter also tend to undertake their own first drafts; the latter does so in a hand-written draft since he is the only justice who does not use a word processor in his chambers. The first drafts of all the other justices' opinions are usually prepared by their clerks. Still, only after a justice is satisfied with an initial draft does the opinion go to the other justices for their reactions.

The circulation of opinions among the chambers added to the Court's workload and changed the process of opinion writing. The practice of circulating draft opinions began around the turn of the century and soon became pivotal in the Court's decision-making process. The circulation of opinions provides more opportunities for the shifting of votes and further coalition building or fragmentation within the Court. Chief Justice Marshall, with his insistence on unanimity and nightly conferences after dinner, achieved unsurpassed unanimity. Unanimity, however, was based on the reading of opinions at conferences. No drafts circulated for other justices' scrutiny. Throughout much of the nineteenth century, when the Court's sessions were shorter and the justices had no law clerks, opinions were drafted in about two weeks and then read at conference.[113] If at least a majority agreed with the main points, the opinion was approved.

In this century, the practice became that of circulating draft opinions, initially carbon copies and now two photocopies, for each justice's examination and comments. Because they gave more attention to each opinion, the justices found more to debate. The importance of circulating drafts and negotiating language in an opinion was underscored when Jackson announced from the bench, "I myself have changed my opinion after reading the opinions of the members of the Court. And I am as stubborn as most. But I sometimes wind up not voting the way I voted in conference because the reasons of the majority didn't satisfy me."[114] Similarly, Brennan noted, "I converted more than one proposed majority into a dissent before the final decision was announced. I have also, however, had the more satisfying experience of rewriting a dissent as a majority opinion for the Court." In one case, Brennan added, he "circulated 10 printed drafts before one was approved as the Court's opinion."[115]

As the amount of time spent on the considering of proposed opinions grew, so did the workload. More law clerks were needed, and they were also given a greater role in opinion writing. Though clerks are now largely responsible for drafting and commenting on opinions, they remain subordinates when it comes to negotiating opinions for the Court. There are exceptions. Frankfurter often tried to use his clerks as lobbyists within the Court. And Rutledge once found that during his absence "at the request of Justice Black two minor changes were made by [his] staff in the final draft of the opinion, but apparently that draft was not circulated to show those changes."[116] But even if a clerk is delegated or assumes responsibility for working on an opinion, the justice ultimately must account for what is circulated.

How long does opinion writing take? In the average case, Tom Clark observed, about three weeks' work by a justice and his clerks is required before an opinion circulates. "Then the fur begins to fly."[117] The time spent preparing an opinion depends on how fast a justice works, what his style is, how much use of law clerks he makes, and how controversial the assigned case is. Holmes and Benjamin Cardozo wrote opinions within days after being assigned, with little assistance from law clerks. Even into his eighties, Holmes "thirsted" for opinions. Chief Justice Hughes held back assignments from Cardozo because the justice's law clerk, Melvin Segal, complained that Cardozo would spend his weekends writing his opinions and thus he had little to do during the week. Cardozo later gave his clerk responsibility for checking citations and proofreading drafts. But Cardozo still overworked himself, and Hughes continued to hold back assignments for fear that the bachelor's health would fail.[118] By comparison, Frankfurter relied a great deal on his clerks and was still notoriously slow. As he once said, in apologizing to his brethren for the delay in circulating a proposed opinion, "The elephant's period of gestation is, I believe, eighteen months, but a poor little hot dog has no such excuse."[119]

A number of factors affect how long it takes a justice to complete opinion assignments for the Court. Some justices work quickly, as already noted, while others are notoriously slow. In a study of the Vinson Court (1946–1952), Jan Palmer and Saul Brenner found further confirmation for Black's and Douglas's reputation as expeditious opinion writers, and that Frankfurter consistently took more time than his colleagues to complete his

Justice Byron White working at one of the Court's word processors in his chambers. (*ABAJ/Lillian O'Connell*)

opinions. They also found that over the years Chief Justice Vinson, while striving to equalize his opinion assignments, tended to favor "speedy" writers like Black and Douglas, despite his ideological disagreements with them. Among other factors associated with prolonging the time taken to produce an opinion for the Court are (1) the importance and divisiveness of a case, (2) the size of the voting majority at conference, (3) whether the initial vote was to affirm rather than reverse a lower court, (4) whether one or more of the justices later switched their votes, and (5) whether a case had to be reassigned or carried over for another term.[120]

The interplay of professional and psychological pressures on a justice writing the Court's opinion is a complex but crucial part of the Court's decision making. When the practice, in the 1920s and 1930s, was to return comments within twenty-four hours after receipt of a draft, the pressures were especially great. There are no time limits now, but the pressures persist, especially during the last two months of a term, when the justices concentrate on opinion writing.[121]

Whether drafting or commenting on a proposed opinion, justices differ when trying to influence each other. They look for emotional appeals, sometimes personal threats. Justice Clark thought that Warren was the greatest chief justice in the history of the Court and sought his approval of a revised opinion. But he received this disturbing response: "Tom: Nuts. E. W."[122] Shortly after coming to the Court, Brennan wrote Black, "I welcome, as always, every and any comment you will be good enough to make on anything I ever write—whether we vote together at the time or not."[123] By contrast, Justice Marshall had a tendency to simply scribble "B.S." on drafts circulated by Rehnquist.[124]

Douglas could be a real charmer—if he wanted to be—when appealing for modifications in proposed opinions. "I would stand on my head to join with you in your opinion," he told James Byrnes, though continuing, "I finally concluded, however, that I cannot." His strategy was that of the "Yes, but game." This is evident in his response to one of Reed's drafts: "I like your opinion in No. 18 very much. You have done an excellent job in a difficult field. And I want to join you in it. *But*—"[125] He then set forth the changes that would have to be made.

By contrast, the style of McReynolds was abrupt—sometimes rude—and usually left little room for negotiation. "This statement makes me sick," he once observed.[126] Frankfurter's approach also could be irritating. He was not above making personal attacks. To threaten his ideological foe Hugo Black, Frankfurter circulated but did not publish the following concurring opinion:

I greatly sympathize with the essential purpose of my brother (former Senator) Black's dissent. His roundabout and turgid legal phraseology is a *cris de coeur.* "Would I were back in the Senate," he seems to say, "so that I could put on the statute books what really ought to be there. But here I am, cast by Fate into a den of judges devoid of the habits of legislators, simple fellows who have a crippling feeling that they must enforce the laws as Congress wrote them and not as they ought to have been written. . . ."[127]

Frankfurter nonetheless usually tempered his criticisms by making fun of his own academic proclivities: "What does trouble me is that you do not disclose what you are really doing." He wrote Douglas, "As you know, I am no poker player and naturally, therefore, I do not believe in poker playing in the disposition of cases. Or has professing for twenty-five years disabled me from understanding the need for these involutions?"[128]

More typically when commenting on circulated drafts, justices appeal to professionalism and jurisprudential concerns. Even McReynolds, perhaps at the prompting of Taft, once appealed to Stone's basic conservatism: "All of us get into a fog now and then, as I know so well from my own experience. Won't you 'Stop, Look, and Listen'?"[129] Such appeals may carry subtly or explicitly the threat of a concurring or dissenting opinion. Stone, in one instance, candidly told Frankfurter, "If you wish to write [the opinion] placing the case on the ground which I think tenable and desirable, I shall cheerfully join you. If not, I will add a few observations for myself."[130]

Justices may suggest minor editorial or major substantive changes. Before joining one of Arthur Goldberg's opinions, Harlan requested that the word "desegregation" be substituted for "integration" throughout the opinion. As he explained, " 'Integration' brings blood to Southerners' eyes for they think that 'desegregation' means just that—'integration.' I do not think that we ought to use the word in our opinions."[131] Likewise, Stewart strongly objected to some of the language in Abe Fortas's proposed opinion in *Tinker v. Des Moines School District*

(1969), which upheld the right of students to wear black arm-bands in protest of the government's involvement in Vietnam. "At the risk of appearing eccentric," Stewart wrote, "I shall not join any opinion that speaks of what is going on in Vietnam as a 'war' [since Congress never formally declared a war in Viet-nam]."[132] Frankfurter was more caustic when he wrote Reed that "all talk about 'jurisdictional facts' and 'constitutional facts' seems to be rubbish—worse than rubbish misleading irrele-vances." He further explained:

For all I know you probably think me very persnickety or, at least, academic in fussing about your reference to "constitutional facts" and *Crowell v. Benson*. Well, the fact is that I am academic and I have no excuse for being on this Court unless I remain so. By which I mean that Harvard paid me a high salary for the opportunity of understand-ing the problems covered by the phrase "judicial review." . . . The fact of the matter is that probably the deepest source of error and darkness in the law is the loose use of language reflecting too often a disregard of the history of doctrines.[133]

Editorial suggestions may also be directed at a justice's use of precedents and basic conceptualization. Douglas, for instance, sent Brennan a letter outlining fourteen changes he thought necessary in the proposed opinion for the watershed reapportionment decision in *Baker v. Carr* (1962).[134] Likewise, Brennan sent a twenty-one-page list of revisions on Earl War-ren's initial draft of *Miranda v. Arizona* (1966), which upheld the right of criminal suspects to remain silent at the time of police questioning. At the outset, Brennan expressed his feeling of guilt "about the extent of the suggestions." But he emphasized the importance of careful drafting. Brennan explained, "[T]his will be one of the most important opinions of our time and I know that you will want the fullest expression of my views."[135]

Occasionally, proposed changes lead to a recasting of the entire opinion. Douglas was assigned the Court's opinion in *Griswold v. Connecticut* (1965), in which he announced the creation of a constitutional right of privacy based on the "penumbras" of various guarantees of the Bill of Rights. His initial draft, however, did not develop this theory. Rather, Douglas sought to justify the decision on the basis of earlier cases recognizing a First Amendment right of associational privacy. The analogy and precedents, he admitted, "do not decide this case." "Marriage does not fit precisely any of the categories of First Amendment rights. But it is a form of association as vital in the life of a man or a woman as any other, and perhaps more so." Both Black and Brennan strongly objected to Douglas's extravagant reliance on First Amendment precedents. In a three-page letter, Brennan detailed an alternative approach, as the following excerpt indicates:

I have read your draft opinion in *Griswold v. Connecticut*, and, while I agree with a great deal of it, I should like to suggest a substantial change in emphasis for your consideration. It goes without saying, of course, that your rejection of any approach based on *Lochner v. New York* is absolutely right. [In *Lochner* (1905), a majority read into the Fourteenth Amendment a "liberty of contract" in order to strike down economic legislation. Although the Court later abandoned the doctrine of a "liberty of contract," *Lochner* continues to symbolize the original sin of constitutional interpretation—that is, the Court's creation and enforcement of unenumerated rights.] And I agree that the association of husband and wife is not mentioned in the Bill of Rights, and that that is the obstacle we must hurdle to effect a reversal in this case.

But I hesitate to bring the husband-wife relationship within the right to association we have constructed in the First Amendment context. . . . In the First Amendment context, in situations like *NAACP v. Alabama* [1964], privacy is necessary to protect the capacity of an association for fruitful advocacy. In the present context, it seems to me that we are really interested in the privacy of married couples quite apart from any interest in advocacy. . . . Instead of expanding the First Amendment right of association to include marriage, why not say that what has been done for the First Amendment can also be done for some of the other fundamental guarantees of the Bill of Rights? In other words, where fundamentals are concerned, the Bill of Rights guarantees are but expressions or examples of those rights, and do not preclude applications or extensions of those rights to situations unanticipated by the Framers.

The restriction on the dissemination and use of contraceptives, Brennan explained,

would, on this reasoning, run afoul of a right to privacy created out of the Fourth Amendment and the self-incrimination clause of the Fifth, together with the Third, in much the same way as the right of association has been created out of the First. Taken together, those amendments indicate a fundamental concern with the sanctity of the home and the right of the individual to be alone.

"With this change of emphasis," Brennan concluded, the opinion "would be most attractive to me because it would require less departure from the specific guarantees and because I think there is a better chance it will command a Court." Douglas subsequently revised his opinion and based the right of privacy on the penumbras of the First, Third, Fourth, Fifth, and Ninth Amendments.[136]

In order to accommodate the views of others, the author of an opinion for the Court must negotiate language and bargain over substance. "The ground you recommend was not the one on which I voted 'no'—But I think that, as a matter of policy, you are clearly right; and I am engaged in redrafting the opinion on that line," Brandeis wrote to the respected craftsman Van Devanter, adding, "May I trouble you to formulate the rule of law, which you think should be established?"[137]

At times, justices may not feel that a case is worth fighting over. "Probably bad—but only a small baby. Let it go," Sutherland noted on the back of one of Stone's drafts. Hughes was a bit more graphic when responding to another proposed opinion: "I choke a little at swallowing your analysis, still I do not think it would serve any useful purpose to expose my views."[138] Similarly, Pierce Butler agreed to go along with one of Stone's opinions, though noting, "I voted to reverse. While this sustains

Justice William J. Brennan, Jr., in his chambers. (*Collection of the Supreme Court of the United States*)

your conclusion to affirm, I still think reversal would be better. But I shall in silence acquiesce. Dissents seldom aid in the right development or statement of the law. They often do harm. For myself I say: 'Lead us not into temptation.' "[139]

Justices sometimes join an opinion with which they disagree, perhaps with the hope that in some later case other justices will reciprocate and not threaten a dissenting vote or opinion. This tactic was not lost on Stone, who explained to Frankfurter, in language reminiscent of Butler's twenty years earlier: "I voted the other way in this case but I shall acquiesce in the decision unless some of my brethren see the light and point out that you cracked the law in order to satisfy your moral scruples."[140] Disturbed by one of Holmes's draft opinions, Joseph McKenna wrote, "It may be that there is some defect in my mental processes for I can't appreciate the reasoning. But I will not dissent alone."[141] Another of Holmes's circulated opinions prompted Mahlon Pitney to respond, "Cannot agree, but will say nothing."[142]

More than a willingness to negotiate is sometimes required. Judicial temperament and diplomacy are also crucial, as is illustrated by the deliberations behind the landmark decision inaugurating the reapportionment revolution. *Baker v. Carr* (1962) raised two central issues: first, whether the malapportionment of a state legislature is a "political question" for which courts have no remedy; second, the merits of the claim that individuals have a right to equal votes and equal representation. With potentially broad political consequences, the case was divisive, being carried over and reargued for a term. The extreme positions within the Court remained firm, but the center tended to be soft. Allies on judicial self-restraint, Frankfurter and Harlan were committed to their view, expressed in *Colegrove v. Green* (1946), that the "Court ought not to enter this political thicket." At conference, Tom Clark and Charles Whittaker supported their view that the case presented a nonjusticiable political question. By contrast, Warren, Black, Douglas, and Brennan thought that the issue was justiciable. They were prepared to address the merits of the case. The pivotal and youngest justice, Potter Stewart, considered the issue justiciable. But he adamantly refused to address the merits of the case. He would vote to reverse the lower-court ruling that the issue was a political question only if the decision was limited to holding that the lower court had jurisdiction to decide the dispute. Stewart did not want the Court to decide the merits of the case.

Assigned the task of drafting the opinion, Brennan had to hold on to Stewart's vote and dissuade Black and Douglas from writing opinions on the merits that would threaten the loss of the crucial fifth vote. After circulating his draft and incorporating suggested changes, he optimistically wrote Black, "Potter Stewart was satisfied with all of the changes. The Chief also is agreed. It, therefore, looks as though we have a court agreed upon this as circulated."[143] It appeared that the decision would come down on the original five-to-four vote.

Clark, however, had been pondering the fact that in this case the population ratio for the urban and rural districts in the state was more than nineteen to one. As he put it, "city slickers" had been "too long deprive[d] of a constitutional form of government."[144] Clark concluded that citizens denied equal voting power had no political recourse; their only recourse was to the federal judiciary. Clark wrote an opinion abandoning Frankfurter and going beyond the majority to address the merits of the claim.

Brennan faced the dilemma of how to bring in Clark without losing Stewart, and thereby enlarge the consensus. Further negotiations were necessary but limited. Brennan wrote his brethren:

> The changes represent the maximum to which Potter will subscribe. We discussed much more elaborate changes which would have taken over a substantial part of Tom Clark's opinion. Potter felt that if they were made it would be necessary for him to dissent from that much of the revised opinion. I therefore decided it was best not to press for the changes but to hope that Tom will be willing to join the Court opinion but say he would go further as per his separate opinion.[145]

Even though there were five votes for deciding the merits, the final opinion in *Baker v. Carr* was limited to the jurisdictional question. Douglas refrained from addressing the merits in his concurring opinion. Stewart joined with an opinion emphasizing the limited nature of the ruling. Clark filed an opinion explaining his view of the merits. Whittaker withdrew from the case, retiring from the Court two weeks later because of poor health. Only Frankfurter and Harlan were left dissenting.

The Value of Judicial Opinions

Published opinions for the Court are the residue of conflicts and compromises among the justices. But they also reflect changing institutional norms. In historical perspective, changes in judicial norms have affected trends in opinion writing, the value of judicial opinions, and the Court's contributions to public law and policy.

OPINIONS FOR THE COURT

During the nineteenth century and down through most of Hughes's chief justiceship, there were few separate, concurring, or dissenting opinions from the opinion announcing the Court's decision.[146] A norm of consensus on opinions for the Court was forged by Chief Justice John Marshall, who believed that unanimous decisions would build the Court's prestige and legitimacy. He therefore discouraged dissenting opinions and wrote the overwhelming number of the Court's opinions, even when he disagreed with a ruling. The Taney Court and subsequent ones generally emmulated that practice and consensus became an institutional norm.

That norm broke down in the late 1930s and 1940s with the publication of increasing numbers of individual opinions. As the graph on page 296 underscores, throughout the nineteenth century opinions for the Court accounted for 80 to 90 percent of all opinions.[147] That changed dramatically, however, with the percentage of opinions for the Court of the total opinions annually produced falling throughout the 1940s and 1950s, and, then, from 1960 to 1996 never again rising above 50 percent,

**PERCENTAGE OF OPINIONS FOR THE COURT OF TOTAL OPINIONS
ANNUALLY ISSUED, 1801–1996**

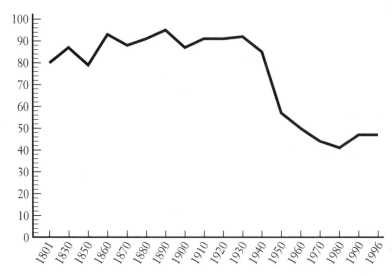

with the exception of two terms. In other words, whereas in the
nineteenth century individual opinions amounted to less than 20
percent of the Court's total opinion production, in the second
half of the twentieth century institutional opinions constituted
less than half of the Court's annual output of opinions. Moreover, while unanimity remains high on case selection (around 80
percent, as was discussed in Chapter Four), unanimity on opinions dropped to around 30–35 percent. Even though the business of the Court is to give institutional opinions, as Justice
Stewart observed, "that view [came] to be that of a minority of
the justices."[148] When compared to the Court's practice half a
century ago, there are approximately ten times the number of
concurring opinions, four times more dissenting opinions, and
seven times the number of separate opinions in which the justices explain their personal views and why they partially concur
in and/or dissent from the Court's opinion.

What explains the rise of individual opinions? In his pioneering work, *The Roosevelt Court: A Study in Judicial Politics and Values, 1937–1947,*[149] C. Herman Pritchett identified the rise in individual opinions with the appointments made by FDR between 1937 and 1943. "Looking backward," he pointed out, "the 1941–42 term was definitely a turning point." Disagreement rates increased and the percentage of opinions for Court of the total opinions issued plunged from 81 percent in Hughes's last term to 67 percent in Stone's first term as chief justice. The percentage continued falling sharply throughout Stone's chief justiceship as well as those of his successors. Pritchett offered two principal explanations for what happened. First, the New Deal justices quickly began working out their competing judicial philosophies. Second, the 1941 term "saw the debut of Stone as Chief Justice" and, as Pritchett observed, "it seems to be agreed that as presiding officer he lacked some of the talents of his very able predecessor."

Subsequent studies attributed the erosion of the Court's consensual norm primarily to Stone.[150] But, the rise of individual opinions (as further illustrated in the graph on page 298) appears largely due to the impact of changes in the Court's composition and was more complex than simply Stone's lack of leadership skills. For one thing, concurring opinions were on the rise prior to Stone's chief justiceship.[151] Moreover, the percentage of unanimous decisions began dropping before his chief justiceship and continued declining during the next three decades.[152] Furthermore, the drop in the percentage of opinions for the Court of the total number issued began during the last four years of the Hughes Court, coinciding with the arrival of FDR's first five appointees (Black, Reed, Frankfurter, Douglas, and Murphy). The traditional norm of consensus, in other words, failed to hold in the last four years of Hughes's chief justiceship.

Why did the norm of consensus collapse with the arrival of the New Deal justices? Simply put, they brought the full force of American legal realism and liberal legalism to bear on the Court. FDR's appointees not only constituted a majority but embodied the intellectual forces of a generation of progressive

OPINION WRITING, 1937–1998

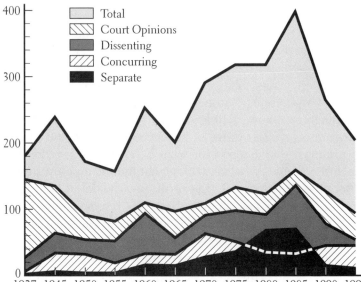

liberals who revolted against the legal formalism of the old conservative order.[153] American legal realism, though, was not so
much a school of thought as an intellectual movement embracing diverse, though generally progressive and pragmatic, positions on judging and legal reform.[154] Legal realism, nonetheless,
highlighted the indeterminacy of law, taught that judges make
law, and advocated judicial pragmatism or the balancing of competing values. Legal realism about matters of degree and judicial
balancing, instead of reliance on fixed formulas and tests, however, also made consensus more difficult and raised the premium on justifying the decisions.

In addition, liberal legalism lacked coherence.[155] At bottom,
as Pritchett explained, were "the short-comings of American liberalism as a social and economic philosophy." On the bench,
liberal legalism inherited from Holmes and Brandeis, and per-

petuated by FDR's appointees, fragmented the justices. Holmes had stood for judicial self-restraint and deference to legislatures, whereas Brandeis championed progressive legal reforms. Although dominating the Court, FDR's New Deal justices split into two camps: Frankfurter-Reed-and-Jackson stood for judicial self-restraint and became more conservative during their time on the bench, while Black-Douglas-Murphy-and-Rutledge pushed toward greater progressive judicial activism. These two camps in turn further fragmented over where and how to draw the line between judicial self-restraint and activism in constitutional interpretation. As a result of their disagreements over the course of liberal legalism and constitutional interpretation, the New Deal justices were inclined to articulate their distinctive views in individual opinions.

Besides these intellectual currents sweeping the Court came other changes in its operation that contributed to the rise of individual opinions. First, throughout most of the nineteenth century, the author of the Court's opinion did not circulate drafts. Instead, drafts were read at conference, where other justices basically only agreed on the key points of the opinion. Under Chief Justice Fuller (1888–1910), the Court began circulating drafts of opinions prior to conference, which became a routine practice by the 1930s. The justices thus had more time to study the actual wording of opinions and to make suggestions for changes or to write separately. Second, coinciding with higher disagreement rates was the Court's move into its own building. Prior to the completion of the building in 1935 (as discussed in Chapter Three), the justices worked alone at home. With their move into the marble temple, the institutional life of the Court changed. The building initially brought about greater interaction and, perhaps, intensified their psychological interdependence and independence. Some, like Frankfurter, constantly tried to lobby the others in their chambers, which often proved counterproductive by heightening personal tensions and undoubtedly contributing to increasing disagreement. Finally, along with settling into the marble temple, the number of law clerks began to increase and opinion writing subsequently proliferated.

In sum, the demise of the norm of consensus preceded Stone's chief justiceship. The New Deal justices infused legal realism and liberal legalism into the Court, but they were not of one mind. They quickly began pursuing their conflicting tenets of liberal legalism in individual opinions. The continued increase in individual opinions long after Stone's departure further undercuts the theory that Stone bears "much of the responsibility for changing the operational norms of the Court."[156] Post–New Deal justices, then, were socialized into higher rates of individual expression. By the end of the Warren Court, the New Deal justices had effectively transformed the Court's norm of consensus into one of individual expression. The devaluation of consensus and the growth in separate individual opinions continued during the Burger Court years.

Although the percent of opinions for the Court of the total annually issued has increased slightly with the Rehnquist Court, there is no indication of a return to the norm of consensus. At conference, there remains little time for more than a mere tally of votes and even less discussion than during the Burger Court years. Another indication of the devaluation of consensus is the larger number of plurality opinions announcing the decision of the Court. A plurality opinion is an opinion for the Court that fails to command a majority, even though at least five justices agree on the decision. For example, a bare majority may decide a case. But only three justices agree on an opinion announcing the decision. The other two justices in the majority usually file separate concurring opinions, explaining why they think the case was correctly decided but how they disagree with the rationalization in the (plurality) opinion announcing the ruling.

Between 1800 and 1900, there were only ten opinions that commanded the support of less than a majority of the Court. Between 1901 and the last year of Chief Justice Warren, 1969, there were 51 cases decided by plurality opinions. By contrast, during the Burger Court years a total of 116 plurality opinions were handed down, more plurality opinions than had been rendered in the entire previous history of the Court.[157]

Under Chief Justice Rehnquist, the Court has tended to hand down fewer plurality opinions. But, for the first time in the Court's history, during the 1990 term the Court handed down what Chief Justice Rehnquist dubbed "doubleheaders or twins": two cases in which there were two opinions announcing different (and somewhat contradictory) parts of the Court's ruling for two different majorities in each case. In the "coerced confession" case of *Arizona v. Fulminante* (1991), for instance, Chief Justice Rehnquist's opinion for the Court commanded four votes for holding that the admission of a coerced confession at a trial may be excused as a "harmless error" when it can be shown that other evidence adequately supports a guilty verdict. Justice Souter provided the key vote in joining the four Reagan appointees to form a majority on that issue. But the lineup changed and was complicated by the justices' stands on other questions presented in the case. Justice White delivered another opinion announcing the Court's decision on two other aspects of the ruling. White deemed the circumstances here of Oreste Fulminante's confession to constitute a coerced confession, whereas Chief Justice Rehnquist and Justices O'Connor, Kennedy, and Souter disagreed. On that issue, Justice Scalia joined White's opinion, which was also joined by Justices Blackmun, Marshall, and Stevens. Moreover, on the final question of whether the use of Fulminante's confession was harmless beyond a reasonable doubt, White commanded a majority for affirming the judgment of the court below and remanding the case back for a new trial at which Fulminante's confession could not be used against him, despite the broader ruling permitting the use of such confessions handed down in Rehnquist's opinion for the Court. On that issue White was joined by Blackmun, Marshall, Stevens, and Kennedy; Rehnquist, O'Connor, and Scalia dissented; and Souter gave no indication of whether or how he voted on that issue.

The other case, *Gentile v. State Bar of Nevada* (1991), that like-wise resulted in two opinions announcing different portions of the Court's ruling, involved a lawyer's First Amendment free speech challenge to a state's disciplinary action against him for holding a press conference and making certain out-of-court statements about a pending trial.

Trends and changes in the justices' consensus building and opinion writing register basic changes in judicial behavior and in the Court's composition as well as in the value of institutional and individual opinions. When individual opinions are more highly prized than opinions for the Court, consensus declines and the Court's rulings and policy-making appear more frag-mented, less stable, and less predictable. Yet, as discussed in the following section, even conservatives, like Justice Scalia, now vigorously defend the filing of individual concurring and dis-senting opinions.

SEPARATE, CONCURRING, AND DISSENTING OPINIONS

The tension between institutional and individual opinions is part of a deeper conflict in judicial behavior between the norms of interdependence and independence. "I defend the right of any justice to file anything he wants," Douglas observed.[158] Yet the proliferation of individual opinions comes at the cost of con-sensus on the Court's policy-making.

In contrast to the author of an opinion for the Court, a justice writing separate, concurring, or dissenting opinions does not carry the burden of massing other justices. But in extraordinary circumstances a separate opinion may prove necessary, the only practical way of obtaining a ruling for the Court. That is what happened in *Regents of the University of California v. Bakke* (1978).

In *Bakke,* the Burger Court addressed the controversy over reverse discrimination and the permissibility of quota systems and affirmative-action programs for minorities in higher edu-cation. Allan Bakke, a white male, was denied admission to the medical school at the University of California at Davis. There were only one hundred openings each year, and sixteen of them were reserved for minority students. Bakke was twice denied admission, even though minorities who had lower grade-point averages and scores on the Medical College Admission Test were admitted. Bakke decided to challenge the admission policy for minorities.

Powell's separate opinion announced the Court's ruling in *Bakke,* upholding affirmative-action programs (but not quota systems like that at Davis) and admitting Bakke to the medical school. But the only part of his opinion joined by another justice was a one-paragraph statement of the facts. Powell delivered the Court's ruling because none of the justices were willing to bend much during conference discussions or afterward. Apart from Powell, they were split four to four on the issues. In the fall, the chief justice and Justices Brennan, Marshall, Rehnquist, Stevens, and White had all circulated memos staking out their positions. As for Powell, he was for diversity but against quotas. He favored a program like that at Harvard College which took various factors into account in order to secure a diverse student body. As he explained in a memo to the conference, "I think that prudential considerations—the desirability of solving a constitutional problem of national importance and one that will not go away—weigh strongly in favor of staying on the course."[159]

Burger, Rehnquist, and Stewart accepted the view of Stevens that the Court need not address the question of whether affirmative-action programs violate the Constitution. They ultimately voted to strike down quota systems as an impermissible racial classification under Title VI of the Civil Rights Act of 1964, without reaching the constitutionality of the University of California at Davis's program, and to admit Bakke. At conference, though, Burger had said that the U.C. at Davis program was an "absolutely clear" violation of Title VI and that he saw no difference between that statute and the Fourteenth Amendment. According to Stewart, "The basic core meaning of [the equal protection] clause is just this: a state may not act adversely against any person because of his race." Rehnquist could not have agreed more, observing that "race may *not* be a factor in any program." Stevens persuaded these justices to avoid the constitutional question and rest with Title VI. The "problem with the constitutional issue," Stevens reasoned, "is that these programs may not be permanent. Negroes may not need protection many more years." Marshall took exception at this, saying, "It will be 100 years." Basically, Stevens approved the University of California at Davis program as a *"temporary* measure," but not as a permanent solution, and "would therefore like to 'duck' the constitutional issue and let the problem work itself out."[160] Although more liberal than the other three, the three most conservative justices on the Court at that time bought his argument. They signed on to his opinion as a kind of damage control, in order to prevent the formation of a majority for a more sweeping opinion.

By contrast, White, Marshall, and Blackmun sided with Brennan in holding affirmative-action programs to be constitutionally permissible remedies for past racial discrimination and voted not to admit Bakke. At conference, Brennan claimed that the commands of the Fourteenth Amendment and Title VI were "essentially the same. We therefore *must* reach the constitutional issue." As to the merits, he insisted that neither "preclude affirmative action programs that do not stigmatize." Brennan even went so far as to say, oddly, that the University of California at Davis setting aside sixteen seats for minorities was "not a quota—just an honest effort to create an affirmative action program." The others of his bloc agreed. As Marshall put it simply, "This is a 'quota' to get someone in—not a quota to get someone out."[161]

After their conference in December, Chief Justice Burger tried to persuade Powell to vote to affirm the lower court. But Powell remained true, in the words of his law clerk Bob Comfort, to his "effort to map out a middle ground which will avoid the dire consequences each side predicts if it should lose."[162] As a result, Burger and Brennan finally conferred in May and decided to "jointly" assign the Court's opinion to Powell.[163] Powell thus gathered the votes, but not the justices' support for his opinion, from each bloc on each of the two key issues. His opinion declared quota systems invalid and that Bakke should be admitted, relying on the four votes of the Stevens bloc. At the same time, Powell upheld the constitutionality of affirmative-action programs in universities and thereby won the vote of the Brennan bloc. Powell, however, refused to accept Brennan's view that past racial discrimination justified the ruling. Instead, Powell ruled that affirmative-action programs are permissible because under the First Amendment universities need a diverse student body to ensure academic freedom and the educational process. Powell's pragmatic rationalization for that controversial decision thus had the support of no other justice.

The Burger Court remained sharply divided after *Bakke* on the permissibility of affirmative-action programs in the workplace. In three out of four cases, affirmative-action programs were approved, with Powell often casting the crucial vote, but the justices could not always agree on the reasons for their decisions.[164] Once Powell stepped down in 1987, however, the Rehnquist Court finally turned the corner. Splitting six to three in *City of Richmond v. J. A. Croson Company* (1989), Reagan's four appointees, along with White and Stevens, stood firmly against the three oldest and most liberal justices: Brennan, Marshall, and Blackmun. In this watershed ruling the Rehnquist Court held that states and localities may not "set aside" quotas for minority-owned businesses when awarding building contracts unless they have a compelling interest and show direct and concrete evidence of past discrimination. O'Connor's opinion for the majority, moreover, announced that the Court would henceforth apply a "strict scrutiny" test when reviewing programs that discriminate on the basis of race, regardless of whether they confer benefits or burdens on racial minorities. By contrast, the Burger Court following Powell's opinion in *Bakke* had upheld affirmative-action programs on a less-demanding test known as "exacting scrutiny." It did so on the ground that if elected officials choose to give racial minorities special benefits as a remedy for past discrimination, those officials could be voted out of office or forced to curtail unpopular programs. But O'Connor rejected that rationale in holding that only the tougher "strict scrutiny" test could protect whites against invidious forms of reverse discrimination. The following year and in his last term on the bench, Justice Brennan managed to forge a bare majority for upholding affirmative action programs adopted by the federal government and mandated by Congress, in *Metro Broadcasting, Inc. v. Federal Communications Commission* (1990). He and two other dissenters in *Croson* were joined by Justices Stevens and White; while Reagan's four appointees banded together in a bitter dissent. However, in the early 1990s four justices—Brennan, Marshall, Blackmun, and White—retired, leaving only Justice Stevens who had voted with the bare majority in *Metro Broadcasting* on the high bench. And in *Adarand Constructors, Inc. v. Pena* (1995), Justice O'Connor commanded a majority for overruling *Metro Broadcasting* and applying the Court's "strict scrutiny" test to strike down most affirmative-action programs adopted by Congress, no less than the states. In that case, dissenting Justice Stevens was joined by Justices Souter, Ginsburg, and Breyer.

Justices usually write separate concurring opinions to explain how the Court's decision could have been otherwise rationalized. Some are defensible, in Stevens's view, because a compromised opinion would be meaningless. Concurring opinions may be required because of a "greater institutional interest in the forthrightness of differing justices' views."[165] Although agreeing with the result reached in an opinion by Nathan Clifford, for example, Joseph Bradley was dissatisfied with the treatment of the merits of an 1874 case. Bradley explained, "I think I had better, in a few sentences, expressing my conclusion [write] separately instead of our trying to make up a compromise opinion which would mean nothing, and fail to be a frank exposition of our views."[166]

Even though agreeing with the Court's opinion, justices sometimes write concurring opinions for egocentric or political reasons. Angering Warren, Black, and Brennan, and over the strong opposition of Douglas, Frankfurter insisted on publishing a concurring opinion in *Cooper v. Aaron* (1958), the Little Rock school desegregation case. Because many southern lawyers and law professors had been his students at Harvard Law School, Frankfurter insisted that it was important for him to lecture them on the soundness of the Court's decision not to permit delays in school desegregation. At other times, justices try to send "signals" to lower courts about the direction of Supreme Court policy-making. Such concurring opinions, in the view of Stevens, are objectionable because they amount to "advisory opinions."

Concurring opinions were rare for most of the nineteenth and early twentieth centuries. They are no longer uncommon. Every member of the Court now usually writes anywhere from four to twelve concurrences each term. Rehnquist tends to write the fewest (less than four a year), whereas Scalia and Stevens average about twelve.

Ideological differences do not appear to have any bearing on whether justices publish concurrences. Advocates of judicial self-restraint and activism are just as likely to publish concurring opinions. "Centralists," like Powell, Stewart, White, Kennedy, and O'Connor, may tend to write a few more, since their votes are often pivotal to the Court's decisions.

Such factors as personal style and use of law clerks also appear important in determining whether justices write a large number of concurrences. Burger as a matter of practice tried not to write concurrences. He did so only to "nail down" points that the majority had not fully stated or been willing to accept. Like White and Marshall, Burger consistently wrote a small

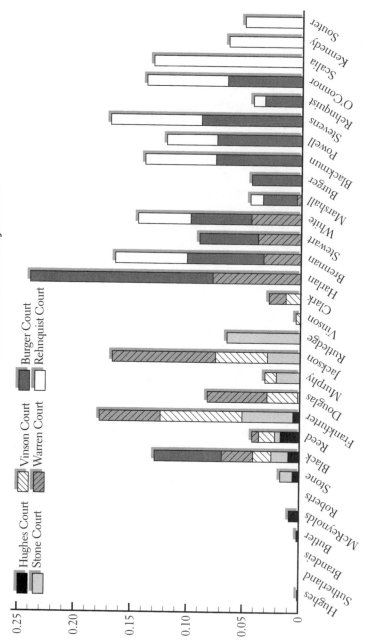

CONCURRING BEHAVIOR OF POST-1937 JUSTICES

Based on the number of dissenting opinions divided by the number of cases decided by written opinion, October 1937 term to 1995–1996 term.

number, about five or six, every year. But the number of concurrences written by some others of the Court more than doubled. What was once true of dissents may now be true about concurrences: "Associate Justices are remembered chiefly by their dissenting opinions, in which they wrote their views without restraint," Justice John Clarke observed.[167]

Dissenting opinions are more understandable and defensible. Dissenting opinions, in the view of Hughes, who rarely wrote dissents, appeal "to the brooding spirit of the law, to the intelligence of a future day, when a later decision may possibly correct the error into which the dissenting judge believes the Court to have been betrayed."[168] Harlan's dissent from the doctrine of "separate but equal" in *Plessy v. Ferguson* (1896) was eventually vindicated in *Brown v. Board of Education* (1954). Dissents may also appeal for more immediate legislative action: James Iredell's dissent in *Chisholm v. Georgia* (1793) invited the adoption of the Eleventh Amendment, overturning the Court's decision; and the dissenters' arguments in *Dred Scott v. Sandford* (1857) lent support to the passage of the Thirteenth, Fourteenth, and Fifteenth Amendments after the Civil War.

A dissenting opinion is a way of undercutting the Court's decision and opinion. The threat of a dissent may thus be useful for a justice trying to persuade the majority to narrow its holding or tone down the language of its opinion. Brandeis, who often dissented, complained, "The Court does not heed dissents sufficiently."[169] Yet he himself at times "suppressed dissents for tactical reasons." "I think this case is wrongly decided," he wrote Holmes. "But you have restricted the opinion so closely to the facts of this case, that I am inclined to think it will do less harm to let it pass unnoticed by dissent."[170]

There is a crucial difference between threatening a dissent and having it published. A number of considerations enter into a decision to publish a dissent. A revised opinion struck Justice Mahlon Pitney as "still indefensible." "But the revision of the opinion," he wrote William Day, "has eliminated some errors of statement, construction, and reasoning that would have wrought far-reaching mischief in the general administration of the law. In view of this, possibly [it would be] better to submit in silence, consoling ourselves that the injustice to the individual defendant in error will, in all human probability, be rectified upon a new trial."[171]

Threats of dissents now carry less force. Although in the nineteenth and early twentieth centuries, justices might threaten (and bargain with) a dissent, they usually withheld publication. "I should now, as is my custom, when I have the misfortune to differ from this Court," Chief Justice Marshall observed, "acquiesce silently in its opinion."[172] Similarly, Chief Justice Salmon P. Chase noted in his diary that he seldom filed dissents because he thought "that except in very important causes [filing a] dissent [was] inexpedient."[173]

Lower dissent rates in the nineteenth century do not reflect more agreement within the Court.[174] Instead, institutional decisions were more highly prized. Taft, who suppressed more than two hundred dissents during his service on the high bench, wrote, "I don't approve of dissentings generally, for I think in many cases where I differ from the majority, it is more important to stand by the Court and give its judgment weight than merely to record my individual dissent where it is better to have the law certain than to have it settled either way."[175]

Published dissents are a manifestation of "institutional disobedience."[176] But justices differ in how far they carry that disobedience. Holmes and Brandeis were among "the great dissenters." Yet Holmes was "reluctant to [dissent] again after he had once had his say on a subject."[177] Likewise, Tom Clark would dissent once from the Court's rulings with which he disagreed and thereafter in similar cases silently acquiesce.[178] In contrast, Black and Douglas noted every dissent and frequently issued a dissenting opinion, even when they had previously made clear their disagreements with the majority. In Black's words,

"Dissents keep the boys on their toes." For Black, a dissenter is an advocate. He once told Blackmun, "That's the way to do it, Harry—strike for the jugular, strike for the jugular."[179]

As the publishing of dissenting opinions gradually spread, the practice became an acceptable form of institutional disobedience. The change in judicial norms is evident from a com-

COMPARISON OF DISSENT RATES

Justice	Number of Dissenting Opinions	Average per Term
"THE GREAT DISSENTERS"		
W. Johnson, 1804–1834	30	1.0
J. Catron, 1837–1865	26	0.9
N. Clifford, 1858–1881	60	2.6
J. Harlan, 1877–1911	119	3.5
O. Holmes, 1902–1932	72	2.4
L. Brandeis, 1916–1939	65	2.9
H. Stone, 1925–1946	93	4.6
H. Black, 1937–1971	310	9.1
F. Frankfurter, 1939–1962	251	10.9
J. Harlan, 1955–1971	242	15.1
THE BURGER AND REHNQUIST COURTS		
W. Douglas, 1969–1974	231	38.5
J. Stevens, 1975–1997	449	20.4
W. Brennan, Jr., 1969–1990	402	19.1
T. Marshall, 1969–1991	335	15.4
W. Rehnquist, 1972–1997	277	11.0
H. Blackmun, 1970–1994	245	10.2
L. Powell, Jr., 1972–1987	159	9.9
B. White, 1969–1993	233	9.3
A. Scalia, 1986–1997	89	7.5
W. Burger, 1969–1986	111	6.5
S. O'Connor, 1981–1997	101	6.3
S. Breyer, 1994–1997	18	6.0
C. Thomas, 1991–1997	33	5.5
A. Kennedy, 1988–1997	45	5.0
D. Souter, 1990–1997	32	4.5
R. Ginsburg, 1993–1997	16	4.0

parison of current rates of dissenting opinions with those of "the great dissenters," those who wrote a disproportionate number of dissents during earlier periods of the Court's history. Although the number of dissenting opinions rose dramatically during the 1970s and early 1980s (as indicated in the table "Comparison of Dissent Rates" on page 311), after Chief Justice Burger left the bench in 1986 the dissenting justices tended to more frequently join each other in a single dissent, rather than file multiple dissents. In their last years on the Court as senior associate justices in dissent, Brennan and Marshall often assigned themselves or others to write a joint dissent, except in especially controversial and important cases.[180] In *Cruzan by Cruzan v. Director, Missouri Department of Health* (1990), for instance, the Rehnquist Court split five to four when confronting for the first time a claim of a constitutional "right to die." After Justices Brennan, Marshall, Blackmun, and Stevens found themselves outvoted at conference, Brennan wrote the other three: "We four are in dissent in [*Cruzan*]. I suggest that, because of the significance of this case, perhaps each of us might want to write his own."[181] But, as Justice O'Connor has noted, the prevailing practice in the 1990s has been for the senior associate justice in the minority to assign an author to write a dissent to the majority's ruling.[182]

The proliferation of separate dissenting and concurring opinions concerned some of the justices and was criticized by the practicing bar and scholars, as Rehnquist noted in a 1981 memo to the conference. At that time, he proposed that writers of opinions for the majority hold a " 'rump' session" in their chambers "to thrash out any differences in the wording or content of the opinion." Rehnquist conceded that, "It could well lead to a certain amount of 'log-rolling' on relatively minor issues in the case, but I would not regard this as an evil." Still, the proposal did not fly and Stevens expressed "reservations about adopting a regular practice of conferences that do not include the entire court."[183]

Justice Scalia, however, staunchly defended the practice of filing dissenting and concurring opinions in a 1994 address to the Supreme Court Historical Society, quoting a couplet of Thomas à Becket in T. S. Eliot's *Murder in the Cathedral*, when Becket is tempted by the devil to resist Henry II, he rebuffs him with the retort, "That would be greatest treason, to do the right deed for the wrong reason." The same principle applies to judicial opinions, claimed Scalia, "to get the reasons wrong is to get it all wrong, and that is worth a dissent, even if the dissent is called a concurrence." Scalia praised separate opinions for their internal and external consequences. "The most important internal effect of a system permitting dissents and concurrences is to improve the majority opinion." The prospect of a dissent, he emphasized, may make the majority's opinion writer receptive to suggested changes, and a draft dissent "often causes the majority to refine its opinion, eliminating the more vulnerable assertions." Also, Scalia added, "a system of separate opinions renders the profession of a judge—and I think even the profession of a lawyer—more enjoyable." In addition, Scalia contended that "dissents augment rather than diminish the prestige of the Court. When history demonstrates that one of the Court's decisions has been a truly horrendous mistake, it is comforting— and conducive of respect for the Court—to look back and realize that at least some of the Justices saw the danger clearly, and gave voice, often eloquent voice, to their concern." "A second external consequence of a concurring or dissenting opinion is that it can help change the law," as well as "inform the public in general, and the bar in particular, about the state of the Court's collective mind." Finally, Scalia stressed that, "By enabling, indeed compelling, the Justices of our Court, through their personally signed majority, dissenting and concurring opinions, to set forth clear and consistent positions on both sides of the major legal issues of the day, it has kept the Court in the forefront of the intellectual development of the law . . . . The Court itself is not just the central organ of legal *judgment;* it is center stage for significant legal *debate.*"[184]

DISSENTING BEHAVIOR OF POST-1937 JUSTICES

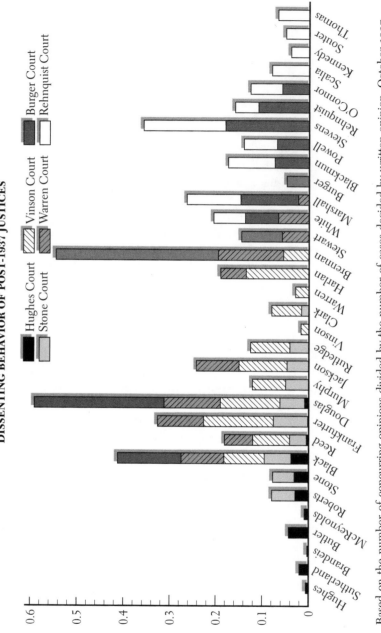

Based on the number of concurring opinions divided by the number of cases decided by written opinion, October 1937 term to 1995–1996 term.

Institutional and Individual Opinions

The devaluation of opinions for the Court and the greater premium placed on individual opinions may affect the implementation of Supreme Court policy-making. Even Black, who had no qualms about threatening or filing separate opinions, recognized the importance of institutional opinions. Black wrote Tom Clark about one of his proposed opinions:

I have no idea what troubles you about my treatment of the [case]. . . . It is rather bad I think to have less than a majority for a court opinion. Consequently, I would be glad to see if your objections, whatever they are, can be met. I feel so strongly that one should have a court opinion that I would be willing to have the case reassigned if that would help.[185]

By contrast, Frankfurter came to value individual expression more than the compromises and cooperation essential to achieving institutional opinions. "Unanimity is an appealing abstraction," Frankfurter concluded, but "a single Court statement on important constitutional issues and other aspects of public law is bound to smother differences that in the interests of candor and of the best interest of the Court ought to be expressed.[186]

A number of realities lie behind the changing norms and patterns of institutional and individual opinions. Individual opinion writing, as noted earlier became institutionalized after the arrival of the New Deal justices. In addition, personal and ideological differences contribute. The contemporary Court's virtually complete discretionary jurisdiction also enables it to select primarily cases of national importance for public law and policy. The Court now decides principally major questions of constitutional and statutory interpretation. These are areas in which the justices are most likely to disagree and to be least inclined to compromise. Constitutional interpretation, in Frankfurter's words, "is not at all a science, but applied politics,"[187] and thus proves especially divisive. Cases granted oral argument and decided by opinion are also the most thoroughly researched and considered cases. They are the ones to which the justices devote the most of their time, and hence those on which they have most clarified their own thinking and differences.

The increasing caseload may also have contributed to changes in norms of opinion writing. The "proliferation of concurring opinions and even some dissenting opinions is a result of these pressures" of a greater workload, Burger claimed, "and the consequent lack of time to try to hammer out differences."[188] In the nineteenth and early twentieth century, the justices spent more time in conference discussing each case and were more inclined to try to reach compromises. There is now less direct communication and more formal, written exchanges among the justices. The justices' "isolation" in their chambers may now also play a part, for, according to Justice Thomas, "there is no going to each other's chambers," as they once did in order to hammer out differences.[189] There are more law clerks as well, along with greater delegation of a responsibility for drafting concurring and dissenting opinions. Justices in turn are less willing to withdraw concurring or dissenting opinions because of the time their clerks devoted to them. As one justice put it, even though his concerns had been accommodated in the majority's opinion, "it would break [his] law clerk's heart" to suppress his concurring opinion.[190]

Accompanying the trend toward more separate opinions has been "the ascendency of the law-review type of opinion" and an "increased length of opinions."[191] Opinions have become not merely more numerous but also longer. Opinions in 1938 averaged about eight pages, by 1970 slightly more than nine pages, and by the 1980s eleven pages. That increase may seem small, but the justices were also writing more than twice as many opinions each term as they did fifty years ago.[192] The Rehnquist Court has cut back on the number of cases decided by full written opinion as well as the length of some of its opinions. Still, the reduction in the number of cases has not led to a corresponding decline in the length of the Court's opinions. In its 1988 term, for instance, the Court handed down 133 decisions with opinions that averaged 7.5 pages in *U.S. Law Week*. By contrast, in the 1993 term 84 full written opinions averaged 8.8 per decision. In other words, the 41 percent decline in the number of signed opinions was accompanied by only a 28 percent decline in the number of pages per opinion.[193]

The justices' opinions also contain a large amount of "boiler plate," restatement of facts, and discussions of nonconstitutional matters, even in constitutional cases. In an analysis of the content of opinions written by Justices Rehnquist and Brennan in constitutional cases between 1973 and 1982, political scientists Glenn Phelps and John Gates found that about half of the (8,368) paragraphs dealt either with the case's facts or matters other than constitutional interpretation. Those two ideologically-opposed justices, moreover, were just as likely to marshall the same kinds of constitutional arguments, though for different ends. As a judicial conservative, Rehnquist champions an *interpretivist* approach to constitutional interpretation, while Brennan was labeled a *non-interpretivist*. Interpretivists generally hold that constitutional interpretation should be confined to the text and historical context of provisions of the Constitution. By contrast, non-interpretivists maintain that constitutional interpretation frequently requires going beyond text and historical context to structural arguments grounded in the Constitution and to broader principles of constitutional politics. Yet, neither approach is inexorably wedded to either a conservative or liberal

COMPARATIVE CONSTITUTIONAL APPROACHES IN OPINIONS

Type of Argument Advanced in Opinions	Rehnquist	Brennan
	Number of Paragraphs (%)	
Doctrinal	1,492 (34.2)	1,513 (37.7)
Statements of Facts	1,320 (30.2)	1,045 (26.0)
Nonconstitutional	942 (21.6)	934 (23.3)
Extrinsic (Non-textual)	391 (8.9)	389 (9.7)
Textual	77 (1.7)	34 (0.8)
Structural	73 (1.6)	42 (1.0)
Historical	67 (1.5)	49 (1.2)
Total	4,362 (99.7)	4,006 (99.7)

political philosophy.[194] And a comparison of opinions by Rehnquist and Brennan reveals not only that, respectively, 51 and 49 percent of the paragraphs in their opinions were devoted to nonconstitutional matters. When the kinds of constitutional arguments made in their opinions were compared, Phelps and Gates found that both overwhelmingly advanced arguments based on *stare decisis* and developing legal doctrines.[195] Besides writing opinions consisting largely in statements of facts and reviewing nonconstitutional matters, as well as drawing heavily on doctrinal arguments, Rehnquist did not significantly appeal to history any more often than Brennan, nor were the latter's opinions significantly more likely to advance non-interpretivist arguments than Rehnquist's.

Less agreement and more numerous and longer opinions invite uncertainty and confusion about the Court's rulings, interpretation of law, and policy-making. As individual opinions came to predominate, they also became more idiosyncratic. "It is a genuine misfortune to have the Court's treatment of the subject be a virtual Tower of Babel, from which no definite principles can be clearly drawn," Rehnquist lamented in his dissent in *Metromedia v. City of San Diego* (1981), adding, "I regret even more keenly my contribution to this judicial clamor, but find that none of the views expressed in the other opinions written in the case came close enough to mine to warrant the necessary compromise to obtain a Court opinion."

SIX

The Court and American Life

W HY DOES the Supreme Court pass the school desegregation case?" asked one of Chief Justice Vinson's law clerks in 1952. *Brown v. Board of Education of Topeka, Kansas* had arrived on the Court's docket in 1951, but it was carried over for oral argument the next term and then consolidated with four other cases and reargued in December 1953. The landmark ruling did not come down until May 17, 1954. "Well," Justice Frankfurter explained, "we're holding it for the election"—1952 was a presidential election year. "You're holding it for the election?" The clerk persisted in disbelief. "I thought the Supreme Court was supposed to decide cases without regard to elections." "When you have a major social political issue of this magnitude," timing and public reactions are important considerations, and, Frankfurter continued, "we do not think this is the time to decide it."[1] Similarly, Tom Clark recalled that the Court awaited, over Douglas's dissent, additional cases from the District of Columbia and other regions, so as "to get a national coverage, rather than a sectional one." Such political considerations are by no means unique. "We often delay adjudication. It's not a question of evading at all,"

Clark concluded. "It's just the practicalities of life—common sense."[2]

Denied the power of the sword or the purse, the Court must cultivate its institutional prestige. The power of the Court lies in the persuasiveness of its rulings and ultimately rests with other political institutions and public opinion. As an independent force, the Court has no chance to resolve great issues of public policy. *Dred Scott v. Sandford* (1857) and *Brown v. Board of Education* (1954) illustrate the limitations of Supreme Court policy-making. The "great folly," as Senator Henry Cabot Lodge characterized *Dred Scott,* was not the Court's interpretation of the Constitution or the unpersuasive moral position that blacks were not persons under the Constitution. Rather, "the attempt of the Court to settle the slavery question by judicial decision was simple madness." As Lodge explained:

Slavery involved not only the great moral issue of the right of one man to hold another in bondage and to buy and sell him but it involved also the foundations of a social fabric covering half the country and caused men to feel so deeply that it finally brought them beyond the question of nullification to a point where the life of the Union was at stake and a decision could only be reached by war.[3]

A hundred years later, political struggles within the country and, notably, presidential and congressional leadership in enforcing the Court's school desegregation ruling saved the moral appeal of *Brown* from becoming another "great folly."

Because the Court's decisions are not self-executing, public reactions inevitably weigh on the minds of the justices. Justice Stone, for one, was furious at Chief Justice Hughes's rush to hand down *Powell v. Alabama* (1932). Picketers protested the Scottsboro boys' conviction and death sentence. Stone attributed the Court's rush to judgment to Hughes's "wish to put a stop to the [public] demonstrations around the Court."[4] Opposition to the school desegregation ruling in *Brown* led to bitter, sometimes violent confrontations. In Little Rock, Arkansas,

Governor Orval Faubus encouraged disobedience by southern segregationists. The federal National Guard had to be called out to maintain order. The school board in Little Rock unsuccessfully pleaded, in *Cooper v. Aaron* (1958), for the Court's postponement of the implementation of *Brown's* mandate. In the midst of the controversy, Frankfurter worried that Chief Justice Warren's attitude had become "more like that of a fighting politician than that of a judicial statesman." In such confrontations between the Court and the country, "the transcending issue," Frankfurter reminded the others, remains that of preserving "the Supreme Court as the authoritative organ of what the Constitution requires."[5] When the justices move too far or too fast in their interpretation of the Constitution, they threaten public acceptance of the Court's legitimacy.

The Court's institutional prestige and role in American politics occasionally weighs heavily on the justices, particularly when confronting major controversies. The plurality opinion issued by Justices Kennedy, O'Connor, and Souter in *Casey*, declining to overrule "the essence of *Roe v. Wade*" while rejecting much of its analysis, as discussed in Chapter One, illustrates that concern. So too, the Court sought to avoid igniting another major controversy in its 1997 rulings in *Washington v. Glucksberg* and *Vacco v. Quill*. There, the Court refused to extend its 1990 ruling in *Cruzan v. Cruzan*, recognizing the right of terminally ill patients to have life-support systems withdrawn, to embrace a right to physician-assisted suicide. Chief Justice Rehnquist's opinion for the Court, and several concurring opinions, emphasized that that claim of the so-called "right to die with dignity" movement should continue to play out in state legislatures and the political process, while not completely ruling out in the future the Court's reconsideration of such a constitutional claim.

The political struggles of the Court (and among the justices) continue after the writing of opinions and final votes. Announcements of decisions trigger diverse reactions from the media, interest groups, lower courts, Congress, the President, and the general public. Their reactions may enhance or thwart compliance and reinforce or undermine the Court's prestige. Opinion days thus may reveal something of the political struggles that might otherwise remain hidden within the marble temple. They may also mark the beginning of larger political struggles for influence in the country.

Opinion Days

The justices announce their decisions in the courtroom, typically crowded with reporters, anxious attorneys, and curious spectators. When several decisions are to be handed down, the justices delivering the Court's opinions make their announcements in reverse order of seniority. Authors of concurring or dissenting opinions are free to give their views orally as well. Before 1857, decisions were announced on any day the Court was in session. Thereafter the practice was to announce decisions only on Mondays, but in 1965 the Court reverted to its earlier practice. In 1971, the Court further broke with the late-nineteenth-century tradition of "Decision Mondays." On Mondays, the Burger Court generally released only orders and summary decisions and admitted new attorneys to its bar. The Rehnquist Court followed that practice until 1995, when it decided that it would immediately release (but not announce in the courtroom) which cases were granted after the Friday conference, instead of waiting until Mondays, so it could speed up the scheduling of oral arguments. In those weeks when the justices hear oral arguments (October through April), the Court usually announces opinions on Tuesdays and Wednesdays, and then on any day of the week during the rest of the term (May, June, and, sometimes, the first week of July). By tradition, there is no prior announcement as to when cases will be handed down.

Even as late as Warren's last term, in 1968–1969, entire days were devoted to the delivery of opinions and admission of attorneys.[6] In 1971, Burger managed to persuade the others, over the strong objections of Black, to make only brief summary announcements. But he failed to get the justices to agree to put an end to what he considered an "archaic practice" of orally announcing opinions from the bench.[7] Justices now announce most opinions in two to four minutes, merely stating the result in each case.

The erosion of the practice of reading the full text of opinions was only partly due to its time-consuming nature. The practice sometimes occasioned outbursts and caustic exchanges among the justices, publicly dramatizing the struggles within the Court. Once, when vigorously dissenting, McReynolds hit the bench with his fist, exclaiming, "The Constitution is gone!" and then explained why he thought so. Frankfurter tended to monopolize opinion days, just as he liked to dominate oral arguments and conference discussions. In one instance, after he had ad-libbed at length when delivering the Court's opinion, Chief Justice Stone snidely remarked, "By God, Felix, if you had put all that stuff in the opinion, never in my life would I have agreed to it."[8] On another occasion, in a relatively minor case, Frankfurter took nearly fifteen minutes to attack the majority's ruling as nonsense. His sharp criticism prompted Chief Justice Warren, who had not even written an opinion in the case, to offer a rebuttal in open Court. Warren then turned to Frankfurter and invited him to respond. Not to be outdone, the latter told the courtroom, "The Chief Justice urges me to comment on what he said, but of course I won't. I have another case."[9] Such extemporaneous exchanges are less common now, with the prevalence of summary announcements.

Communicating Decisions to the Media

"Sir, we write the opinions, we don't explain them." That was the response of New Jersey State Supreme Court Chief Justice Arthur Vanderbilt to a reporter's request that he explain a passage in an opinion. Members of the Supreme Court generally agree with that motto. Opinions, Brennan has observed, "must stand on their own merits without embellishment or comment from the judges who write or join them."[10] Reporters nonetheless complain about the secrecy surrounding the Court's decision making, while justices complain that their decisions are distorted by the media.

Justices appreciate that compliance with their decisions depends on public understanding of their opinions. Sometimes they are particularly sensitive to this consideration. Chief Justice Hughes, for instance, permitted President Roosevelt to run a telephone line from the White House to the Court in order to learn immediately the Court's decision in the *Gold Clause* cases (1935). This decision was vital to the New Deal in upholding FDR's removal of the gold standard and the devaluation of the dollar. In Frankfurter's view, Hughes "established the very bad precedent of pandering to journalist impatience" by pushing for quick decisions and brief opinions.[11] When *Brown v. Board of Education* was decided, Warren insisted that "the opinion should be short, readable by the lay public, non-rhetorical, unemotional and, above all, non-accusatory."[12]

Media coverage of the Court has grown in the last sixty years. In the 1930s, less than half a dozen reporters covered the Court on a regular basis. During Hughes's chief justiceship, a "Press Office" was established in the Office of the Marshal. The single "press officer"—a former reporter—would announce those cases on the Court's conference list and those set for oral argument. Later, in the 1940s, he began distributing an edited list of the cases. Reporters had six small cubicles on the ground floor, just below the courtroom, where they received copies of opinions sent down through a pneumatic tube.[13] By the late 1950s, there were full-time reporters from the United Press International (UPI), the Associated Press (AP), a few major newspapers, and a couple of more specialized legal periodicals, such as *U.S. Law Week*. In the last three decades, the number of reporters steadily increased to about thirty, with a core group of regular journalists about half that number. All three major television networks, along with Cable News Network, once had regular reporters at the Court, but dropped them in the 1980s.

Despite the growing media attention, the justices remain somewhat indifferent to the problems of journalists who try to make the Court's decisions understandable for the public. Inevitably at odds with the Court's traditions, journalists are at times frustrated by their limited access to the justices. Shortly after coming to the Court, Burger was confronted with a petition of grievances by the corps of reporters covering the Court. They presented "an outline of some problems which [they perceived to be] of mutual concern to the Court and to the press" and suggested changes "so that the public may be better informed about the Court." Not all of the demands appeared reasonable from the Court's perspective. The Court was unreceptive to demands for reasons why justices sometimes disqualify themselves from cases and for "access to the staff of the justices." The Court also rejected a proposed press privilege of having—"on a confidential basis"—advance notification and copies of the opinions to be handed down.[14]

But changes have been made, though not without opposition from some justices. On opinion days, journalists now receive copies of the headnotes—prepared by the Reporter of Decisions and summarizing the main points of a decision. Justice Black disapproved on the ground that "the press will understand the opinions better."[15] The Court also now has an expanded Public Information Office, which makes available all filings and briefs for cases on the docket, the Court's conference lists and final opinions, as well as speeches made by the justices. Reporters thus may follow cases from the time of filing to acceptance for oral argument, and then listen to oral arguments and the delivery of decisions as well as immediately read the final published opinions. Even so, the media's access to the justices remains limited. No cameras are permitted in the courtroom when the Court is in session, nor does that prospect appear likely in the near future. As Justice Souter put it in 1996 when testifying before a House of Representatives appropriations committee hearing: "I think the case [against cameras in the courtroom] is so strong that I can tell you that the day you see a camera coming into our courtroom, it's going to roll over my dead body."

In light of these changes, Burger felt that "except for its decision conferences, the Supreme Court literally operates 'in a goldfish bowl.' "[16] But reporters feel differently. They do not have the kind of access to the Court that they do to Congress, the President, and the executive branch. As the *New York Times'* Linda Greenhouse observed, "Sources, leaks, casual contact with newsmakers—none of these hallmarks of Washington journalism exists on the Court beat. . . ."[17] To some the secrecy within the marble temple is disturbing, though others are less troubled by it. "It is more valuable to have a Justice on the record [in a printed opinion] saying what he or she means than hearing some Hill aide anonymously explain the actions of a senator or congressman." As the former *Washington Post* reporter Fred Barbash remarked, "No other institution explains itself at such length, such frightening length."[18]

Some of the difficulties of covering the Court are inherent in the business of journalism—press deadlines, the problems of condensing complex decisions into a 180-second "news slot" or "sound-bite," and possibly, even the training of reporters. The Court has tried to address even such practical matters. For example, in opening the session at ten in the morning rather than at noon, the Warren Court provided a couple of extra hours so as to relieve some of the pressures of reporters' deadlines. "Decision Mondays" were also abandoned in response to complaints that the "massing of opinions" on a single day made conscientious reporting virtually impossible. Reporters continue to complain that the Court hands down too many of its major decisions during the last week of the term.

The public learns through the media something about only

a few of the Court's rulings each term. Usually, only the most controversial rulings by the Court are reported. Studies of media coverage of the Court's rulings indicate that the major television networks report on no more than half of the most important decisions each term, and the bulk of the Court's work receives no attention.[19]

Within a short period of time, both print and broadcast reporters must condense often complex and lengthy opinions in an understandable way for the public. Only about half of the reporters who cover the Court have law degrees. Not surprisingly, they disagree about the importance of formal legal education. "Lawyer-reporters tend to use less jargon," claims NBC's former Court reporter Carl Stern. "Non-lawyers fear to stray from the literal words used by the Court." By contrast, the veteran reporter Lyle Denniston has maintained, "A law degree inhibits one's ability to cover the Court." Law schools, he has insisted, "train you to have too much respect for authority" and "teach you to believe that things are done better the higher you go."[20]

Regardless of whether reporters have a legal background, the interpreting of opinions remains difficult. Some decisions are "literally impossible to decipher," the *New York Times* reporter Linda Greenhouse has noted.[21] Some problems in communicating decisions are of the Court's own making. Since opinions for the Court must meet the approval of a majority of the justices, ambiguity results from the negotiations and compromises necessary to reach agreement. Hughes, for instance, met opposition to one of his opinions because of "the insertion of the word 'reasonable' in certain places," even though he "put in the word out of abundant caution" to qualify the Court's holding. Since it was not "worth while to have a division in the Court over its use in the present case," he omitted the word from the opinion.[22] Ambiguities may also be prudent. They leave problems open for later cases, and the Court preserves its policy-making options. For example, reporters, school boards, and citizens celebrated or cursed *Brown v. Board of Education* for not mandating integration rather than merely ending segregation. But justices like Stanley Reed had no doubt about that "big distinction." They would never have gone along with a ruling mandating integration. As Warren later emphasized, the justices "decided only that the practice of segregating children in public schools solely because of their race was unconstitutional. This left other questions to be answered"—answered in later cases, after the justices had gauged public reactions and further deliberated among themselves.[23]

Misunderstanding also results when opinions include extraneous matter, statements of personal philosophy, and other forms of *obiter dicta*—words entirely unnecessary for the decision of the case. These problems are exacerbated by longer, more heavily footnoted opinions. The justices are particularly confusing when they divide five to four and issue numerous concurring and dissenting opinions.

Implementing Rulings and Achieving Compliance

When deciding major issues of public law and policy, justices must consider strategies for getting public acceptance of their rulings. When striking down the doctrine of "separate but equal" facilities in 1954 in *Brown v. Board of Education (Brown I)*, for instance, the Warren Court waited a year before issuing, in *Brown II*, its mandate for "all deliberate speed" in ending racial segregation in public education.

Resistance to the social policy announced in *Brown I* was expected. A rigid timetable for desegregation would only intensify opposition. During oral arguments on *Brown II*, devoted to the question of what kind of decree the Court should issue to enforce *Brown*, Warren confronted the hard fact of southern resistance. The attorney for South Carolina, S. Emory Rogers, pressed for an open-ended decree—one that would not specify when and how desegregation should take place. He boldly proclaimed:

> Mr. Chief Justice, to say we will conform depends on the decree handed down. I am frank to tell you, right now [in] our district I do not think that we will send—[that] the white people of the district will send their children to the Negro schools. It would be unfair to tell the Court that we are going to do that. I do not think it is. But I do think that something can be worked out. We hope so.

"It is not a question of attitude," Warren shot back, "it is a question of conforming to the decree." Their heated exchange continued as follows:

> CHIEF JUSTICE WARREN: But you are not willing to say here that there would be an honest attempt to conform to this decree, if we did leave it to the district court [to implement]?
> MR. ROGERS: No, I am not. Let us get the word "honest" out of there.
> CHIEF JUSTICE WARREN: No, leave it in.
> MR. ROGERS: No, because I would have to tell you that right now we would not conform—we would not send our white children to the Negro schools.[24]

The exchange reinforced Warren's view "that reasonable attempts to start the integration process is [*sic*] all the court can expect in view of the scope of the problem, and that an order to immediately admit all negroes in white schools would be an absurdity because impossible to obey in many areas. Thus, while total immediate integration might be a reasonable order for Kansas, it would be unreasonable for Virginia, and the district judge might decide that a grade a year or three grades a year is [*sic*] reasonable compliance in Virginia."[25] Six law clerks were assigned to prepare a segregation research report. They summarized available studies, discussed how school districts in different regions could be desegregated, and projected the effects and reactions to various desegregation plans.

The Court's problem, as one of Reed's law clerks put it, was to frame a decree "so as to allow such divergent results without making it so broad that evasion is encouraged."[26] The clerks agreed that there should be a simple decree but disagreed on whether there should be guidelines for its implementation. One clerk opposed any guidelines. The others thought that their absence "smacks of indecisiveness, and gives the extremists more time to operate." The problem was how precise a guideline should be established. What would constitute "good-faith" compliance? "Although we think a 12-year gradual desegregation plan permissible," they confessed, "we are not certain that the opinion should explicitly sanction it."[27]

At conference, Warren repeated these concerns. Black and Minton thought that a simple decree, without an opinion, was enough. As Black explained, "the less we say the better off we are." The others disagreed. A short, simple opinion seemed advisable for reaffirming *Brown I* and providing guidance for dealing with the inevitable problems of compliance. Harlan wanted *Brown II* expressly to recognize that school desegregation was a local problem to be solved by local authorities. The others also insisted on making clear that school boards and lower courts had flexibility in ending segregation. In Burton's view, "neither this Court nor district courts should act as a school board or formulate the program" for desegregation.

Agreement emerged that the Court should issue a short opinion-decree. In a memorandum, Warren summarized the main points of agreement. The opinion should simply state that *Brown I* held racially segregated public schools to be unconstitutional. *Brown II* should acknowledge that the ruling created various administrative problems, but emphasize that "local school authorities have the primary responsibility for assessing and solving these problems; [and] the courts will have to consider these problems in determining whether the efforts of local school authorities" are in good-faith compliance. The cases, he concluded, should be remanded to the lower courts "for such proceedings and decree necessary and proper to carry out this

Court's decision." The justices agreed, and along these lines Warren drafted the Court's short opinion-decree.[28]

The phrase "all deliberate speed" was borrowed from Holmes's opinion in *Virginia v. West Virginia* (1911), a case dealing with how much of the state's public debt, and when, Virginia ought to receive at the time West Virginia broke off and became a state. It was inserted in the final opinion at the suggestion of Frankfurter. Forced integration might lead to a lowering of educational standards. Immediate, court-ordered desegregation, Frankfurter warned, "would make a mockery of the Constitutional adjudication designed to vindicate a claim to equal treatment to achieve 'integrated' but lower educational standards." The Court, he insisted, "does its duty if it gets effectively under way the righting of a wrong. When the wrong is deeply rooted state policy the court does its duty if it decrees measures that reverse the direction of the unconstitutional policy so as to uproot it 'with all deliberate speed.' "[29] As much an apology for not setting precise guidelines as a recognition of the limitations of judicial power, the phrase symbolized the Court's bold moral appeal to the country.

Ten years later, after school closings, massive resistance, and continuing litigation, Black complained: "There has been entirely too much deliberation and not enough speed" in complying with *Brown*. "The time for mere 'deliberate speed' has run out."[30] *Brown*'s moral appeal amounted to little more than an invitation for delay. At the beginning of the school year in 1964, President Johnson was apprised of the piecemeal progress and continuing resistance:

Arkansas: Desegregation expanded in schools in Little Rock and Fort Smith. About 870 Negroes reported in previously white schools, compared to 390 last year. Twenty-one districts desegregated, compared to 13 last year.

Florida: Four counties integrated, bringing to 21 the number admitting Negroes (State has 67 counties). No trouble. Estimated 8,000 Negroes attending all-white schools.

Mississippi: Biloxi—Seventeen Negro children attended integrated classes in four previously all-white elementary schools, after 10 years of angry resistance. *Canton*—Nineteen Negro students attempted to enroll in the all-white high school but left quietly when rejected by school officials. Civil rights workers said earlier they would not oppose school officials if the youngsters were turned away, but would follow with court action later.

Virginia: Virginia will have 25 newly-desegregated districts this year—including Prince Edward County [which had previously closed rather than desegregate its schools]—making 80 of 128 in the State with some integration. About 6,000 Negroes are attending once-white schools.[31]

With no federal leadership, implementation of *Brown* was deliberately slow and uneven. Ruby Martin, an attorney for the U.S. Commission on Civil Rights in the early 1960s, has recalled that "the work of the lawyers from 1954 to 1964 resulted in two percent of the Negro kids in the Southern states attending schools with white students."[32] The Department of Justice had little role in ending school segregation before the passage of the Civil Rights Act of 1964. The department had participated in a few school desegregation cases but ordinarily only by filing *amici* briefs. The Civil Rights Division within the department was created after Congress passed the Civil Rights Act of 1957, which expanded federal jurisdiction over voting rights and which was the first such legislation in eighty-seven years. But the division had virtually no authority, expertise, or resources to enforce *Brown* until the passage of the 1964 act. The litigation strategy during the Kennedy administration sought to secure voting rights for blacks and thereby "encourage the inevitable integration but never at the cost of disturbing the social equilibrium."[33]

Even after the Department of Justice assumed a role in enforcing school desegregation, it initially gave little attention to areas outside the South or to problems other than ending *de jure* segregation—segregation enforced by laws prohibiting the integration of public schools. The department paid almost no attention to *de facto* segregation, caused by socioeconomic conditions such as housing patterns, in the North and the West. President Johnson's special assistant Joseph Califano was advised by the attorney general, "There are no current federal programs directly related to the problem of *de facto* school segregation. Title VI of the Civil Rights Act is of doubtful applicability." Attorney General Nicholas de B. Katzenbach admitted, "[O]ne of our difficulties is that we don't know enough about *de facto* segregation."[34] The Department of Health, Education, and Welfare (HEW) was subsequently given responsibility for the federal government's role in ending segregated schools. It had authority to issue guidelines and review plans for integration. More important, HEW had the power to cut off federal funding if school districts refused to submit to or comply with desegregation plans.

By the mid-1960s, the Departments of Justice and HEW had assumed leadership in implementing *Brown*. But it took time to build records and evidence of segregation in northern and western school districts and to challenge local authorities in the courts. Not until the summer of 1968 did the outgoing Johnson administration initiate the first school desegregation cases in the North and the West and try to achieve the national coverage that the Court envisioned in *Brown*.[35]

In 1969, Black impatiently observed "there is no longer the slightest excuse, reason, or justification for further postponement of the time when every public school system in the United States will be a unitary one."[36] In *Alexander v. Holmes County Board of Education* (1969), the Burger Court agreed on a brief *per curiam* opinion holding that the Fifth Circuit Court of Appeals should deny further requests for delay from southern school districts. In its opinion, the Court observed that the "standard allowing 'all deliberate speed' for desegregation is no longer constitutionally permissible." *Alexander* sent a message to the Nixon administration that "the obligation of every school district is to terminate dual school systems at once and to operate now and hereafter only unitary schools."[37]

The message in *Alexander*, like that in *Brown*, was still ambiguous. Justice Marshall could not win unanimity on finally setting a "cut-off" date for school desegregation. Black threatened a dissenting opinion noting that "all deliberate speed," as Frankfurter understood when suggesting the Holmesian phrase, connotes delay, not speed. Black concluded that the Court's emphasis on "all deliberate speed" had been a "self-inflicted wound." "The duty of this Court and of the others," he implored, "is too simple to require perpetual litigation and deliberation. That duty is to extirpate all racial discrimination from our system of public schools NOW." On the Court less than four months, Burger vigorously opposed setting any final cut-off date for desegregation. Brennan sought consensus, but the justices could not agree on a more precise order than that of proceeding with desegregation plans "here and now." *Alexander*, White lamented in an unpublished memo, "neither says the order is to be entered now, within six months or even with deliberate speed. Hugo," he added, "is convinced that a mistake was made in 1954–1955 with respect to the deliberate speed formula. I am beginning to understand how mistakes like that happen. Nevertheless, I join, expecting the Court of Appeals to make sure that the shortcomings of this order never come to light."[38]

The shortcomings of *Alexander* came to light when the court of appeals delayed yet again. The Court, in *Carter v. West Feliciana Parish School Board* (1970), scolded about the continued failure to proceed with desegregation. This time Burger, Rehnquist, and Stewart voiced their disagreement and insistence on maintaining a flexible approach to implementation. The fifth circuit, they said, "is far more familiar than we with the various situations of these several school districts, some large, some small, some rural and some metropolitan, and has exhibited responsibility and fidelity to the objectives of our holdings in school desegregation cases."

Twenty years after *Brown*, some schools remained segregated. David Mathews, secretary of the Department of Health,

Education, and Welfare, reported to President Ford the results of a survey of half of the nation's primary and secondary public schools, enrolling 91 percent of all students: of these, 42 percent had an "appreciable percentage" of minority students, 16 percent had undertaken desegregation plans, while 26 percent had not, and 7 percent of the school districts remained racially segregated.[39]

For over four decades, problems of implementing and achieving compliance with *Brown* persisted. Litigation by civil rights groups forced change, but it was piecemeal, costly, and modest. The judiciary alone could not achieve desegregation. Evasion and resistance were encouraged by the reluctance of Presidents and Congress to enforce the mandate. Refusing publicly to endorse *Brown*, Eisenhower would not take steps to enforce the decision until violence erupted in Little Rock, Arkansas. He then did so "*not* to enforce integration but to prevent opposition by violence to orders of a court."[40] Later the Kennedy and Johnson administrations lacked congressional authorization and resources to take major initiatives in enforcing school desegregation. Not until 1964, when Congress passed the Civil Rights Act, did the executive branch have such authorization.

Enforcement and implementation required the cooperation and coordination of all three branches. Little progress could be made, as Assistant Attorney General Stephen Pollock has explained, "where historically there had been slavery and a long tradition of discrimination [until] all three branches of the federal government [could] be lined up in support of a movement forward or a requirement for change."[41] The election of Nixon in 1968 then brought changes both in the policies of the executive branch and in the composition of the Court. The simplicity and flexibility of *Brown*, moreover, invited evasion. It produced a continuing struggle over measures, such as gerrymandering school district lines and busing in the 1970s and 1980s, because the mandate itself had evolved from one of ending segregation to one of securing integration in public schools. Republican and

Democratic administrations in turn differed on the means and ends of their enforcement policies in promoting integration.

Over forty years after *Brown,* over 500 school desegregation cases remained in the lower federal courts. At issue in most was whether schools had achieved integration and become free of the vestiges of past segregation. Although lower courts split over how much proof school boards had to show to demonstrate that present *de facto* racial isolation was unrelated to past *de jure* segregation, the Court declined to review major desegregation cases from the mid-1970s to the end of the 1980s. During that time the dynamics of segregation in the country changed, as did the composition and direction of the Court.

In the 1980s support for mandated school desegregation waned and the Reagan and Bush administrations encouraged localities to escape the "burdens" of *Brown* by fighting courts' desegregation orders. The federal bench also grew more conservative and integration proved elusive. By the 1990s resegregation was on the rise in many parts of the country, particularly in the Midwest and Northeast for blacks and in the West for Hispanics. A 1992 report for the National School Boards Association found that there had been no significant progress on the integration of blacks since 1972, and Hispanics were increasingly segregated due to housing patterns, declining white public school enrollments, and the continuing movement away from central cities to the suburbs. Blacks and Hispanics are almost ten times as likely as whites to attend schools in the largest, predominately minority-populated central cities. And resegregation followed the move of both blacks and whites into many suburban areas. However, the South became one of the most integrated regions in the country. Whereas 99 percent of blacks in the South attended all-black schools in 1963, only 24 percent went to schools enrolling 90–100 percent minorities in the late 1980s–1990s. By comparison, 48 percent in the Northeast attended predominantly non-white schools, 42 percent in the Midwest, and 28 percent in the West. Although the Northeast and Midwest have less than half the old Confederacy's proportion of black students, they have twice the South's level of intense segregation. As a result, a "black family moving from Michigan or New Jersey to Georgia or Tennessee is more likely now to see their child grow up in integrated schools than if they had remained in the North."[42]

The war over *Brown*'s mandate for ending state-imposed segregation was won. But fights over achieving integration continued in even more intractable ways because of demographic changes pushing toward renewed *de facto* segregation, profound disagreement over how much could and should be done to root out the vestiges of past discrimination, and the apparent futility of court-ordered integration in regions that were fast becoming racially segregated. Support for the judiciary's continued efforts to force integration also quietly ebbed with each change in the Court's composition. In its 1989 term the Court in *Missouri v. Jenkins* (1990) (*Jenkins I*) upheld the authority of federal judges to order school boards to raise taxes in order to pay for desegregation plans. But Reagan's four appointees—Rehnquist, O'Connor, Scalia, and Kennedy—stood together in disagreeing with the majority's analysis. With the retirements of Justice Brennan in 1990 and a year later of Justice Marshall, the Rehnquist Court signaled a gradual end to the *Brown* era.

Following the appointment of David Souter to replace Brennan, Chief Justice Rehnquist commanded a bare majority in *Board of Education of Oklahoma City Public Schools v. Dowell* (1991), holding that school districts that once intentionally segregated may achieve unitary status and court-ordered busing may stop, despite the fact that some schools remain overwhelming black or white, if they have complied with court orders over a reasonable period of time, are unlikely to return to their former ways, and have for all practical purposes eliminated the vestiges of prior discrimination. But in one of his last dissents, Justice Marshall, joined by Blackmun and Stevens, took a widely different view of *Brown*'s legacy and the vestiges of segregation.

The dissenters would have ruled that the persistence of racially-identifiable schools per se demonstrates that the vestiges of racial discrimination have not been eliminated.

Dowell was not the last word from the Rehnquist Court on judicial supervision of desegregation in the 1990s. Like *Brown,* the ruling was ambiguous, though each pointed in opposite directions. *Brown*'s mandate for "all deliberate speed" provided no guidance for how far lower courts' remedial decrees should go, while *Dowell* offered little guidance for when courts may withdraw and return full responsibility to local school boards. Both the majority and the dissenters in *Dowell* reaffirmed the Warren Court's last major desegregation case, *Green v. New Kent County School Board* (1968), in which it held that lower courts should examine "every facet of school operations," including student assignments, faculty, staff, transportation, extracurricular activities, and facilities. But *Dowell* left undecided the most important issues: how much proof school districts must show in demonstrating that currently racially isolated schools are unrelated to past intentional discrimination, and whether other factors (such as housing patterns) promote the vestiges of segregation and justify continued judicial supervision.

Barely a month after *Dowell* the Court agreed to review several other desegregation cases, including *Freeman v. Pitts,* in order to clarify its new stance. *Freeman* raised the question of how long federal courts should supervise desegregation in DeKalb County, Georgia. The DeKalb County School District, Georgia's largest, with 80,000 students, had a population that was 57 percent black. Half of the black students attended schools that were at least 90 percent black, while a quarter of the white students attended schools in which over 90 percent of the students were white. A federal district, nevertheless, concluded that DeKalb County's schools were integrated and it no longer bore responsibility for continuing supervision. But the Court of Appeals for the Eleventh Circuit reversed, holding on the basis of *Green* that no school could be declared fully integrated until "it maintains at least three years of racial equality in six categories: student assignment, faculty, staff, transportation, extracurricular activities and facilities."

Just days before the Court's scheduled date for oral arguments in *Freeman v. Pitts* on the opening day of the 1991 term, Justice Marshall abruptly retired, after earlier announcing that he would step down upon his successor's confirmation. Since Justice Thomas had not yet been confirmed, he did not participate in the case, which came down six months later on March 31, 1992. Although unanimous in their decision, the justices were not of one mind on how quickly or on what basis lower courts should halt their desegregation orders. Justice Kennedy's opinion for the Court, which only Chief Justice Rehnquist and Justices White, Scalia, and Souter joined, represented a rough compromise on the closing of the *Brown* era.

In reversing the appellate court's decision in *Freeman,* Kennedy held that lower courts may withdraw from supervising discrete categories of school operations, as identified in *Green,* once school districts show compliance with desegregation orders. Lower courts, he added, need neither wait for a period of years before doing so, nor await desegregation in all areas of a school system before they disengage. Yet, his opinion did not go far enough for Scalia, who in a concurrence urged an immediate end to all judicial supervision of schools that no longer intentionally discriminated. At the same time, Kennedy's opinion went too far for Justices Blackmun, Stevens, O'Connor, and Souter. They countered in separate concurrences that lower courts should undertake a probing analysis of a school district's record before abandoning desegregation orders. *Dowell* and *Freeman* thus charted a new course, not a dramatic reversal, pointing to a new period of litigation—a period not unlike that immediately after *Brown* but in which lower courts gradually move to relinquish, rather than assert, control over public schools.

The new course signaled in *Dowell* and *Freeman* was further underscored in *Missouri v. Jenkins* (1995) (*Jenkins II*). There, writing for a bare majority, Chief Justice Rehnquist ruled that a lower federal court exceeded its power in ordering the creation of magnet schools and greater funding for the Kansas City school district, which is predominantly black due to "white flight," in order to make the city's schools more attractive to white students living in the suburbs. By contrast, dissenting Justices Breyer, Ginsburg, Souter, and Stevens disagreed. "Given the deep, inglorious history of segregation in Missouri," in Justice Ginsburg's words, "to curtail desegregation at this time and in this manner is an action at once too swift and too soon."

By the end of the 1990s, numerous court-ordered desegregation orders throughout the country had been lifted and many school districts were reverting to some version of a neighborhood school district, including Austin, Texas; Broward County, Florida; Cleveland, Ohio; Denver, Colorado; and Norfolk, Virginia. *Dowell, Freeman*, and *Jenkins II* had, indeed, signaled the end of *Brown*'s era of court-ordered desegregation. And the twentieth century ended with states and local school districts increasingly facing the problems of racial disparities and of finding ways to equalize financial disparities among and within school districts so as to address the continuing problems of academic performance and to provide equal educational opportunities.[43]

"By itself," the political scientist Robert Dahl observed, "the Court is almost powerless to affect the course of national policy."[44] Another political scientist, Gerald Rosenberg, goes much farther in claiming that "courts can *almost never* be effective producers of significant social reform."[45] *Brown*'s failure to achieve immediate and widespread desegregation is instructive, Rosenberg contends, in developing a model of judicial policy-making on the basis of two opposing theories of judicial power. On the theory of a "Constrainted Court" three institutional factors limit judicial policy-making: "[t]he limited nature of constitutional rights"; "[t]he lack of judicial independence"; and "[t]he judiciary's lack of powers of implementation." On the other hand, a "Dynamic Court" theory emphasizes the judiciary's freedom "from electoral constraints and [other] institutional arrangements that stymie change," and thus enable the courts to take on issues that other political institutions might not or cannot. But neither theory is completely satisfactory, according to Rosenberg, because occasionally courts do bring about social change. The Court may do so when the three institutional restraints identified with the "Constrained Court" theory are absent and at least one of the following conditions exist to support judicial policy-making: when other political institutions and actors offer either (a) incentives or (b) costs to induce compliance; (c) "when judicial decisions can be implemented by the market"; or (d) when the Court's ruling serves as "a shield, cover, or excuse, for persons crucial to implementation who are *willing to act*." On the historical basis of resistance and forced compliance with *Brown*'s mandate, Rosenberg concludes that "*Brown* and its progeny stand for the proposition that courts are impotent to produce significant social reform."

Brown, nonetheless, dramatically and undeniably altered the course of American life in ways and for reasons that Rosenberg underestimates. Neither Congress nor President Eisenhower would have moved to end segregated schools in the 1950s, as their reluctance for a decade to enforce *Brown* underscores. The Court lent moral force and legitimacy to the civil rights movement and to the eventual move by Congress and President Johnson to enforce compliance with *Brown*. More important, to argue that the Court is impotent to bring about social change overstates the case. Neither Congress nor the President, any more than the Court, could have single-handedly dismantled racially segregated public schools. As political scientist Richard Neustadt has argued, presidential power ultimately turns on a President's power of persuasion,[46] the Court's power depends on the persuasiveness of its rulings and the magnitude of change in social behavior mandated.

The Court raises the ante in its bid for compliance when it appeals for massive social change through a prescribed course of action, in contrast to when it simply says "no" when striking down a law. The unanimous but ambiguous ruling in *Brown* reflects the justices' awareness that their decisions are not self-enforcing, especially when they deal with highly controversial issues and their rulings depend heavily on other institutions for implementation. Moreover, the ambiguity of *Brown's* remedial decree was the price of achieving unanimity. Unanimity appeared necessary if the Court was to preserve its institutional prestige while pursuing revolutionary change in social policy. The justices sacrificed their own policy preferences for more precise guidelines, while the Court tolerated lengthy delays in recognition of the costs of open defiance, building consensus, and gaining public acceptance. But in the ensuing decades *Brown's* mandate was also transformed from that of a simple decree for putting an end to state-imposed segregation into the more vexing one of achieving integrated public schools. With that transformation of *Brown's* mandate the political dynamics of the desegregation controversy evolved, along with a changing Court and country.

PUBLIC OPINION AND PARTISAN REALIGNMENT

Public opinion serves to curb the Court when it threatens to go too far or too fast in its rulings. The Court has usually been in step with major political movements, except during transitional periods or critical elections.[47] It would nevertheless be wrong to conclude, along with Finley Peter Dunne's fictional Mr. Dooley, that "th' supreme court follows th' iliction returns."[48] To be sure, the battle over FDR's "Court-packing" plan and the Court's "switch in time that saved nine" in 1937 give that impression. Public opinion supported the New Deal, but after his landslide reelection in 1936, turned against FDR when he proposed to "pack the Court" by increasing its size from nine to fifteen. In a series of five-to-four and six-to-three decisions in 1935–1936, the Court had struck down virtually every important measure of FDR's New Deal program. But in the spring of 1937, while the Senate Judiciary Committee considered FDR's proposal, the Court abruptly handed down three five-to-four rulings upholding major pieces of New Deal legislation. Shortly afterward, FDR's close personal friend and soon-to-be nominee for the Court, Felix Frankfurter, wrote Justice Stone confessing that he was "not wholly happy in thinking that Mr. Dooley should, in the course of history turn out to have been one of the most distinguished legal philosophers."[49] Frankfurter, of course, knew that justices do not simply follow the election returns. The fact that the Court abandoned its opposition to the New Deal when it did, moreover, significantly undercut public support for FDR's Court-packing plan. Gallup polls taken during the spring of 1937 reveal that the Court's switch-in-time influenced the shift in public opinion away from support for FDR's proposed reforms. In this instance at least, as political scientist Gregory Caldeira concludes, the Court "outmaneuvered the president" and by retreating from its defense of conservative economic policy shaped public opinion in favor of preserving its institutional integrity.[50] However, as noted in Chapter 2, the "switch in time that saved nine," the actual vote to uphold New Deal legislation, took place in conference in December 1936, prior to FDR's introduction of his Court-packing proposal. But, the publication of its opinions upholding progressive legislation in Spring 1937 was, to be sure, timely and influential.

Life in the marble temple is not immune from shifts in public opinion. For one thing, Scalia emphasizes, "it's a little unrealistic to talk about the Court as though it's a continuing, unchanging institution rather than to some extent necessarily a reflection of the society in which it functions. Ultimately, the justices of the Court are taken from the society, [and] if the society changes, you are going eventually to be drawing judges from that same society, and however impartial they may try to be, they are going to bring with them those societ[al] attitudes."[51]

Justice Antonin Scalia, appointed to the Supreme Court by Ronald Reagan in 1986. (*AP/Wide World Photos, Inc.*)

The justices, however, deny being directly influenced by public opinion. In a 1993 interview on ABC's "Nightline," for instance, Justice Blackmun twice mentioned public opinion and support for capital punishment when discussing his opposition to the death penalty. But, when asked, "Why would public opinion have any impact on the thinking of a Supreme Court justice on an issue as vital as the death penalty?" Blackmun responded, "Well, the reference I have just made, of course, I have made because I disagree with it. I don't agree with it, and I am not influenced by it."[52]

The Court's prestige rests on preserving the public's view that justices base their decisions on interpretations of the law, rather than on their personal policy preferences. Yet complete indifference to public opinion would be the height of judicial arrogance. Even one so devoted to the law as Frankfurter was not above appealing to the forces of public opinion. When the Warren Court debated the landmark reapportionment case, Frankfurter asked Stewart—who had the pivotal vote—to consider that *Baker v. Carr* could

bring the Court in conflict with political forces and exacerbate political feeling widely throughout the Nation on a larger scale, though not so pathologically, as the Segregation cases have stirred. The latter . . . resulted in merely regional feeling against the Court, with the feeling of most of the country strongly in sympathy with the Court. But if one is right about the widely scattered assailable apportionment disparities, . . . clash and tension between Court and country and politicians will assert themselves within a far wider area than the Segregation cases have aroused.

Baker v. Carr, Frankfurter feared, would turn the whole country against the Court. But after there was a clear majority for the overturning of laws that denied equal voting rights, Douglas pushed for an early announcement of the decision with the comment "This is an election year."[53]

Changes in the composition of the high bench, as Justice Scalia suggests, appear to register broader changes in the country. A number of political scientists theorize and draw on various kinds of data to support the hypothesis that the Court usually registers public opinion and legitimates policies of the prevailing national alliance, rather than playing the role a counter-majoritarian institution over the long haul.[54] But studies of the Court's relationship to public opinion encounter theoretical and methodological problems because they often draw on indirect measures of public opinion,[55] for example, focusing on polls in relation to only a few landmark rulings, lack consistent data, and fail to control for the effects of eliciting variable responses due to phrasing questions in different ways about complex issues, such as a woman's right to obtain an abortion. Studies matching national polls with the Court's rulings reveal considerable congruence, though levels of agreement vary from one policy area to another.[56] Still, such aggregate analyses do not answer the vexing causal question of whether the Court reacts to public opinion or whether the latter is shaped by the Court. Nor do they address the extent to which other political forces intervene and linkages between the Court and its approval ratings among various constituents.[57]

Whether the Court should or does stay in step with the opinion of dominant national political coalitions remains problematic in other ways as well. As an unelected body, the Court's role is basically counter-majoritarian and therefore whether it ought to "stay in tune with the times" is highly debatable.[58] Whether the Court assumes the role of a majoritarian-reinforcing institution also seems doubtful. Vacancies on the bench occur almost randomly and at times are unrelated to shifts in electoral politics. Moreover, it is unclear that the Court always confers legitimacy on the policies of other nationally democratically accountable institutions.

The Court's bearing on shifts in the electorate and public opinion is complicated and reveals no historically prescribed role. American electoral politics periodically undergoes partisan realignment coinciding with the rise and fall of majority parties.[59] The Federalist-Jeffersonian period of the early Republic ran from 1789 to 1828 and then gave way to the Jacksonian era (1828–1860). Abraham Lincoln's election in 1860 marked the beginning of a Republican era that ended in 1896, only to be followed by a second Republican era lasting until 1932. With FDR's election in 1932 the New Deal-Democratic party coalition came together and prevailed until the late 1960s. Since that coalition's breakup, divided government has persisted with Republicans winning the presidency (except in the 1976 and 1992 elections) and Democrats retaining hold on both houses of Congress (with the exception of the early 1980s when the Senate was lost briefly), until Republicans won back both houses in the 1994 midterm election. These periods of realignment and dealignment arose from issues cutting deeply across existing lines of ideological cleavage and resulting in sharply polarized electorates and parties' redefinition. Cleavages emerged over slavery in the 1850s; between rich and poor in the 1880s and 1890s; over progressive economic regulations in the 1930s; and due to the quest for racial equality, combatting rising crime, and cultural clashes over life-style choices in the 1960s. The party system and dominant national political coalitions have thus been transformed by critical elections and a series of dealigning elections since 1960.

During critical elections in 1860, 1896, 1932, 1960, and 1964, some political scientists argue, the Court supported the reigning party by helping shape its positions on critical issues.[60] Other scholars contend however, that after critical elections the Court stands firm and does battle with the newly emergent majority party. Yet, as political scientist John B. Gates has shown, "neither role appears inevitable," nor has the Court played the same role in each realignment.[61]

Before the 1860 election, *Dred Scott* fanned the flames of sectional conflict over slavery, and prior to the 1896 election, the Court reinforced the laissez-faire economic policies of the old Republican party by overturning federal income tax legislation and restricting the enforcement of antitrust laws. Still, after Lincoln's victory and his securing a new majority of Republican justices on the bench, the Court did not invariably side with him or his party's policies. Prior to the New Deal realignment the Court sent mixed signals on progressive economic policies, yet after the 1932 election virtually went to war with FDR and Congress over the New Deal. During the subsequent constitutional crisis in 1937 the Court then abruptly reversed course, despite no changes in membership. In the 1960s the Warren Court's rulings reinforced the liberal-egalitarian social policies promoted by the Democratic party. At the same time, the Court thereby contributed to the defection of white middle-class voters, especially in the South, and to the breakup of the old New Deal coalition. Already angry over LBJ's pushing the Civil Rights Act of 1964 through the Democrat-controlled Congress, voters grew increasingly bitter over forced integration, rising crime rates, affirmative action, and higher taxes. "Liberal judicial activism," "crime control," and quotas became powerful symbols for Republican presidential candidates from Nixon to Bush.[62] In short, the Court has not consistently played a prescribed role either before or after partisan realignments.

The relationship between the Court and public opinion remains subtle, complex, and difficult to measure. Most of the Court's decisions attract neither media nor widespread public attention. The public tends to identify with the Court's institutional symbol as a temple of law rather than of politics—impartial and removed from the pressures of special partisan interests.[63] Yet there is a strong relationship between diffuse public support for the Court and agreement with its recent rulings, political ideology, and partisanship.[64] Issues like school desegregation and abortion focus public attention and may mobilize public support for or opposition to the Court. In the last fifty years, public confidence in the Court has ebbed and flowed with changes in the direction of its policy-making on major issues affecting American life. From the mid-1960s to the mid-1980s, confidence declined in relation to the Court's rulings protecting the rights of the accused, invalidation of state and federal laws, and to presidential popularity.[65] But the Court's composition changed dramatically in the late 1980s and 1990s with Reagan's, Bush's, and Clinton's appointees. The Court continues to be generally held in high regard by the public and polls indicate that the Court's move in more conservative directions—

on the rights of the accused, for instance—is in accord with public opinion.[66]

Does the Court influence public opinion or does the latter influence the Court? There is no simple answer. Much depends on the Court's composition, what and how it decides particular issues, and its salience for the public in the short and long run; in Caldeira's words, "Sometimes opinion moves against the Court; at other times it follows the Court; and at still others it scarcely moves at all."[67]

CONSTITUENTS AND PUBLICS

Less concerned about public opinion than are elected public officials, justices are sensitive to the attitudes of the Court's immediate constituents: the solicitor general, the attorney general, and the Department of Justice, counsel for federal agencies, states' attorneys general, and the legal profession. Their responses to the Court's rulings shape public understanding and determine the extent of compliance.

The solicitor general, attorney general, and agency counsel interpret the Court's decisions and advise the White House and agencies on compliance. Justices may find a favorable or unfavorable reception from the executive branch. Immediately after *Alexander*, for instance, Nixon directed his staff to begin work on how to combat both the Court's implicit sanctioning of busing and its eventual approval of court-ordered busing in *Swann v. Charlotte-Mecklenburg Board of Education* (1971). The solicitor general decides which and what kinds of cases to take to the Court. In selecting cases, he tries to offer the Court (or a majority) opportunities for pursuing its policy goals and those of the President.

The attorney general, cabinet heads, and agency counsel may likewise extend or thwart the Court's policies. They do so through their advisory opinions, litigation strategies, and development of agency policy and programs. During the Ford administration and the continuing controversy over busing, for

instance, the Department of Justice tried to achieve retrenchment from court-ordered busing by its selection of cases and
relitigation of busing issues. At the same time, White House
counsel and HEW sought ways to avoid busing and to "depolit-
icize" the controversy.[68]

The reactions of the fifty state attorneys general are no less
important. They have a pivotal role in advising governors, may-
ors, police chiefs, and others in their states. Their responses tend
to reflect state and local reactions to the Court's rulings.
Regional differences were evident in responses to the 1962 and
1963 school prayer decisions. The Court struck down a state-
composed prayer in *Engel v. Vitale* (1962) and the reciting of
the Lord's Prayer in public schools in *Abington School District
v. Schempp* (1963). Long-standing practices of school prayer in
the East and the South were not to be easily relinquished. Voluntary school prayer, silent meditation, and "the objective study
of the Bible and of religion" were viewed as still permissible.
Where school prayer received support in state constitutions or
legislation, state and local officials denied the legitimacy of the
Court's decrees and refused to obey.

Local and regional opposition to rulings like those on school
desegregation and prayer does not emerge in a vacuum. Opposition tends to reflect broader national political debates. Southern resistance to *Brown* was encouraged in 1957 by 101 U.S.
senators and representatives who signed the "Southern Manifesto," challenging the authority of the Court and declaring:

> We pledge ourselves to use all lawful means to bring about a rever-
> sal of this decision [*Brown v. Board of Education*] which is contrary
> to the Constitution and to prevent the use of force in its implemen-
> tation.
>
> In this trying period, as we seek to right this wrong, we appeal to
> our people not to be provoked by the agitators and trouble makers
> invading our states and to scrupulously refrain from disorder and law-
> lessness.[69]

Congressional and presidential responses to the school

prayer rulings similarly have tended to legitimize opposition to the Court's decisions. Within three days after *Engel*, more than fifty proposed constitutional amendments to override or limit the decision were introduced in Congress. Two decades later, the number had swelled into the hundreds. Both the House of Representatives and the Senate at various times voted in favor of constitutional amendments but failed to achieve their enactment. Congress did pass appropriations bills for the Department of Education specifying that no funds "shall be used to prevent the implementation of programs of voluntary prayer and meditation in the public schools." In 1982, Reagan asked Congress to pass the following constitutional amendment:

Nothing in this Constitution shall be construed to prohibit individual or group prayer in public schools or other public institutions. No person shall be required by the United States or by any State to participate in prayer.[70]

Over twenty years after *Engel*, compliance remained uneven. Twenty-two states had laws calling for silent or voluntary prayers at the beginning of the school day in public schools. Arizona, Connecticut, and Rhode Island permitted classes to begin with a moment of silent meditation. But in *Wallace v. Jaffree* (1985), the Court reaffirmed its earlier rulings. Over the dissent of Burger, White, and Rehnquist, the Court struck down an Alabama law requiring each school day to begin with a moment of silent prayer or meditation. The majority held that states may not require silent prayer, though meditation may be allowed so long as states do not expressly try to promote religion in the classroom. *Wallace v. Jaffree* intensified opposition and congressional and presidential attempts to thwart, if not reverse, the Court's rulings on school prayer.[71]

Seven years after *Wallace*, and the elevation of Rehnquist to chief justice and the appointments of Scalia, Kennedy, Souter, and Thomas, the Court reconsidered the issue of prayer in public schools in *Lee v. Weisman* (1992). That case posed a challenge to school authorities allowing the inclusion of brief prayerful mentions of God in invocations and benedictions during graduation ceremonies. The Bush administration joined the suit in an *amicus* brief, asking the Court to jettison earlier rulings barring prayer in public schools and to legitimate "the practice under assault [as a] non-coercive, ceremonial acknowledgement of the heritage of a deeply religious people." However, in a somewhat surprising decision, given the changes in the Court's composition, a bare majority rejected that invitation to abandon its prior rulings and held that even non-sectarian benedictions violate the First Amendment's bar to government establishment of religion.

Justice Kennedy announced *Lee v. Weisman* because he cast the deciding vote in a ruling that otherwise split the justices four to four. The school district's supervision of graduation ceremonies, according to Kennedy, "places public pressure, as well as peer pressure, on attending students to stand as a group or, at least, maintain respectful silence during the Invocation and Benediction. This pressure, though subtle and indirect, can be as real as any overt compulsion." And he concluded that under any of the Court's First Amendment tests "the government may not coerce anyone to support or participate in religion or its exercise." Kennedy's opinion, though, held out the possibility that government may endorse religion in other ways, and that he might join the four dissenters here in other cases allowing governmental involvement with religion outside of public schools, as with official displays of creches and other religious symbols.

When the Court attempts to forge major changes, its rulings galvanize special-interest groups. *Brown* sent a signal to groups like the NAACP and the ACLU to use the judicial process to achieve what they could not through the political process. The school prayer and abortion decisions, likewise, fragmented the Court's public. Polarized by the Court's decisions and often divided over its authority to decide major issues of public policy, special-interest groups fuel political struggles at all levels of government.

The justices may also consider the anticipated reactions of the immediate audience of the Court's rulings. One example is that of Chief Justice Warren in *Miranda v. Arizona* (1966), which held that police must read suspects their Fifth and Sixth Amendment rights to remain silent and to consult and have an attorney present during police questioning.

When working on *Miranda*, Warren recalled a controversy involving a law professor's seminar for Minneapolis-area police and Minnesota's state attorney general (and later Senator and Vice President) Walter Mondale. At the seminar, police were told how to adhere to the Court's decisions and still maintain past interrogation practices. "For instance, you're supposed to arraign a prisoner before a magistrate without unreasonable delay," the law professor advised. "But if the magistrate goes hunting for the weekend on a Friday afternoon at 3:00 p.m., you can arrange to arrest your suspect at 3:30. That way you've got the whole weekend." Mondale took the law professor to task. At a news conference, he responded, "Some persons claim the Supreme Court has gone too far. Others claim to know how constitutional protections may be avoided by tricky indirection. Both viewpoints are wrong—this [seminar] was called to assist us in better fulfilling our sworn duty to uphold the Constitution. It was not called to second guess the Supreme Court." Warren knew full well that not all state attorneys general and police supported the Court's rulings on criminal procedure. He therefore strove to outline in *Miranda* a code for police procedures governing the interrogation of criminal suspects that police could not easily evade. There was considerable antagonism toward the *Miranda* warnings, but they became widely accepted in police practice.[72]

Policy considerations, such as the cost of compliance, may also persuade the justices to limit the scope and application of their decisions. In another controversial decision, *Mapp v. Ohio* (1961), the Warren Court reversed an earlier holding in *Wolf v. Colorado* (1949). In *Wolf*, the Court had held that the Fourth

Amendment's prohibition against "unreasonable searches and seizures" applied to the states and the national government. But the Court refused also to extend to the states the Fourth Amendment's exclusionary rule, forbidding the use at trial of evidence obtained in violation of requirements for a proper search and seizure. *Mapp* reversed *Wolf* by holding that the exclusionary rule applies in state as well as in federal courts. The decision raised the possibility that all convictions secured in state courts before 1961 on the basis of illegally obtained evidence would be challenged and new trials demanded.

The Court's decisions have traditionally applied retroactively, permitting individuals to have retrials. In *Linkletter v. Walker* (1965), however, the Court refused to apply *Mapp* retroactively. Justice Clark reasoned that the exclusionary rule was designed to deter police misconduct and that retrials "would tax the administration of justice to the utmost." The Burger Court subsequently developed what became known as its "ambulatory-retroactively doctrine" in other areas of criminal law as well. "That doctrine," Harlan explained, "was the product of the Court's disquietude with the impacts of its fast-moving pace in constitutional innovation in the criminal field." But he also objected that the doctrine merely rationalizes the Court's freedom "to act, in effect, like a legislature, making its new constitutional rules wholly or partially retroactive or only prospective as it deems wise."[73]

The Court has no direct means of mobilizing support for its rulings. Justices may appeal, as Frankfurter unsuccessfully did during the Little Rock school desegregation crisis in *Cooper v. Aaron*, to the legal profession for understanding and assistance. He felt compelled to do so because many of his former students at Harvard Law School were leading members of the southern bar and because the ex-justice (and former governor of South Carolina) James Byrnes had called on the country to curb the Court. Byrnes had published an attack on *Brown* and an article written by one of Frankfurter's favorite former law clerks, Alexander Bickel. As a clerk, Bickel had prepared a lengthy research report on school desegregation when the Court first considered *Brown*. Later, when back at Harvard, Bickel revised and published it in the *Harvard Law Review*. Given Byrnes's attack, Frankfurter personally felt the need to lecture southern lawyers on the legitimacy of the Court's ruling in *Brown*.[74]

Justices usually maintain close relationships with members of the legal profession, which provides the justices with a natural constituency. A former president of the American Bar Association (ABA), Lewis Powell urged bar associations to lobby for congressional legislation to limit the availability of criminal appeals.[75] Burger repeatedly appealed to the ABA to lobby Congress for improvements in the administration of justice. Mobilizing the ABA depends on the issue and on ideological compatibility. Whereas Burger enjoyed the support of most of the leadership of the ABA, his predecessor resigned as a member and refused to attend any meetings of the association. Warren did so because the ABA castigated the Court for its desegregation and "pro-Red" rulings. The ABA contributed to the hysteria of the McCarthy era and lent credibility to campaigns, like that of the John Birch Society, to "Impeach Earl Warren." The ABA does not represent the views of all members or of the legal profession as a whole, but its resources and prestige are useful political weapons for or against the Court.

The Court is an instrument of political power, but the justices remain dependent on the attitudes and actions of their immediate constituents, elected officials, and the dynamics of pressure-group politics and public opinion. Implementation and compliance largely depend on lower courts, Congress, and the President.

COMPETITION AND COMPLIANCE IN LOWER COURTS

The Court's "bare bones" opinion-decree in *Brown II* maximized flexibility. "Local passions aroused by [*Brown I*] would thereby be absorbed or tempered," Frankfurter insisted. But, he pointed out, "local conflicts would be left on the doorsteps of local judges." The Court left the job of achieving compliance to the lower courts. Unloading "responsibility upon lower courts most subject to community pressures without any guidelines for them except our decision of unconstitutionality," Frankfurter prophetically observed, "would result in drawn-out, indefinite delay without even colorable compliance."[76]

Lower-court judges bore the social and psychological burdens of opposition to *Brown*. Initially, for many southern judges, social ostracism became a fact of life. As the political scientist Jack Peltason describes in his book *Fifty-eight Lonely Men: Southern Federal Judges and School Desegregation*:

The District judge is very much a part of the life of the South. He must eventually leave his chambers and when he does he attends a Rotary lunch or stops at the club to drink with men outraged by what they consider "judicial tyranny." A judge who makes rulings adverse to segregation is not likely to be honored by testimonial dinners, or to read flattering editorials in the local press, or to partake in the fellowship at the club.

There were also less gentle and subtle pressures on judges. They were forced "to discontinue the public listing of their telephone number to avoid anonymous and obscene telephone calls made round the clock. Their mail [was] loaded with threatening letters. Some [were] forced to seek police protection for themselves and their families."[77] Others, like Judge J. Skelly Wright in Louisiana, were denied elevation from district to circuit courts. Their rulings angered southern senators, who invoked "senatorial courtesy" to veto their appointments.

When trial judges decide wide-ranging disputes over desegregation or the environment, community pressures may confront them with hard choices. The more responsive to local community values judges are, the more threatened their legitimacy as dispassionate enforcers of national law. Circuit court of appeals judges are, to an extent, geographically removed from local community pressure. Still, the decentralized structure of the federal judiciary encourages them to apply the Court's decisions in ways that accommodate regional and local values. Federal appellate judges fashion a law of the circuit. Among the circuits, the political scientist J. Woodford Howard has found, "[i]nformal norms are national in scope but regionally enforced."[78] Unlike southern circuit judges after *Brown*, for instance, northern appellate court judges ordered massive busing and redistricting of school lines in order to achieve integration. Appellate court judges thus regionalize public law and policy.

Compliance with the Court's decisions by lower courts is invariably uneven. They may extend or limit decisions in anticipation of later rulings by the high court. Following the watershed ruling on privacy in *Griswold v. Connecticut* (1965), lower courts interpreted the newfound constitutional right of privacy as striking down a wide range of laws, from those limiting the length of male employees' and students' hair, to ones forbidding certain sexual acts between consenting adults and the use of marijuana, to ones requiring psychological tests of applicants for government jobs, and to ones governing access to financial and medical records. The Court reversed or would not approve the extension of the right of privacy in many of these areas.

A simple model of compliance is not very useful: decisions handed down by the Court on major issues of public policy are not necessarily or readily applied by lower courts. Ambiguity and plurality or five-to-four decisions invite lower courts to pursue their own policy goals. Crucial language in an opinion may be treated like *dicta*. Differences between the facts on which the Court ruled and the circumstances of a case at hand may be emphasized so as to distinguish or reach a result opposite to the Court's decision. Lower courts, for example, interpreted *Abington School District v. Schempp*, which struck down compulsory reciting of the Lord's Prayer in public schools, as permitting voluntary and nondenominational prayer in public schools. Likewise, Texas courts refused to extend the ruling in *Norris v. Alabama* (1935), forbidding racial discrimination against blacks in jury selection. They did not forbid the exclusion of Hispanics from juries until *Hernandez v. Texas* (1954) directly ordered them to do so. Lower courts may thus effectively delay implementation and compliance.

Lower courts may also make "exceptions" when applying Supreme Court rulings in anticipation, as the Court's composition changes, that the justices will eventually approve of them and thereby limit earlier rulings. For example, lower courts and finally the Supreme Court carved out a good-faith exception to the Fourth Amendment's exclusionary rule, which prohibits the use in trials of evidence obtained by police in violation of the amendment's requirements for a reasonable search and seizure. In two 1984 rulings, *Massachusetts v. Sheppard* and *United States v. Leon*, the Court upheld the good-faith exception in holding that the exclusionary rule does not bar the use of evidence that police found when conducting a search based on a warrant which they believed to be good but which was later found to be defective. Over a sharp dissent by Justices O'Connor, Brennan, Marshall, and Stevens, the Rehnquist Court in *Illinois v. Krull* (1987) further extended the good-faith exception, when holding that the Fourth Amendment does not require the exclusion of evidence found by police acting under a statute which authorized warrantless searches, but which was later struck down as unconstitutional. Subsequently, by a seven-to-two vote in *Arizona v. Evans* (1995), the Rehnquist Court expanded the "good faith" exception to the exclusionary rule to include police reliance on mistaken computer records of outstanding arrest warrants.

Open defiance is infrequent but not unprecedented. In *Jaffree v. Board of School Commissioners* (1983), a federal district court judge in Alabama directly challenged the legitimacy of the Court. Here the judge upheld the daily recitation of the Lord's Prayer in public schools and expressly rejected the Court's twenty-year-old rulings in *Engel* and *Abington* that the First Amendment's ban on the establishment of religion applies to the states and that compulsory school prayer violates the establishment clause. A majority of the Court rebuffed the lower court when it decided an appeal of the ruling and struck down the "moment of silence" law in *Wallace v. Jaffree* (1985).

Federal and state judges frequently express their disagreements and criticisms of the Court at judicial conferences, at bar association meetings, and in legal publications and correspondence. The Conference of State Chief Justices in 1958 went so far as to pass a resolution condemning the Warren Court for its erosion of federalism and its tendency "to adopt the role of policymaker without proper judicial restraint."[79] The Warren Court's rulings in cases like *Gideon*, *Mapp*, and *Miranda* revolutionized criminal procedure by holding that the rights of the accused guaranteed in the Bill of Rights apply in state no less than in federal courts. The Warren Court thus drew intense criticism from state judges. That criticism is exemplified by the reaction to *Katz v. United States* (1967). *Katz* held that the Fourth Amendment "protects people, not places" and that police must obtain a search warrant before tapping telephone lines, even those of a public telephone booth. Writing to Harlan, one of the most conservative members of the Court at the time, Georgia State Supreme Court Chief Justice William Duckworth castigated the ruling and expressed the views of many critics of the Warren Court:

By such nearsighted decisions you victimize the innocent public and force them to endure crime, solely because some individual officer personally violated rights of the criminal. . . . If your court would recognize that State courts are capable of honestly and intelligently enforcing criminal laws—and by experience know more than most of you about how to do it within the Constitution, the flood-tide of crime would abate. No honest judge can or will deny that the Constitution is the Supreme Law. But Justices of the Supreme Court, although given the final word, are not superior in qualification, dedication and honor in deciding cases.[80]

Surprised by the frankness of the criticism, Harlan responded
that "the great debates that have been taking place, both within
and without the judiciary [are] the product of the extraordinary
era in which we are living and not of any change in the basic
point of view of the federal judiciary."[81]

Opposition and defiance by federal and state judges reflect
their own policy preferences and the political currents of the
time. When the Warren Court handed down *Mapp v. Ohio*
(1961), the California state attorney general (and later state
supreme court justice) Stanley Mosk told Justice Douglas,
"Thank the good Lord for *Mapp v. Ohio*." He explained that a
bare majority of the California State Supreme Court had just
interpreted its state constitution to incorporate the exclusionary
rule. Its decision was attacked by the press and local politicians.
Mosk explained that "with the system of elective judges they
have in California, pressure on the trial courts was very, very
great not to apply [the decision] or to find there were more
exceptions to it, or in others, try to get around it." *Mapp*, Douglas reported to his brethren, took "the pressure off the local
judges to create exceptions and to follow the exclusionary rule
and all its ramifications."[82]

Whether state judges oppose or comply with the Court's
leadership depends on their political views and the direction of
the Court's policy-making. During the Warren Court revolutions
in school desegregation, criminal procedure, and reapportionment, state judges like Georgia's Chief Justice Duckworth complained about the nationalization of public law and policy. The
autonomy of state judges appeared eroded by the Warren
Court's rulings that they respect and apply basic guarantees of
the Bill of Rights. *Miranda*'s safeguards against coerced confessions, for example, established a minimal threshold requirement
that all fifty states had to respect. State courts could guarantee
more procedural safeguards than the Court, but they could not
grant fewer.

From the 1970s through the 1990s, the direction of the
Court's policy-making gradually changed, reflecting the more

conservative views of the appointees of Nixon, Reagan, and Bush. Although not always outright reversing Warren Court rulings, the Court refused further extensions and achieved retrenchment in some areas. More liberal state supreme courts accordingly refused to follow rulings of the Burger and Rehnquist Courts. "Why should we always be the tail being wagged by the Federal dog?" asked New Hampshire State Supreme Court Justice Charles Douglas and other state judges. "Liberal state courts have taken the doctrines of federalism and states' rights, heretofore associated with [conservatives] like George C. Wallace," California's Justice Stanley Mosk has explained, "and adapted them to give citizens more rights under their state constitutions rather than to oppress them." Indeed, since 1969 state supreme courts have handed down hundreds of rulings vindicating rights broader than, or left unprotected by, the Burger and Rehnquist Courts.[83] In *Commonwealth of Kentucky v. Wasson* (1992), for example, the Supreme Court of Kentucky expressly rejected the Court's analysis in *Bowers v. Hardwick* (1986) (discussed in Chapter Five) and struck down its state law against homosexual sodomy as a violation of its state constitution's guarantee of a right of privacy. Several other state supreme courts have done the same, including the Supreme Court of Georgia, which struck down its state law against sodomy in *Powell v. Georgia* (1998) that *Bowers* had previously upheld. Such developments in state constitutional law, in the view of Brennan, are a sign of "the strength of our federal system." By contrast, the Court's conservative members have sought to bring state courts into line by reversing decisions vindicating broader constitutional rights than they approved.[84] In *Michigan v. Long* (1983), the Court announced that when state courts defend rights broader than approved by it, they must clearly and explicitly rest their decisions on "adequate and independent state grounds"—namely, their state constitutions or state constitutional laws. Otherwise, O'Connor observed, in her opinion for the majority, the Court would assume that state courts are relying on federal constitutional law and feel free to review and reverse those decisions with which it disagrees.

CONGRESSIONAL ACTION AND REACTION

Legislators frequently "have gone after the Supreme Court because it doesn't cost anything," Attorney General Nicholas Katzenbach once observed.[85] On the floor of the Senate or the House of Representatives, rhetoric is cheaper than building coalitions. The views of constituents also constrain congressional action. As a senator from Texas in the 1950s, Lyndon Johnson expressed his reservations about the wisdom of *Brown v. Board of Education*. But when responding to his constituents, LBJ was more antagonistic and responsive to their views. "Unfortunately," he wrote to one of them, "the edict was handed down by men many miles removed from our part of the country and in most cases men who had no first-hand knowledge of conditions in the South and Southwest." He assured another, "[T]he people of Texas can depend on me to stand firmly against forced integration."[86]

Major confrontations between Congress and the Court have occurred a number of times. With the election of Thomas Jefferson in 1800, Republicans gained control of Congress. The defeated President John Adams and the outgoing Federalists in Congress passed the Judiciary Act of 1801, creating new circuit court judgeships and stipulating that when the next vacancy on the Court occurred, it should go unfilled. That attempt to maintain influence in the judiciary was quickly countered. In 1802 the Republican Congress repealed the act of 1801, abolishing the judgeships and returning the number of justices to six. Congress also postponed the Court's next term in order to preclude it from immediately hearing a challenge, in *Stuart v. Laird* (1803), to its repealing legislation. When the Court decided *Stuart*, it upheld Congress's power to repeal the Judiciary Act of 1801. The Jeffersonian Republicans then impeached Justice Samuel Chase for expounding Federalist doctrine. Though the

Senate acquitted him, it would not confirm nominees for federal judgeships unless they were Republicans.

The Marshall Court approved the expansion of national governmental power, but in response, Congress in the 1820s and 1830s threatened to remove the Court's jurisdiction over disputes involving states' rights. After the Civil War, Congress succeeded in repealing the Court's jurisdiction over certain denials of writs of *habeas corpus*—orders commanding that a prisoner be brought before a judge and that cause be shown for his imprisonment. In *Ex parte McCardle* (1869), the Court upheld the repeal of its jurisdiction and thus avoided deciding a controversial case attacking the constitutionality of Reconstruction legislation.

At the turn of the century, Progressives in Congress unsuccessfully sought to pressure the Court—dominated at the time by advocates of laissez-faire social and economic policy. They proposed requiring a two-thirds vote by the justices when striking down federal statutes, and permitting Congress to overrule the Court's decisions by a two-thirds majority. The confrontation escalated with the Court's invalidation of the early New Deal program in the 1930s. Although Congress refused to go along with FDR's Court-packing plan, it passed legislation allowing justices to retire, after ten years of service at age seventy, with full rather than half salary. Congress thus made retirement more financially attractive and gave FDR opportunities to appoint justices who shared his political philosophy. Later the Warren Court faced almost persistent attempts to curb its jurisdiction and reverse specific decisions. And the Burger Court's rulings on abortion generated numerous proposals to curb the Court's jurisdiction and overturn or modify its decisions.

Congress may put pressure on the Court in a number of ways. The Senate may try to influence judicial appointments and may impeach justices. More often, Congress uses institutional and jurisdictional changes as weapons against the Court.

Congress has tried to pressure the Court when setting its

terms and size and when authorizing appropriations for salaries, law clerks, secretaries, and office technology. Only once, in 1802, when repealing the Judiciary Act of 1801 and abolishing a session for a year, did Congress actually set the Court's term in order to delay and influence a particular decision.

The size of the Court is not preordained, and changes generally reflect attempts to control the Court. The Jeffersonian Republicans' quick repeal of the act passed by the Federalists in 1801, reducing the number of justices, was the first of several attempts to influence the Court. Presidents James Madison, James Monroe, and John Quincy Adams all claimed that the country's geographical expansion warranted enlarging the size of the Court. But Congress refused to do so until the last day of Andrew Jackson's term, in 1837. During the Civil War, the number of justices increased to ten, ostensibly because of the creation of a tenth circuit in the West. This gave Abraham Lincoln his fourth appointment and a chance to secure a pro-Union majority on the bench. Antagonism toward President Andrew Johnson's Reconstruction policies led to a reduction from ten to seven justices. After General Ulysses S. Grant was elected President, Congress again authorized nine justices—the number that has prevailed. In the nineteenth century, at least, Congress rather successfully denied Presidents additional appointments in order to preserve the Court's policies and increased the number of justices so as to change the ideological composition of the Court.

Although Article III of the Constitution forbids reducing justices' salaries, Congress may withhold salary increases as punishment, especially in times of high inflation. In 1964, when authorizing the first pay increase in almost a decade for federal employees, Congress gave the justices $3,000 less than other top-level employees. Members of Congress did so as a way of expressing their disapproval of Warren Court rulings on reapportionment. Representative (and later Senate leader) Robert Dole, a Kansas Republican, even proposed that for the justices "the effective date of the pay increase, if adopted by this House, would be the date the Supreme Court reverses" its reapportionment decisions.[87]

More direct attacks are possible. Under Article III, Congress is authorized "to make exceptions" to the appellate jurisdiction of the Court. That authorization has been viewed as a way of denying the Court review of certain kinds of cases. But Congress succeeded only once, with the 1868 repeal of jurisdiction over writs of *habeas corpus*, which the Court upheld in *Ex parte McCardle* (1869).[88]

Court-curbing legislation is not a very effective weapon. Rather than limit judicial review, Congress has given the Court the power to set its own agenda and decide major issues of public law and policy—precisely the kinds of issues that Congress then seeks to deny the Court review. The Court has also suggested that it would not approve repeals of its jurisdiction that were merely attempts to dictate how particular kinds of cases should be decided.[89] Most proposals to curb the Court, of course, are simply that. During the McCarthy era, for instance, Republican Senator William Jenner spearheaded a drive to forbid review of cases challenging legislative committees investigating un-American activities. Another unsuccessful attempt was made in 1968 to amend the Omnibus Crime Control and Safe Streets Act so as to prevent the Court from reviewing state criminal cases raising *Miranda* issues. In 1979, Senator Jesse Helms of North Carolina succeeded in persuading the Senate to pass, by a vote of fifty-one to forty, an amendment eliminating federal court jurisdiction over school prayer cases, but the House of Representatives never considered the bill.[90] Given the overwhelming failure of Court-curbing attempts, the political scientist C. Herman Pritchett has pointed out, "Congress can no longer claim with good conscience the authority granted by Article III, Section 2, and every time proposals to exercise such authority are rejected," he adds, "the Court's control over its appellate jurisdiction is correspondingly strengthened."[91]

Congress has had somewhat greater success in reversing the Court by constitutional amendment. Congress must pass a constitutional amendment, which three-fourths of the states must then ratify. The process is cumbersome, and thousands of amendments to overrule the Court have failed. But six decisions have been overturned by constitutional amendment. *Chisholm v. Georgia* (1793), holding that citizens of one state could sue another state in federal courts, was reversed by the Eleventh Amendment, guaranteeing sovereign immunity for states from suits by citizens of another state. The Thirteenth and Fourteenth Amendments, abolishing slavery and making blacks citizens of the United States, technically overturned the ruling in *Dred Scott v. Sandford* (1857) that blacks were not persons under the Constitution. With the ratification in 1913 of the Sixteenth Amendment, Congress reversed *Pollock v. Farmers' Loan and Trust Co.* (1895), which had invalidated a federal income tax. In 1970, an amendment to the Voting Rights Act of 1965 lowered the voting age to eighteen years for all elections. Though he signed the act into law, Nixon had Attorney General John Mitchell challenge the validity of lowering the voting age by simple legislation rather than by constitutional amendment. Within six months, in *Oregon v. Mitchell* (1970), a bare majority of the Burger Court held that Congress had exceeded its power by lowering the voting age for state and local elections. Less than a year later, the Twenty-sixth Amendment was ratified, extending the franchise to eighteen-year-olds in all elections.

In 1920 the Nineteenth Amendment extended voting rights to women and basically nullified *Minor v. Happersett* (1874), in which the Court rejected the claim that women could not be prohibited from voting under the Fourteenth Amendment's equal protection clause. The Twenty-fourth Amendment, ratified in 1964, prohibits the use of poll taxes as a qualification for voting, and thus invalidated the Court's rejection of a Fourteenth Amendment challenge to poll taxes in *Breedlove v. Suttles* (1937). Finally, it bears noting that several leaders in the

Reconstruction Congress maintained that provisions of what became the Fourteenth Amendment in 1868 would effectively override *Barron v. Baltimore* (1833) and apply the Bill of Rights to the states as well as the federal government. Shortly after that amendment's ratification, however, the Court denied that interpretation of the amendment in the *The Slaughterhouse Cases* (1873). But subsequently, in the early and mid-twentieth century, the Court selectively incorporated the major guarantees of the first eight amendments into the Fourteenth Amendment and applied them to the states.[92]

More successful than Court-curbing and Constitution-amending efforts are congressional enactments and rewriting of legislation in response to the Court's rulings. For example, the Court held in *Pennsylvania v. Wheeling and Belmont Bridge Co.* (1852) that a bridge built across the Ohio River obstructed interstate commerce and violated a congressionally approved state compact. Congress immediately passed a statute declaring that the bridge did not obstruct interstate commerce.

Congressional reversals usually relate to nonstatutory matters involving administrative policies. In *Zurcher v. The Stanford Daily* (1978), however, the Court held that there was no constitutional prohibition against police searching newsrooms without a warrant for "mere evidence," photographs, of a crime. Congress basically reversed that holding by passing the Privacy Protection Act of 1980, prohibiting unannounced searches of newsrooms and requiring that such evidence be obtained by a subpoena.

Congressional reversals of the Court's statutory interpretations have historically been less frequent. Congress usually has been constrained by the lobbying efforts of beneficiaries of the Court's rulings. Recently, however, Congress has tended to reverse more statutory decisions of the Court. Between 1967 and 1990, Congress overrode 121 of the Court's statutory decisions; by contrast, between 1945 and 1957 only 21 rulings were overridden.[93] Morever, Congress has increasingly overruled lower federal court decisions as well, as indicated in the table.[94] Notably, 73 percent (89) of the 121 decisions were overturned less than ten years after they had been decided by the Court. Almost 40 percent reversed conservative rulings, while 20 percent reversed liberal holdings, and in slightly more than 40 percent there was no clean liberal-conservative split in the ruling of the Court. The leading subject matter of the decisions reversed involved civil rights, criminal law, antitrust, bankruptcy, jurisdiction and procedure, and environmental law.

Congress's reversal of more and more of the federal judiciary's statutory rulings may be due to a number of factors. The federal bench became more conservative in the 1980s due to the appointments of Presidents Reagan and Bush, while Democrats retained control of both houses of Congress except for the early part of the 1980s when a Republican majority controlled the Senate. Besides the persistence of divided government and a growing conservative federal bench, in the 1970s and 1980s Congress passed more omnibus legislation and expanded the number of federal judgeships. As a result, there are both more federal laws for courts to construe and more lower federal court decisions to which Congress may respond. In addition, organized interest groups proliferated, along with the size of congressional staffs. Both interest groups and larger congressional staffs apparently contributed to an increased monitoring of federal courts' rulings and thus to congressional overrides of their decisions.

The Court may also invite Congress to reverse its rulings when legislation appears ambiguous. Burger suggested as much in *Tennessee Valley Authority v. Hill* (1978), when holding that a TVA dam could not be put into operation, because it would destroy the only habitat of a tiny fish—the snail darter—protected under the Endangered Species Act of 1973. Congress subsequently modified the act by authorizing a special board to decide whether to allow federally funded public works projects when they threaten an endangered species.

CONGRESSIONAL REVERSALS OF STATUTORY DECISIONS

Congress	Number of Statutes	Supreme Court Decisions Overridden	Lower Federal Court Decisions Overridden	Total Reversals
90th (1967–68)	14	6	10	16
91st (1969–70)	8	2	13	15
92nd (1971–72)	7	8	4	12
93rd (1973–74)	10	7	7	14
94th (1975–76)	17	12	22	34
95th (1977–78)	14	19	24	43
96th (1979–80)	20	8	23	31
97th (1981–82)	17	8	16	24
98th (1983–84)	16	15	29	44
99th (1985–86)	25	18	27	45
100th (1987–88)	24	12	27	39
101st (1989–90)	15	9	18	27
Total:	*187*	*124*	*220*	*344*

When Congress redrafts legislation, the Court occasionally refuses to yield. During the Vietnam War, the Warren Court ruled in *United States v. Seeger* (1965) that the Selective Service Act's exemption from military service for "reason of religious training or belief" applied to conscientious objectors who did not necessarily believe in a Supreme Being but who had strong moral and philosophical beliefs. Congress rewrote the statute to make clear that the religious exemption applied only to those who objected to war on the basis of traditional religious beliefs in a Supreme Being. In *Welsh v. United States* (1970), the Court nevertheless granted Elliott Welsh II draft exemption because of his philosophical beliefs. The Court ruled that those beliefs may be held with the same "strength of more traditional religious convictions."

Congress cannot overturn the Court's interpretations of the Constitution by mere legislation. But Congress can enhance or thwart compliance with the Court's rulings. After the Warren Court's landmark decision in *Gideon v. Wainwright* (1963) that indigents have a right to counsel, Congress provided attorneys for indigents charged with federal offenses. By contrast, in the Crime Control and Safe Streets Act of 1968, Congress permitted federal courts to use evidence obtained from suspects who had not been read their *Miranda* rights, if their testimony appeared voluntary on the basis of the "totality of the circumstances" surrounding their interrogation. Congress thus attempted to return to a pre-*Miranda* standard for police questioning of criminal suspects.

The Supreme Court underscored its power, in *City of Boerne v. Flores* (1997), when striking down the Religious Freedom Restoration Act of 1993 (RFRA), which Congress enacted in an attempt to override the Court's 1990 decision in *Employment Division, Department of Human Resources of Oregon v. Smith*. In *Smith*, the Court set aside the balancing test for religious minorities laid down in *Sherbert v. Verner* (1963), holding instead that the First Amendment guarantee for the free exercise of religion does not require making exceptions for religious minorities from generally applicable laws like education, traffic, and unemployment compensation regulations. A broad coalition of religious organizations persuaded Congress to reestablish the *Sherbert* test as a matter of federal law in RFRA. But, in striking down the RFRA, the Court ruled that Congress does not have the power, under the Fourteenth Amendment's enforcement power in Section 5, to enforce constitutional rights broader than recognized by the Court. Since a majority of the justices no longer held to *Sherbert*, Congress exceeded its powers in trying to reestablish its test for accommodating religious minorities.

Congress may, nonetheless, openly defy the Court's rulings. When holding, in *Immigration and Naturalization Service v. Chadha* (1983), that Congress may not delegate decision-making authority to agencies and still retain the power of vetoing decisions with which it disagrees, the Court invalidated over two hundred provisions for one-house vetoes of administrative actions. Congress responded by deleting or substituting joint resolutions for one-house veto provisions. But in the years since

Chadha, Congress also passed no fewer than two hundred new provisions for legislative vetoes.[95]

Congress indubitably has the power to delay and undercut implementation of the Court's rulings. For example, Congress delayed implementation of *Brown* by not authorizing the executive branch to enforce the decision prior to the Civil Rights Act of 1964. Then, by cutting back on appropriations for the Departments of Justice and HEW during the Nixon and Ford administrations, Congress registered increasing opposition to busing and further attempts at achieving integrated public schools. "What the Congress gave in Title VI of the 1964 Civil Rights Acts," Joseph Califano observed, "it took away in part through the annual HEW appropriations bills by forbidding the use of any funds to bus school children."[96]

On major issues of public policy, Congress is likely to prevail or, at least, temper the impact of the Court's rulings. In a study of the Court's invalidation of legislation between 1790 and 1957, Robert Dahl found that Congress ultimately prevailed 70 percent of the time. Congress was able to do so by reenacting legislation and because of changes in the composition and direction of the Court.[97] But the Court forges public policy not only when invalidating federal legislation but also by overturning state and local laws and practices, and Dahl failed to take note of that important fact.[98] The continuing controversies over decisions striking down state laws on school desegregation, school prayer, and abortion are a measure of how the Court's policy-making may elevate issues to the national political agenda and influence American life.

CAMPAIGN POLITICS AND PRESIDENTIAL LEADERSHIP

Charged with the responsibility of taking "care that the laws be faithfully executed," the President is the chief executive officer under the Constitution. As the only nationally elected public official, the President represents the views of the dominant national political coalition. A President's obligation to faithfully execute the laws, including decisions of the Court, may thus collide with his own perceived electoral mandate.

The Court has often been the focus of presidential campaigns and power struggles. But Presidents seldom openly defy particular decisions by the Court. Presidential defiance is, perhaps, symbolized by the following famous remark attributed to Andrew Jackson: "John Marshall has made his decision, now let him enforce it." Jackson's refusal to enforce the decision in *Worcester v. Georgia* (1832), which denied state courts jurisdiction over crimes committed on Indian lands, in fact simply left enforcement problems up to the courts and legislatures. During the Civil War, Lincoln ordered his military commanders to refuse to obey writs of *habeas corpus* issued by Chief Justice Taney. On less dramatic occasions, Presidents have also instructed their attorneys general to refuse to comply with other court orders.

In major confrontations, Presidents generally yield to the Court. Nixon complied with the ruling in *New York Times Co. v. United States,* which struck down, as a prior restraint on freedom of the press, an injunction against the publication of the *Pentagon Papers*—a top-secret report detailing the history of America's involvement in Vietnam. Then, in 1974, he submitted to the Court's decision in *United States v. Nixon,* ordering the release of White House tape recordings pertinent to the trial of his former Attorney General John Mitchell and other presidential assistants for conspiracy and obstruction of justice.

Although Presidents seldom directly defy the Court, their reluctance to enforce rulings may thwart implementation. Eisenhower's reaction to the school desegregation decision was quite similar to Jackson's earlier one. *Brown* was "a hot potato handed to [him] by the judiciary," Attorney General Herbert Brownell has recalled. "After the Court decision [the President] realized that it then became his job as head of the executive branch of government to enforce it. And he went about doing that in what he thought was the right way—it was a long-term way."[99] Eisenhower told his brother, "You keep harping on the Constitution, I should like to point out that the meaning of the Constitution is what the Supreme Court says it is."[100] Eisenhower would not assume leadership for enforcing *Brown.* He disapproved of the Court's bold attempt to mandate a change in the way of life of many Americans. "Laws are rarely effective unless they represent the will of the majority," and, he reasoned, *Brown* removed the "cloak of legality to segregation in all its forms," which the Court itself had given in *Plessy v. Ferguson* (1896), when proclaiming the doctrine of "separate but equal" in public transportation. "After three score years of living under these patterns," Eisenhower concluded, "it was impossible to expect complete and instant reversal of conduct by mere decision of the Supreme Court."[101]

Styles and strategies of political leadership vary, but presidential persuasion can significantly influence compliance with the Court's rulings. By the late 1960s, considerable progress had been made toward ending segregated public schools. This was due largely to the leadership of Presidents Kennedy and Johnson. In the 1968 presidential campaign, though, Nixon won the southern vote with antibusing pledges and promises to take a "middle-of-the-road" approach to school desegregation. After his election, he observed, "[T]here are those who want instant integration and those who want segregation forever. I believe that we need to have a middle course between these two extremes."[102] Surprised by the unanimous decision in *Alexander v. Holmes County School Board* (1969), he became the first President to disagree publicly with one of the Court's rulings on school desegregation. *Alexander* did not deter Nixon from keeping his campaign promises. His strategy was to return the problems of compliance to the courts by curtailing the Department of Justice's prosecution of school districts that refused to desegregate and to cut back on the funding and jurisdiction of HEW for enforcing integration.

In both the short and the long run, Presidents may undercut

Supreme Court policy-making. By issuing contradictory direc-
tives to federal agencies and by assigning low priority to enforcement by the Department of Justice, they may limit the Court's
decisions. Although most of the early New Deal program was
invalidated by the Court, after 1937 FDR persuaded Congress
to reenact major provisions of his social and economic policies.
Presidents may also make broad moral appeals in response to
the Court's rulings, and those appeals may transcend their limited time in office. The Court put school desegregation and
abortion on the national agenda. But Kennedy's appeal for civil
rights captivated a generation and encouraged public acceptance
of the Court's rulings. Similarly, Reagan's opposition to abortion
served to legitimate resistance to the Court's decisions.

During his presidency Reagan worked major changes in the
national debate over abortion in five ways that underscore
the power of a President to undercut controversial rulings of the
Court. First, his anti-abortion rhetoric effectively erased the distinction between private and public morality. In doing so Reagan
distinguished himself from Nixon, Ford, and Carter, who had
said they privately opposed abortion but would not seek to
enforce publicly their private views. Reagan also thereby lent
presidential legitimacy to the anti-abortion movement's morality. Second, his administration supported a constitutional
amendment aimed at reversing *Roe*. Third, and in many ways
most importantly, Reagan's Department of Justice carefully
scrutinized potential appointees to the federal bench, screening
out those deemed supportive of the pro-choice side of the abortion controversy. Fourth, during Reagan's second term his solicitor general, Charles Fried, aggressively pressed the Supreme
Court to abandon *Roe*. Finally, his appointees worked for regulatory reforms that would limit the availability of abortions. In
particular, the head of Health and Human Services (HHS), Dr.
Otis R. Bowen, enacted new regulations, under Title X of the
Public Health Services Act of 1970, that forbid organizations
receiving federal funding from providing abortion counseling or

promoting abortion in any way. The new "abortion gag-order" restrictions were immediately challenged as an unconstitutional violation of doctors' First Amendment freedom of speech, women's right of privacy, and for running contrary to Congress's intent when enacting Title X. For almost two decades, organizations like the Planned Parenthood Federation of America had received grants under Title X, and Congress had consistently appropriated funding for the program. Yet, the Reagan administration bet that a majority of the Rehnquist Court would uphold its reinterpretation of Title X and anti-abortion regulations. In *Rust v. Sullivan* (1991) the Court did just that by a five-to-four vote, with Justices Blackmun, O'Connor, Marshall, and Stevens dissenting. Writing for the Court, Chief Justice Rehnquist held that when a congressional statute is ambiguous and its intent unclear the Court would defer to the executive branch's interpretation. Moreover, Rehnquist dismissed the First Amendment and privacy challenges on the ground that whenever government awards grants or contracts out for services it may impose limitations on recepients' freedom of speech and expression. In sum, the Reagan administration's combined strategies of packing the federal bench and enacting regulatory reforms (which it gauged would be challenged before Reagan-appointed judges) enabled the President to both achieve what he failed to persuade Congress to do and move the Court and constitutional law in the direction of his legal-policy goals.

Presidential influence over the Court in the long run remains largely contingent on appointments to the Court. Vacancies occur at the rate of one every twenty-two months. Four Presidents—including, most recently, Jimmy Carter—had no opportunities to appoint members of the Court. There is no guarantee how a justice will vote or that the addition of his or her vote will prove instrumental in limiting or reversing past rulings with which a President disagrees. But through their appointments, especially when they fill a number of seats in short order, Presidents may leave their mark on Supreme Court policy-making and possibly align the Court and the country or precipitate later confrontations.

The Supreme Court and American Life

"The powers exercised by this Court are inherently oligarchic," Frankfurter once observed when pointing out that "[t]he Court is not saved from being oligarchic because it professes to act in the service of humane ends."[103] Judicial review is antidemocratic. But the Court's power stems from its duty to give authoritative meaning to the Constitution, and rests with the persuasive forces of reason, institutional prestige, the cooperation of other political institutions, and, ultimately, public opinion. The country, in a sense, saves the justices from being an oligarchy by curbing the Court when it goes too far or too fast with its policy-making. Violent opposition and resistance, however, threaten not merely the Court's prestige but the very idea of a government under law.

Some Court watchers, and occasionally even the justices, warn of "an imperial judiciary" and a "government by the judiciary."[104] For much of the Court's history, though, the work of the justices has not involved major issues of public policy. In most areas of public law and policy, the fact that the Court decides an issue is more important than what it decides. Relatively few of the many issues of domestic and foreign policy that arise in government reach the Court. When the Court does decide major questions of public policy, it does so by bringing political controversies within the language, structure, and spirit of the Constitution. By deciding only immediate cases, the Court infuses constitutional meaning into the resolution of the larger surrounding political controversies. But by itself the Court cannot lay major controversies to rest.

The Court can profoundly influence American life. As a guardian of the Constitution, the Court sometimes invites controversy by challenging majoritarian sentiments to respect the rights of minorities and the principles of a representative democracy. The Court's influence is usually more subtle and indirect, varying over time and from one policy issue to another. In the end, the Court's influence on American life cannot be measured precisely, because its policy-making is inextricably bound up with that of other political institutions. Major confrontations in constitutional politics, like those over school desegregation, school prayer, and abortion, are determined as much by what is possible in a system of free government and in a pluralistic society as by what the Court says about the meaning of the Constitution. At its best, the Court appeals to the country to respect the substantive value choices of human dignity and self-governance embedded in our written Constitution.

Appendix

MEMBERS OF THE SUPREME COURT OF THE
UNITED STATES

	Appointing President	Dates of Service
CHIEF JUSTICES		
Jay, John	Washington	1789–1795
Rutledge, John	Washington	1795–1795
Ellsworth, Oliver	Washington	1796–1800
Marshall, John	Adams, J.	1801–1835
Taney, Roger Brooke	Jackson	1836–1864
Chase, Salmon Portland	Lincoln	1864–1873
Waite, Morrison Remick	Grant	1874–1888
Fuller, Melville Weston	Cleveland	1888–1910
White, Edward Douglass	Taft	1910–1921
Taft, William Howard	Harding	1921–1930
Hughes, Charles Evans	Hoover	1930–1941
Stone, Harlan Fiske	Roosevelt, F.	1941–1946
Vinson, Frederick Moore	Truman	1946–1953
Warren, Earl	Eisenhower	1953–1969
Burger, Warren Earl	Nixon	1969–1986
Rehnquist, William Hubbs	Reagan	1986–

	Appointing President	Dates of Service
ASSOCIATE JUSTICES		
Rutledge, John	Washington	1790–1791
Cushing, William	Washington	1790–1810
Wilson, James	Washington	1789–1798
Blair, John	Washington	1790–1796
Iredell, James	Washington	1790–1799
Johnson, Thomas	Washington	1792–1793
Paterson, William	Washington	1793–1806
Chase, Samuel	Washington	1796–1811
Washington, Bushrod	Adams, J.	1799–1829
Moore, Alfred	Adams, J.	1800–1804
Johnson, William	Jefferson	1804–1834
Livingston, Henry Brockholst	Jefferson	1807–1823
Todd, Thomas	Jefferson	1807–1826
Duvall, Gabriel	Madison	1811–1835
Story, Joseph	Madison	1812–1845
Thompson, Smith	Monroe	1823–1843
Trimble, Robert	Adams, J. Q.	1826–1828
McLean, John	Jackson	1830–1861
Baldwin, Henry	Jackson	1830–1844
Wayne, James Moore	Jackson	1835–1867
Barbour, Philip Pendleton	Jackson	1836–1841
Catron, John	Van Buren	1837–1865
McKinley, John	Van Buren	1838–1852
Daniel, Peter Vivian	Van Buren	1842–1860
Nelson, Samuel	Tyler	1845–1872
Woodbury, Levi	Polk	1845–1851
Grier, Robert Cooper	Polk	1846–1870
Curtis, Benjamin Robbins	Fillmore	1851–1857
Campbell, John Archibald	Pierce	1853–1861
Clifford, Nathan	Buchanan	1858–1881
Swayne, Noah Haynes	Lincoln	1862–1881
Miller, Samuel Freeman	Lincoln	1862–1890
Davis, David	Lincoln	1862–1877
Field, Stephen Johnson	Lincoln	1863–1897
Strong, William	Grant	1870–1880
Bradley, Joseph P.	Grant	1870–1892
Hunt, Ward	Grant	1873–1882

	Appointing President	Dates of Service
Harlan, John Marshall	Hayes	1877–1911
Woods, William Burnham	Hayes	1881–1887
Matthews, Stanley	Garfield	1881–1889
Gray, Horace	Arthur	1882–1902
Blatchford, Samuel	Arthur	1882–1893
Lamar, Lucius Quintus C.	Cleveland	1888–1893
Brewer, David Josiah	Harrison	1890–1910
Brown, Henry Billings	Harrison	1891–1906
Shiras, George, Jr.	Harrison	1892–1903
Jackson, Howell Edmunds	Harrison	1893–1895
White, Edward Douglass	Cleveland	1894–1910
Peckham, Rufus Wheeler	Cleveland	1896–1909
McKenna, Joseph	McKinley	1898–1925
Holmes, Oliver Wendell	Roosevelt, T.	1902–1932
Day, William Rufus	Roosevelt, T.	1903–1922
Moody, William Henry	Roosevelt, T.	1906–1910
Lurton, Horace Harmon	Taft	1910–1914
Hughes, Charles Evans	Taft	1910–1916
Van Devanter, Willis	Taft	1911–1937
Lamar, Joseph Rucker	Taft	1911–1916
Pitney, Mahlon	Taft	1912–1922
McReynolds, James Clark	Wilson	1914–1941
Brandeis, Louis Dembitz	Wilson	1916–1939
Clarke, John Hessin	Wilson	1916–1922
Sutherland, George	Harding	1921–1938
Butler, Pierce	Harding	1923–1939
Sanford, Edward Terry	Harding	1923–1930
Stone, Harlan Fiske	Coolidge	1925–1941
Roberts, Owen Josephus	Hoover	1930–1945
Cardozo, Benjamin Nathan	Hoover	1932–1938
Black, Hugo Lafayette	Roosevelt, F.	1937–1971
Reed, Stanley Forman	Roosevelt, F.	1938–1957
Frankfurter, Felix	Roosevelt, F.	1939–1962
Douglas, William Orville	Roosevelt, F.	1939–1975
Murphy, Frank	Roosevelt, F.	1940–1949
Byrnes, James Francis	Roosevelt, F.	1941–1942
Jackson, Robert Houghwout	Roosevelt, F.	1941–1954
Rutledge, Wiley Blount	Roosevelt, F.	1943–1949

	Appointing President	Dates of Service
Burton, Harold Hitz	Truman	1945–1958
Clark, Thomas Campbell	Truman	1949–1967
Minton, Sherman	Truman	1949–1956
Harlan, John Marshall	Eisenhower	1955–1971
Brennan, William Joseph, Jr.	Eisenhower	1956–1990
Whittaker, Charles Evans	Eisenhower	1957–1962
Stewart, Potter	Eisenhower	1958–1981
White, Byron Raymond	Kennedy	1962–1993
Goldberg, Arthur Joseph	Kennedy	1962–1965
Fortas, Abe	Johnson, L.	1965–1969
Marshall, Thurgood	Johnson, L.	1967–1991
Blackmun, Harry A.	Nixon	1970–1994
Powell, Lewis Franklin, Jr.	Nixon	1972–1987
Rehnquist, William Hubbs	Nixon	1972–1986
Stevens, John Paul	Ford	1975–
O'Connor, Sandra Day	Reagan	1981–
Scalia, Antonin	Reagan	1986–
Kennedy, Anthony	Reagan	1988–
Souter, David H.	Bush	1990–
Thomas, Clarence	Bush	1991–
Ginsburg, Ruth Bader	Clinton	1993–
Breyer, Stephen G.	Clinton	1994–

Notes

YA   Yale University Library, New Haven, Connecticut
YU   Yeshiva University, Cardozo School of Law, New York, New York

ONE

A Struggle for Power

1. Quoted by L. Shearer, "Intelligence Report," *Parade* magazine (January 23, 1983). See also Norma McCorvey, *I AM ROE: My Life, Roe v. Wade, and Freedom of Choice* (New York: Harper Collins, 1994).
2. Rowan television interview, "In Search of Justice," WUSA (September 14, 1987); "Jane Roe Speaks Out," *Village Voice* 44 (April 11, 1989).
3. A. L. Goodstein, " 'Jane Roe' Renounces Abortion Movement," *The Washington Post* F1 (August 15, 1995).
4. Docket Book, William J. Brennan, Jr., Papers, Box 417, LC.
5. The discussion of the oral arguments in *Roe v. Wade* is based on recordings of the arguments available at NARS, and transcripts (which do not contain the names of the justices asking the questions) in *Landmark Briefs and Arguemnts of the Supreme Court of the United States,* ed. P. Kurland and G. Casper (Arlington, Va.: University Publications of America, 1974). On the basis of the author's experience, a judgment was made as to which justices were asking what questions, but all quotations are from the transcripts of the oral argument.
6. Docket Book, Brennan Papers, Box 420A, LC.
7. Memos, December 18 and 20, 1971, Brennan Papers, Box 281, LC.
8. Memos, May 18 and 19, 1972, from Douglas and Brennan, and Memos to Conference, May 18 and 25, 1972, from Blackmun, Brennan Papers, Box 281, LC.
9. Memorandum to the Conference, May 31, 1972, Brennan Papers, Box 281, LC.
10. Memo to Blackmun, May 31, 1972, Brennan Papers, Box 281, LC.
11. Memorandum for Conference, June 1, 1972, Brennan Papers, Box 281, LC.
12. Memo to Chief Justice Burger, June 1, 1972, Brennan Papers, Box 281, LC.
13. Memo to Blackmun, January 4, 1973, Brennan Papers, Box 281, LC.
14. Memorandum to the Conference, January 16, 1973, Brennan Papers, Box 281, LC.
15. Quoted in *New York Times* A1, A20 (January 23, 1973).
16. Quoted ibid., at A20.
17. See, e.g., J. H. Ely, "The Wages of Crying Wolf: A Comment on *Roe v. Wade*," 82 *Yale Law Journal* 920 (1973).
18. See D. M. O'Brien, *Privacy, Law, and Public Policy* (New York: Praeger, 1979).
19. Senate Committee on the Judiciary, *Constitutional Amendments Relating to Abortion: Hearings before the Subcommittee on the Constitution,* 97th Cong., 1st sess., vol. 1, at 90 (Washington, D.C.: GPO, 1983); S. Okie, "Abortion Since Roe v. Wade," *Washington Post* A1 (March 21, 1989); A. Torres and J. Forrest, "Why Do Women Have Abortions?," 20 *Family Planning Perspectives* 169 (July–August 1988).
20. J. Gross, "Separate Paths of Pain Lead to Abortion Clinic," *New York Times* A1 (May 8, 1989). See also Barbara Hickson Craig and David M. O'Brien, *Abortion and American Politics* (Chatham: Chatham House, 1993), chap. 7.
21. See, e.g., *Planned Parenthood v. Danforth,* 428 U.S. 52 (1976) (written consent of woman, after doctor's explanation of dangers of abortion, permissible; but spousal consent unconstitutional if husband is allowed to prohibit abortion); *Bellotti v. Baird,* 443 U.S. 622 (1979) (parental veto of minor's abortion unconstitutional);

> *H. L. v. Matheson,* 450 U.S. 398 (1981) (upheld requirements that parents be notified of minor's decision to have an abortion); and *Bigelow v. Virginia,* 421 U.S. 809 (1975) (states may not ban advertisements for abortion clinics).

22. See *Poelker v. Doe,* 432 U.S. 519 (1977) (upholding city's policy of refusing non-therapeutic abortions in public hospitals); *Beal v. Poe,* 432 U.S. 438 (1977), and *Maher v. Roe,* 432 U.S. 464 (1977) (upholding restrictions on the funding of non-therapeutic abortions).
23. See K. Lewis and T. Carr, *Abortion: Judicial and Legislative Central, Issue Brief* (Washington, D.C.: Congressional Research Service, August 3, 1984).
24. See R. Davidson, "Procedures and Politics in Congress," in G. Steiner, ed., *The Abortion Dispute and the American System* (Washington, D.C.: The Brookings Institution, 1983).
25. Table is based on a list of cases in *The Constitution of the United States of America: Analysis and Interpretation* 1595–97 (Washington, D.C.: Library of Congress, 1973), supplementary materials provided by the Congressional Research Service, Library of Congress, and tabulations by the author.

TWO

The Cult of the Robe

1. W. Rehnquist, "Presidential Appointments to the Supreme Court" (Lecture, University of Minnesota, October 9, 1984) appearing in 2 *Constitutional Commentary* 319 (1985).
2. Memorandum to the President, January 6, 1965, John Macy Papers, Box 726, "Judgeships File," JPL.
3. Oral History Interview with Justice Frankfurter, at 52–53, KPL. See also Letter, May 15, 1964. Charles Wyzanski Papers, Box 1, File 26, HLS.
4. Letter to Alexander Bickel, March 18, 1963, Felix Frankfurter Papers, Box 206, HLS.
5. H. Abraham, "A Bench Happily Filled: Some Historical Reflections on the Supreme Court Appointment Process," 66 *Judicature* 282, 286 (1983).
6. *Jacobellis v. Ohio,* 378 U.S. 184, 197 (1964).
7. Based on an updating of data collected in A. Blaustein and R. Mersky, *The First One Hundred Justices* 20–21 (Hamden, Conn.: Archon, 1978).
8. Letter, October 9, 1928, Harlan F. Stone Papers, Box 24, LC.
9. Ibid.
10. Quoted in "The Second Woman Justice: Ruth Bader Ginsburg Talks Candidly About a Changing Society," *ABA Journal* 40 (October, 1993), at 41.
11. Letter to Henry Stimson, February 17, 1932, quoted in letter from H. Gotlieb to Frankfurter, October 23, 1961, WHCF-FG, Box 194, KPL.
12. Letter, February 20, 1932, White House Central Files (WHCF), Box 878, HPL.
13. See I. Carmen, "The President, Politics and the Power of Appointments: Hoover's Nomination of Mr. Justice Cardozo," 55 *Virginia Law Review* 616 (1969).
14. WHCF, Box 193, HPL. (The undated note from Justice Stone appears in a file of endorsements of Hughes for chief justice. Justice Stone may have also suggested Cardozo for the chief justiceship, but the note, with President Hoover's notations, appears to have been intended for filling Justice Sanford's vacancy.) See also Benjamin Cardozo Papers, Box 11, CU and YU.
15. See materials on the Parker Nomination, WHCF, Boxes 192 and 193, HPL; and Stone Papers, Box 17, LC.

16. Homer Cummings Diaries, UV; and White House Central Files—President's Secretary's Files (WHCF-PSF), Box 231, TPL.

17. See C. Cameron, A. Cover, and J. Segal, "Senate Voting on Supreme Court Nominees: A Neoinstitutional Model," 84 *American Political Science Review* 525 (1990).

18. See J. Massaro's excellent study, *Supremely Political: The Role of Ideology and Management in Unsuccessful Supreme Court Nominations* (Albany, N.Y.: SUNY Press, 1990).

19. See L. Berkson, S. Beller, and M. Grimaldi, *Judicial Selection in the United States: A Compendium of Provisions* (Chicago: American Judicature Society, 1980); and V. Flango and C. Ducat, "What Difference Does Method of Judicial Selection Make?" 5 *Justice System Journal* 25 (1979).

20. See James Eastland Oral History Interview, at 14–15, JPL; and Kennedy Interview, at 603–7, KPL.

21. Kennedy Interview, at 603, KPL. See also WHCF-FG, Boxes 505 and 530, KPL.

22. W. Mitchell, "Appointment of Federal Judges," 17 *American Bar Association Journal* 569 (1931). See also William Mitchell Papers, Box 7, MHS; and WHCF, Box 441, HPL.

23. Letter, October 17, 1975, WHCF-FG, Box 50; Letter from Baroody, November 19, 1975, WHCF-FG, Box 51; Telephone Logs, WHCF-FG, Box 17, FPL. For further discussion, see D. O'Brien, "The Politics of Professionalism: President Gerald Ford's Appointment of John Paul Stevens," 21 *Presidential Studies Quarterly* 103 (1991).

24. See ABA, *Standing Committee on Federal Judiciary: What It Is and How It Works* (ABA, 1983). See also E. Slotnick, "The ABA Standing Committee on Federal Judiciary: A Contemporary Assessment," 66 *Judicature* 349 (1983); and White House Central Files—General Files (WHCF-GF), Box 67, EPL.

25. Leon Jaworski Oral History Interview, at 15, JPL.

26. Letter to Thomas Reed Powell, October 15, 1928, Stone Papers, Box 24, LC.

27. Records of the Department of Justice, Harold Burton Files, NARS; William O. Douglas Interview with Walter Murphy, MLPU; Tom C. Clark Oral History Interview, TPL; and White House Central Files—Confidential Files (WHCF-CF), Box 5, TPL.

28. See, generally, D. Danelski, *A Supreme Court Justice Is Appointed* (New York: Random House, 1964).

29. Letter to the President, November 12, 1938, Hugo Black Papers, Box 63, LC.

30. File on Wiley Rutledge, Records of the Attorney General, Department of Justice, NARS; also, Papers as President, President's Secretary's Files (PSF), Box 186, RPL.

31. Douglas Interview, at 86–89, MLPU.

32. See R. Evans, Jr., and R. Novak, *Nixon in the White House* 159–71 (New York: Random House, 1971).

33. See, e.g., Memos to the President on Lower Court Appointments, WHCF-FG, Box 505; Larry Temple Papers, Box 1; Barefoot Sanders Papers, Box 1; and John Macy Oral History Interview, Tape 3, at 13, JPL.

34. Letters, November 22, 1954, and September 10, 1941, Wyzanski Papers, Box 1, Files 13 and 18, HLS.

35. L. R. Wilfry to the President, October 31, 1910, Edward White Papers, LC.

36. See Memorandum for the Attorney General, November 27, 1942, and Comparative List Showing Religion of Judges Appointed during the Periods of 1922–1933 and 1933–1942, Francis Biddle Papers, Box 2, RPL.

37. Note on telephone conversation with Attorney General Brownell, September 9, 1956, Dwight David Eisenhower (DDE) Diaries, Box 11, EPL.

38. Quoted in Memorandum on Confirmation of Justice Louis Brandeis, WHCF, Fortas/ Thornberry Series, Chron. File, JPL. See, generally, A. T. Mason, *Brandeis: A Free Man's Life* (New York: Viking Press, 1946).

39. Kennedy Interview, at 319, KPL.

40. Letter to the President, July 19, 1965, WHCF-FG, Box 535, JPL.

41. Letter from Paul Carrington, March 13, 1967, to Joseph Califano, Records of Department of Justice, NARS.

42. Thurgood Marshall Oral History Interview, at 7, JPL.

43. See J. Segal and H. Spaeth, "Decisional Trends on the Warren and Burger Courts," 73 *Judicature* 103 (1989); D. O'Brien, "The High Court Changes Course," *The Public Perspective* 6 (1991); and L. Baum, "Membership Change and Collective Voting Change in the United States Supreme Court," 54 *The Journal of Politics* 3 (1992).

44. White House Central Files—Office Files (WHCF-OF), 41A, Box 212, TPL.

45. Macy Papers, Box 726, JPL.

46. R. Nixon, *RN: The Memories of Richard Nixon* 423 (New York: Grosset & Dunlap, 1978).

47. Materials in WHCF-FG 51, FPL.

48. Ginsburg, *ABA Journal*, supra note 10, at 41.

49. Letter to Thomas Reed Powell, October 15, 1928, Stone Papers, Box 24, LC.

50. "The Black Controversy," Robert Jackson Papers, LC.

51. Statement Appended to Letter to Virginia Hamilton, April 7, 1968, Black Papers, Box 31, LC. (I am grateful to Professor Howard Ball for directing me to this note.) See also materials in Black Papers, Box 234, LC; and Cummings Diaries, UV.

52. Cummings Diaries, UV; Stanley Reed Interview, 3–35, CUOHP; and Stanley Reed Papers, Boxes 282 and 370, UK.

53. Cummings Diaries, UV.

54. Henry Morgenthau Diaries, vol. 69, p. 308, RPL; and G. Kanin, "Trips to Felix," *Atlantic Monthly* 55, 60 (1964).

55. Interview Session, Justice Felix Frankfurter and Gerald Gunther, Felix Frankfurter Papers, Box 201, HLS; and Cummings Diaries, UV.

56. Papers as President, PSF, Box 77, RPL.

57. Douglas Interview, at 2–15; MLPU. See also President Roosevelt's correspondence with Senator Schwellenbach, Papers as President, PSF, Box 186, RPL.

58. Cummings Diaries, UV.

59. Robert Jackson Interview, at 779, CUOHP; and Robert Jackson Papers, LC.

60. On Hughes's appointment, compare M. Pusey, *Charles Evans Hughes*, vol. 2, at 651 (New York: Macmillan, 1951), with F. B. Wiener, "Justice Hughes' Appointment—The Cotton Story Re-examined," *Yearbook of the Supreme Court Historical Society 78* (1981). A dispute has arisen over whether President Hoover was telephoned and encouraged by his acting secretary of state, Joseph Cotton, to offer the chief justiceship to Hughes on the basis of his belief that the latter would decline the offer and thus leave President Hoover free to appoint someone else— like Learned Hand, as Cotton apparently hoped—or elevate the President's good friend Justice Stone. That dispute is unlikely to be finally resolved since the telephone logs for the period in question are missing from both the Hoover Presidential Library and the Hoover Institution on War, Revolution, and Peace, where the papers of the President were initially stored. Apart from the conjectures in the above article and book, there is also evidence that Justice Holmes and Brandeis conferred with President Hoover before his nomination of Hughes and may have indicated their preference for the appointment of Hughes rather than for the ele-

vation of Justice Stone. Hoover Papers, Boxes 62 and 317, HI; Mitchell Papers, Box 7, MHL; WHCF, Boxes 22 and 191, HPL; Appointment Books and Telephone Logs, HPL; Post-Presidential Series (PPS), Box 370, HPL; Felix Frankfurter Papers, Box 169, HLS; and Stone Papers, Box 13, LC.

61. Notes on "H. F. S. & C. J.' ship," Felix Frankfurter Papers, Box 172, HLS.

62. Jackson Interview, at 1086–87, CUOPH; and Robert Jackson Papers, LC.

63. Fred Vinson Papers, Box 218, UK; Reed Papers, Box 325, UK; WHCF-PSF, Boxes 221 and 231, and Office Files, Box 212, TPL; Eban Ayers Papers, 1947 Diary in Box 26, TPL; and Jackson Papers, LC.

64. Letter, June 11, 1946, reprinted in R. Ferrell, ed., *Off the Record: The Private Papers of Harry S. Truman* 90 (New York: Harper & Row, 1980).

65. Tom Clark Oral History Interview, at 16, UK.

66. William Rogers Oral History Interview, UK.

67. Douglas Interview, at 265–66, MLPU.

68. There is no doubt that Nixon and Knowland found the appointment fortunate. See Letter from Senator Knowland to the President, September 25, 1953 (the letter arrived at the White House after the appointment of Warren was announced), WHCF-OF, Box 371, EPL.

69. Herbert Brownell Oral History Interview, at 6–11, EPL; Brownell Interview, at 60–65, BLUC; and DDE Diary, Box 4, EPL.

70. October 8, 1953, DDE Diary, Box 4; and letter to Edgar Eisenhower, White House Central Files—Name Series (WHCF-NS), Box 11, EPL.

71. Bernard Shanley Papers, Box 1, EPL.

72. Letter, WHCF-NS, Box 11, EPL.

73. Nixon, supra note, 59, at 419–20.

74. Memorandum for H. R. Haldeman (March 25, 1969), WHCF-FG 50, Box 1; and Memorandum for the President (May 6, 1969), WHCF-EXFG 51, Box 1, Nixon Presidential Materials, NACP.

75. Letter to the President (May 8, 1969), Nixon Presidential Materials, WHCF-EXFG 51, Box 1, NACP.

76. For further discussion, see D. M. O'Brien, "The Reagan Judges: His Most Enduring Legacy?" in C. O. Jones, ed., *The Reagan Legacy* (Chatham, N.J.: Chatham House, 1988); and S. Goldman, "Reagan's Judicial Legacy," 72 *Judicature* 318 (1989).

77. Quoted and discussed by O'Brien, *Judicial Roulette* (New York: Twentieth Century Fund, 1988). See also S. Alumbaugh and C. K. Rowland, "The Links Between Platform-Based Appointment Criteria and Trial Judges' Abortion Judgments," 74 *Judicature* 153 (1990).

78. For a listing of solo dissenters from 1953 to 1991, see L. Epstein, J. Segal, H. Spaeth, and T. Walker, *The Supreme Court Compendium: Data, Decisions, & Developments,* 502 (Washington, D.C.: *Congressional Quarterly,* 1993).

79. See *Arizona v. Hicks,* 480 U.S. 321 (1987); and *National Treasury Employees Union v. Von Raab,* 489 U.S. 656 (1989).

80. See *Morrison v. Olsen,* 487 U.S. 654 (1988) (Scalia, J., dis. op.); and *Mistretta v. United States,* 488 U.S. 361 (1989) (Scalia, J., dis. op.).

81. Statement from Justice Powell, Marshall Papers, Box 406, LC.

82. For further discussion, see O'Brien, "Epilogue: The Bork Controversy," *Judicial Roulette,* loc. cit., at 99.

83. See E. Meese, "The Attorney General's View of the Supreme Court: Toward Jurisprudence of Original Intention," *Law and Public Affairs,* ed. C. Wise and D. M. O'Brien, 45 *Public Administration Review* 701 (1985); and R. Bork, "Tradition and

Morality in Constitutional Law," in M. Cannon and D. M. O'Brien, eds., *Views from the Bench* 166 (Chatham, N.J.: Chatham House, 1985).

84. H. J. Abraham, *Justices and Presidents* (New York: Oxford University Press, 3rd ed., 1991).

85. M. Miller, *Plain Speaking: An Oral Biography of Harry S. Truman* 225–26 (New York: Berkley, 1973).

86. Letter, July 9, 1952, WHCF-PSF, Box 118, TPL.

87. Handwritten note by the President, President's Personal Files (PPF), Box 6, TPL.

88. *McGrath v. Kristensen,* 340 U.S. 162, 172 (1950) (Jackson, J., con. op., quoting Baron Bramwell).

89. Quoted in Abraham, supra note 84, at 72.

90. Clark Interview, at 212–13, TPL.

91. Kennedy Interview, KPL.

92. Rehnquist, supra note 1, at 23–24.

93. See L. Tribe, *God Save This Honorable Court,* chap. 2 (New York: Random House, 1985).

94. Jackson Interview, at 1104, CUOHP; "The Black Controversy," Jackson Papers, LC; and Sidney Fine Interview with William Douglas, at 8, BHLUM.

95. Letter, February 2, 1955, Felix Frankfurter Papers, Box 1, HLS.

96. J. Lash, ed., *From the Diaries of Felix Frankfurter* 155 (New York: W. W. Norton, 1974).

97. This is based on the definitive study of extrajudicial activities by William Cibes, "Extra-Judicial Activities of Justices of the United States Supreme Court, 1790–1960" (Ph. D. diss., Princeton University, 1975) (based on public and presidential papers); and the author's own study of papers of the justices and other presidential papers.

98. For a further discussion of off-the-bench commentaries, see A. Westin, "Out of Court Commentary by United States Supreme Court Justices, 1790–1962: Of Free Speech and Judicial Lockjaw," 62 *Columbia Law Review* 633 (1962); and D. M. O'Brien, ed., *Judges on Judging,* Introduction (Chatham; Chatham House, 1997).

99. Letter, August 8, 1793, reprinted in H. P. Johnson, ed., *The Correspondence and Public Papers of John Jay* 488–89 (New York: Putnam's, 1890). For other correspondence see John Jay Papers, CU.

100. A. T. Mason, *William Howard Taft: Chief Justice* (New York: Simon & Schuster, 1965).

101. Cummings Diaries, UV; Memorandum, March 1, 1943, PSF, Box 76, RPL.

102. Newton Minow Oral History Interview, at 14. UK; Vinson Papers, Box 229, UK; Ayers, Box 26, TPL.

103. Notes of telephone conversations, June 19, 1957, John Foster Dulles Papers, Box 12; and Papers as President—Ann Whitman Diary Series, EPL.

104. J. Ehrlichman, *Witness to Power: The Nixon Years* 132–33 (New York: Simon & Schuster, 1982.

105. See Nixon Presidential Materials, WHSF-President's Personal Files, Box 6; and WHCF-EXFG 51, Box 1, NACP.

106. E. Warren, *The Memoirs of Chief Justice Earl Warren,* 339 (New York: Doubleday, 1977); and Justice Brennan's memo on the Landau interviews, Earl Warren Papers, Box 348, LC.

107. Senate Committee on the Judiciary, *Hearings on the Nomination of Abe Fortas of Tennessee to the Chief Justice of the United States,* 90th Cong., 2d sess., September 13, 1968, at 1303.

108. A. Lief, *Brandeis: The Personal History of an American Ideal* 409 (Harrisburg, Pa.: Telegraph Press, 1936).
109. B. Murphy, *The Brandeis/ Frankfurter Connection* (New York: Oxford University Press, 1982).
110. Based on conversations with the former solicitor general and dean of Harvard Law School Erwin Griswold (1983) and the Washington lawyer-lobbyist Thomas ("Tommy the Cork") Corcoran (1982).
111. Note to President, October 26, 1938, PPF, Box 4877, RPL.
112. Justice Murphy's notes on his meetings with President Roosevelt during 1940–1943 are in Eugene Gressman Papers, BHLUM; and Justice Byrnes's memoranda to the President and other White House advisers are in James F. Brynes Papers, box 1229, CLE. See also Alpha Files, Boxes 607, 4877, and 6389, and PSF, Box 186, RPL.
113. WHCF-PSF, Boxes 118 and 284; PPF, Box 504, TPL. Kennedy Interview and Robert Kennedy Papers, Box 16, KPL. WHCF-NS, Letter of 22 March 1966; White House-Famous Names, Letter of February 25, 1964; WHCF-FG, 535 and 505 / 9, JPL.
114. Goldberg attended less than half of the cabinet meetings held during his first two and one-half years as ambassador to the United Nations. Memoranda and other materials in White House Central Files—Official Files of the President, Goldberg File, JPL.
115. Memo from Jim Jones to the President, November 2, 1967, White House Notes File; Meetings Notes File, November 2, 1967; March 20 and 27, 1968, Meetings Notes Files, JPL.
116. Diary Backup, Boxes 43, 60, 63, and 66, JPL.
117. Thruston Morton Oral History Interview, at 22, JPL.
118. WHCF, Fortas/ Thornberry Series, Box 1, JPL; Diary Backup, Box 45, WHCF-Name File (Douglas); and Macy Papers (Fortas File), JPL.
119. Memorandum to Temple, WHCF, Fortas/ Thorberry Series, Chron. File, JPL; and Letter, September 9, 1968, Warren Christopher Papers, Box 18, JPL.
120. Clark Clifford Oral History Interview, Tape 4, at 29; Paul Porter Interview, at 28–34; Macy Interview, at 726; and Larry Temple Oral History Interview, JPL.
121. Letter, September 6, 1968; WHCF, Fortas/ Thornberry Series, Chron. File, JPL.
122. Eastland, in Senate Committee on the Judiciary, *Report on the Nomination of Abe Fortas,* 90th Cong. 2d sess., at 41 (Washington, D.C.: GPO, 1968).
123. Letter, July 25, 1968, Warren Papers, Box 352, LC.
124. Letter, July 24, 1968, John M. Harlan Papers, Box 531, MLPU.
125. Letter, May 14, 1969, Harlan Papers, Box 606, MLPU; and Warren Papers, (Statement of Wolfson), Box 353, LC.
126. See *Shapero v. Kentucky Bar Association,* 486 U.S. 466 (1988); *Liljeberg v. Health Services Acquisition Corporation,* 486 U.S. 847 (1988); and, more generally, J. Mackenzie, *The Appearance of Justice* (New York: Scribners, 1974).
127. Letters in Willis Van Devanter Papers, Box 35, LC; and Stone Papers, LC.
128. Correspondence in PPF, File 1662, and PSF, Box 186, RPL; and Felix Frankfurter Papers, Box 170, File 12, HLS.
129. Letter to Truman, February 13, 1946, Harold Burton Papers, Box 49, LC.
130. Address, Fordham-Stein Award Dinner (October 25, 1978).
131. Letters to and from the Justices, Supreme Court of the United States Papers, NARS.
132. Quoted in C. Fairman, *Mr. Justice Miller and the Supreme Court* 404 (Cambridge: Harvard University Press, 1939).

133. Quoted in Mason, supra note 100, at 271.
134. See correspondence in William Day Papers, Box 29; Van Devanter Papers, Boxes 32, 33, 34 and 35, LC; and further discussion in Chapter Three.
135. Letters of April 8, 1937 (to and from Frankfurter and Stone), Felix Frankfurter Papers, Box 171, HLS; and Letter, December 21, 1939, Stone Papers, Box 13, LC; and Charles Evans Hughes Papers, LC.
136. See, generally, P. Fish, *The Politics of Federal Judicial Administration* (Princeton: Princeton University Press, 1973); and J. Spaniol, "Making Federal Rules: The Inside Story," 69 *American Bar Association Journal* 1645 (1983).
137. R. Hartmann, *Palace Politics* 60 (New York: McGraw-Hill, 1980). For a somewhat different view, compare G. Ford, *A Time to Heal* 90 (New York: Harper & Row, 1979).
138. News Release, December 16, 1970, by Congressman Ford, Robert Hartmann Papers, Box 17, FPL. Also, Letter to Congressman Celler, Chairman of the Committee on the Judiciary, July 29, 1970, Hartmann Papers, Box 12, FPL.
139. Ford, in *Cong. Rec.*, 91st Cong., 2d sess., 11912, 11913 (April 15, 1970).

THREE

Life in the Marble Temple

1. Undated letters to Elizabeth Woodbury, Levi Woodbury Papers, Box 7, LC.
2. B. Cardozo, *The Nature of the Judicial Process* 168 (New Haven: Yale University Press, 1921).
3. Quoted by C. Warren, *The Supreme Court in United States History,* vol 1, at 48 n. 1 (Boston: Little, Brown, 1922).
4. C. Fairman, *Reconstruction and Reunion,* 1864–1888, at 69 n. 138 (New York: Macmillan, 1975).
5. *American State Papers, Misc.* I, no. 32.
6. Letter to Rufus King, December 19, 1793, in C. R. King, ed., *The Life and Correspondence of Rufus King,* at 126 (New York: Putnam's, 1894).
7. Quoted by G. Hazelton, *The National Capitol* 141 (New York: Taylor, 1911).
8. C. Swisher, *History of the Supreme Court of the United States: The Taney Period, 1836–64* (New York: Macmillan, 1974).
9. This was particularly true of Justice Joseph Story, who taught at Harvard and served as president of two banks and as a consultant to a number of firms and other organizations. See G. Dunne, *Justice Joseph Story and the Rise of the Supreme Court,* 121–23, 66–68 (New York: Simon and Schuster, 1970), on Justice John McKinley's frequent absence from Court sessions and his private legal practice.
10. The requirement of circuit riding was finally abolished by the Circuit Court of Appeals Act of March 3, 1891, Ch. 517, 26 Stat. 826. In 1793, Congress had provided a rotation system in order to cut back on the circuit riding of the justices, and in 1801 it eliminated the duties, only to reinstate the practice in 1802. Congress modified the requirements in 1803, 1837, and 1866. For discussions of the burdens of circuit riding, see S. J. Field, *Personal Reminiscences of Early Days in California* (New York: De Capo, 1968); and J. Frank, *Justice Daniel Dissenting* (Cambridge: Harvard University Press, 1964).
11. Quoted in Warren, supra note 3, vol. 1, at 460–61.
12. See 5 Peters, preceding page 1, and 724 (Justice Baldwin dissenting) (1832); and 6 Wheaton v (1821). Henry Baldwin's papers, NARS. For a history of the rules

governing briefs and records in the nineteenth century, see Morrison Waite Papers, Box 40 (Misc. File) LC.

13. See 44 Stat. 433 (1867), providing for the employment of messengers. The provision for hiring stenographic clerks for the justices is in 24 Stat. 254 (1886).

14. A. Beveridge, *The Life of John Marshall*, vol. 4, at 90 (Boston: Houghton Mifflin, 1919).

15. Letter from Marshall to Story, July 13, 1821, reprinted in 14 *Proceedings of the Massachusetts Historical Society*, 2d ser. 328 (1900–1901). See also Letter from Justice Story to Chief Justice Marshall, June 26, 1831. John Marshall Papers, CWM (original in Joseph Story Papers, Massachusetts Historical Society).

16. See Letters from Marshall to Story, May 3, 1831, July 26, 1831, October 12, 1831, and November 19, 1831, reprinted in J. Oster, *The Political and Economic Doctrines of John Marshall* 132–39 (New York: Neale, 1914). See also G. Haskins and H. Johnson, *Foundations of Power: John Marshall, 1801–1815*, 382–89 and Table I, at 652 (New York: Macmillan, 1981).

17. *Philadelphia Union*, April 24, 1819, quoted by D. Morgan, *Justice William Johnson: The First Dissenter* 173 (Columbia: University of South Carolina Press, 1954).

18. Letter to Jefferson, December 10, 1822, Thomas Jefferson Papers MS, LC, quoted by D. Morgan, "Mr. Justice William Johnson and the Constitution," 57 *Harvard Law Review* 328, 222–24 (1944).

19. Undated letter, John McLean Papers, Box 18, LC.

20. Justices Daniel, Campbell, and Curtis strongly objected to Chief Justice Taney's refusal to let the Clerk give copies of his opinion in *Dred Scott* to other members of the Court. See Letters from Justices Daniel and Campbell, March 10 and 18, 1857, Office of the Clerk of the Supreme Court, NARS. Justice Curtis's lengthy correspondence on this matter is also reprinted in G. Curtis, ed., *Life and Writings of Benjamin Robbins Curtis*, 2 vols. (Boston: Little, Brown, 1879).

21. C. Fairman, *Mr. Justice Miller and the Supreme Court, 1862–1890*, 279 (New York: Russell & Russell, 1939).

22. Id., at 121. See also Fairman, supra note 4, at 67–69; and Horace Gray Papers, Box 2; John M. Harlan (the elder) Papers; and Rufus Peckham Papers, LC.

23. W. King, *Melville Weston Fuller: Chief Justice of the United States, 1888–1910*, 191–92 (New York: Macmillan, 1950).

24. I am indebted to Erwin N. Griswold for this and other items of history of the Court.

25. "Recollections of Justice Holmes," Arthur Sutherland Papers, HLS.

26. D. Acheson, *Morning and Noon* 41 (Boston: Houghton Mifflin, 1965).

27. See, e.g., Memorandum by Howard Westwood, Harlan F. Stone Papers, Box 48, LC. For a fascinating account of Justice McReynolds, see J. Knox, "Experiences as Law Clerk to Mr. Justice James C. McReynolds of the Supreme Court of the United States" (unpublished manuscript); and James McReynolds Papers, UV.

28. F. Frankfuter, "Chief Justices I Have Known," reprinted in P. Kurland, ed., *Felix Frankfurter in the Supreme Court* 491 (Chicago: Chicago University Press, 1970).

29. Quoted by C. Wyzanski, Jr., *Whereas — A Judge's Premises* 61 (Boston: Little, Brown, 1944).

30. See, e.g., Letters from Chief Justice Taft to Joseph Guerin, December 21, 1922, and to Justice Stone, May 28, 1925, William Howard Taft Papers, LC. See also H. F. Pringle, *The Life and Times of William Howard Taft*, vol. 2, at 1075–80 (New York: Farrar and Rinehart, 1939); and A. T. Mason, *William Howard Taft: Chief Justice* (New York: Simon & Schuster, 1965).

31. Letter from Chief Justice Fuller to Representative Joseph Cannon, December 21,

1896, Melville Fuller Papers, Box 4, LC. See also Letter of February 1, 1928, reprinted in *Cong. Rec.* 3285–86 (April 14, 1892). Congress had several times around the turn of the century considered but failed to pass legislation for the construction of a building for the Court. Records of the Marshal's Office, NARS.

32. See Letter to Senator Reed Smoot, President of the Building Commission, June 8, 1926, signed by the chief justice and by Justices Van Devanter, Butler, Sanford, and Stone, Stone Papers, Box 81, LC.

33. See Letter from Librarian, October 12, 1947, Stone Papers, Box 83, LC.

34. W. H. Taft, "The Jurisdiction of the Supreme Court under the Act of February 25, 1925." 35 *Yale Law Journal* 1, 2 (1925).

35. For a good discussion of nineteenth-century breaches of secrecy, see Fairman, supra note 21, at 121–37.

36. See William O. Douglas Papers, Box 228 (Memoranda to the Chief Justice, January 6, 1944, and May 21, 1945), LC; and Stone Papers, Box 74 (Memorandum from Justice Douglas, January 5, 1944), LC. But see also A. Charns, *Cloak and Gavel: FBI Wiretaps, Bugs, Informers, and the Supreme Court* (Urbana: University of Illinois Press, 1992), which provides further evidence of Justice Fortas's indiscretions in discussing pending cases with members of the executive branch.

37. See C. Newland, "Personal Assistants to Supreme Court Justices: The Law Clerks," 40 *Oregon Law Review* 299, 310 (1961).

38. See notes on proposed draft of "Code of Conduct for Supreme Court Law Clerks," Marshall Papers, Box 570, LC. See also Box 452, LC.

39. Edward Lazarus, *Closed Chambers: The First Eyewitness Account of the Epic Struggles Inside the Supreme Court* (New York: Time Books, 1998).

40. See, e.g., David Garrow, "A Dissenting Opinion," *New York Times Book Review* 26 (April 19, 1998); and David O'Brien, "A Disturbing Portrait," 81 *Judicature* 214 (1998).

41. Memorandum for Conference, December 9, 1990, Marshall Papers, Box 524, LC.

42. See correspondence of the justices, Marshall Papers, Boxes 379 and 435, LC.

43. Letter from Chief Justice Rehnquist, October 27, 1989, Marshall Papers, LC.

44. Letters from Justice Stevens, February 11, 1988, and August 30, 1990, Marshall Papers, Boxes 435 and 494, LC.

45. Memorandum to Conference, Agreement with Archives Concerning Tapes of Oral Argument, May 1, 1986, Marshall Papers, Box 378, LC.

46. Memorandum to the Conference from Justices Brennan and Marshall, December 9, 1987, Marshall Papers, LC.

47. See Memorandum to the Conference, October 2, 1975, and letter from Justice Brennan, December 13, 1974, Marshall Papers, Box 574, LC.

48. See, e.g., Memorandum to Justice Douglas from the Marshal on his appointment to the Court, Douglas Papers, Box 229, LC.

49. Much of this and the subsequent discussion about the bureaucratization of the Court draws on personal observations and conversations with Mark Cannon, Administrative Assistant to the Chief Justice.

50. Waite Papers, undated note and record of vote, Box 40, LC.

51. See, e.g., Douglas Papers, Box 218, LC (Memo from Justice Rehnquist concerning the posting of opinions to be announced because "he goofed in failing to announce Bill Douglas' dissenting opinion").

52. See Memoranda in Marshall Papers, Boxes 435, 452, and 493, LC.

53. Memorandum from Chief Justice Burger, April 9, 1986, in Marshall Papers, Box 378, LC.

54. Letter from Justice Blackmun, September 30, 1988, Marshall Papers, Box 461, LC.

55. Felix Frankfurter Papers, Box 108, File 2267, LC.
56. E. Warren, "A Conversation with Earl Warren," WGBH-TV Educational Foundation, transcript (Boston: WGBH Educational Foundation, 1972).
57. L. Powell, "What the Justices Are Saying . . ." *American Bar Association Journal* 1454, 1454 (1976).
58. See 260 U.S. X (1922); and Letter from W. H. Taft to R. Taft, October 26, 1922 (commenting, "This is a fair sample of McReynold's personal character and the difficulty of getting along with him"), Taft Papers, LC. For Justice Black's refusal to sign a letter to Justice Roberts, see Hugo Black Papers, Box 62, LC; and Stone Papers, Box 81, LC.
59. Based on figures in House Committee on Appropriations, *The Judiciary Appropriations for 1952: Hearings before the Subcommittee,* 82d Cong., 1st sess., at 2 (Washington, D.C.: GPO, 1951); and House Committee on Appropriations, *Departments of Commerce, Justice, and State, the Judiciary, and Related Agencies Appropriations for 1984: Hearings before a Subcommittee,* 98th Cong., 1st sess., at 297 (Washington, D.C.: GPO, 1983).
60. P. Stewart, "Reflections on the Supreme Court," 8 *Litigation* 8, 12 (1982).
61. Powell, supra note 57, at 1454.
62. J. M. Harlan, Jr., "A Glimpse of the Supreme Court at Work," 11 *University of Chicago Law School Record* 1, 1 (1963).
63. H. Blackmun, "A Justice Speaks Out: A Conversation with Harry Blackmun," Cable News Network, transcript, at 4 (December 4, 1982).
64. See prepared statements of Justices White and Blackmun, in House Committee on Appropriations, *Departments . . . : Hearings before a Subcommittee,* 94th Cong., 2d sess., at 26 (Washington, D.C.: GPO, 1976); and Statement of Justice Powell, in House Committee on Appropriations, *Departments . . . : Hearings before a Subcommittee,* 95th Cong., 2d sess., at 181 (Washington, D.C.: GPO, 1978).
66. See, e.g., William J. Brennan Papers, Box 336, LC. In 1972, Justice Rehnquist requested, and the other justices agreed, to send all draft opinions and "join letters" in duplicate. See Brennan Papers, Box 279, LC.
66. Memorandum from Clerk, September 26, 1990, Marshall Papers, Box 523, LC.
67. W. Rehnquist, "Are the Old Times Dead?" (Mac Swinford Lecture, University of Kentucky, September 23, 1983) (copy on file with the author).
68. This is the view of Justice Powell. See his former law clerk's discussion of Justice Powell's selection and working relations with his law clerks in J. Harvie Wilkinson III, *Serving Justice* 52–54 (New York: Charterhouse, 1974).
69. The figures here come from a study by Tony Mauro, "Corps of Clerks Lacking in Diversity," *USA Today* 12A (March 13, 1998). See also Mark Brown, "Gender Discrimination in the Supreme Court's Clerkship Selection Process," 75 *Oregon Law Review* 359 (1996).
70. Letter of January 21, 1974, Stone Papers, Box 48, LC.
71. Memo to Clerks from Justice Burton, John M. Harlan Papers, Box 561, MLPU.
72. Benno Schmidt Interview, at 8, CUOHP.
73. D. Acheson, "Recollections of Service with the Federal Supreme Court," 18 *Alabama Lawyer* 335, 364 (1957).
74. S. Fine, *Frank Murphy: The Washington Years* 161 (Ann Arbor: University of Michigan Press, 1984). Justice Frank Murphy's Papers, at the University of Michigan, contain a large number of case files in which the law clerks' handwritten draft opinion is attached to a typewritten copy with the justice's comments and changes. BHLUM.
75. Memo from Justice Rutledge to the Chief Justice, May 17, 1948; and undated note to Justice Rutledge, Wiley Rutledge Papers, Box 166, LC.

76. *United States v. Carolene Products Co.*, 304 U.S. 144, 152 n. 4 (1938). See Stone Papers, Box 67, LC. The note was initially drafted by Louis Lusky, who went on to be a Columbia law professor.

77. Stone Papers, Box 48, LC.

78. See Black Papers, Box 60, LC.

79. Douglas, *The Court Years* 173 (New York: Random House, 1980). See also John Sapieza Oral History Interview, UK; and William Oliver Oral History Interview, BLUC.

80. Howard Trienens and Newton Minow Oral History Interviews, UK. For a good example, see files on *Dennis v. United States*, Fred Vinson Papers, Box 270, UK.

81. Quoted in Letter from Frankfurter to Reed, December 3, 1941, Stanley Reed Papers, Box 171, UK.

82. Arthur Rosett Oral History Interview, UK.

83. On Warren's practice, see Schmidt Interview, at 256, CUOHP; and Martin Richman Oral History Interview, at 4–5, BLUC. The discussion of Rehnquist's practice is based on his remarks at the Jefferson Literary Society and Debating Meeting, Charlottesville, Va., September 20, 1985; and interviews in PBS Special, "This Honorable Court" (1988), and on C-SPAN, "Book Notes," (October 25, 1998).

84. Arthur Rosett Interview, UK. See also Gordon Davidson Interview, UK.

85. Recalled in F. Alley Allen Interview, UK.

86. Quoted in B. Schwartz and S. Lesher, *Inside the Warren Court* 39 (New York: Doubleday, 1983). Chief Justice Warren's instructions to his clerks on the preparation of *cert.* memos in Ifp cases are outlined in Memorandums for the Law Clerks, at 5–7; Earl Warren Papers, Box 398, LC. See also Suggestions in the Matter of Being a Law Clerk, Robert Garner Papers, Box 1, TPL.

87. See S. M. Shapiro, "*Certiorari* Practice: The Supreme Court's Shrinking Docket," 24 *Litigation* 25 (1998).

88. W. J. Brennan, Jr., "The National Court of Appeals: Another Dissent," 40 *University of Chicago Law Review* 473 (1973).

89. J. P. Stevens, "Some Thoughts on Judicial Restraint," 66 *Judicature* 177, 179 (1982).

90. Memorandum for Conference, September 24, 1986, Marshall Papers, Box 379, LC.

91. Bench memos, it bears emphasizing, serve two purposes: first, preparing justices for oral argument; and, second, providing a preliminary outline of a justice's possible opinion, particularly when a justice plans to write an opinion in the case, because of either their subject matter or the anticipated vote on the merits at conference. Warren Papers, Box 398, LC.

92. Like other justices, Frankfurter normally worked from a memorandum written by one of his law clerks, whether drafting an opinion for the Court or a concurring or dissenting opinion. See Felix Frankfurter Papers, Box 177, Law Clerks File, HLS. See also "Notes to Law Clerks," Tom C. Clark Papers, UT; Burton's instructions to his clerks and those of Harlan in the Harlan Papers, Boxes 561 and 583, MLPU; Fred Vinson Papers, UK; and Warren Papers, Box 398, LC.

93. Douglas, supra note 79, at 175.

94. W. Rehnquist, "Remarks," Ninth Circuit Conference, Corodano, California, July 17, 1982, printed draft delivery copy, at 24 (copy on file with the author).

95. W. Rehnquist, "Who Writes Decisions of the Supreme Court?" *U.S. News & World Report* 74 (December 13, 1957).

96. Vinson Papers, Box 217, UK. Justice Rehnquist has recalled that when he clerked, that was true for Justice Jackson as well. Interview, November 16, 1984, SC.

97. Bickel, "Supreme Court Law Clerks" (draft of manuscript in response to Rehn-

quist's article), Frankfurter Papers, Box 215 (Bickel File), LC. For a different view of the practices of law clerks, see "Views of a Leading Lawyer who in his day was one of the most esteemed of Mr. Justice Brandeis' law clerks," Felix Frankfurter Papers, Box 177, File 1, HLS.

98. Memo, Robert Jackson Papers, LC. For a further discussion, see R. Kluger, *Simple Justice* 606—9 (New York: Vintage, 1977).

99. See, e.g., Memorandum to Conference on *United States v. Nixon,* Brennan Papers, Box 329, LC.

100. Brennan Papers, Box 336 (Memorandum, February 27, 1975), LC.

101. Memorandum to Justice Marshall, August 9, 1990, Marshall Papers, Box 494, LC. See also Memorandum to Justice Marshall, July 22, 1987, Box 406, LC.

102. Letter to author from Mary Ann Willis, Counsel of Legal Office (October, 9, 1998).

103. See Memorandum to the Court from Chief Justice Taft, February 12, 1928, Willis Van Devanter Papers, Box 35, LC; Memorandum Respecting the Compensation of the Clerk, Douglas Papers, Box 229, LC; and "Historical Note to the Clerk's Office Personnel," Felix Frankfurter Papers, Box 182, File 11, HLS.

104. Jay to Fisher Ames, November 27, 1789, reprinted in H. Johnston, ed., *The Correspondence and Public Papers of John Jay,* vol. 3, at 379 (New York: Franklin, 1970). For similar incidents, see correspondence—especially, from Justice Duval, Taney, and Wayne—in Records of the Clerk of the Supreme Court, NARS.

105. Justice Grier's correspondence, as well as that of Justice Curtis, may be found in the Records of the Clerk of the Supreme Court, Letters to and from the Justices, NARS. See also, Benjamin Curtis Papers, LC.

106. For further discussion of this history of the Office of the Reporter, see Letter from John Marshall to Dudley Chase, February 7, 1817, reprinted in Oster, supra note 16, at 80–83; and, generally, G. Dunne, "Early Court Reporters," *Supreme Court Historical Society Yearbook* 61 (1976).

107. Quoted in Swisher, supra note 8, at 50.

108. This story is detailed in Frank, supra note 10, at 170–72.

109. See, e.g., C. P. Magath, *Morrison R. Waite: The Triumph of Character* 254–67 (New York: Macmillan, 1963).

110. Because of controversies surrounding the writing of headnotes, the justices voted on what the Reporter should and should not include in his headnotes. See Memorandum as to Reports, February 28, 1856, Records of the Office of the Marshal, NARS. The Court formally recognized that headnotes are not part of an opinion in *United States v. Detroit Lumber Co.,* 200 U.S. 321, 337 (1906). Note, however, that in this case the Reporter thought it sufficiently important to note in a headnote that headnotes are prepared by the Reporter and not considered binding by the Court. See also C. Butler, *A Century at the Bar of the Supreme Court of the United States* 80 (New York: Putnam's, 1942).

111. For a wonderful discussion of this event and its significance, see McGrath, supra note 109, at 224–25.

112. Quoted by C. Fairman, "What Makes a Great Justice? Mr. Justice Bradley and the Supreme Court," *Boston University Law Review* 49, 100 (1949/ 1950). For other illustrations of the problems of editing justices' opinions, see the interview with Henry Putzel, former Reporter for the Court: "Double Revolving Peripatetic Nitpicker," *Supreme Court Historical Society Yearbook* 10 (1980).

113. See F. Barbash, "That Opinion Was Here Somewhere . . ." *Washington Post* A5 (June 10, 1983).

114. See Memorandum to the Conference, Re: *Jimenez v. Weinberger* (July 5, 1975), Brennan Papers, Box 363, LC. Occasionally, other close Court watchers, like the

solicitor general, will find errors in preliminary prints of opinions and suggest modifications before an opinion is published in the official *United States Reports*. See
Sherman Minton Papers, Box 6, TPL.
115. See, e.g., *Barclay's Bank, Ltd. v. Franchise Tax Board of California*, 512 U.S. 298
(1994), where Justice Ginsburg inserted a bracketed statement clarifying the decision. See also Mark Tushnet, "Sloppiness in the Supreme Court, O. T. 1935–O. T.
1944," 3 *Constitutional Commentary* 73 (1986).
116. Memorandum for Conference, April 22, 1986, Marshall Papers, Box 378, LC.
117. Memorandum for Conference from Chief Justice Burger, in Brennan Papers, Box
640, LC.
118. Memorandum, November 3, 1983, in Brennan Papers, Box 640, LC. *Keeton v.
Hustler Magazine, Inc.*, 465 U.S. 770 (1984).
119. Letter to author from Shelley Dowling, Librarian of the Court (July 22, 1998). See
Ms. Dowling's essay on the library in L. Gasaway and M. Chiorazzi, eds., *Law
Librarianship: Historical Perspectives* (Littleton: F. B. Rothman, 1996). The early
history of the Supreme Court's library is set forth in a Memorandum by the Law
Librarian of the Library of Congress, November 1, 1940, Felix Frankfurter Papers,
Box 182, File 19, HLS.
120. A partial listing of these responsibilities may be found as Appendix A in D. Meador,
"The Federal Judiciary and Its Future Administration," 65 *Virginia Law Review*
1055–59 (1979). See also Warren Papers, Box 658, LC.
121. Quoted by A. Mason, *Harlan Fiske Stone: Pillar of the Law* 719 (New York: Viking,
1956). In the Stone Papers, LC, there are numerous other letters expressing his
astonishment at the time-consuming administrative responsibilities of the chief
justiceship.
122. Interview with Chief Justice Warren E. Burger, *U.S. News & World Report* 32, 43
(December 14, 1970). The changes and reforms that he initiated are examined in
E. A. Tamm and P. Reardon, "Warren E. Burger and the Administration of Justice," 3 *Brigham Young University Law Review* 447 (1981), excerpt reprinted in
M. Cannon and D. M. O'Brien, eds., *Views from the Bench: The Judiciary and
Constitutional Politics* (Chatham, N.J.: Chatham House, 1985).
123. See House Committee on Appropriations, *Departments . . . Hearings before a Sub-
committee*, 92d Cong., 1st sess., at 127–28 (Washington, D.C.: GPO, 1971); Judicial
Conference, *Report of the Proceedings* 25 (1971); and House Committee on the
Judiciary, *Administrative Assistant to the Chief Justice: Hearings before Subcommittee No. 5*, 92d Cong., 1st sess. (Washington, D.C.: GPO, 1971).
124. James Duff (November 13, 1998). Some of the functions of the Office of Administrative Assistant to the Chief Justice have been described by M. Cannon in "An
Administrator's View of the Supreme Court," 22 *Federal Bar News* 109 (1975);
and "Administrative Change and the Supreme Court," 57 *Judicature* 334 (1974).
125. Toni House to the author (May 1998).
126. Interview with Chief Justice Rehnquist (November 13, 1998).
127. Data on filings and total docket for 1800–1913 were gathered by examining the
Docket Books of the Supreme Court of the United States (available at the National
Archives, Washington, D.C.). Figures for the number of filings and docket for
1913–1997 are taken from Annual Reports of the Office of the Clerk, Supreme
Court of the United States. Cases disposed of each term include both cases given
plenary consideration and those summarily decided or otherwise disposed of. Figures for cases disposed of and carried over for the years 1800–1810, 1820, 1822–
1846, 1850, 1860, 1870, 1880, and 1890 are based on the author's tabulation of
cases contained in the Docket Books of the Supreme Court of the United States.

Figures for 1890–1910 were taken from *Annual Reports of the Attorney General of the United States* (Washington, D.C.: GPO, 1891, 1901, 1911). David Brewer Papers, Box 13, YA. Data for 1913–1997 were taken from Statistical Sheet, Office of the Clerk, Supreme Court. This section draws on the author's article "The Supreme Court: A Co-equal Branch of Government," *Supreme Court Historical Society Yearbook* 90 (1984).

128. See F. Frankfurter and J. Landis, *The Business of the Supreme Court,* 105–10 (Cambridge: Harvard University Press, 1927).

129. See Letter of Chief Justice Taft to Justice Van Devanter, Van Devanter Papers, Box 34, LC.

130. See W. Taft, "The Jurisdiction of the Supreme Court under the Act of February 13, 1925," 35 *Yale Law Journal* (1925); Letter to Senator Copeland, December 9, 1925, reprinted in *Cong. Rec.,* 68h Cong., 2d sess., 2916, 2920 (1925); and testimony of Chief Justice Taft and Justices Van Devanter, McReynolds, and Sutherland on the bill, in House Committee on the Judiciary, *Jurisdiction of Circuit Courts of Appeals and of the Supreme Court of the United States,* 68th Cong., 2d sess. House Report 8206, at 6–30 (Washington, D.C.: GPO, 1925). In a letter to Mr. George Rose, Justice Van Devaner discusses the drafting of the bill by a committee of justices of the Supreme Court. Van Devanter Papers (Letter of March 9, 1925), Box 29, LC. Committees of justices drafted legislation altering the Court's jurisdiction earlier as well. See correspondence among Chief Justice White and Justices Van Devanter and Day in 1911 and 1914, William Day Papers, Boxes 27 and 29, LC.

131. Chief Justice Burger, "Annual Report on the State of the Judiciary" (Address to the American Bar Association, New Orleans, February 6, 1983); quoting *Dick v. New York Life Insurance Co.,* 359 U.S. 437, 458–59 (1959) (Frankfurter, J., dis. op.).

132. Testimony of Justice White, in House Committee on Appropriations, *Departments . . . : Hearings before a Subcommittee,* 95th Cong., 1st sess., at 55 (Washington, D.C.: GPO, 1977).

133. Letter to Congressman Robert Kastenmeier, June 17, 1982, signed by all nine justices supporting the passage of H.R. 2406. Congress finally enacted legislation eliminating most of the Court's remaining mandatory appellate jurisdiction in 1988. See Public Law, 100–352.

134. *Report of the Study Group on the Caseload of the Supreme Court,* 57 *Federal Rules and Decisions* 573–650 (1973).

135. See, e.g., E. Warren and W. Burger, "Retired Chief Justice Attacks, Chief Justice Burger Defends Freund Study Group's Composition and Proposal," 59 *American Bar Association Journal* 721 (1973); and W. Brennan, supra note 88.

136. See J. P. Stevens, "The Life Span of a Judge-Made Rule," 58 *New York University Law Review* 1 (1983).

137. Commission on Revision of the Federal Court Appellate System, *Structure and Internal Procedures: Recommendations for Change* (Washington, D.C.: CRFCAS, 1975).

138. See, e.g., "DOJ Report Favoring Creation of Intercircuit Court," *Legal Times* 38 (May 23, 1983); and Statement of Jonathan Rose, assistant attorney general Office of Legal Policy, "Concerning the Workload of the Supreme Court," before the House Committee on the Judiciary, Subcommittee on Courts, Civil Liberties, and the Administration of Justice, November 10, 1983. See also D. M. O'Brien, "Managing the Business of the Supreme Court," 45 *Public Administration Review* 667–678 (1985); and S. Estreicher and J. Sexton, *Redefining the Supreme Court's Role* (New Haven: Yale University Press, 1986).

139. See Statement of Judges Wilfred Feinberg and Donald Lay, on the Intercircuit Tribunal Bill, before the House Committee on the Judiciary, Subcommittee on Courts, Civil Liberties, and the Administration of Justice, September 22, 1983. See, generally, House Committee on the Judiciary, *Supreme Court Workload,* 98th Cong., 1st sess. (Washington, D.C.: GPO, 1984).
140. Letter from Justice Stevens to Congressman Kastenmeier, October 25, 1983.

FOUR

Deciding What to Decide

1. J. M. Harlan, Jr., "A Glimpse of the Supreme Court at Work," 11 *University of Chicago Law School Record* 1, 4 (1963).
2. A. Lewis, *Gideon's Trumpet* 208 (New York: Random House, 1964).
3. Testimony of Justice Rehnquist at appropriations hearings for the Supreme Court. House Committee on Appropriations, *Departments . . . : Hearings before a Subcommittee,* 96th Cong., 1st sess., at 21 (Washington, D.C.: GPO, 1980).
4. Congress may alter the jurisdiction of federal courts by changing the criteria for "federal questions" and diversity suits (where federal courts consider disputes over state law when the parties are from two different states) and raise or eliminate the dollar amount required for filing such suits. In 1980, Congress eliminated, in certain cases, the requirement of $10,000 in a dispute, but maintained a dollar amount required for bringing diversity suits. See 31 U.S.C. 1331–32 (1982).
5. 27 Stat. 252 (1892), 28 U.S.C. Sec. 1915 (1966).
6. C. E. Hughes, *Addresses of Charles Evans Hughes* 185–86 (New York: Putnam's, 1916).
7. *United States v. Butler,* 297 U.S. 1 (1936).
8. *Flast v. Cohen,* 392 U.S. 83, 94–95 (1968).
9. See Stewart Jay, *Most Humble Servants: The Advisory Role of Early Judges.* (New Haven: Yale University Press, 1997).
10. *Muskrat v. United States,* 219 U.S. 346, 362 (1911).
11. *Duke Power Co. v. Carolina Environmental Study Group,* 438 U.S. 59, 103 (1978) (con. op.). See also *Bellotti v. Baird,* 443 U.S. 622 (1979).
12. *Aetna Life Insurance Co. v. Haworth,* 300 U.S. 277 (1937).
13. *Data Processing Service v. Camp,* 397 U.S. 150, 151 (1970).
14. *Braxton County Court v. West Virginia,* 208 U.S. 192, 197 (1908); *Coleman v. Miller,* 307 U.S. 433, 464 (1931) (Frankfurter, J., dis. op.).
15. *Frothingham v. Mellon,* 262 U.S. 447, 487–88 (1923).
16. See, *Laird v. Tatum,* 408 U.S. 1 (1972); and *Sierra Club v. Morton,* 405 U.S. 727 (1972).
17. *Linda R. S. v. Richard D.,* 410 U.S. 614 (1973) (dis. op.). Two other important rulings that cut back the law of standing are: *Valley Forge Christian College v. Americans United for Separation of Church and State,* 454 U.S. 464 (1982); and *Allen v. Wright,* 468 U.S. 737 (1984).
18. *Ex parte Baez,* 177 U.S. 378 (1900).
19. A. de Tocqueville, *Democracy in America,* ed. P. Bradley, vol. 1, at 288 (New York: Vintage, 1945).
20. See *Colegrove v. Green,* 328 U.S. 549 (1946).
21. J. Roche, "Judicial Self-Restraint," 49 *American Political Science Review* 762, 768 (1955).
22. L. Henkin, "Is There a 'Political Question' Doctrine?" 85 *Yale Law Journal* 597, 606 (1976).

23. Draft of opinion, George Sutherland Papers, Box 7, LC.
24. *Burnet v. Coronado Oil,* 285 U.S. 393 (1932) (Brandeis, J., dis. op.).
25. W. O. Douglas, Interview, "CBS Reports," transcript, at 13 (New York: CBS News, September 6, 1972).
26. Quoted, cited, and discussed by R. Collins and D. O'Brien, "Just Where Does Judge Bork Stand?" *National Law Journal* 13 (September 7, 1987).
27. L. Powell, *"Stare Decisis* and Judicial Restraint," Leslie H. Arps Lecture before the Association of the Bar of the City of New York (October 17, 1989).
28. For further discussion see C. Banks, "The Supreme Court and Precedent: An Analysis of Natural Courts and Reversals Trends," 75 *Judicature* 262 (1992).
29. R. Jackson, "The Task of Maintaining Our Liberties: The Role of the Judiciary," 39 *American Bar Association Journal* 962, 962 (1953).
30. Memoranda, March 21, 1989, and March 17, 1988, Marshall Papers, Boxes 452 and 435, LC.
31. Letters to Justice O'Connor from Justices Brennan, Powell, and Rehnquist, Marshall Papers, Box 331, LC.
32. Letter to Chief Justice Burger, September 28, 1982, Marshall Papers, Box 307, LC.
33. See E. N. Griswold and E. Gellhorn, "200 Cases in Which Justices Recused Themselves," *Washington Post* A25 (October 18, 1988).
34. See, e.g., "Memorandum on Disqualification or Recusal of Justices" (November 3, 1988), Marshall Papers, Box 568, LC.
35. Letter to Frankfurter, March 30, 1937, Harlan F. Stone Papers, Box 13, LC. See also Letter from Clerk to Chief Justice Taft, March 27, 1928, Willis Van Devanter Papers, Box 34, LC.
36. H. Wiley, "Jurisdictional Statements on Appeals to the United States Supreme Court," 31 *American Bar Association Journal* 239 (1945).
37. F. Vinson, Address before the American Bar Association, September 7, 1949, reprinted in 69 S.Ct. v, vi (1949).
38. See Commission on Revision of the Federal Court Appellate System, *Structure and Internal Procedures; Recommendations for Change* 11–19, 76–79, 91–111 (Washington, D.C.: CRFCAS, 1975). The commission's estimate was criticized as too high by G. Casper and R. Posner, *The Workload of the Supreme Court* (Chicago: American Bar Foundation, 1976). But see T. E. Baker and D. D. McFarland, "The Need for a New National Court," 100 *Harvard Law Review* 1400 (1987).
39. For further discussion, see S. M. Shapiro, *"Certiorari* Practice: The Supreme Court's Shrinking Docket," 24 *Litigation* 25 (1998).
40. In *re Jesse McDonald,* 489 U.S. 180 (1989).
41. See *In re Amendment Rule 39,* 500 U.S. 13 (1991). See also Memoranda from Chief Justice Rehnquist and Justice Kennedy, Marshall Papers, Box 524, LC.
42. Memorandum to the Conference by Frankfurter, 1951, 1953–1961, SC. These items are also in the John M. Harlan Papers, Boxes 499 and 587, MLPU; in the Felix Frankfurter Papers at HLS; as well as in the Tom C. Clark Papers, UT. For an excellent discussion of Frankfurter's efforts, see D. Hutchinson, "Felix Frankfurter and the Business of the Supreme Court, O.T. 1946–O.T. 1961," *The Supreme Court Review* 143, ed. P. Kurland and G. Casper (Chicago: University of Chicago Press, 1980).
43. Brandeis-Frankfurter Conversations, at 17 and 30; Felix Frankfurter Papers, Box 224, LC.
44. See, e.g., Memorandum for the Conference by Chief Justice Warren, October 7, 1957, Frankfurter Papers, Box 220, File 4051, LC.

45. Letter from Justice Douglas to Justice Frankfurter, October 13, 1960, Felix Frankfurter Papers, Box 152, Folder 9, HLS. The letter is also in the Harlan Papers, Box 49, MLPU.
46. Letter from Justice Black to Justice Frankfurter, October 13, 1960, Felix Frankfurter Papers, Box 152, Folder 9, HLS. See also Memorandum to Conference by Justice Clark, October 7, 1957, Clark Papers, UT.
47. Based on statistics compiled by the Office of the Administrative Assistant to the Chief Justice.
48. This chart is based on data for 1935–1971 contained in *Report of the Study Group on the Caseload of the Supreme Court*, 57 *Federal Rules and Decisions* 573, 614 (1973). Data for 1971–1997 are compiled from the Statistical Sheets (Final), Office of the Clerk, Supreme Court. Note that cases on the Court's original docket are included in the total number of filings but do not usually appear in the number for paid and unpaid filings. Note also that at various times between 1935 and 1971 the method of assigning cases to the Miscellaneous Docket changed and that there thus may be some minor variations in the composition of the Miscellaneous Docket. The Miscellaneous Docket was created in 1945, and beginning in 1947, all petitions for *certiorari in forma pauperis* were transferred to that docket, and appeals *in forma pauperis* were likewise docketed and transferred in 1954. After the creation of the Miscellaneous Docket, a case was transferred from it to the Appellate Docket once *certiorari* was granted or an appeal noted. Since 1971, the Clerk of the Supreme Court reports as a category all *in forma pauperis* petitions.
49. Memorandum of Justice Frankfurter on In Forma Pauperis Petitions, November 1, 1954, Felix Frankfurter Papers, Box 205, Folder 5, HLS. See also Stanley Reed Papers, Memo, November 1, 1944, Box 172, UK.
50. Memorandum from Chief Justice Burger, Hugo Black Papers, Box 58, LC.
51. Memorandum from the Chief Justice and NARS Report, Hugo Black Papers, Boxes 58, and 426, LC. See also Letter to Harlan, July 15, 1970, and Memoranda to the Conference, July 16 and 30, 1970, Harlan Papers, Box 490, MLPU. At other times, justices share the law clerks assigned to retired justices. See Memorandum from Chief Justice Burger, 1974, Clark Papers, UT.
52. Quoted in Bernard Schwartz, *Decision: How the Supreme Court Decides Cases* (New York: Oxford University Press, 1996), p. 257.
53. Interview quoted in D. M. O'Brien, "Managing the Business of the Supreme Court," 45 *Public Administration Review* 667, 670 (1985).
54. Quoted by T. Clark, "Internal Operations of the United States Supreme Court," 43 *Judicature* 45, 48 (1959).
55. K. W. Starr, "Supreme Court Needs a Management Revolt," *Wall Street Journal* A23 (October 13, 1993).
56. Memos in Marshall Papers, LC, quoted by Tony Mauro, "Ginsburg Jumps In: Last One Into the Cert. Pool is a Rotten Egg," *Connecticut Law Tribune* 1 (September 27, 1993).
57. Quoted in Tony Mauro, "Justices Give Pivotal Role to Novice Lawyers," *USA Today* A1, A2 (March 13, 1998).
58. The preceding observations are based on conversations with law clerks. Law clerks frankly admit their lack of maturity in screening filings when they begin their year at the Court. Similar observations by former law clerks may be found in the Harlan F. Stone Papers, LC.
59. See, e.g., Letter from Hughes to Stone, October 1, 1931, Stone Papers, Box 75, LC.

60. Quoted in "The Supreme Court: How It Operates in Private Chambers outside Courtroom," *Smithsonian* magazine, special report (1976).
61. Memorandum, Marshall Papers, Boxes 427 and 492, LC.
62. Memorandum, Marshall Papers, Box 452, LC.
63. See W. J. Brennan, Jr., "The National Court of Appeals: Another Dissent," 40 *University of Chicago Law Review* 473, 478–79 (1973). See also, G. Caldeira and J. Wright, "The Discuss List: Agenda Building in the Supreme Court," 24 *Law & Society Review* 807 (1990).
64. J. F. Byrnes, *All in One Lifetime* 154 (New York: Harper, 1958).
65. Interview with Chief Justice Rehnquist, PBS Special, "This Honorable Court" (outtake).
66. See, e.g., Memorandum to Justice Brennan, June 27, 1984, Brennan Papers, LC.
67. Rehnquist Interview, PBS Special, "This Honorable Court" (outtake).
68. W. O. Douglas, *The Court Years* 223, 226, and 227 (New York: Random House, 1980).
69. O. Roberts, Address, Meeting of the Association of the Bar of the City of New York and the New York County Lawyers' Association, December 12, 1946; and Robert Jackson Papers, LC.
70. Memorandum of Howard Westwood, Stone Papers, Box 48, LC. See also Memorandum of talk with HFS, March 2, 1965, Felix Frankfurter Papers, Box 171, File 14, HLS.
71. Powell, quoted in "The Reasonable Man," *ABA Journal* 69 (October 1990), at 72; Rehnquist, from interview on "Booknotes," C-Span, July 5, 1992.
72. Memo to chief justice, June 20, 1975, William J. Brennan Papers, Box 336, LC. For a similar incident, see Frankfurter's lengthy memo to Stone, December 12, 1939, Reed Papers, Box 171, UK.
73. See, e.g., Memos between the chief justice and Blackmun, October 3, 1975, Brennan Papers, Box 363, LC.
74. Justice Blackmun, Speech at Eighth Circuit Judicial Conference, St. Louis, Missouri, July 15, 1988.
75. April 24, 1987 Memorandum, Marshall Papers, Box 407, LC.
76. Memorandum, May 8, 1990, Marshall Papers, Box 493, LC.
77. Memorandum, November 24, 1989, Marshall Papers, Box 492, LC.
78. Letter from Justice Stevens, December 19, 1989, Marshall Papers, Box 492, LC.
79. Comments at George Washington National Law Center, February 16, 1988, quoted in "Ruling Fixed Opinions," *New York Times* A16 (February 22, 1988).
80. Rehnquist Interview, PBS Special, "This Honorable Court" (outtake).
81. B. White, "The Work of the Supreme Court: A Nuts and Bolts Description," 54 *New York State Bar Journal* 346, 383 (1982).
82. Clark, supra note 54, at 50.
83. See J. Palmer, *The Vinson Court Era: The Supreme Court's Conference Votes* (New York: AMS Press, 1990), at 29.
84. H. Black, "Justice Black and the Bill of Rights," CBS Special, transcript, at 5 (New York: CBS News, December 3, 1968).
85. H. Blackmun, "A Justice Speaks Out: A Conversation with Harry A. Blackmun," Cable News Network, transcript, at 4 (December 4, 1982). See also Letters to Conference, discussing the voting procedure, from Justice Blackmun (September 23, 1980), Stewart (September 18, 1980), and Stevens (September 16, 1980), Marshall Papers, Box 263, LC.

86. Memorandum to Conference, October 1, 1986, Marshall Papers, Box 427, LC.
87. M. Provine, *Case Selection in the United States Supreme Court* 32 (Chicago: University of Chicago Press, 1980).
88. Data gathered from Memorandum to Conference, September 30, 1986, from Justice White, Marshall Papers, Box 427, LC.
89. Based on Justice Thurgood Marshall's docket books for the 1990 term, Marshall Papers, Boxes 561–566, LC.
90. W. H. Taft, testimony, in *Hearings before the House Committee on the Judiciary*, 67th Cong., 2d sess., at 2 (Washington, D.C., 1922).
91. P. Linzer, "The Meaning of Certiorari Denials," 79 *Columbia Law Review* 1227, 1302 (1979). See also S. Brenner, "The New Certiorari Game," 41 *Journal of Politics* 649 (1979).
92. Testimony of McReynolds, in *Hearings on H.R. 8206 before the Committee on the Judiciary*, 68th Cong., 2d sess., 1924.
93. Ibid.
94. C. E. Hughes, "Reason as Opposed to the Tyranny of Force" (Speech delivered to the American Law Institute, May 6, 1937), reprinted in *Vital Speeches of the Day* 458, 459 (1937).
95. Letter from Reed, October 12, 1940, Douglas Papers, Box 228 (Frankfurter File), LC. See also his note to Burton, March 5, 1952, Harold Burton Papers, Box 336, LC.
96. Memorandum for Conference, March 11, 1943, Douglas Papers, Box 228 (Frankfurter File), LC.
97. Memorandum for Conference, April 6, 1944, Stone Papers, Box 24, LC.
98. See Memorandum to Conference from Stevens, May 14, 1976, Brennan Papers, Box 363, LC. Conversely, the crucial fourth vote may be lost if a justice decided to deny rather than grant a case after the conference vote. See Letter from Harlan, December 13, 1965, Clark Papers, UT. See also Letter from Frankfurter to Burton, February 1, 1965, Felix Frankfurter Papers, Box 169, File 6, HLS.
99. See, e.g., *Maryland v. Baltimore Radio Show, Inc.*, 338 U.S. 912 (1950); *Brown v. Allen*, 344 U.S 443 (1953); and *Daniels v. Allen*, 344 U.S. 443 (1953).
100. Memorandum from Justice Frankfurter on the Integrity of the *Certiorari* process to Justice Harlan (February 21, 1957), Harlan's Papers, Box 532, MLPU.
101. This discussion draws on D. M. O'Brien, "Join-3, Votes, the Rule of Four, the Cert. Pool, and the Supreme Court's Shrinking Plenary Docket," 13 *The Journal of Law & Politics* 779 (1997); and D. M. O'Brien, "The Rehnquist Court's Shrinking Docket," 81 *Judicature* 58 (1997).
102. Data for 1941–1971 are taken from *Report of the Study Group on the Caseload of the Supreme Court* (the Freund report), 57 *Federal Rules and Decisions* 573, 615 (1973). Data for 1981, and 1990–1991 are based on the author's analysis of the docketbook of Thurgood Marshall, Marshall Papers, Boxes 561–566, LC.
103. Based on Bench Memoranda, Marshall Papers, Boxes 375–376 and 513–514, LC. Excluded here are three cases granted by an equally divided Court and one case in which five justices voted to grant, but which was ultimately denied at the request of the Solicitor General.
104. J. P. Stevens, "The Life Span of a Judge-Made Rule" (Lecture delivered at New York University School of Law, October 27, 1982), excerpt reprinted in M. Cannon and D. M. O'Brien, eds., *Views from the Bench: The Judiciary and Constitutional Politics* (Chatham, N.J.: Chatham House, 1985).
105. Memorandum for Conference from Justice Marshall, September 21, 1983, in Brennan Papers, Box 640, LC.

106. Letter from Justice Stevens to Chief Justice Burger (August 31, 1983), in Brennan Papers, Box 540, LC.
107. Interview with Justice Stevens, October 16, 1988.
108. This discussion draws on D. M. O'Brien, "Join-3, Votes, the Rule of Four, the *Cert.* Pool, and the Supreme Court's Shrinking Plenary Docket," 13 *The Journal of Law & Politics* 779 (1997).
109. Letters to author from Chief Justice Rehnquist (October 21, 1996) and Justice Blackmun (October 10, 1996) and telephone interview with Justice Stevens (October 8, 1996).
110. *Singleton v. Commissioner of Internal Revenue,* 439 U.S. 940, 942 (1978) (Stevens, J., op. respecting denial of *certiorari*).
111. *United States v. Carver,* 260 U.S. 482, 490 (1922).
112. *Brown v. Allen,* 344 U.S. 443, 542 (1953).
113. *Maryland v. Baltimore Radio Show,* 338 U.S. 912, 917–19 (1950).
114. *Brown v. Allen,* 344 U.S. 443, 542 (1953).
115. *Rogers v. Missouri Pacific Railroad Co.,* 352 U.S. 500, 528 (1957).
116. See ibid., and *McBride v. Toledo Terminal Co.,* 354 U.S. 517, 519–20 (1957).
117. *United States v. Shannon,* 342 U.S. 288, 298 (1952).
118. *Darr v. Burford,* 339 U.S. 200, 226 (1950) (Frankfurter, J., dis. op.).
119. *Daniels v. Allen,* 344 U.S. 443, 491 (1953).
120. Letter to Frankfurter, March 30, 1937, Stone Papers, Box 13.
121. See, e.g., *Brown v. Texas,* 117 S.Ct. 355 (1997) (Stevens, Souter, Breyer, and Ginsburg, opinion respecting the denial of *certiorai*).
122. *Liles v. Oregon,* 425 U.S. 963, 963 (1976).
123. See *Callins v. Collins,* 510 U.S. 1141 (1994).
124. *Drake v. Zant,* and *Westbrook v. Balkcom,* 449 U.S. 999 (1980) (dissenting opinions by Justices Brennan, joined by Marshall, Stewart, and White). See also *Triangle Improvement Council v. Ritchie,* 402 U.S. 497 (1970), where the four justices who voted to grant review joined in a dissent from the majority's decision to override the rule of four and dismiss the case as improvidently granted.
125. Memorandum to Conference, June 25, 1984, Marshall Papers, Box 331, LC.
126. See A. Hellman, " 'Granted, Vacated, and Remanded'—Shedding Light on a Dark Corner of Supreme Court Practice," 67 *Judicature* 390, 391 n. 10 (1984).
127. Letter from the justices to Congressman Kastenmeier, June 17, 1982, attachment, p. 5.
128. *Hicks v. Miranda,* 422 U.S. 332, 345 (1975), quoting *Doe v. Hodgson,* 478 F. 2d 537, 539, *cert.* denied sub. nom., *Doe v. Brennan,* 414 U.S. 1096 (1973). See also *Colorado Springs Amusements, Ltd. v. Rizzo,* 428 U.S. 913 (1976) (Brennan, J., dis. op.) (reviewing the problems of confusion created by the Court's position).
129. See *Lawrence v. Chater,* 116 S.Ct. 604 (1996) and *Stutson v. United States,* 116 S.Ct. 600 (1996).
130. J. Goebel, Jr., *Antecedents and Beginnings to 1801,* Appendix, at 804 (New York: Macmillan, 1971).
131. This table incorporates data from and updates the statistics compiled in F. Frankfurter and J. Landis, *The Business of the Supreme Court,* Table 1, at 302 (New York: Macmillan, 1927) (data for 1825, 1875, and 1925); F. Frankfurter and J. Landis, "The Business of the Supreme Court in the October Term 1930," 45 *Harvard Law Review* 271, Table 9, at 9 (1930) (data for 1930); and E. Gressman, "Much Ado about Certiorari," 52 *Georgetown Law Journal* 742, 756–57 (1964) (data for 1935, 1945, and 1955). Data for 1960, 1965, 1970, 1975, 1980 and 1990 were compiled by the author, and those for 1985 by one of my esteemed graduate

students, William Mandell. The table aims only to illustrate trends. The classification in this and other tables necessarily invites differences of opinion as to the dominant issue in a case.

132. Vinson, supra note 37, at vi.

133. *NAACP v. Button,* 371 U.S. 415, 429–30 (1963).

134. L. Powell, *The Powell Memorandum: Attack on American Free Enterprise System* 7 (August 24, 1971) (Chamber of Commerce of the United States, Washington, D.C.).

135. See B. Weisbrod, J. Handler, and N. Komesar, eds., *Public Interest Law: A Economic and Institutional Analysis* (Berkeley: University of California Press, 1978); L. Epstein, *Conservatives in Court* (Knoxville: University of Tennessee Press, 1985); N. Aron, *Liberty and Justice for All: Public Interest Law in the 1980s and Beyond* (Boulder, Col.: Westview Press, 1989); and K. O'Connor, *Women's Organizations' Use of the Court* (Lexington, Mass.: Lexington Books, 1980).

136. R. Jackson, *The Struggle for Judicial Supremacy* 287 (New York: Knopf, 1951).

137. See R. Kluger, *Simple Justice: The History of Brown v. Board of Education and Black America's Struggle for Equality* (New York: Alfred Knopf, 1976); C. Vose, *Caucasians Only: The Supreme Court, the NAACP and the Restrictive Covenant Cases* (Berkeley: University of California Press, 1959); and M. Tushnet, *The NAACP's Legal Strategy against Segregated Education, 1925–1950* (Chapel Hill: University of North Carolina Press, 1987).

138. S. Wasby, "Civil Rights Litigation by Organizations: Constraints and Choices," 68 *Judicature* 337 (1985). See also S. Lawrence, *The Poor in Court: The Legal Services Program and Supreme Court Decision Making* (Princeton, N.J.: Princeton University Press, 1990).

139. For a study of interest-group litigation in the lower federal courts, see L. Epstein and C. K. Rowland, "Debunking the Myth of Interest Group Invincibility in the Courts," 85 *American Political Science Review* 205 (1991).

140. See S. Olson, "The Political Evolution of Interest Group Litigation," in R. Gambitta, M. May, and J. Foster, eds., *Governing through Courts* (Beverly Hills, Calif.: Sage, 1981); J. Kobylka, "A Court-Created Context for Group Litigation: Libertarian Groups and Obscenity," 49 *Journal of Politics* 1061 (1987); and J. Stewart and J. Sheffield, "Does Interest Group Litigation Matter? The Case of Black Political Mobilization in Mississippi." 49 *Journal of Politics* 780 (1987).

141. See S. Behuniak-Long, "Friendly Fire: Amici Curiae and *Webster v. Reproductive Health Services,*" 74 *Judicature* 261 (1991).

142. See Lee Epstein, Jeffrey Segal, Harold Spaeth, and Thomas Walker, *The Supreme Court Compendium: Data, Decisions & Developments,* Table 7-22, 582 (Washington, D.C.: *Congressional Quarterly,* 1993).

143. See G. Caldeira and J. Wright, "Organized Interests and Agenda Setting in U.S. Supreme Court," 82 *American Political Science Review* 1108 (1988).

144. See J. Tanenhaus, M. Schick, M. Muraskin, and D. Rosen, "The Supreme Court's Certiorari Jurisdiction: Cue Theory," in *Judicial Decisionmaking,* ed. G. Schubert, at 111-32 (New York: Free Press, 1963); V. Armstrong and C. Johnson, "Certiorari Decisions by the Warren & Burger Courts: Is Cue Theory Time Bound?" *Polity* 141 (1983); D. M. Provine, "Deciding What to Decide: How the Supreme Court Sets Its Agenda," 64 *Judicature* 321 (1981).

145. See S. S. Ulmer, "Selecting Cases for Supreme Court Review: An Underdog Model," 72 *American Political Science Review* 902 (1978); S. S. Ulmer, W. Hintze, and L. Kirklosky, 6 *Law & Society* 637 (1972); G. Rathjen and H. Spaeth, "Denial of Access and Ideological Preferences: An Analysis of the Voting Behavior of the

Burger Court Justices, 1969–1976," *Western Political Quarterly* 70 (1983); G. Caldiera and J. Wright, "Organized Interests and Agenda-Setting in the U.S. Supreme Court," 82 *American Political Science Review* 1111 (1988).

146. Data taken from Jonathan Rose, assistant attorney general, Department of Justice, "The Workload of the Supreme Court," Testimony before the House Committee on the Judiciary, Subcommittee on Courts, Civil Liberties, and the Administration of Justice, at 5–6 (November 10, 1983). Compared with the situation fifty years earlier, the government is now participating in more argued cases each term and winning slightly more as well. During 1928–1936, the government's success rate averaged 67 percent each term; between 1937 and 1944, it averaged 74 percent. Memorandum for the Attorney General by Solicitor General Stanley Reed, June 1, 1937, Felix Frankfurter Papers, Box 170, File 16, HLS; and Report to the Attorney General, June 20, 1945, Francis Biddle Papers, Box 2, RPL. R. Chamberlin, "Mixing Politics and Law: The Office of the Solicitor General" 2 *Journal of Law & Politics* 379 (1988); and see Lee Epstein, Jeffrey Segal, Harold Spaeth, and Thomas Walker, *The Supreme Court Compendium:* Data, Decisions of Development, Table 7-10 (Washington, D.C.: *Congressional Quarterly,* 1993); see also G. Uelman, "The Influence of the Solicitor General upon the Supreme Court Disposition of Federal Circuit Court Decisions," 69 *Judicature* 361 (1986).

147. See conference notes on *Melkonyan v. Sullivan*, Marshall Papers, Box 563, LC.

148. W. O. Douglas, Interview, "CBS Reports," transcript, at 12 (New York: CBS News, September 6, 1972).

149. See R. Pacelle, Jr., *The Transformation of the Supreme Court's Agenda: From the New Deal to the Reagan Administration* (Boulder, Colo.: Westview Press, 1991), at 149.

150. See R. Galloway, *Justice for All: The Rich and Poor in Supreme Court History, 1790–1990* (Durham, N.C.: Carolina Academic Press, 1991).

151. Pacelle, loc. cit.

152. D. J. Garrow, "The Rehnquist Years," *New York Times Magazine* 65 (October 6, 1996).

153. Quoted by S. Duffy, "Inside the Highest Court," *Pennsylvania Law Weekly* 11 (April 17, 1965).

154. Interview with Tony Mauro, "Justices Give Pivotal Role to Novice Lawyers," *USA Today* A2 (March 13–15, 1998).

155. Black, supra note 84, at 5.

156. Letter to Senator Burton Wheeler, reprinted in Senate Committee on the Judiciary, *Hearings on the Reorganization of the Federal Judiciary,* 75th Cong., 1st sess., 1937, Senate Report 711, at 40.

157. J. Clarke, "Observations and Reflections on Practice in the Supreme Court," 8 *American Bar Association Journal* 263, 263 (1922).

158. J. Harlan, "Manning the Dikes," 13 *Record of the New York City Bar Association* 541, 547 (1958); Douglas, supra note 148; Rehnquist, Remarks at the Jefferson Literary and Debating Society, Charlottesville, Virginia, September 20, 1985.

159. *Ex parte Brummett,* 295 U.S. 719 (1935); 299 U.S. 514 (1936); 302 U.S. 644 (1937); 303 U.S. 570 (1938); 306 U.S. 615 (1939); 309 U.S. 625 (1940); *Ex parte Brummitt,* 304 U.S. 545 (1938); 311 U.S. 614 (1940); 313 U.S. 548 (1941); and 314 U.S. 585 (1941).

160. Brennan, supra note 63.

161. See *In re Reverend Clovis Carl Green,* 669 F.2d 779, 781 (1981).

162. Memorandum to Conference, May 25, 1971, Harlan Papers, Box 434, MLPU.

163. W. O. Douglas, "The Supreme Court and Its Caseload," 45 *Cornell Law Quarterly* 401, 413–14 (1960).

FIVE

Deciding Cases and Writing Opinions

1. See *Buchanan v. Wade*, 401 U.S. 989 (1971); and *Commonwealth's Attorney for the City of Richmond v. Doe*, 425 U.S. 901 (1976).
2. *Board of Education of Oklahoma City v. National Gay Task Force*, 470 U.S. 903 (1985).
3. Justice White's proposed dissent of October 17, 1985 is in the *Bowers v. Hardwick* file, Lewis F. Powell, Jr. Papers, WLLS. It also may be located in Thurgood Marshall's Papers, Box 393, LC.
4. Memo to Mike [Mosman], March 31, 1986, Lewis F. Powell, Jr. Papers, WLLS.
5. See John C. Jefferies, Jr., *Justice Lewis F. Powell, Jr.: A Biography* (New York: Scribners, 1994), at 511–530, for the best discussion in print of Justice Powell's deliberations.
6. Memo of April 1, 1986, and Memo of April 2, 1986, *Bowers v. Hardwick* file, Lewis F. Powell, Jr. Papers, WLLS.
7. Docket Book, Ibid.
8. Letter from Chief Justice Burger, April 3, 1986, Ibid.
9. Interview with Powell (February 16, 1987). See also David M. O'Brien, "For the Majority," *The Los Angeles Times*, Opinion, 1–2 (May 3, 1987); and *Bowers v. Hardwick*, 478 U.S. 186 (1986).
10. See Anand Agneshwar, "Ex-Justice Says He May Have Been Wrong," *National Law Journal* 3 (November 5, 1990).
11. Interview with Stewart, February 28, 1985, SC.
12. Memorandum, William J. Brennan Papers, Box 14, LC; and Interview with Justice Brennan, September 30, 1985, SC.
13. *Abbate v. United States*, 359 U.S. 187 (1959). Brennan wrote the opinion for the Court but added a separate concurring opinion. Justice O'Connor did the same in *Bush v. Vera*, 116 S. Ct. 1941 (1996); as did Justice Blackmun in *Logan v. Zimmerman Brush Co.*, 455 U.S. 422 (1982); and Justice Jackson in *Wheeling Steel Corp. v. Glander*, 337 U.S. 562. (1949).
14. Memorandum, May 28, 1974, Brennan Papers, Box 423, LC.
15. Transcript of Oral Arguments. The transcript may be found in *Landmark Briefs and Arguments of the Supreme Court of the United States: Constitutional Law*, vol. 79, ed. P. Kurland and G. Casper (Arlington, Va.: University Publications of America, 1975).
16. Docket Book, 1972 Term, Brennan Papers, Box 423, LC.
17. Memorandum to the Conference, July 14, 1974, Brennan Papers, Box 329, LC.
18. Memorandum, July 22, 1974, Brennan Papers, Box 329, LC.
19. Handwritten note to Brennan on a Letter to Burger, July 12, 1974, Brennan Papers, Box 329, LC.
20. Letter to Burger, July 18, 1974, Brennan Papers, Box 329, LC.
21. Interview with Justice Brennan, 1987.
22. C. E. Hughes, *The Supreme Court of the United States* 61 (New York: Columbia University Press, 1928).
23. W. J. Brennan, quoted in Report of the Commission on Revision of the Federal

Court Appellate System, *Structure and Internal Procedures: Recommendation for Change,* 67 *Federal Rules and Decisions* 195, 254 (1975).

24. W. Rehnquist, "Oral Advocacy: A Disappearing Art" (Brainerd Currie Lecture, Mercer University School of Law, October 20, 1983), ms p. 4 (on file with the author).

25. Quoted by A. Beveridge, *The Life of John Marshall,* vol. 4, at 249–50 (Boston: Houghton Mifflin, 1919).

26. Quoted by C. Warren, *The Supreme Court in United States History,* vol. 1, at 603 (Boston: Little, Brown, 1922).

27. *Bridge Proprietors v. Hoboken Co.,* 68 U.S. 116 (1863).

28. J. Clarke, "Reminiscences of the Court and the Law," 5 *Proceedings of the Fifth Annual Meeting of the California State Bar* 20 (1932).

29. Letter to Pollock, March 17, 1898, reprinted in *Holmes-Pollock Letters,* ed. M. Howe, 81 (Cambridge: Harvard University Press, 1946).

30. Undated note, Hugo Black Papers, Frankfurter File, Box 60, LC.

31. Speech before ABA Tenth Annual Appellant Advocate Institute Luncheon (May 13, 1996).

32. See Kevin McGuire, *The Supreme Court Bar: Legal Elites in the Washington Community* (Charlottesville: University Press of Virginia, 1993).

33. F. Frankfurter, *Proceedings in Honor of Mr. Justice Frankfurter and Distinguished Alumni* 18 (Occasional Paper No. 3 of the Harvard Law School, 1960).

34. W. Rutledge, "The Appellate Brief," 28 *American Bar Association Journal* 251, 251 (1942).

35. See C. H. Butler, *A Century at the Bar of the Supreme Court of the United States* 88 (New York: Putnam's, 1942).

36. Rehnquist, supra note 24, at 19.

37. Quoted in the *Philadelphia Inquirer* (April 9, 1963), cited by H. Abraham, *The Judicial Process* 203 (New York: Oxford University Press, 4th ed., 1980); and "Seminar with Mr. Chief Justice Warren," University of Virginia Legal Forum, at 9 (April 25, 1973).

38. Reported by J. Frank, *The Marble Palace* 105 (New York: Knopf, 1958).

39. Interview with Justice Kennedy in film "The Supreme Court of the United States" (York Associates, 1997).

40. Blackmun Speech before Eighth Circuit Judicial Conference (July 15, 1988); Scalia Interview, PBS Special, "This Honorable Court;" and Rehnquist, as quoted by Mary Stallcup, "Questions from the Bench," *Manhattan Lawyer* (May 24, 1988).

41. Interview, supra note 39.

42. L. F. Powell, "What Really Goes On at the Court," printed in M. Cannon and D. O'Brien, eds., *Views from the Bench: The Judiciary and Constitutional Politics* (Chatham, N.J.: Chatham House, 1985).

43. Memo from Justice Douglas to Conference, October 23, 1961, Black Papers, Box 60, LC.

44. W. O. Douglas, *The Court Years* 34 (New York: Random House, 1980).

45. H. Hart, Jr., "Foreword: The Time Chart of the Justices," 73 *Harvard Law Review* 84 (1959). See also Henry M. Hart Papers, HLS. Hart's estimate of the number of hours devoted to conference was slightly high. During the 1949–1952 terms, the justices in fact met an average 119 hours per term. Earl Warren Papers, Box 660, LC.

46. The estimated amount of conference time is based on the assumption that the justices hold twenty-six regular conferences, running for about five hours each, and that they meet on Wednesdays for an hour and half every week in which they hear oral arguments.

47. Letter from Frankfurter to Burton, Harold Burton Papers, Box 101, LC.
48. H. Blackmun, "What Have I Learned," Lecture at Aspen Summer Institute, C-SPAN (September 12, 1992).
49. C. Thomas, Address to the National Center for Policy Analysis, Dallas, Texas (aired on C-SPAN, October 13, 1996).
50. Interview with Scalia, PBS Special, "This Honorable Court" (outtake).
51. For further discussion see A. Melone, "Revisiting the Freshman Effect Hypothesis: The First Two Terms of Justice Anthony Kennedy," 74 *Judicature* 6 (1990); and S. Johnson and C. Smith, "David Souter's First Term on the Supreme Court: The Impact of a New Justice," 75 *Judicature* 238 (1992).
52. D. Danelski, "The Influence of the Chief Justice in the Decisional Process," in W. Murphy and C. H. Pritchett, eds., *Courts, Judges, and Politics* 568 (New York: Random House, 4th ed., 1986).
53. A. T. Mason, *William Howard Taft: Chief Justice* 220–21 (New York: Simon & Schuster, 1965).
54. Letter to the author from Blackmun, November 8, 1984.
55. E. Warren, "A Conversation with Earl Warren," WGBH-TV educational foundation, transcript, at 12 (Boston: WGBH Educational Foundation, 1972). Warren Papers, Box 571 and, Docket Book in, Box 367, LC; Robert Jackson Papers, LC; and *Diary,* Burton Papers, Box 3, LC. For an excellent further discussion, see D. Hutchinson, "Unanimity and Desegregation: Decisionmaking in the Supreme Court, 1948–1958," 68 *Georgetown Law Journal* 1 (1979).
56. Warren to Conference, October 7, 1957, Black Papers, Box 320, LC. See also Tom Clark Memo to Conference, October 7, 1957, Tom C. Clark Papers, UT.
57. Vinson to Frankfurter, October 11, 1951, William O. Douglas Papers, Box 224, LC.
58. Burger, "Supreme Court Film," transcript, at p. 12 (film shown to visitors to the Supreme Court until 1987).
59. Brennan Papers, Box 283, LC. See also letter from Chief Justice Taft, April 22, 1927, Willis Van Devanter Papers, Box 34, LC.
60. Douglas Memorandum to Conference, Black Papers, Box 60, LC. See also Justice Frankfurter's Memorandum on *Baker v. Carr,* Clark Papers, UT.
61. Quoted by D. Dorin, "Social Leadership, Humor, and Supreme Court Decision-making," 66 *Judicature* 462 (1983). See also Tom C. Clark Oral History Interview, at 50, UK.
62. Memorandum for Frankfurter, Clark Papers, UT.
63. W. J. Brennan, Jr., "A Remembrance of William O. Douglas," 1990 *Journal of Supreme Court History* 104 (1991), at 105.
64. Quoted by W. Burger, "In Memoriam: John M. Harlan," 92A S. Ct. 5, 44 (1972).
65. S. O'Connor, "Thurgood Marshall: The Influence of a Raconteur," 44 *Stanford Law Review* 1217 (1992). See also A. Kennedy, "The Voice of Thurgood Marshall," 44 *Stanford Law Review* 1221 (1992).
66. Quoted by E. Gerhart, *America's Advocate: Robert H. Jackson* 274 (New York: Bobbs-Merrill, 1958).
67. Note to Clark, May 3, 1968, Clark Papers, UT. Justice Douglas later told the story in his autobiography, supra note 43, at 226.
68. The story is told in W. King, *Melville Weston Fuller: Chief Justice of the United States* 290 (New York: Macmillan, 1950).
69. Conference Notes, Frank Murphy Papers, Box 69, File 32, BHLUM.
70. Undated note, Black Papers, Box 61, LC.
71. Undated note, Felix Frankfurter Papers, Box 170, File 9, HLS.
72. Sidney Fine Interview with William O. Douglas, October 24, 1964, BHLUM.

73. Letter to Murphy, February 10, 1947, Felix Frankfurter Papers, Box 170, File 14, HLS.
74. Note from Murphy, Felix Frankfurter Papers, Box 170, File 13, HLS.
75. Letter, Black Papers, Box 60, LC.
76. Unsigned note, January 4, 1941, Black Papers, Box 261, LC.
77. J. Harlan, "A Glimpse of the Supreme Court at Work," 11 *University of Chicago Law School Record* 1, 7 (1963).
78. Memo from Burger, December 20, 1971, Brennan Papers, Box 281, LC.
79. Memo to Conference, Brennan Papers, Box 306, LC.
80. Quoted by A. T. Mason, Review of *The Holmes-Einstein Letters,* in *New York Review of Books* 60 (November 22, 1964).
81. Oliver W. Holmes Papers, Box 42 File 35, HLS.
82. Interview with Justice Blackmun, "All Things Considered," National Public Radio (December 28, 1993).
83. Tom C. Clark Oral History Interview, at 5, UK.
84. Quoted by J. McLean, *William Rufus Day* (Baltimore: Johns Hopkins Press, 1946).
85. See King, 332–35 loc. cit.
86. See Danelski, supra note 52. Obviously, what "important constitutional cases" are is a matter of debate, and so the figures are only rough approximations of each chief justice's practice.
87. Memorandum of Howard Westwood, Stone Papers, Box 48 LC.
88. "Chief Justice Vinson and His Law Clerks," 49 *Northwestern University Law Review* 26, 31 (1954). The charts are in the Vinson Papers, Box 217, UK. See also S. Brenner and J. Palmer, "The Time Taken to Write Opinions as a Determinant of Opinion Assignments," 72 *Judicature* 179 (1988).
89. W. J. Brennan, "Chief Justice Warren," 88 *Harvard Law Review* 1, 2, 5 (1974).
90. Based on data collected each term by the Clerk of the Supreme Court, Sheet: Number of Printed Opinions and Memorandum, SC, and the author's own tabulations.
91. For further discussion see S. Davis, "Power on the Court: Chief Justice Rehnquist's Opinion Assignments," 74 *Judicature* 66 (1990); and F. Maltzman and P. Wahlbeck, "May It please the Chief? Opinion Assignments in the Rehnquist Court," 40 *American Journal Political Science* 421 (1996).
92. Memorandum to the Conference, November 24, 1989, Marshall Papers, Box 492, LC.
93. See Memorandum, May 27, 1948, Douglas Papers, Box 217, LC.
94. Quoted by A. McCormack, "A Law Clerk's Recollections," 46 *Columbia Law Review* 710, 712 (1946). For another, though less successful, switch of position when writing the Court's opinion, see Memo on *Bryan v. United States* (1950), Sherman Minton Papers, Box 1, TPL.
95. See *Hodel v. Virginia Surface Mining,* 452 U.S. 264 (1981); *FERC v. Mississippi,* 456 U.S. 742 (1982); *United Transportation Union v. Long Island Railroad Company,* 455 U.S. 678 (1982); and *EEOC v. Wyoming,* 460 U.S. 222 (1983).
96. See S. Brenner, "Fluidity on the United States Supreme Court: A Reexamination," 24 *American Journal of Political Science* 526 (1980); and S. Brenner, "Fluidity on the Supreme Court: 1956–1967," 26 *American Journal of Political Science* 388 (1982).
97. In another seven cases, Harlan circulated opinions as to why they should be granted or otherwise disposed of than as voted at the initial conference. After a subsequent change in the conference vote, these opinions were not filed. Harlan Papers, Boxes 4, 18, 37, 55, 76, 101, 131, 154, 185, 214, 272, 295, 326, 369, and 407, MLPU.

For a further discussion, see D. O'Brien, "John Marshall Harlan's Unpublished Opinions: Reflections of a Supreme Court at Work," *Journal of Supreme Court History* 1991, at 27.

98. Danelski, supra note 52, at 503. See also W. Murphy, *Elements of Judicial Strategy* (Chicago: University of Chicago Press, 1964).

99. Studies of the opinion assignment practices of chief justices vary in their data base and, to some extent, in their conclusions. See Danelski, supra note 45; S. Ulmer, "The Use of Power in the Supreme Court: The Opinion Assignments of Earl Warren, 1953–1960," 19 *Journal of Public Law* 49 (1970); W. McLauchlan, "Ideology and Conflict in Supreme Court Opinion Assignment, 1946–1962," 25 *Western Political Quarterly* 16 (1972); and S. Brenner, "Strategic Choice and Opinion Assignment on the U.S. Supreme Court: A Reexamination," 35 *Western Political Quarterly* 204 (1982).

100. The story is ably told by Mason, *Harlan Fiske Stone* 614–15 (New York: Viking, 1956).

101. See J. Frank, *Justice Daniel Dissenting* 181–83 (Cambridge: Harvard University Press, 1964).

102. See Mason, *Taft* 206–8, loc. cit. On occasion, however, Taft did make assignments for expressly political reasons. He explained his assignment of one First Amendment case to Justice Pierce Butler as follows: "He is the only one to whom I can properly give it. He was appointed by Harding and not by Wilson, and I rather think we ought to have somebody other than an appointee of Wilson to consider and decide the case." Letter to Justice Van Devanter, July 9, 1926, Van Devanter Papers, Box 35, LC.

103. See D. Atkinson, "Opinion Writing on the Supreme Court, 1949–1956: The Views of Justice Sherman Minton," 49 *Temple Law Quarterly* 105 (1975).

104. See J. Howard, *Mr. Justice Murphy* 237 (Princeton, N.J.: Princeton University Press, 1968); and S. Brenner, "Another Look at Freshman Indecisiveness on the Supreme Court," 16 *Polity* 320 (1983).

105. See T. Bowen and J. Scheb, "Freshman Opinion Writing on the U.S. Supreme Court, 1921–1991," 76 *Judicature* 239 (1993); and E. Slotnick, "Who Speaks for the Court? Majority Opinion Assignments from Taft to Burger," 23 *American Journal of Political Science* 60 (1979).

106. See, e.g., C. Smith, J. Baugh, T. Hensely, and S. Johnson, "The First-Term Performance of Justice Ruth Bader Ginsburg," 78 *Judicature* 74 (1994).

107. Letter to Vinson, November 13, 1947, Douglas Papers, Box 217, LC.

108. Quoted by A. Lewis in "A Talk with Warren on Crime, the Court, the Country," *New York Times Magazine* 130 (October 19, 1969), as quoted by Abraham, supra note 37, at 210.

109. See also S. Brenner, "Issue Specialization as a Variable in Opinion Assignment on the U.S. Supreme Court," 46 *Journal of Politics* 1217 (1984); and S. Brenner and H. S. Spaeth, "Issue Specialization in Majority Opinion Assignment on the Burger Court," 39 *Western Political Quarterly* 520 (1986).

110. Walter Murphy Interview with Douglas, at 148, MLPU.

111. Waite's Papers contain numerous examples of justices complaining about opinion assignments, as do other papers of the justices with regard to Vinson and Burger. See, e.g., Morrison Waite Papers, Box 40. Files for the 1878, 1879, and 1883 Terms, LC; Melville Fuller Papers, Boxes 4 and 6, LC; Frankfurter Papers, Box 108, File 2268, LC; and Vinson Papers, Box 215, UK; Douglas Papers and Brennan Papers, LC.

112. Letter to Brennan, RE: No. 30, Felix Frankfurther Papers, Box 169, File 5, HLS.

113. See Letters from Gray to Fuller on the problems of reading opinions aloud at conference. Fuller Papers, Box 5, LC.
114. Quoted in A. Westin, *The Anatomy of a Constitutional Law Case* 123–24 (New York: Macmillan, 1958).
115. W. J. Brennan, Jr., "State Court Decisions and the Supreme Court," 31 *Pennsylvania Bar Association Quarterly* 393, 405 (1960).
116. Memorandum, April 23, 1948, Douglas Papers, Box 217, LC.
117. T. Clark, "Internal Operation of the United States Supreme Court," 43 *Judicature* 45, 51 (1959).
118. Conversation with Paul Freund. And see Douglas, "Mr. Justice Cardozo," 588 *Michigan Law Review* 549 (1960).
119. Memo, Douglas Papers, Box 228, LC.
120. See J. Palmer and S. Brenner, "The Amount of the Time Taken by the Vinson Court to Process its Full-Opinion Cases," 1990 *Journal of Supreme Court History* 142 (1991).
121. See, e.g., Letter to Justice Byrnes, November 1, 1941, Stone Papers, Box 79, LC.
122. Clark Papers, UT. See also Oral History Interview with Tom Clark, JPL.
123. Undated note, Black Papers, Box 58, LC.
124. Marshall Papers, LC.
125. Memos to Byrnes and Reed, 1941, Douglas Papers, Box 228, LC.
126. Quoted by M. Pusey, *Charles Evans Hughes*, vol. 2, at 671 (New York: Macmillan, 1951).
127. Harlan F. Stone Papers, Box 75, LC.
128. Letter December 20, 1940, Black Papers, Box 261, LC.
129. Quoted by A. T. Mason, *The Supreme Court from Taft to Burger* 65 (Baton Rouge: Louisiana University Press, 3d ed., 1979).
130. Quoted by Mason, supra note 100, at 501.
131. Note, May 20, 1963, Harlan Papers, Box 538, MLPU.
132. Note, January 2, 1969, Harlan Papers, Box 338, MLPU; Abe Fortas Papers, YA.
133. Letter to Reed, December 2, 1941, Douglas Papers, Box 128, LC.
134. Letter to Brennan, January 29, 1962, Brennan Papers, Box 145, LC.
135. Letter to Warren, May 11, 1966, Brennan Papers, Box 145, LC. See also Memo, September 13, 1966, Warren Papers, Box 348; and Warren Papers, Boxes 616 and 617, LC.
136. Letter of April 24, 1965, Brennan Papers, Box 130, LC. For the conference discussion, see Brennan Papers, Box 411; and Warren Papers, Box 267, LC. Douglas's first draft is in Brennan Papers, Box 130, LC.
137. Letter of May 19, 1926, Van Devanter Papers, LC; reprinted in M. Urofsky and D. Levy, eds., *Letters of Justice Louis D. Brandeis*, vol. 5, at 128 (New York: SUNY, 1978).
138. Quoted by Murphy, supra note 98, at 53. Likewise, Sutherland wrote Holmes, "I voted 'yes' and would prefer that result. I am inclined to acquiesce and will." Holmes Papers, "Opinion Book 1926," HLS. For other instances, see Louis Brandeis Papers, HLS.
139. Quoted by Murphy, supra note 98, at 52. On another occasion, Justice Butler indicated his preference for the opposite result but decided to acquiesce "unless someone initiates opposition." Note to Justice Holmes, "Opinion Book 1926," HLS.
140. Memo, January 25, 1945, Stone Papers, Box 75, LC.
141. Note on draft opinion, Holmes Papers, "Opinion Book 1919," HLS.
142. Response on draft of *Beaumont v. Prieto*, Holmes Papers, "Opinion Book 1918," HLS.

143. Letter to Black, January 31, 1962, Brennan Papers, Box 68, LC.
144. Letter to Frankfurter, February 3, 1962, Clark Papers, UT.
145. Memorandum, March 10, 1962, Brennan Papers, Box 68, LC.
146. This discussion draws on the author's more extensive analysis, "Institutional Norms and Supreme Court Opinions: On Reconsidering the rise of Individual Opinions," in C. Clayton and H. Gillman, eds., *Supreme Court Decision-making: Institutional Approaches to the Supreme Court* 91–113 (Chicago: University of Chicago Press, 1999).
147. Opinions refer to the number of opinions for the Court disposing of one or more cases on merits. Prior to 1801, the Supreme Court maintained the practice of issuing its opinions *seriatim*. Here each case disposed of in such a manner is counted as only one opinion. This practice was largely abandoned shortly before John Marshall became chief justice. The figures for the number of opinions for the terms 1791–1800 are taken from J. Goebel, Jr., *History of the Supreme Court of the United States (1790–1800)*, Table XII, at 811 (New York: Macmillan, 1971). The number for those terms between 1800 and 1815 are taken from G. Haskins and H. A. Johnson, *Foundations of Power: John Marshall (1801–1815)*, Table 2, at 653 (New York: Macmillan, 1981). The numbers for the 1810, 1820, 1830, 1840, 1850, 1860, 1870, 1890, 1900, and 1910 terms are based on an analysis of decisions in *United States Reports* for those years. Excluded from those figures are short *per curiam* or memorandum orders denying review or not reaching the merits of a case or otherwise disposing of a case. Data for the October terms after 1913 are taken from Statistical Sheet, Office of the Clerk, Supreme Court.

  Total number of opinions refers to both signed and *per curiam* opinions for the Court and dissenting, concurring, or separate opinions in cases given plenary consideration. Excluded, for example, are dissenting opinions from the denial of a petition for *certiorari*. Data for 1801–1814 are taken from Haskins and Johnson, *Foundations*. Figures for the 1800, 1810, 1820, 1830, 1840, 1850, 1860, 1870, 1880, 1890, 1900, and 1910 terms are based on an examination and tabulation by the author of opinions in *United States Reports* for those years. Figures for the October terms after 1913 are taken from the Annual Statement of Number of Printed Opinions, Office of the Clerk, Supreme Court, with the exception of the 1924–1936 terms, for which the number of total opinions was taken from the *Harvard Law Review's Annual Survey* of those terms.

  Cases disposed of during term include both those given plenary consideration and those summarily decided or otherwise disposed of. Figures for cases disposed of and carried over for the years 1791–1810, 1820, 1822–1846, 1850, 1860, 1870, 1880, and 1890 are based on the author's tabulation of cases contained in the Docket Books of the Supreme Court of the United States (available at the National Archives, Washington, D.C.). Figures for the terms between 1890 and 1910 are taken from the *Annual Reports of the Attorney General of the United States* (Washington, D.C.: GPO, 1891, 1901, 1911). Figures for October terms after 1913 are taken from Statistical Sheet, Office of the Clerk, Supreme Court.
148. Interview with Stewart, February 28, 1985, SC.
149. C. Herman Pritchett, *The Roosevelt Court: A Study in Judicial Politics and Values, 1937–1947* (New York: Macmillan, 1948).
150. See Thomas Walker, Lee Epstein, and William Dixon, "On the Mysterious Demise of Consenual Norms in the United States Supreme Court," 50 *The Journal of Politics* 361 (1988).
151. See Stacia Haynie, "Leadership and Consensus on the U.S. Supreme Court," 54 *The Journal of Politics* 1158 (1992).

152. See Lee Epstein, Jeffrey Segal, Harold Spaeth, and Thomas Walker, *The Supreme Court Compendium*, Table 3-1, 147–148 (Washington, D.C.: C.Q. Press, 1994).

153. For further discussion, see Morton White, *Social Thought in America: The Revolt against Formalism* (Boston: Beacon Press, 1957).

154. See Wilfred Rumble, *American Legal Realism: Skepticism, Reform, and the Judicial Process* (Ithaca: Cornell University Press, 1968); and William Fisher, Morton Horowitz, and Thomas Reed, eds., *American Legal Realism* (New York: Oxford University Press, 1993).

155. For further discussion, see Laura Kalman, *The Strange Career of Legal Liberalism* (New Haven: Yale University Press, 1996).

156. Walker, Epstein, and Dixon, supra note 150, at 386.

157. For plurality decisions before the 1969 term, see J. F. Davis and W. Reynolds, "Juridicial Cripples: Plurality Opinions in the Supreme Court," 1974 *Duke Law Journal* 59. For the 1969–1979 terms, see Note, "Plurality Decisions and Judicial Decisionmaking," 94 *Harvard Law Review* 1127, Appendix, at 1147 (1981). Plurality decisions in the 1980–1996 terms were tabulated by the author.

158. Memorandum to Conference, October 28, 1961, Black Papers, Box 60, L.C.

159. Memo to Conference, November 22, 1977, *The Regents of the University of California v. Bakke* file, Lewis F. Powell, Jr. Papers, WLLS.

160. Notes on Conference of 12/9/77, Ibid.

161. Ibid.

162. Bench Memo, August 19, 1977, Ibid.

163. Memorandum to the Conference, May 2, 1978, in Ibid.

164. Voting five to four in *Wygant v. Jackson Board of Education*, 476 U.S. 267 (1986), the Court struck down a program for laying off white teachers before minority group teachers with less seniority. But the Court upheld affirmative-action programs in the promotion of women and minorities in the workplace, in *Johnson v. Transportation Agency*, 480 U.S. 616 (1987), and in *United States v. Paradise*, 480 U.S. 149 (1987); as well as approved Congress's setting aside of minority contracts, in *Fullilove v. Klutznick*, 448 U.S. 448 (1980). The Burger Court also upheld private affirmative-action programs, in *United Steelworkers of America v. Weber*, 443 U.S. 193 (1979); and programs resulting from consent decrees and lower-court remedial orders, in *Local 93 of the International Association of Firefighters v. City of Cleveland*, 478 U.S. 501 (1986), and *Local 28 of the Sheet Metal Workers v. EEOC*, 478 U.S. 421 (1986).

165. Interview with Stevens, April 5, 1985, SC.

166. Letter, April 20, 1874, Records of the Clerk of the Supreme Court, NARS.

167. Quoted by McLean, supra note 84, at 60.

168. Hughes, supra note 22, at 68.

169. Frankfurter-Brandeis Conversations, Frankfurter Papers, Box 224, File 4101, LC. The original transcript of these conversations is in the Brandeis Papers, Box 114, HLS.

170. Quoted in A. Bickel, *The Unpublished Opinions of Mr. Justice Brandeis* 18 (Chicago: University of Chicago Press, 1967).

171. Letter, December 8, 1915, Day Papers, Box 30, LC.

172. *Bank of the United States v. Dandridge*, 25 U.S. 64, 90 (1827). See also letters from Justice Story by the Reporter in 1818, telling of his agreement with the Court's opinion and providing a copy of a dissenting opinion that he suppressed. W. W. Story, *Life and Letters of Joseph Story*, vol. 1, 303–8 (Boston: Little, Brown, 1851).

173. John Niven, ed., *The Salmon P. Chase Papers: Journals, 1829–1872*, vol. 1 (Kent, Ohio: Kent State University Press, 1993), at 517.

174. Holmes's "Opinion Books" contain numerous examples of justices asquiescing in a unanimous decision even though as many as three or more disagreed with the ruling. See, e.g., Letter from Justice Brown to Holmes, April 25, 1899, in which he says, "The opinion was not quite so unamimous as it appears to be. There were three members of the Court who . . . threatened to dissent, but they finally acquiesced in the result." Holmes Papers, Box 45, File 24, HLS.

175. Quoted by Mason, supra note 53, at 61 and 223.

176. J. Campbell III, "The Spirit of Dissent," 66 *Judicature* 305 (1983).

177. L. Brandeis, quoted by Bickel, supra note 170, at 18.

178. See D. Dorin, " 'Seize the Time': Justice Tom Clark's Role in *Mapp v. Ohio*," in V. Swigert, ed., *Law and the Legal Process* 21 (Beverly Hills, Calif.: Sage, 1982).

179. Quoted by Burger, "In Memoriam: Hugo L. Black," 92 S.Ct. 5, 79 (1972).

180. See, for example, memoranda in Boxes 492, 523, and Memoranda for Conference from Justice Marshall on *Rust v. Sullivan*, Box 530, Marshall Papers, LC. See also B. Blair Cook, "Justice Brennan and the Institutionalization of Dissent Assignment," 79 *Judicature* 17 (1995).

181. Memoranda from Justice Brennan, December 11, 1989, Marshall Papers, Box 502, LC.

182. Justice O'Connor, Lecture at the Marshall-Wythe School of Law, Williamsburg, Virginia, November 14, 1994, reported in *Amicus Curiae* (November 21, 1994). For other examples of justices assigning dissents or requesting such assignments, see memos in Marshall Papers, Boxes 423, 454, 470, 473, 511, and 602, LC.

183. Memoranda to Conference, November 10, 1981, Marshall Papers, Box 579, LC.

184. A. Scalia, "Dissenting Opinions," *Journal of Supreme Court History 1994*, at 33–44.

185. Undated Conference Note, Clark papers, UT.

186. Memorandum for Conference, November 5, 1959, Harlan Papers, Box 486, MLPU.

187. F. Frankfurter, "The Zeitgeist and the Judiciary," in A. MacLeish and E. Prichard, Jr., eds., *Law and Politics* (New York: Harcourt, Brace, 1939).

188. Burger, Annual Judicial Conference, Second Judicial Circuit, Buck Hill Falls, Pennsylvania (May 10, 1980) (unpublished manuscript on file with the author).

189. C. Thomas, Speech at Trinity United Methodist Church, aired on C-SPAN (April 12, 1997).

190. Interview with Chief Justice Burger (1985).

191. Memorandum to Conference, October 28, 1961, Black Papers, Box 60, LC. See also M. Handler, "The Supreme Court's Footnote Addiction," *New York State Bar Journal* (December 1986).

192. Included in the number of opinion pages are those for signed majority, concurring, dissenting, and *per curiam* opinions. For the 1960, 1965, 1970, 1975, and 1979 terms, see House Committee on Appropriations, *Departments. . . . Hearings before a Subcommittee,* 97th Cong., 2d sess., pt. 4, at 380 (Washington, D.C.: GPO, 1982). Figures for the 1938 term and tabulations for the average length of opinions are the author's.

193. David Stewart, "Quiet Times," *ABA Journal* 40 (October, 1994).

194. For a further discussion of the sources of interpretivist versus non-interpretivist approaches to constitutional interpretation, see D. O'Brien, *Constitutional Law and Politics,* Ch. 1 of either Vol. 1 or Vol. 2 (New York: Norton, 4th ed., 2000).

195. G. Phelps and J. Gates, "The Myth of Jurisprudence," 31 *Santa Clara Law Review* 567 (1991), at 589. Their content analysis is further developed in J. Gates and G.

Phelps, "Intentionalism in Constitutional Opinions," 49 *Political Research Quarterly* 245 (1996).

SIX

The Court and American Life

1. Newton Minow Oral History Interview, at 27–28, UK. See also Conference Lists, Hugo Black Papers, Box 310, LC.
2. Tom Clark Oral History Interview, at 10, UK. *Brown v. Board of Education*, 344 U.S. 1 (1952) (*per curiam* decision on postponement of oral arguments).
3. Letter to Charles Warren, July 19, 1923, Charles Warren Papers, Box 2, LC.
4. Story related in a letter from Herbert Wechsler to Frankfurter, July 22, 1946, Felix Frankfurter Papers, Box 172, HLS.
5. Letter to Harlan, September 2, 1958, Felix Frankfurter Papers, Box 169, HLS.
6. See letter from Stone to Frankfurter, March 17, 1943, Harlan F. Stone Papers, Box 13, LC; Earl Warren Papers, Box 125, LC; and *Supreme Court Journal* for June 21, 1969.
7. Memorandum for Conference, June 27, 1984, in Brennan Papers, Box 670, LC.
8. W. O. Douglas, *The Court Years* 40 (New York: Random House, 1980).
9. "Frankfurter Dissent Provokes Warren to Rebuttal on Bench," *New York Times* A1, col. 4 (March 21, 1961). For another such story, see W. J. Brennan, Jr., "Chief Justice Warren," 88 *Harvard Law Review* 1, 2 (1974).
10. W. Brennan, Jr., Remarks at Student Legal Forum, Charlottesville, Virginia, at 1 (February 17, 1959), SC.
11. Letter to Frankfurter to Reed, February 10, 1936. Felix Frankfurter Papers, Box 170, HLS.
12. Memorandum to Members of the Court, May 7, 1954, Tom C. Clark Papers, UT; Earl Warren Papers, Box 574, LC.
13. See Memorandum to the Chief Justice from the Press Office, September 1, 1948, Stanley Reed Papers, Box 174, UK; and John M. Harlan Papers, Box 498, MLPU.
14. See Letter to the Chief Justice and "Background Paper for the Chief Justice," September 22, 1969, Harlan Papers, Box 606, MLPU.
15. Note, October 12, 1970, William J. Brennan Papers, Box 487, LC.
16. W. E. Burger, foreword to M. Cannon and D. M. O'Brien, eds., *Views from the Bench: The Judiciary and Constitutional Politics* (Chatham, N.J.: Chatham House, 1985).
17. Linda Greenhouse, "Telling the Court's Story," 105 *Yale Law Journal* 1537 (1996).
18. Quoted in M. Tropin, "What, Exactly, Is the Court Saying?" *Barrister Magazine* 14, 68 (Spring 1984). See also R. Sherman, "The Media and the Law," *National Law Journal* 32 (June 6, 1988).
19. See E. Katsh, "The Supreme Court Beat: How Television Covers the U.S. Supreme Court," 67 *Judicature* 6 (1983); and E. Slotnick and J. Segal, "Television News and the Supreme Court," APSA Convention Paper, 1992.
20. Tropin, supra note 18, at 68–69.
21. Quoted ibid., 67. For a further discussion of media coverage of the Court, see E. Slotnick, "Media Coverage of Supreme Court Decision Making: Problems and Prospects," 75 *Judicature* 128 (1991); E. Slotnick, "Television News and the Supreme Court: A Case Study," 77 *Judicature* 21 (1993).
22. Letter to Reed about *Cox v. New Hampshire*, March 28, 1941, Reed Papers, Box 171, UK.

23. E. Warren, *The Memoirs of Earl Warren* 285 (New York: Doubleday, 1977). See also Gordon Davidson Interview, UK; and Reed Papers, Boxes 41, 43, 50, and 331, UK.

24. Transcript of Oral Argument, Reed Papers, Box 43, UK.

25. Memo summarizing conversation with the chief justice by John Fassett for Justice Reed, Reed Papers, Box 331, UK. See also Harold Burton Papers, Box 263, LC; and Clark Papers, UK.

26. Reed Papers, Box 331, UK.

27. Law Clerks' Recommendations for Segregation Decree, Clark Papers, UT; Warren Papers, Box 574, LC.

28. Reed's notes of conference discussion, Reed Papers, Box 43, UK. Burton's "Diaries," Box 3, LC; Felix Frankfurter Papers, HLS; and Warren Papers, Boxes 571 and 574, LC.

29. Memorandum to the Brethren, January 15, 1954, Burton Papers, Box 263, LC (quoting *Virginia v. West Virginia,* 200 U.S. 1 (1911).

30. *Griffin v. Prince Edward County School Board,* 377 U.S. 218, 219, 234 (1964).

31. Memorandum, School Openings and Desegregation, Lee White Papers, Box 5, JPL.

32. Ruby Martin Oral History Interview, at 12, JPL.

33. V. Navasky, *Kennedy Justice* 97–98 (New York: Atheneum, 1971). For a good survey of the activities and accomplishments of the Eisenhower administration in the area of civil rights, see Memorandum to the Attorney General, January 18, 1961, William Rogers Papers, Box 47; and Dwight David Eisenhower (DDE) Diaries, Box 33, EPL.

34. Memorandum on Civil Rights Legislation, White House Central Files—Executive Legislative Series, Hu, Box 65, JPL. See also Stephen Pollack Interview III, at 19; and White House Central Files—Confidential Files (WHCF-CF), Boxes 102 and 127, JPL.

35. See, generally, Lee White Papers, Box 2; and WHCF-CF, Box 102, JPL.

36. *Alexander v. Holmes County Board of Education,* 396 U.S. 1218, 1220 (1969).

37. *Alexander v. Holmes County Board of Education,* 396 U.S. 19 (1969) (per curiam). The Court had previously held, in *Green v. School Board New Kent County,* 391 U.S. 430 (1968), that "freedom of choice" in achieving school desegregation was ineffective.

38. All quotations are from justices' memos; Harlan Papers, Boxes 487, 565 and 606, MLPU; and Brennan Papers, Box 218, LC.

39. Based on figures in Appendix to Memorandum for the President, Ford Papers, WHCF—Special Files, Box 4, FPL. (The report considered districts with an "appreciable percentage" of minority students to have at least 5 percent minority students and segregated districts to have more than 50 percent nonminority students.)

40. Handwritten note of President Eisenhower, Papers as President—Administrative Series, Box 23, EPL.

41. Pollack Interview III, at 19, JPL.

42. See, Council of Urban Boards of Education, *Status of School Desegregation: The Next Generation* (Washington, D.C.: Council of Urban Boards of Education, 1992); National School Board Association, *Status of School Desegregation: 1968–1986* (Washington, D.C.: National School Board Association, 1989); A. Hacker, *Two Nations: Black and White, Separate, Hostile, Unequal* (New York, Scribner's 1992); and G. Orfield, S. Eaton, and the Harvard Project on School Desegregation, *Dismantling Desegregation* (New York: New Press, 1996).

43. See, e.g., W. Hendrie, "Without Court Orders, Schools Ponder How to Pursue Diversity," *Education Week* 36 (April 30, 1997); Hendrie, "Pressure for Community Schools Grows as Oversight Wanes," *Education Week* 23 (June 17, 1998); and Orfield, Eaton, and the Harvard Projection on School Desegregation, op. cit.

44. R. Dahl, "Decision-Making in a Democracy: The Supreme Court as a National Policy-Maker," 6 *Journal of Public Law* 279, 293 (1957).

45. G. Rosenberg, *The Hollow Hope: Can Courts Bring About Social Change?* (Chicago: University of Chicago Press, 1991).

46. R. Neustadt, *Presidential Power and the Modern Presidents* (New York: Free Press, 1990).

47. Dahl, op. cit. and R. Funston, "The Supreme Court and Critical Elections," 69 *American Political Science Review* 795 (1975). See also G. Caldeira, "Neither the Purse nor the Sword: Dynamics of Public Confidence in the Supreme Court," 80 *American Political Science Review* 1209 (1986).

48. F. P. Dunne, "On the Supreme Court's Decisions," in *Mr. Dooley in Peace and in War* (1898).

49. Letter, October 15, 1937, Stone Papers, Box 13, LC.

50. G. Caldeira, "Public Opinion and the U.S. Supreme Court: FDR's Court-Packing Plan," 81 *American Political Science Review* 1139 (1987).

51. Interview with Scalia, PBS Special, "This Honorable Court," 1988.

52. Interview with Justice Blackmun, ABC's "Nightline," November 18, 1993.

53. Letter, April 24, 1961, Felix Frankfurter Papers, Box 171, HLS. Memo to Conference, March 2, 1962, Clark Papers, UT. For another example of Frankfurter's appeal to the forces of public opinion, see his memorandum on *Reid v. Covert*, June 5, 1957, Warren Papers, Box 434, LC.

54. See R. Dahl, "Decision-making in a Democracy: The Supreme Court as a National Policy-Maker," 6 *Journal of Public Law*, 279 (1957); R. Funston, "The Supreme Court and Critical Elections," 69 *American Political Science Review* 795 (1975); and J. Casper, "The Supreme Court and National Policymaking," 70 *American Political Science Review* 50 (1976).

55. See D. Barnum, "The Supreme Court and Public Opinion: Judicial Decisionmaking in the Post New Deal Period," 47 *Journal of Politics* 652 (1985).

56. See T. Marshall, *Public Opinion and the Supreme Court* (Boston: Unwin Hyman, 1989).

57. For an excellent overview and criticisms of research on courts and public opinion, see G. Caldeira, "Courts and Public Opinion," in J. Gates and C. Johnson, eds., *The American Courts: A Critical Assessment* 303 (Washington, D.C.: Congressional Quarterly Press, 1991).

58. See and compare, J. H. Ely, *Democracy and Distrust: A Theory of Judicial Review* (Cambridge: Harvard University Press, 1980); W. Lasser, *The Limits of Judicial Power: The Supreme Court in American Politics* (Chapel Hill: University of North Carolina Press, 1988); and D. O'Brien, "The Framers' Muse on Republicanism and the Supreme Court, and Pragmatic Constitutional Interpretivism," 53 *The Review of Politics* 251 (1991).

59. See V. O. Key, "A Theory of Critical Elections," 17 *Journal of Politics* 3 (1955); and J. Sundquist, *Dynamics of the Party System* (Washington, D.C.: The Brookings Institution, 1973).

60. See D. Adamany, "The Supreme Court's Role in Critical Elections," in B. Campbell and R. Trilling, eds., *Realignment in American Politics* (Austin: University of Texas Press, 1980).

61. See J. Gates, *The Supreme Court and Partisan Realignment* (Boulder, CO.: Westview Press, 1992); M. Graber, "The Nonmajoritarian Difficulty: Legislative Deference to the Judiciary" in 7 *Studies in American Political Development* 35 (1993); and W. Lasser, "The Supreme Court in Periods of Critical Realignment," 47 *Journal of Politics* 1174 (1985).
62. For a further discussion, see T. Edsall and M. Edsall, *Chain Reaction: The Impact of Race, Rights, and Taxes on American Politics* (New York: Norton, 1991).
63. See "Institutions: Confidence Even in Difficult Times," *Public Opinion* 33 (1981); Hearst Report, *The American Public, the Media and the Judicial System* (New York: Hearst Corporation, 1983); W. Murphy J. Tanenhaus, and D. Kastner, *Public Evaluations of Constitutional Courts: Alternative Explanations* (Beverly Hills, Calif.: Sage, 1973); and W. Murphy and J. Tanenhaus, "Public Opinion and the United States Supreme Court," 2 *Law and Society Review* 357 (1968).
64. See G. Casey, "Popular Perceptions of Supreme Court Rulings," 4 *American Politics Quarterly* 3 (1976); D. Jaros and R. Roper, "The Supreme Court, Myth, Diffuse Support, Specific Support, and Legitimacy," 8 *American Politics Quarterly* 85 (1980); and P. Secret, J. Johnson, and S. Welch, "Racial Differences in Attitudes Toward the Supreme Court's Decision on Prayer in Public Schools," 67 *Social Science Quarterly* 877 (1986).
65. See G. Caldeira, "Neither the Purse nor the Sword: Dynamics of Public Confidence in the Supreme Court," 80 *American Political Science Review* 1209 (1986).
66. See e.g., J. Scheb II and W. Lyons, "Public Holds U.S. Supreme Court in High Regard," 77 *Judicature* 273 (1994); and Michael Comiskey, "The Rehnquist Court and American Values," 77 *Judicature* 261 (1994); for an analysis to the contrary, see W. Mishler and R. Sheehan, "The Supreme Court as a Countermajoritarian Institution? The Impact of Public Opinion on Supreme Court Decisions," 87 *American Political Science Review* 87 (1993).
67. Caldeira, supra note 57, at 307.
68. Memorandum to the President from Jim Cannon (June 1, 1976), and Memorandum from HEW Secretary David Mathews (March 29, 1974), Ford Papers, WHCF—Special Files, Box 4, FPL. See also Edmund Schmults Papers, Box 9, FPL.
69. "Text of 96 Congressman's Declaration on Integration," *New York Times* 19 (March 12, 1956). (Five congressmen later joined the manifesto.)
70. *Cong. Rec.*, 97th Cong., 2d sess., S5428 (May 18, 1982) and H2852 (May 25, 1982) (daily ed.)
71. For further discussion see E. Keynes, with R. Miller, *The Court vs. Congress: Prayer, Busing, and Abortion* (Durham, N.C.: Duke University Press, 1989).
72. Notes and Correspondence, *Miranda* File, Warren Papers, Box 617, LC; and Abe Fortas Papers, YA.
73. *Williams v. United States*, 401 U.S. 675, 677 (1971). See also *Gregg v. Georgia*, 428 U.S. 153, 180 (1976) and *Woodson v. North Carolina*, 428 U.S. 280, 299 (1976).
74. Frankfurter and Byrnes, both appointed by Roosevelt, had maintained a close relationship through the years; in 1953–1954, the latter, as governor, had made well known to Frankfurter his views that the Court would exceed its constitutional power in striking down segregation. See letters and memos, Warren Papers, Boxes 574 and 353, LC; discussion of *Cooper v. Aaron* in Chapter Five; J. Byrnes, "The Supreme Court Must Be Curbed," *U.S. News & World Report* 50 (May 18, 1956); and A. Bickel, "Frankfurter's Former Clerk Disputes Byrnes's Statement," *U.S. News & World Report* 132 (June 15, 1956) (a copy of Bickel's original and more

extensive rebuttal of Byrnes's article may be found in Warren Papers, Box 353, LC).

75. See L. Powell Jr., "Are the Federal Courts Becoming Bureaucracies?" 68 *American Bar Association Journal* 1370 (1982).

76. Memorandum on the Segregation Decree, Warren Papers, Box 574. LC.

77. J. Peltason, *Fifty-eight Lonely Men: Southern Federal Judges and School Desegregation* 9–10 (New York: Harcourt, Brace and World, 1961).

78. J. W. Howard, *Courts of Appeals in the Federal Judicial System* (Princeton, N.J.: Princeton University Press, 1981).

79. *Report of the Committee on Federal-State Relationships as Affected by Judicial Decisions,* reprinted in *Cong. Rec.,* 73d Cong., 2d sess., Appendix, A7784, A7787 (daily ed., August 25, 1958).

80. Letter, December 28, 1967, Harlan Papers, Box 301, MLPU.

81. Letter, January 29, 1968, Harlan Papers, Box 301, MLPU.

82. Letter to Clark, January 25, 1962, Clark Papers, UT.

83. See R. Collins, P. Galie, and J. Kincaid, "State High Courts, State Constitutions, and Individual Rights Litigation Since 1980: A Judicial Survey," 16 *Publius* 141 (1986). Note, though, that state supreme courts have not uniformly moved in more liberal directions; see B. Latzer, "The Hidden Conservativism of the State Court 'Revolution,' " 74 *Judicature* 190 (1991).

84. See *Florida v. Meyers,* 466 U.S. 380, 383 (1984) (Stevens, J., dis. op.).

85. Nicholas Kazenbach Oral History Interview, at 41, JPL.

86. Letter, October 8, 1956, quoted by D. Fuerth, "Lyndon B. Johnson and Civil Rights" (Ph.D. diss., University of Texas, 1974); and Letter, April 2, 1957, Senate Papers, Box 289, JPL.

87. Quoted by J. Schmidhauser and L. Berg, *The Supreme Court and Congress: Conflict and Interaction, 1945–1968* 10 (New York: Free Press, 1972).

88. In *Lauf v. E. G. Shinner,* 303 U.S. 323 (1938), the Court upheld the Norris-LaGuardia Act's removal of the power of lower federal courts to issue injunctions in labor disputes.

89. *United States v. Klein,* 80 U.S. 128 (1872).

90. See *Cong. Rec.,* 94th Cong., 2d sess., S4128 (daily ed., April 5, 1979) and S4138 (daily ed., April 9, 1979).

91. C. H. Pritchett, *Congress versus the Supreme Court, 1957–1960,* 122–23 (Minneapolis: University of Minnesota Press, 1961).

92. For a further discussion of the Court's nationalization of the Bill of Rights, see D. O'Brien, *Constitutional Law and Politics: Civil Rights and Civil Liberties* Ch. 4 (New York: Norton, 4th ed., 2000).

93. See Note, "Congressional Reversals of Supreme Court Decisions," 71 *Harvard Law Review* 1324 (1958).

94. This data is derived from William N. Eskridge, Jr., "Overriding Supreme Court Statutory Interpretation Decisions," 101 *Yale Law Journal* 331, 338 (1991).

95. See L. Fisher, "Separation of Powers: Interpretation Outside of Courts," 18 *Pepperdine Law Review* 57 (1990); and R. Paschall, "The Continuing Colloquy: Congress and the Finality of the Supreme Court," 8 *Journal of Law & Politics* 143 (1992).

96. J. Califano, *Governing America* 227 (New York: Simon & Schuster, 1981).

97. Dahl, supra note 44.

98. See J. Casper, "The Supreme Court and National Policy-Making," 70 *American Political Science Review* 60 (1976).

99. Herbert Brownell Oral History Interview, at 33, EPL.

100. Letter to Edgar Eisenhower, November 8, 1954, DDE Diaries, Box 8, EPL.

101. Letter to Swede Hazlett, July 22, 1957, DDE Diaries, Box 25, EPL.

102. Quoted in R. Evans, Jr., and R. Novak, *Nixon in the White House* 156 (New York: Random House, 1971).

103. *American Federation of Labor v. American Sash & Door Company,* 335 U.S. 538, 555–56 (1946).

104. See N. Glazer, "Toward an Imperial Judiciary," 40 *The Public Interest* 104 (1975); D. Horowitz, *The Courts and Social Policy* (Washington, D.C.: Brookings Institution, 1977); and R. Berger, *Government by the Judiciary* (Cambridge: Harvard University Press, 1977). But see D. M. O'Brien, "The 'Imperial Judiciary': Of Paper Tigers and Socio-Legal Indicators," 2 *Journal of Law & Politics* 1 (1985); and for a more extreme argument that courts cannot bring about social change see G. Rosenberg, *The Hollow Hope: Can Courts Bring About Social Change?* (Chicago: University of Chicago Press, 1991) and M. J. Klarman, "Rethinking the Civil Rights and Civil Liberties Revolution," 82 *Virginia Law Review* 1 (1996).

Glossary

Advisory opinion   An opinion or interpretation of law that does not have binding effect. The Court does not give advisory opinions, for example, on hypothetical disputes; it decides only actual cases or controversies.

Affirm   In an appellate court, to reach a decision that agrees with the result reached in a case by the lower court.

Amicus curiae   A friend of the court, a person not a party to litigation, who volunteers or is invited by the court to give his views on a case.

Appeal   To take a case to a higher court for review. Generally, a party losing in a trial court may appeal once to an appellate court as a matter of right. If the party loses in the appellate court, appeal to a higher court is within the discretion of the higher court. Most appeals to the Supreme Court are within its discretion to deny or grant a hearing.

Appellant   The party that appeals a lower-court decision to a higher court.

Appellee   One who has an interest in upholding the decision of a lower court and is compelled to respond when the case is appealed to a higher court by the appellant.

Brief   A document prepared by counsel to serve as the basis for an argument in court, setting out the facts and legal arguments in support of his or her case.

Case   A general term for an action, cause, suit, or controversy, at law or equity; a question contested before a court.

Case law   The law as defined by previously decided cases, distinct from statutes and other sources of law.

Certification, writ of   A method of taking a case from appellate court to the Supreme Court in which the lower court asks that some question or interpretation of law be certified, clarified, and made more certain.

Certiorari, writ of   A writ issued from the Supreme Court, at its discretion and at the request of a petitioner, to order a lower court to send the record of a case to the Court for its review.

Civil law   The body of law dealing with the private rights of individuals, as distinguished from criminal law.

Class action   A lawsuit brought by one person or group on behalf of all persons similarly situated.

Common law   The collection of principles and rules, particularly from unwritten English law, that derive their authority from long-standing usage and custom or from courts recognizing and enforcing those customs.

Concurring opinion   An opinion by a justice that agrees with the result reached by the Court in a case but disagrees with the Court's rationale for its decision.

Controversies   *See* Justiciable controversy.

Criminal law   The body of law that deals with the enforcement of laws and the punishment of persons who, by breaking laws, commit crimes against the state.

Declaratory judgment   A court pronouncement declaring a legal right or interpretation but not ordering a special action.

De facto   In fact, in reality.

Defendant   In a civil action, the party denying or defending itself against charges brought by a plaintiff. In a criminal action, the person indicted for the commission of an offense.

De jure   As a result of law, as a result of official action.

Dicta   *See Obiter dictum.*

Discretionary jurisdiction   Jurisdiction that a court may accept or reject in particular cases. The Supreme Court has discretionary jurisdiction in over 90 percent of the cases that come to it.

Dismissal   An order disposing of a case without a hearing or trial.

Dissenting opinion   An opinion by a justice that disagrees with the result reached by the Court in a case.

Docket   All cases filed in a court.

Due process   Fair and regular procedure. The Fifth and Fourteenth Amendments guarantee persons that they will not be deprived of life, liberty, or property by the government until fair and usual procedures have been followed.

Error, writ of   A writ issued from an appeals court to a lower court requiring that it send the record of a case so that it may review it for error.

Ex parte   From, or on, only one side. Application to a court for some ruling or action on behalf of only one party.

Exclusionary rule   An evidentiary rule requiring that evidence obtained in violation of an individual's constitutional rights under the Fourth Amendment must be excluded at trial.

Habeas corpus   Literally, "you have the body"; a writ issued to inquire whether a person is lawfully imprisoned or detained. The writ demands that the persons holding the prisoner justify his detention or release him.

In forma pauperis   In the manner of a pauper, without liability for the costs of filing cases before a court.

Injunction   A court order prohibiting a person from performing a particular act.

Judgment   The official decision of a court.

Judicial review   The power to review and strike down any legislation or other government action that is inconsistent with federal or state constitutions. The Supreme Court reviews government action only under the Constitution of the United States.

Jurisdiction   The power of a court to hear a case or controversy, which exists when the proper parties are present and when the point to be decided is among the issues authorized to be handled by a particular court.

Justiciable controversy   A controversy in which a claim of right is asserted against another who has an interest in contesting it. Courts will consider only justiciable controversies, as distinguished from hypothetical disputes.

Majority opinion   An opinion in a case that is subscribed to by a majority of the justices who participated in the decision.

***Mandamus*, writ of** "We command"; an order issued from a superior court directing a lower court or other government authority to perform a particular act.

Mandatory jurisdiction Jurisdiction that a court must accept. The Supreme Court must decide cases coming under its appellate jurisdiction, though it may avoid giving them plenary consideration.

Moot Unsettled, undecided. A moot question is also one that is no longer material, or that has already been resolved, and has become hypothetical.

Motion A written or oral application to a court or judge to obtain a rule or order.

Obiter dictum A statement by a judge or justices expressing an opinion and included with, but not essential to, an opinion resolving a case before the court. Dicta are not necessarily binding in later cases.

Opinion for the court The opinion announcing the decision of a court.

Original jurisdiction The jurisdiction of a court of first instance, or trial court. The Supreme Court has original jurisdiction under Article III of the Constitution.

Per curiam "By the court"; an unsigned opinion of the court.

Petitioner One who files a petition with a court seeking action or relief, including the plaintiff or appellant. When a writ of certiorari is granted by the Supreme Court, the party seeking review is called the petitioner, and the party responding is called the respondent.

Plenary consideration Full consideration. When the Supreme Court grants a case review, it may give it full consideration, permitting the parties to submit briefs on the merits of the case and to present oral arguments, before the Court reaches its decision.

Plurality opinion An opinion announcing the decision of the Court, but having the support of less than a majority of the Court.

Political question Questions that courts refuse to decide because they are deemed to be essentially political in nature or because their determination would involve an intrusion on the powers of the executive or legislature.

Remand To send back. After a decision in a case, the case is often sent back by a higher court to the court from which it came for further action in light of its decision.

Respondent The party that is compelled to answer the claims or questions posed in a court by a petitioner.

Reverse In an appellate court, to reach a decision that disagrees with the result reached in a case by a lower court.

Ripeness When a case is ready for adjudication and decision; the issues presented must not be hypothetical, and the parties must have exhausted other avenues of appeal.

Seriatim Separately, individually, one by one. The Court's practice was once to have each justice give his opinion on a case separately.

Standing Having the appropriate characteristics to bring or participate in a case; in particular, having a personal interest and stake in the outcome.

Stare decisis "Let the decision stand." The principle of adherence to settled cases, the doctrine that principles of law established in earlier cases should be accepted as authoritative in similar subsequent cases.

Statute A written law enacted by a legislature.

Subpoena An order to present oneself before a grand jury, court, or legislative hearing.

Subpoena duces tecum An order to produce specified documents or papers.

Summary decision A decision in a case that does not give it full consideration; when the Court decides a case without having the parties submit briefs on the merits of the case or present oral arguments before the Court.

Tort An injury or wrong to the person or property of another.

Vacate To make void, annul, or rescind the decision of a lower court.

Writ An order commanding someone to perform or not perform acts specified in the order.

Selected Further Readings

Abraham, Henry. *The Judicial Process*. 7th ed. New York: Oxford University Press, 1998.

——. *Justices and Presidents*. 3d ed. New York: Oxford University Press, 1992.

Abraham, Henry, and Barbara Perry. *Freedom and the Court: Civil Rights and Liberties in the United States*. 7th ed. New York: Oxford University Press, 1998.

Baum, Lawrence. *The Puzzle of Judicial Behavior*. Ann Arbor: University of Michigan Press, 1997.

Bickel, Alexander. *The Least Dangerous Branch: The Supreme Court at the Bar of Politics*. New York: Bobbs-Merrill, 1963.

——, and Benno Schmidt. *The Judiciary and Responsible Government, 1910–21*. New York: Macmillan, 1984.

Black, Charles. *Structure and Relationship in Constitutional Law*. Baton Rouge: Louisiana University Press, 1969.

Black, Hugo. *A Constitutional Faith*. New York: Knopf, 1969.

Canon, Bradley, and Charles Johnson. *Judicial Policies: Implementation and Impact*. 2d ed. Washington, D.C.: CQ Press, 1999.

Cardozo, Benjamin. *The Nature of the Judicial Process*. New Haven: Yale University Press, 1921.

Clayton, Cornell, and Howard Gillman, eds. *Supreme Court Decision Making: New Institutionalist Approaches*. Chicago: University of Chicago Press, 1999.

Cortner, Richard. *The Supreme Court and the Second Bill of Rights: The*

Fourteenth Amendment and the Nationalization of Civil Liberties. Madison: University of Wisconsin Press, 1981.

Craig, Barbara. *Chadha.* New York: Oxford University Press, 1988.

Ely, John Hart. *Democracy and Distrust: A Theory of Judicial Review,* Cambridge: Harvard University Press, 1980.

Epstein, Lee, Jeffrey Segal, Harold Spaeth, and Thomas Walker. *The Supreme Court Compendium.* Washington, D.C.: Congressional Quarterly, 1994.

Epstein, Lee, and Jack Knight. *The Choices Justices Make.* Washington, D.C.: C.Q. Press, 1998.

Fairman, Charles. *Reconstruction and Reunion, 1864–1888.* New York: Macmillan, 1975.

Fish, Peter. *The Office of Chief Justice.* Charlottesville: University of Virginia Press, 1984.

Fiss, Owen. *Troubled Beginnings of the Modern State, 1888–1910.* New York: Macmillan, 1993.

Friedman, Leon, and Fred Israel, eds. *The Justices of the United States Supreme Court, 1789–1978: Their Lives and Major Opinions.* 5 vols. New York: Chelsea House, 1980.

Gates, John. *The Supreme Court and Partisan Realignment.* Boulder: Westview Press, 1992.

Goebel, Julius. *Antecedents and Beginnings to 1801.* New York: Macmillan, 1971.

Hall, Kermit, ed. *The Oxford Companion to the Supreme Court of the United States.* New York: Oxford University Press, 1993.

Haskins, George, and Herbert Johnson. *Foundations of Power: John Marshall, 1801–1815.* New York: Macmillan, 1981.

Irons, Peter. *The Courage of Their Convictions.* New York: Free Press, 1988.

Kahn, Ronald. *The Supreme Court & Constitutional Theory, 1953–1993.* Lawrence: University of Kansas Press, 1994.

Lasser, William. *The Limits of Judicial Power.* Chapel Hill: University of North Carolina Press, 1988.

Lazarus, Edward. *Closed Chambers: The First Eyewitness Account of the Epic Struggles Inside the Supreme Court.* New York: Time Books, 1998.

Levy, Leonard. *Original Intent and the Framers' Constitution.* New York: Macmillan, 1988.

Lewis, Anthony. *Gideon's Trumpet.* New York: Random House, 1964.

Marshall, Thomas. *Public Opinion and the Supreme Court.* Boston: Unwin Hyman, 1989.

McGuire, Kevin. *The Supreme Court Bar: Legal Elites in the Washington Community.* Charlottesville: University of Virginia Press, 1993.

Murphy, Bruce. *The Brandeis/ Frankfurter Connection: The Secret Political Activities of Two Supreme Court Justices.* New York: Oxford University Press, 1982.

Murphy, Walter. *Elements of Judicial Strategy.* Chicago: University of Chicago Press, 1964.

O'Brien, David. *Judicial Roulette.* New York: Twentieth Century Fund/ Priority Press, 1988.

———. *Constitutional Law and Politics.* 2 vols. New York: Norton, 4th ed., 2000.

———. *Supreme Court Watch.* New York: Norton, 1991–.

———, ed. *Judges on Judging: Views from the Bench.* Chatham: Chatham House, 1997.

———, ed. *The Lanahan Readings in Civil Rights and Civil Liberties.* Baltimore: Lanahan Publishers, 1999.

Pacelle, Richard. *The Transformation of the Supreme Court's Agenda.* Boulder: Westview Press, 1991.

Perry, H. W. *Deciding to Decide Agenda Setting in the United States Supreme Court.* Cambridge: Harvard University Press, 1991.

Pritchett, C. Herman. *The Roosevelt Court: A Study in Judicial Politics and Values.* New York: Macmillan Co., 1948.

Rehnquist, William H. *The Supreme Court.* New York: Morrow, 1987.

Rosenberg, Gerald. *The Hollow Hope: Can Courts Bring About Social Change?* Chicago: University of Chicago Press, 1991.

Rossiter, Clinton, with Richard Longaker. *The Supreme Court and the Commander in Chief.* Ithaca: Cornell University Press, 1976.

Schwartz, Bernard. *Super Chief: Earl Warren and His Supreme Court—A Judicial Biography.* New York: New York University Press, 1983.

———. *The Ascent of Pragmatism: The Burger Court in Action.* Reading: Addison-Wesley, 1990.

Slotnick, Elliot, and Jennifer A. Segal. *Television News and the Supreme Court: All the News That's Fit to Air?* New York: Cambridge University Press, 1998.

Stern, Robert, Eugene Gressman, and Stephen Shapiro. *Supreme Court Practice.* 7th ed. Washington, D.C.: Bureau of National Affairs, 1993.

Supreme Court Historical Society: *Journal of Supreme Court History.* Washington, D.C.: SCHS, 1976–.

Warren, Charles. *The Supreme Court in United States History.* 3 vols. Boston: Little, Brown, 1922.

White, G. Edward. *The Marshall Court and Cultural Change, 1815–1835.* New York: Macmillan, 1988.

INDEX